Dunkirk: Nine Days That Saved An Army

Dunkirk: Nine Days That Saved An Army

A Day by Day Account of the Greatest Evacuation

John Grehan

FRONTLINE
BOOKS

First published in Great Britain in 2018 by
FRONTLINE BOOKS
An imprint of
Pen & Sword Books Ltd
Yorkshire - Philadelphia

ISBN 978 1 52672 484 7

A CIP catalogue record for this book is
available from the British Library

Typeset in INDIA by Geniies IT & Services Private Limited
Printed and bound by TJ International Ltd, Padstow, Cornwall

Pen & Sword Books Ltd incorporates the Imprints of Aviation, Atlas,
Family History, Fiction, Maritime, Military, Discovery, Politics, History,
Archaeology, Select, Wharncliffe Local History, Wharncliffe True Crime,
Military Classics, Wharncliffe Transport, Leo Cooper, The Praetorian Press,
Remember When, Seaforth Publishing and Frontline Publishing.

For a complete list of Pen & Sword titles please contact
PEN & SWORD BOOKS LTD
47 Church Street, Barnsley, South Yorkshire, S70 2AS, England
E-mail: enquiries@pen-and-sword.co.uk
Website: www.pen-and-sword.co.uk
Or
PEN AND SWORD BOOKS
1950 Lawrence Rd, Havertown, PA 19083, USA
E-mail: Uspen-and-sword@casematepublishers.com
Website: www.penandswordbooks.com

Contents

Preface

From my upstairs window I can look down on my yacht, berthed in a small marina at Shoreham-by-Sea in West Sussex. It is not an imposing vessel, but its length overall is thirty feet. It is just long enough, and close enough to Ramsgate, to have been considered suitable by the Admiralty for use in Operation *Dynamo*. It has, however, a long fin keel, giving it a draft of 5.5 feet and it would have been of little practical value off the beaches of Malo-les-Bains, Bray-Dunes or La Panne.

Two berths along from my yacht is a former 1920s' Admiral's barge. Though the owner was told when he bought it that it was one of the Little Ships of Dunkirk, and it would indeed have been eminently suitable for ferrying troops from the beaches to the larger ships anchored off shore, there is no documentary evidence to support this claim. But the name of every boat that took part in the great evacuation is not known and it is not impossible that this lovely old boat really did cross the Channel to risk bombs, shells, mines and wrecks to help save a few tired and desperate soldiers surrounded by the enemy and under frequent attack from the skies over Dunkirk. Had either my neighbour or myself or our boats been at Shoreham in the spring of 1940, we might, just might, have been part of the greatest evacuation in history.

This was certainly the case with one of the famous boats that went to Dunkirk. The comedian Tommy Trinder's boat *Chalmondesleigh* (named after the fictional character he frequently mentioned in his act) was moored at Shoreham when it was requisitioned by the Admiralty. Just a little further down the River Adur from where *Chalmondesleigh* would most probably have been moored, is the Shoreham lifeboat station. Its 41-foot boat, *Rosa Woodd and Phyllis Lunn*, with its 3.6-foot draft, made three trips to Dunkirk with a Royal Navy crew.

Chalmondesleigh, now *Chumley* has been restored and is still afloat, as are many of the Little Ships, including the tug *Challenge* which I was privileged to be shown around when she was temporarily berthed at Shoreham. I have also been on board the Thames barge *Pudge,* whose home is at Maldon in Essex. But would I have volunteered to go to Dunkirk with my boat or my neighbour's? It is a question I have often asked myself. Of course, I believe I would. Not really from any humanitarian convictions nor of ardent patriotism (though these would certainly have been factors that might have impelled me to go), but simply because it would have seemed like a fun adventure.

I am sure that many of those civilians who volunteered to crew merchant ships and smaller civilian craft would have felt the same. Here was a chance to be part of some great escapade, some jolly jaunt. Little could they have realised just what they were letting themselves in for. Some clearly did, as there were instances of crews refusing to go over to Dunkirk. This is a little reported fact, for it does not conform to the much-vaunted 'Dunkirk spirit', but true it is.

Yet the Little Ships, contrary to the popular myths, played only a minor role in Operation *Dynamo* which was principally a Royal Navy accomplishment. Fortunately, the captains of the various warships submitted reports after the operation, and this included those civilian craft that had been requisitioned by the Admiralty and were skippered by Royal Navy officers. It is these reports that enable us to piece together exactly what happened during those nine days in the summer of 1940 when the British Expeditionary Force was saved from annihilation. No one believed it was possible, indeed the evacuation was quite rightly regarded as a 'miracle'. What follows is the story of that remarkable evacuation as told principally by those who were there, almost eighty years ago. It is quite a tale.

John Grehan
Shoreham-by-Sea
December 2017

Maps

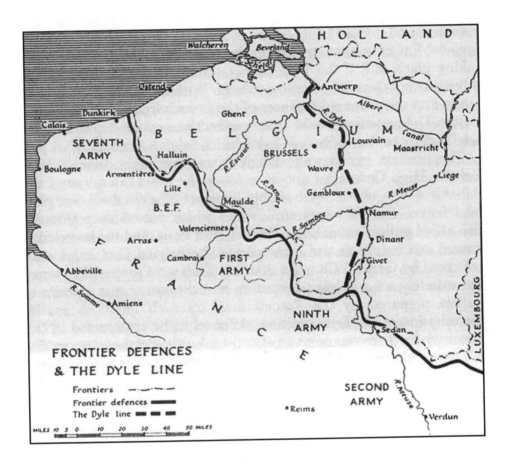

FRONTIER DEFENCES
& THE DYLE LINE

Frontiers ―――――――
Frontier defences ━━━━━
The Dyle line ▬▬ ▬▬ ▬▬

MILES 10 5 0   10   20   30   40   50 MILES

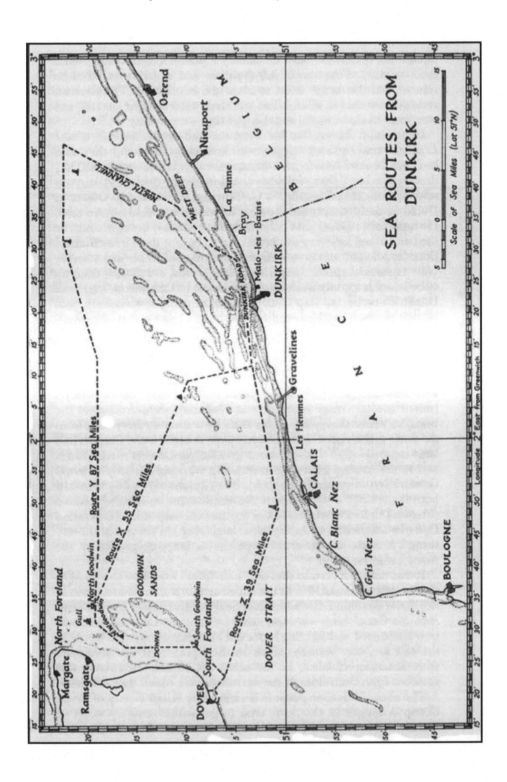

SEA ROUTES FROM DUNKIRK

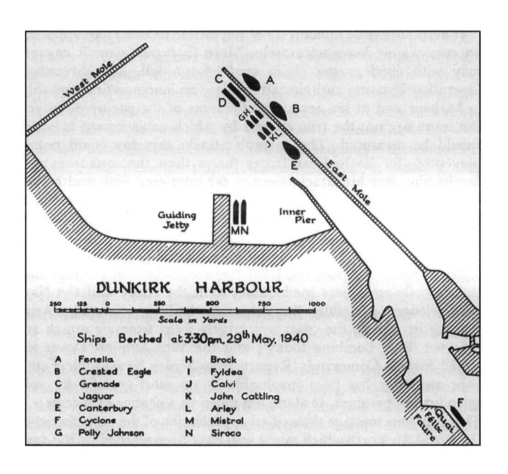

DUNKIRK   HARBOUR

Scale in Yards

Ships   Berthed   at 3·30pm, 29ᵗʰ May, 1940

A	Fenella	H	Brock
B	Crested Eagle	I	Fyldea
C	Grenade	J	Calvi
D	Jaguar	K	John Cattling
E	Canterbury	L	Arley
F	Cyclone	M	Mistral
G	Polly Johnson	N	Siroco

Chapter 1

The British Expeditionary Force In France

U nlike the euphoria that had greeted the declaration of war in August 1914, few welcomed the start of another global conflict in September 1939. The memories, and the scars, of the First World War were still too fresh to be forgotten. It was consternation rather than celebration that marked the news that a British Expeditionary Force (BEF) was crossing the Channel once again to defend France.

This time there was a new factor for the staff of General Headquarters to consider. In 1914, there was no threat from the air, for the few aircraft available to the enemy were employed only in reconnaissance. Now the *Luftwaffe* was Germany's most potent weapon, its fighters and bombers having demonstrated their deadly proficiency in the Spanish Civil War.

Unless the troops could be transported across to France swiftly and secretly, they might never reach the Continent. With the bulk of the German armed forces engaged in the invasion of Poland, now was the time to ship the troops to France, and the advanced units of the BEF were on the move on 4 September, within twenty-four hours of war being declared.

In addition, rather than transporting the troops across the Channel to the northern French ports of Calais or Dunkirk where they would be within easy range of German aircraft, it was arranged for them to be shipped further south, and they were landed at Cherbourg, with their stores and vehicles being despatched to Nantes, St. Nazaire, and Brest.

Ahead of the troops, were sent units of the Docks and Transportation services and within forty-eight hours of arriving at the French ports, these men who, in the main, had been recruited from port authorities around Britain, had the berths allocated to the BEF operating at maximum capacity.

The current BEF had only been formed in 1938 following Germany's annexation of Austria and Hitler's threatened dismemberment of Czechoslovakia. Before Prime Minister Neville Chamberlain secured a deal with Hitler, which gave the German leader a free hand in Czechoslovakia in return for a vague promise that the *Führer* would make no further territorial demands, it looked as if there would be war in Europe. Though there was a relaxation of tension following the Munich Agreement of 29 September 1938, senior British and French officers continued to plan for war and for the defence of the French border. This meant that when war finally came, plans were already in hand for the deployment of the BEF and within two weeks of the declaration of war in 1939, General The Viscount Gort VC, Commander-in-Chief of the BEF, had already established his headquarters at Le Mans.

As his troops landed, they were passed rapidly through transit camps and their vehicles were cleared at once to Vehicle Marshalling Parks, from where they were despatched in convoys, while the troops themselves left by rail on the same day as they marched off the ships.

Since the troops and their vehicles were landed at different ports they had to be collected in an assembly area. The area selected was in the region around Le Mans and Laval, and it took Gort's force around six days to assemble there. Le Mans and Laval are fifty miles apart, the troops being so widely dispersed in case of attack by the *Luftwaffe*. This area is also around 150 miles from the disembarkation ports. Feeding and supplying the troops spread over such distances proved a significant logistical challenge, and the roads and railways of western France were soon choked with traffic.

I Corps of the British Expeditionary Force, commanded by Lieutenant General Michael George Henry Barker, consisted of a headquarters' force and three infantry divisions –1st, 2nd and 48th (South Midland) – each of which was composed of three infantry brigades with accompanying artillery and engineers. II Corps, under the command of Lieutenant General Alan Brooke, was similarly composed of three infantry divisions, in this case the 3rd, 4th and 50th (Northumbrian), and the same support arms. Each division also had its own armoured regiment and a machine-gun battalion

Before the troops could be moved up to the French border ready to face the enemy, the exact sector to be manned by the BEF had to be firmly established. On 22 September, Gort received a message from *Général* Alphonse Georges, Commander of the French Front of the North-East, which informed Gort that his area of responsibility would be from 'Maulde exclusive to Halluin inclusive, and thence a defensive flank along river Lys/Armentières'. To help Gort defend this sector of the line, Georges placed the 51st French Division

(*Général de Brigade* Gillard) under his command. Gort decided to employ it on the left of the sector, covering the towns of Roubaix and Tourcoing.

It had been originally intended that as soon as it had completed its reorganisation in the assembly area, the BEF should move to a concentration point in the north of France, and remain there in readiness to occupy the line not earlier than 5 October. *Général* Georges decided, however, that it was inadvisable to await the arrival of the whole British Expeditionary Force in the concentration area and expressed a wish that I Corps should move up to the front without delay. Gort agreed and he told Georges that I Corps would take over its sector of the line on 2 October, and that II Corps would follow ten days later.

I Corps began the 250-mile move from the assembly area on 26 September. Tanks, tracked vehicles, and slow-moving artillery went by train, with the rest of the of the corps advancing on three parallel routes. Three days were allotted for the move of each formation. Two staging areas were arranged on each road, south of the rivers Seine and Somme respectively. With the fear of aerial attack defining the nature of every movement, anti-aircraft guns were set up to defend these river crossings. Luckily, the weather was fine throughout the whole period of the move, and there was little attention from the German Air Force.

The first stage of the journey north was 120 miles. An average of 500 vehicles moved daily over each stage of the route, maintaining a distance of 100 yards between each vehicle as a precaution against the constant concern over air attack. A halt of one day for maintenance purposes was made after the first day's move. Nevertheless, I Corps completed its move on schedule, taking over from the French the sector Maulde-Gruson on the Belgian frontier. This sector lay between that of the 1st French Army and the 16th French Corps.

Likewise, II Corps moved into its position on the Belgium border on 12 October. General Headquarters was established in and around Habarcq, some eight miles west of Arras.

The BEF was in position ready to face the enemy just five weeks after the declaration of war.

ON THE FRONT LINE

France's main line of defence' of course, was the famous Maginot Line. It was named after the French Minister of War, André Maginot, who secured funding for a series of fortifications to guard France's eastern frontier, using such emotive language as 'concrete is less expensive than a wall of chests.'[1] The Line was built following a national debate which took place in France after the terrible experience of the First World War, on how to prevent the Germans from invading France in the future. It was said that the foundations of the Maginot Line were the war cemeteries of France.[2] Work began on the Line in 1930. The series of defences ran from the Alps, where the forts defended the border with Italy, along France's eastern frontier until it reached Luxemburg and Belgium.

An advance by the Germans through Luxembourg was discounted because the heavily-wooded Ardennes hills extended along this border region. By contrast, an advance through Belgium, as had happened in 1914, was considered highly likely and France wanted Belgium to participate in this defensive scheme.

But the Belgians did not want to do anything that would compromise their stated position as neutrals. If they would have participated in continuing the Line along their frontier with Germany it would have implied that they viewed the Germans as their enemy – which the Belgian Government feared would provoke an immediate German invasion.

On the other hand, as it was perceived at the time, if France would have stretched the Maginot Line along its border with Belgium, then that small country would have been left with little choice other than to abandon its neutrality and align itself with Germany. So, the northern flank of the magnificent, impenetrable Maginot Line remained open and exposed and it was there where the BEF was deployed – where the main German attack was most likely to be delivered. It must be noted at this point that France's policy was not merely defensive. Wars are not won by static defences. The Maginot Line was only expected to hold back the Germans long enough for France (and possibly its allies) to mobilize forces powerful enough to take the offensive and carry the fight to the enemy.

This was, in effect, a replica of the success of the First World War when the Germans were held by the trench network that stretched along the Western Front, before the Allies mounted the attacks that helped precipitate the collapse of German resolve in 1918. But it is axiomatic that generals always prepare for the last war, and there can be few more egregious examples than that of the French military planners of the inter-war years.

As soon as the British troops arrived on the Belgian border they found that French engineers had already built an almost continuous anti-tank ditch along the frontier covered by concrete blockhouses that were equipped with anti-tank weapons and machine-guns. It had been agreed earlier that the French engineers would continue to add to these defences in conjunction with the BEF, and a massive building programme of reinforced concrete pillboxes and trenches therefore began in earnest. The BEF was digging-in.

Along the 200 miles from the end of the Maginot Line at Longuyon to the North Sea coast were five armies. Along the first sector to Sedan stood the French Second Army; from Sedan to the valley of the Oise was the Ninth Army; the First Army then occupied a line from the Oise to Maulde. The BEF was posted between Maulde to Bailleul, and then the French Seventh Army took over the front to the coast.

This was the start of the 'Phoney War', the 'Bore War' or 'Sitzkreig,' as it was variously called, with the Germans showing no sign of risking an attack upon France or Belgium. As the months passed by with no indication of movement by the enemy, discussions were even held about reducing the strength of the BEF and transferring the troops to other theatres where they would be of more use.[3]

Bored though the British were, they were not allowed to be idle during their time on the Belgian border and by early May 1940, more than 400 concrete pillboxes of varying size had been completed with over 100 more under construction, while work on the improvement of field defences, barbed-wire and other obstacles proceeded continuously on the original front and in the sector north of Armentières recently taken over from the French.

Chiefly by the use of excavator machinery, in excess of forty miles of revetted anti-tank ditch had been added to that prepared by the French Army during peace time. Machines had also been used to assist the troops in constructing earthwork defences, as well as in mixing concrete and burying signal cables.

Most of the French divisions on either side of the BEF were no more gainfully employed than their British counterparts, with nothing other than the construction of fieldworks to occupy them. It was only those positioned along the Saar front, ahead of the Maginot Line, that came into contact with the enemy. The French actually undertook an offensive along this sector in September 1939 in a bid to draw German troops away from their attack on Poland. However, the French had little interest in provoking the Germans and the operation was called off after little more than a week. The French troops returned to the security of their positions along the Maginot Line.

Whilst no further large-scale operations took place, the Saar front was not completely quiet. Engagements between the French and the Germans were not uncommon, though few risks were taken by either side, the troops being quite content to stay safely within their own lines.

Nevertheless, there were calls for the British troops to take their share of the limited fighting on the Saar and in response to this call the 3rd Brigade of the BEF's 1st Division of I Corps was selected to be the first British brigade to go into the Maginot Line.

MANNING THE MAGINOT LINE

Not only was this an opportunity for the men to gain combat experience but it would also counter the German propaganda taunts that 'Britain would fight the war to the last Frenchman'. By putting these troops in the front line, it would show the French just what the British were capable of and help overcome the morale-sapping effects of indefinite inaction in the waterlogged defensive positions on the Belgian border.

On 27 November 1939, the 1st Battalion of the King's Shropshire Light Infantry, along with the 1st Battalion Duke of Wellington's Regiment, the 2nd Battalion Sherwood Foresters, and the 3rd Infantry Brigade Anti-Tank Company, were transferred to Metz, before moving up to the Maginot Line itself.

They were now in Lorraine and as the Shropshires' commanding officer pointed out to his men, the older Frenchmen in whose farms and houses they were billeted in had served in the First World War as conscripts for the German Army.

Indeed, some people in this border region were still clearly pro-German as the following incident shows, which is recorded in the battalion's written history: 'The attitude of some inhabitants was not quite what was expected, for instance an ex-Uhlan NCO deliberately drove his sheep into one of the company billets saying he preferred they should be comfortably accommodated rather than the British troops!'

The Shropshires' first impression of the Maginot Line defences was a mixed one. 'We were all astonished at the "Maginot Line,"' wrote one officer. 'As I drove through I hardly noticed anything more than a strong anti-tank obstacle of rails, several strong belts of barbed wire and a few pillboxes, so well were the main forts concealed in our sector. The forts were tunnelled out of a small line of hills. The inside of the forts resembled a battleship, each having engine rooms, living accommodation, kitchen, command post and control rooms, turrets, magazines, hospital and so on.'

Another Shropshire officer had quite a different impression of the Maginot Line: 'We were given a lecture by the French divisional commander on the infantry dispositions – the line of contact, the line of "recoil", the line of reserve. In fact, we discovered none of these lines had been prepared in any way – no trenches, no wire, nothing.'[4]

The 3rd Brigade was placed under the command of the French 42nd Division and when the Shropshires moved up to the front the French troops offered the British plenty of advice – but only on how to avoid trouble. This included removing a vital part from each Bren gun just in case someone was stupid enough to fire one at the Germans! The British troops were also advised never to fire at enemy patrols unless they were actually cutting the wire in front of the Allied trenches, just in case the Germans fired back.[5]

Although the French were reluctant to leave the security of the *ligne de contact*, the line of contact, the most advanced of the Maginot Line's defences, the BEF was there to fight – indeed, the Army's first gallantry medals of the war were won on the Maginot Line. The battalions in the line of contact sent out 'battle' patrols at night to engage the enemy. It was later found that large patrols were difficult to control in the dark and twelve seems to have become established as the best number of men for these missions.

A number of men in each patrol were armed with sub-machine guns, the rest carried grenades, rifles and bludgeons. They blackened their faces, wore cap comforters and long, leather sleeveless Army jerkins. It was, declared one man from another brigade, like playing Boy Scouts.

There was, of course, a serious side to this deadly game of patrol and skirmish, trap and ambush amongst the deserted houses and empty fields of No Man's Land. It was on one of these patrols that Corporal Thomas William Priday met his death, the first British soldier to die in combat in the Second World War.

'As soon as dark fell the khaki-clad patrols climbed over the parapet and crawled out through the gaps in the wire into the unknown,' ran one report.

'They moved here and there, searched houses and villages whose civilian population had long since been evacuated, ever on the lookout for traces of the passage of their opposite numbers in the German ranks. Always they had to be on the very tip-top of alertness, with hands ready to shoot and eyes keen for the slightest suggestion of a well-placed "booby trap" such as both sides delighted to plant.'

Sadly, it was one of those devices, in fact a British booby trap, which detonated and killed Priday near the small village of Monneren. Some accounts state that he was leading a patrol out, others that the men were returning.

Priday was buried with full military honours. During the ceremony, the French divisional commander gave a long address, saluting Priday as '*Le premier soldat qui est mort pour France*'. Unfortunately, the coffin was dropped upside down into the grave with the Union Flag and the accoutrements underneath. Both had to be retrieved and the entire process repeated from the start.

The 2nd Battalion Royal Norfolk Regiment was the first complete infantry unit of the BEF to land in France, and it soon took its turn on the Saar front. Two patrols undertaken on the night of 4/5 January 1940, near the village of Grindoff, resulted in a pair of 'firsts' – one saw the first occasion in which British troops penetrated German territory, whilst the other led to the award of the BEF's first gallantry medals of the Second World War. Captain Francis Barclay was the recipient of a Military Cross, and Lance Corporal H. Davis was awarded the Military Medal. The other members of the patrol, Second Lieutenant C.R. Murray Brown, Lance Corporal A. Harris and Lance Corporal A. Spooner, were Mentioned in Despatches. Unfortunately, these successes were marred by another first for the Norfolks and the BEF – that of losing the first officer in combat. The casualty from the second patrol was Second Lieutenant Patrick Anthony Clement Everitt, the son of Sir Clement and Lady Everitt of Sheringham, Norfolk. Buried with full military honours by the Germans, his body today lies in Rheinberg War Cemetery.

Following the publication of the BEF's first casualties on 30 January 1940, the French issued a communiqué: 'The British now have their wounded and even their dead, on French soil once again.'[6]

However, the French Prime Minister Édouard Daladier was keen to play down the events on the Saar front. 'Military operations have not yet developed with that violence and that vast and brutal extension over wide fronts which they seemed likely to assume,' he told the French National Assembly. 'But we ought not to take this initiative. This war is to us a war for our security and our liberty. Our rule for those who defend us is economy in blood and economy in suffering.'

The economy in lives that the French premier sought certainly seemed valid at that stage of the war when compared with the Great War twenty-five years earlier. Up to December 1939, less than 2,000 British and French Army personnel had lost their lives; by the first Christmas of the First World War that figure had been more than half-a-million.

The first elements of doubt about the continuing low level of activity on the French border began to surface in early January 1940, but no one could quite understand what had happened. On 10 January, a Bf 109 force-landed in Belgium. On board was a German officer carrying the *Luftwaffe*'s Air Fleet II's copy of the *Wehrmacht*'s plans for the invasion of Belgium. The officer was taken prisoner by the Belgians and the plans were passed onto the Allies. What no-one could fathom was whether it was a genuine crash and the documents were real, or that the whole episode had been manufactured by the Germans to mislead the Allies.

The *Oberkommando der Wehrmach* (OKW) was similarly confused. Was the pilot of the Messerschmitt a traitor, taking the officer with the secret plans to the Allies, or did he experience navigational and/or mechanical failures (for he should never have been flying over Belgian air space)?

Both sides now had to consider their positions. Should the Allies adjust their dispositions to counter this attack through Belgium or would that be playing into Hitler's hands? Because of the strength of the Maginot Line, an attack through Belgium was regarded as almost inevitable, and this merely confirmed most people's suspicions. The Germans were seen as being creatures of habit and a repeat of the Schlieffen Plan of the First World War was only to be expected.

The plans carried by Major Hellmuth Reinberger were indeed real, which presented Hitler with a terrible dilemma. Should the invasion plans be altered now that they were known by the enemy? Was there any practical alternative?

It would be the decisions made by the opposing leaders after the German plans were in Allied possession that would determine the outcome of the Battle of France.

THE 'IMPENETRABLE' ARDENNES

The ones in the middle of all this were the Belgians. Assuming that the captured plans were real, as seemed likely, then the only hope the Belgians had of preventing their country from being overrun was to invite the British and French forces to move into Belgium immediately. There were, though, dangers in this for King Leopold and his government. Their tiny country, with its equally small army, would be very much the junior partner and would have to dance to whatever tunes were being played in London and Paris. Leopold, therefore, wanted guarantees that no arrangements would be made without Belgian consent. This was too broad a commitment for the British and French to make and no such guarantees were forthcoming. The British and French troops who were placed on the alert along the Belgian frontier expecting to cross into Belgium, were stood down.

The Belgians were now in a terrible predicament and they felt that their best course of action was to inform Berlin that they had gained possession of the German invasion plans. Hitler could hardly mount an attack when his plans were known to the enemy. Or could he?

It seems that it was General Erich von Manstein, the former Chief of Staff of Army Group A, who first presented a viable alternative plan for an attack against France and the Low Countries to Hitler. This was for the original advance through Belgium to go ahead on a somewhat reduced scale, thus luring the French and British forces into Belgium. Once these forces had been committed, the main German thrust would be delivered to the south-east through the Ardennes and across the Meuse into France through Sedan. As we have seen, an attack by Germany through the Ardennes had been discounted as being impracticable and the French defences in this area were far from strong. It was a bold, but dangerous, scheme that Manstein proposed. Everything would depend on its execution.

What in retrospect now seems remarkable, is that information of just such an attack was transmitted to the Allies, and what is just as surprising is that it came from the German military counter-intelligence branch, the *Abwehr*.

Colonel Hans Oster, second-in-command of the *Abwehr*, was a leading figure in the small group of German officers who sought to remove Hitler from power before he led Germany to disaster.

Oster had repeatedly warned the Dutch Military Attaché in Berlin, Major Gijbertus Sas, of the imminence of an attack in the West. Sas had passed this information onto the Dutch and Belgian governments, pronouncing specific dates for the attack in November and then December 1939, then on 13 January 1940, after the capture of Major Reinberger and the invasion plans. On this last occasion, the Belgian Chief of Staff, General Édourd Van den Bergen, had taken the threat seriously and, without reference to either King Leopold or the King's military advisor, General Raoul Van Overstraeten, had broadcast an announcement ordering all Belgian soldiers on leave to return to their regiments. The warning from Sas proved to be false, but the tension between Germany and Belgian was raised to dangerous levels and Van den Bergen was quickly removed from his post.

So, the months passed with no further alarms. Altogether nine British brigades served on the Maginot Line until, in April 1940, it was decided that the British commitment to the defence of the Line would be increased to divisional strength. The unit chosen for the first – and what would prove to be the last – divisional tour of duty on the Maginot Line was the 51st (Highland) Division.

Commanded by Major General Victor Fortune, the 51st (Highland) Division was a powerful, self-contained formation. It was composed of three infantry brigades, the 152nd Brigade (2nd and 4th Battalions Seaforth Highlanders, 4th Battalion Cameron Highlanders), 153rd Brigade (1st and 5th Battalions Gordon Highlanders, 4th Battalion Black Watch) and 154th Brigade (1st Battalion Black Watch, 7th and 8th Battalions Argyll & Sutherland Highlanders), with an Armoured Reconnaissance Regiment of light tanks and Bren carriers, plus three regiments of field artillery and one anti-tank regiment.

To this force were attached another two artillery regiments, two machine-gun battalions and two battalions of Pioneers. General Fortune also had a composite squadron of the RAF under his command, one flight of which was fighters, the other a flight of Westland Lysander Army Co-operation aircraft. The entire force totaled around 21,000 men.[7]

III CORPS

The 51st Division was the first element of what was to become III Corps, which was to be formed in France throughout February and March 1940 as increasing numbers of trained troops became available from the UK. The other two divisions of III Corps were the 42nd (East Lancashire) and the 44th (Home Counties). With the increase in size of the BEF, so the front Gort's men would be responsible for was to be similarly extended.

The comparative inactivity that had persisted all through the winter along the Saar front continued during the early days of the 51st Division's occupation of the Line. When the Scots moved up to the *ligne de contact*, they found that the French had settled into a comfortable routine of doing nothing that would upset the Germans. When Major James Grant of the 2nd Seaforths suggested a joint patrol against the German lines to his French counterpart, the French officer almost fainted!

Things appeared to change at night, however. 'Punctually at 21.00 hours the fun began,' recalled Sergeant John Mackenzie. 'The whole valley was filled with an ear-splitting volume of sound. Things banged, boomped, screeched, whee-ed, whistled, and thumped. Light flickered from gun-flash and shell-burst. Out in front sped line upon line of tracer, looking like red-hot bees, down and across the valley.' But this drama was an act played out for the generals and the newsreels, the bullets and the shells flying harmlessly over the heads of the men sheltering safely in their trenches. There was no real intention of doing any harm.[8]

Towards the end of April, German patrols became increasingly active against the *ligne de contact*. There was some intense fighting in which the artillery of both sides joined in. Then from the beginning of May this activity died down and an 'uncanny' quiet descended upon the Highlanders' sector of the Line.

This period of calm ended on 6 May 1940, when the German artillery shelled the British positions. Then, on 10 May, less than a month after the 51st Division had arrived on the Maginot Line, the great German offensive began. In response, the French Commander-in-Chief, Général Gamelin, issued an 'Order of the Day' at 14.05 hours:

> The attack which we have been anticipating since last October has been launched this morning. It is the beginning of a fight to the death

between Germany and ourselves. The watchword for all the Allies is: calm, energy, confidence.[9]

Within just a few days all confidence had evaporated and panic replaced calm. France was about to suffer its greatest defeat and the BEF face the prospect of disaster on an unimaginable scale.

Chapter 2

'The Greatest Battle Of History'

On the morning of 10 May 1940, the Germans launched their predicted invasion of Belgium, and a message was issued from French Headquarters to implement 'Plan D'. This plan called for the BEF to move into Belgium to take up a position on the River Dyle. It meant that the Germans had violated Belgium neutrality, and Britain was treaty-bound to march to her defence.

The formulation of this plan had occupied the minds of Gort and the French commanders, *Général* Georges and *Général* Gamelin, throughout the first months of the war. Between them they had at first decided that, in the event of a German attack through Belgium, the BEF should continue to hold the frontier defences, pushing forward mobile troops to the line of the River Escaut, while the French 7th Army on the British left was to delay the enemy on the line of the Messines Ridge and the Yser Canal. This plan was soon discarded, however, in favour of moving the entire BEF up to the Escaut, where they would hold the line of the river from the point at which it crosses the frontier at Maulde northwards to the neighbourhood of Ghent, where the Belgian Army was concentrated. This became known as 'Plan E'.

This plan was also abandoned because, in Gort's words, 'as information became available regarding the defences of the Belgian Army, and its readiness for war, the French High Command formed the opinion that it would be safe to count on the Belgian defence holding out for some days on the Eastern frontier, and the Albert Canal'.

The Belgians had, in fact, been building considerable defensive structures which, though not on the scale of the Maginot Line, were still impressive – or at least that was what they claimed.

It was accepted by the Belgians that they would be unable to stop the Germans on the frontier, so they decided to build a fortified line in the heart of the country. The time taken for the Germans to advance into Belgium up to the fortified line would allow the army to fully mobilise and dig-in – and for Belgium's Allies to come to its help.

The fortified line, then, was intended to run from Antwerp in the north through Leuven and Wavre along the River Dyle, and then on to Namur and Givet (France) along the Meuse. Unfortunately, it was incomplete when the Germans attacked, with the vital stretch from Namur to the French border still devoid of fortifications.

Nevertheless, the line of the Dyle was, from the military point of view, a better one than that of the Escaut. 'It was,' Gort explained, 'shorter, it afforded greater depth and its northern portion was inundated, in addition, it represented smaller enemy occupation of Belgian territory.' This latter factor was not merely a political move; the region that would be saved included Belgium's industrial heartland.

What such a move up to the Dyle meant was that the positions on the border which the British and French had been strengthening all winter would be abandoned. It also meant that the moment the Allies were informed of the German invasion of Belgium, the BEF would have to rush some sixty miles up to the Dyle to get there before the Germans and to occupy positions which the troops were unfamiliar with. Of possibly even greater significance was that this move left a large gap in the Allied front around Gembloux where there was no natural anti-tank obstacle. Earmarked to fill this gap was France's strongest force, the First Army, supported by a full half of its armoured reserves.

So it was, that at approximately 06.15 hours on 10 May, that Gort received instructions to put Plan D into effect. Gort then sent instructions to his corps commanders to begin their move into Belgium at 13.00 hours. 'It was hard to believe,' said Alan Brooke in command of II Corps, 'on a most glorious spring day with all nature looking quite at its best, that we were taking the first step towards what must become one of the greatest battles of history!'[1]

The 12th Royal Lancers, with its Morris CS9/Light Armoured Cars, was the first regiment to cross into Belgium, leading the way to the Dyle, through cheering crowds. It reached the Dyle, unopposed, at 22.30 hours. Everything appeared to be going according to plan, with the French armies on the right and left of the BEF reported as advancing on time. Already, though, the BEF's headquarters at Arras had come under heavy bombardment with the *Luftwaffe* targeting the airfields, railways and supply bases of the Expeditionary Force.

On the 11th, the bulk of the BEF reached the Dyle on schedule, despite encountering the first of the refugees abandoning their homes ahead of the advancing Germans. But already there was bad news from elsewhere, only one day into the battle. The Germans had 100 kilometers of Belgian territory to cross, with its waterways and strongpoints manned by the Belgian Army. It was expected that it would take the Germans a week or two to reach the Dyle position, by which time the British and French would have dug themselves well in. But, the speed of the German move into Belgium had taken the Belgian Army by surprise and its engineers had failed to demolish important bridges over the Albert Canal and the River Meuse which the Germans were already crossing. Furthermore, when the French on Gort's right reached their pre-arranged positions, they found that the strong defences the Belgians had boasted of were incomplete and badly sighted. After consultations with *Général* Georges, it was agreed that despite the unexpectedly poor defences, with a few modifications, they would continue with Plan D. The Germans, after all, were behaving exactly as anticipated and were marching straight towards the waiting Allied forces – or so it seemed. But just as the Germans were moving into Belgium as expected, the Allied armies had marched into Belgium just as the Germans had expected. The British and French divisions braced themselves for the first clash with the enemy, unaware that they had marched into a trap.

'WE HAVE LOST THE BATTLE'

On the 13th, the first skirmishes took place along the British sector, though there was no engagement of any consequence. But some seventy miles to the south of the forward British and French positions there were reports of German forces having marched through the Ardennes and crossed the Belgian stretch of the River Meuse. At this early stage in the unfolding battle the true consequences of this approach by the Germans was not fully appreciated. The French high command considered the densely-wooded and hilly terrain of the Ardennes to be effectively impenetrable to a modern army with all its motorised encumbrances and the line of the River Meuse easily defendable against light forces. This misconception meant that the border along the Ardennes had received comparatively little attention from the French military planners and only a small number of pillboxes and bunkers had been built. To

Général Gamelin, the French Army's Commander-in-Chief, it simply did not seem worth tying up men and materiel where the Germans could never attack. Gamelin was completely, and catastrophically wrong.

It was *Generalmajor* Erwin Romel's 7th Panzer Division of *Generalleutnant* Heinz Guderian's XIX Corps that led the way over the Meuse supported by the *Luftwaffe* which carried out the heaviest bombardment of the war to that date and, it is claimed, the most intense the Germans mounted at any stage in the war. XIX Corps was part of *Generaloberst* Gert von Rundstedt's Army Group A which was composed of no less than forty-five divisions, seven of which were panzer divisions, the bulk of Hitler's armoured resources. The force that had attacked the BEF and the French First Army, *Generaloberst* Fedor von Bock's Army Group B, was far less formidable, with only twenty-nine divisions, just two of which were armoured.

With the BEF and the French First Army holding off von Bock's attacks and the French Second and Third armies manning the Maginot Line and associated areas which were coming under pressure from *Generaloberst* von Leeb's Army Group C (nineteen divisions, none armoured), now that the panzers were across the river there was little to stop them racing into northern France. All Gamelin's plans and all the preparations the Allies had made were, at a stroke, made redundant. Worse still, was that the vast sums of money and enormous resources that had been sunk into the magnificent Maginot Line had been for nothing, as the German armoured divisions merely swept by its northern flank. The French forces were thrown into chaos.

The following day, 14 May, brought more distressing news for the Allies with the announcement that Holland had been overrun and its government had surrendered. Though this had no immediate effect on the BEF which continued to only be lightly engaged, the news came as a terrible shock to the Belgians, eroding their already shaky morale.

After breaking through the French 55th and 71st divisions on the Meuse, Guderian's panzers struck and dispersed the hurriedly-formed French Sixth Army at its assembly area west of Sedan. As the panzers continued to move westwards, *Général* Corap's French Ninth Army found the Germans had swept round behind its southern flank and almost the entire force surrendered over the next few days – and still the 7th Panzer Division pushed on. Against orders to halt and wait for the rest of XIX Corps and Army Group A to consolidate the ground won, Rommel continued to drive deeper into France. The Belgian, British and French forces in Belgium were in danger of being isolated and cut off from the rest of the French Army.

On 15 May 1940, just five days after the start of the German onslaught, the newly-appointed French Prime Minister, Paul Reynaud, rang his equally recently-installed counterpart in London, Winston Churchill, to announce that: 'We have been defeated. We are beaten; we have lost the battle ... The front is broken near Sedan: they [the Germans] are pouring through in great numbers with tanks and armoured cars.'[2]

At the same time that the French armies were collapsing to the south, Gort was writing that: 'By the night of 15th May the movements envisaged in Plan D were all running ahead of schedule.' That situation was about to change drastically. The French First Army, on the right of the BEF, came under heavy pressure on its front as the enemy smashed a gap 5,000 yards wide in the French line. With the French Ninth Army to its right no longer existing as an effective fighting force. *Général d'armée* Gaston Billotte had no choice but to fall back to the south-west to find a narrower and more defensible position. Much as in 1914, when the BEF of the First World War was compelled to withdraw from Mons in line with the French withdrawal, so the BEF of the Second World War had to conform to the movements of the French First Army to maintain the integrity of the Allied front. Likewise, the Belgian Army on the left of the BEF, though not yet seriously engaged, also had to fall back. The decision was taken to revert to Plan E and retreat to the line of the River Escaut.

Lieutenant General Alan Brooke, saw that the Belgians were 'in a very shaky and jumpy condition' and with the fall of Holland, the Germans would be able to bring an increased number of troops against them. 'The BEF is therefore likely to have both its flanks turned,' he wrote in his diary of 15 May, 'and will have a very unpleasant time in extricating itself out of its current position'.[3]

The BEF had been shipped over to France through the ports of Cherbourg, Brest, St Nazaire and Nantes. The direction of von Rundstedt's Army Group A was directly north of the Somme, with the potential of placing itself between those ports and the BEF. Once this was understood in the Admiralty, the Ministry of Shipping was informed that the supply lines of the BEF had to switch to the northern ports of Boulogne, Calais, Dunkirk and Ostend. This was no panic measure but a reasoned readjustment of the British lines of communication.

On the afternoon of the 16th, Churchill flew to Paris to discuss the deteriorating situation with the French Prime Minister, the Minister for War, Daladier, and *Général* Gamelin. Gamelin explained that the Germans had pushed sixty miles into northern France, scattering the French armies as they advanced. Churchill, then asked, 'Where is the strategic reserve?' Gamelin shrugged his shoulders, and replied with one a single word, 'Aucune' – 'none'. The whole purpose of the Maginot Line was that France would not need to mass all its troops on the border, thus enabling the formation of a strategic reserve that could move to any threatened point. The fact that the French, contrary to all the pre-war plans, had no reserve shocked Churchill.

The reality was that the French already believed they had been defeated. The other factor was the speed of the German advance, which baffled the French commanders who were never able to organise a defensive line before the Germans had either pushed through or around them.

Churchill, typically, said that instead of retreating as they had been doing, the Allied armies should counter-attack. Indeed, this was exactly the opinion of Colonel Charles de Gaulle, who saw that German communications through Sedan were exposed and vulnerable. On the 17th he led his 4e Division Cuirassée de Réserve against the German-held village of Montcornet. After some initial success, de Gaulle's attack was driven off. Two days later de Gaulle tried again to cut the German lines of communication, but again failed. At this point, Prime Minister Reynard dismissed Gamelin who had completely lost his nerve, being replaced by *Général* Maxime Weygand

The withdrawal to the Escaut was accomplished without too many problems. Unfortunately, the French First Army had opened the sluices along the Scheldt to inundate the ground around Valenciennes and this had reduced the depth of the river in the sector held by the BEF to just three feet. Yet there, after advancing and retreating for the last nine days, the Allied armies in the north halted.

In the areas taken up by the British, the Belgian civilians who had not already moved out were ordered to leave their homes by midnight on the 15th. The reason for this was to make sure that the enemy could not receive any assistance from pro-German elements in the local population. One such incident was recorded in the War Diary of the 7th Field Regiment, Royal Artillery:

During the morning [of the 15th] a civilian was apprehended on suspicion, sent to 9 Inf Bde for interrogation and released by them … In the evening, the suspected civilian who had been apprehended in the morning was again found in the village, and it was discovered that he had been cutting marks in the grass. He was again taken to 9 Inf Bde for interrogation, and five minutes later was, by order of the Brigadier, taken out and shot.

The Allies may have made a stand on the line of the Escaut, but to the south the enemy kept on advancing which meant that the BEF's rear areas were now under imminent threat. The only British units in these areas were those of the lines of communication troops. It had never been expected that these troops would have to fight, but now every man and every gun was needed to halt the German advance. Amongst the line of communication troops were three infantry divisions – the 12th, 23rd and 46th – which had been stripped of their artillery and heavy equipment and sent over to act as a labour force. These men, some of whom had never even fired their rifles, would have to hold back the full might of the German panzer divisions. They would be almost wiped out, suffering casualties on a scale not seen since the First World War (of the 701 men 7th Battalion, Royal Sussex Regiment, for example, who mustered for duty on the morning of the 20th, just seventy survived to be marched into captivity that night). But crucially, they delayed the Germans for a few hours, and by this date, every hour was precious to the BEF.

This was because it had now become sadly evident that the German advance could not be halted and that all the British could do was try and escape back to England. Gort's Deputy Chief of Staff, Brigadier Sir Oliver Leese, had already prepared the first plan for withdrawal and evacuation, and this was put into words for the first time at a meeting at Gort's headquarters which Billotte visited late on 19 May. Gort told the French commander that, 'there was an imminent danger of the forces in the north-eastern area, that is to say the French forces next to the sea, the Belgian Army, the B.E.F. and the bulk of the French 1st Army on our right, being irretrievably cut off from the main French forces in the south.'[4]

If that happened the only course of action available was for the BEF to withdraw north-westwards towards the Channel ports, 'making use of the successive river and canal lines, and of holding a defensive perimeter there, at any rate sufficiently long to enable the force to be withdrawn, preferably in concert with the French and Belgians'.

After what must have been a painful meeting, Gort wrote:

> I realized that this course was in theory a last alternative, and it would involve the departure of the BEF from the theatre of war at a time when the French might need all the support which Britain could give them. It involved the virtual certainty that even if the excellent port facilities at Dunkirk continued to be available, it would be necessary to abandon all the heavier guns and much of the vehicles and equipment. Nevertheless, I felt that in the circumstances there might be no other course open to me.[5]

Gort's pessimistic assessment of the strategic situation seemed barely credible to those far from the fighting in London. The Chief of the Imperial General Staff, General Sir Edmund Ironside, refused to acknowledge Gort's belief that an evacuation of the BEF was an option. Instead, he favoured a march south to link up with the other French armies behind the Somme. The War Cabinet agreed and decided that Ironside should go over to France and see what was happening for himself. 'We therefore sent him to Lord Gort with instructions to move the British Army in a south-westerly direction and to force his way through all opposition in order to join up with the French in the south,' the Prime Minister recalled, 'and that the Belgians should be urged to conform to this movement, or, alternatively, that we would evacuate as many of their troops [the Belgians] as possible from the Channel ports.'[6] Ironside reached Gort's headquarters at Wahagines at 06.00 hours on the 20th. After listening to the British field commander, Ironside visited Billotte and Blanchard at Lens. He found that the French commanders had, 'No plan, no thought of a plan. Ready to be slaughtered.' The CIGS could see that Billotte was 'completely beaten' and he even lost his temper with the general and shook him by the buttons of his tunic.[7]

Eventually, he got Billotte to agree to a counter-attack in conjunction with the BEF, and this information was passed onto Weygand, who agreed to an operation in which elements of the French First Army and the BEF would attack the German communications at Arras from the north whilst at the same time the French Seventh Army would attack from the south. Believing that he had done all he could, Ironside returned to London.

'WE STAND AND FIGHT'

Gort immediately began to prepare for the counter-attack at Arras. The 5th and 50th divisions and the 1st Army Tank Brigade and a few other units were placed under the command of Major General Harold Franklyn, to be then known collectively as Frankforce. The French First Army's contribution took the form of the French Cavalry Corps of light tanks; this, though, had been reduced by that time to only a quarter of its original strength.

On the 21st, Franklyn attacked southwards whilst the *3e Division Légère Mécanique* pushed northwards. The forces employed in the attack were far too weak to have any real chance of stopping the enemy and, after some initial gains, the Germans drove off the counter-attack. Nevertheless, the Battle of Arras had a far greater impact on German operations than is generally appreciated, as Rundstedt later admitted :

> A critical moment in the drive [towards the coast] came just as my forces had reached the Channel. It was caused by a British counter-attack southwards from Arras on May 21st. For a short time it was feared that our armoured divisions would be cut off before the infantry divisions could come up to support them. None of the French counter-attacks carried any threat such as this one.

This concern that the panzer divisions might be cut off from the rest of Army Group A, was transmitted throughout the chain of command, and was one of the factors that led just three days later to Hitler's ill-judged order to halt the tanks. That decision cost Hitler an even more decisive victory than the one he eventually achieved, for it allowed the BEF to reach Dunkirk and establish a strong defensive perimeter. One can only wonder what might have happened if Gort had committed himself fully to the counter-attack, instead of employing little more than two divisions? It might well be that Gort felt he could not weaken his defensive front further by releasing more men. But the Escaut position had been under consideration for a long time, and indeed was regarded as far stronger than the Dyle. One can only conclude that Gort had already set his mind on evacuation, and he only undertook the attack at Arras to satisfy Churchill's and Ironside's demands.

Though he had already decided that a retreat to the coast was all but inevitable, Gort could not let his growing concerns over the perilous state of the Expeditionary Force be communicated to his men. An army's morale is highly fragile and needs to be handled with care, so on 21 May, Gort circulated a message to battalion commanders in a bid to scotch any rumours of an unfolding disaster in the army's rear: 'News from the south reassuring. We stand and fight. Tell your men.'[8] It was a blatant lie, but such rhetoric has inspired soldiers throughout the generations and the men of the BEF responded accordingly. They dug-in and prepared to face the German onslaught. It came soon enough.

At 07.30 hours that morning, German artillery began hammering the British line. 'Suddenly all hell was let loose,' recalled Les Drinkwater with the 3rd Battalion, Grenadier Guards:

> We were lying down behind a bush, bullets were cracking over our bodies, trench mortar bombs and shrapnel shells were exploding. The din was terrible. To our amazement, through all this noise, we could hear the familiar sound of a Bren gun, firing as if it was defying the whole German Army. The Bren was positioned on the other side of the bush, on the canal bank ... Suddenly a terrific explosion rent the air. The Bren gun had received a direct hit. It blasted Guardsman Arthur Rice clean through the bush. He looked a dreadful mess. His knee was smashed, his leg and arm riddled with shrapnel. He also had a head wound ... the other guardsman on the Bren gun lay somewhere on the canal bank. Terrible screams of agony came from him. He had received a nasty head wound, and blood had seeped into his eyes, temporarily blinding him.[9]

Infantry carrying rafts then ran down to the canal bank, but they were easy targets as they tried to row across the water, and all the German attacks were beaten off. Though Gort was holding the line of the Scheldt as requested, the longer the BEF remained stationary facing north, the greater was the risk of his command being cut off from the coast. Gort was acutely conscious of this, as well as the potential threat from his right flank. The First Army had been broken once and there was no certainty that it would not break again. Gort, therefore, had to take measures to protect this flank and for this an impromptu grouping was formed under the command of his Director of Intelligence, Major General Mason-MacFarlane. Macforce, as it was called, comprised a battalion of the Welsh Guards with a brigade of light tanks and carriers, artillery, a machine-gun company and other supporting units, and it bore responsibility for the ground from Maulde to Carvin. Over the following days other such composite forces were created by Gort to meet the different challenges the BEF was to encounter.

The main body of the BEF withdrew on the night of 23/24 May from the Escaut to the Gort Line along the French/Belgian border that it had abandoned just two weeks earlier. Churchill, completely misjudging the state of affairs, was still urging Gort to undertake offensive operations. On the evening of the 23rd he sent a message to Gort ordering him to attack south again, this time with eight divisions. 'Here are Winston's plans again,' complained Lieutenant General Henry Pownall, Gort's Chief of Staff:

> Can nobody prevent him trying to conduct operations himself as a super Commander-in-Chief? How does he think we are to collect eight divisions and attack as he suggests… He can have no conception of our situation and condition. Where *are* the Belgian Cavalry Corps? How is an attack like this to be staged involving three nationalities at an hour's notice? The man's mad.[10]

THE WAR IN THE AIR

Attached to the BEF was an Air Component that consisted of nine squadrons of Lysanders and Bristol Blenhiems for reconnaissance and army co-operation, along with four squadrons of Hawker Hurricane fighters. In addition to this, the Royal Air Force had dispatched to France the Advanced Air Striking Force (AASF) of ten squadrons of light/medium bombers (eight of Fairey Battles and two of Blenheims) and three of Hurricanes. It had also been agreed that if the Germans were to launch an attack a further four squadrons of Hurricanes would be sent to France.

It had been the Battles and Blenheims that had taken on the hazardous, if not suicidal role, of attacking and slowing the advancing German army. Frequently operating in daylight, usually at low level, and often with meagre or non-existent fighter cover, the attacks took a terrible toll on the Bomber Command aircrews as they faced light and heavy flak and a formidable *Luftwaffe* fighter force.

The RAF was also hampered by the mass of refugees as early as 11 May who were moving along the same roads as the Germans, as Charles Gardner described in a BBC broadcast:

> The first thing our men saw near Luxembourg was a crowd of refugees – and behind them was a German motor-cycle column, obviously using the refugees as a temporary screen. The motor-cyclists opened fire on our planes with machine-guns – but we replied, and then went on towards the mechanized units, which were some way behind.[11]

Such problems continued throughout the succeeding days, as revealed in an Air Ministry communiqué:

> From the air, the head of the German advance presented at times a picture of utter chaos. Often bombing was made impossible because of the difficulty of identifying enemy columns between the streams of refugees ... On one enemy road reconnoitered at a height of 1,000 feet, some 40 to 50 green-painted German lorries were seen to be hopelessly intermingled with pedestrians, ambulances, civilian cars, tradesmen's vans and bicycles.[12]

The most notable action took place on 12 May, after it had been discovered that the Dutch engineers had failed to demolish the two important bridges over the Albert Canal near Maastricht. The AASF's commanding officer, Air Marshal Barratt, was well aware how important these bridges were in aiding the German advance westwards and knew that he had to try and destroy them. Barratt appreciated that the bridges would be heavily defended by enemy fighters and anti-aircraft guns, and that any aircraft sent to attack the bridges stood little chance of returning. He could not order men to go on such a mission, so he called for volunteers from the Fairey Battles of 12 Squadron – and every single crew member stepped forward. The names of the six crews selected for the operation had to be drawn from a hat.

They set off in two flights of three, one flight for each of the bridges. Only two men returned from the raid, one of whom was Sergeant G.D. Mansell:

We were given a fighter escort of three aircraft, but when we were about 20 miles from our target, thirty Messerschmitts tried to intercept us. We continued on our course while the three fighters waded into the attack. The odds were 10 to 1, but several of those Messerschmitts were brought down, though as a result, we arrived near Maastricht with no company except more enemy fighters and the anti-aircraft barrage.

The Messerschmitts attacked us from the rear. The first I knew about them was when our rear-gunner shouted: 'Enemy fighters on our tail.' Our pilot turned, and took evasive action, while the gunner shot one of them down. That seemed to frighten the others for they soon sheared off. The barrage was terrific and as we neared our target we saw the first flight of three bombers, now returning home, caught in the thick of the enemy's fire, and all three were lost.

The big bridge looked a sorry mess and was sagging in the middle, hit by the bombs dropped by the three bombers ahead of us. When we delivered our attack, we were about 6000 feet up. We dived to 2000 feet – one aircraft close behind the other – and dropped our bombs. On looking down, we saw that our bridge now matched the other. It sagged in the centre and its iron girders looked far from intact. Immediately after we had dropped our bombs we turned for home, but the barrage was there waiting for us. It was even more intense, and our aircraft began to show signs of heavy damage. The pilot gave orders to abandon aircraft. The rear gunner jumped first and we have seen nothing of him since. Then I jumped. The pilot remained with his aircraft and managed to bring it down safely.[13]

The pilot of Mansell's Battle, Pilot Officer Davey, force-landed near Brussels and survived. The two men who led the mission, Flying Officer Donald

Garland and Sergeant Pilot Tom Gray, were both awarded posthumous Victoria Crosses, the first air VCs of the war.

By the end of 12 May, the AASF had just seventy-two serviceable bombers remaining. An attempt to bomb the bridges over the Meuse on 14 May to stop the German advance saw the AASF lose a further forty aircraft to *Luftwaffe* fighters. One German officer, *Oberstleutnant* Walter von Hippel, watched as the Battles were massacred:

> Again and again an enemy aircraft crashes out of the sky, dragging a long plume of smoke behind it, which after the crash of the succeeding explosion remains for some time perpendicular in the warm air. Occasionally, from the falling machines one or two white parachutes release themselves and float slowly to earth.[14]

The French *Armée de l'Air* likewise suffered badly, losing 795 planes in May and June 1940; 320 due to air action, 235 by accidents, 240 on the airfields.

With the *Luftwaffe* dominating the skies, the French asked Churchill for more fighters. Churchill wanted to support the French as much as possible and he put the request to the War Cabinet. The Prime Minister considered the decision to send more fighters into the battle 'one of the gravest that a British Cabinet had ever had to face.' But as the Germans advanced, the bases of the Air Component and the AASF were in danger of being overrun and the Air Officer Commanding the Air Component was forced to move his headquarters to England.

It was clearly unwise, if not impracticable, to send more squadrons over to France, but a number of fighter squadrons were allowed to operate from the UK against the Germans in France. It was Air Chief Marshal Hugh Dowding, Commander-in-Chief of Fighter Command, who stopped Churchill from committing further aircraft to what was considered a lost cause, famously writing to Churchill on 16 May in stark terms: 'I believe that, if an adequate fighter force is kept in this country, if the fleet remains in being, and if Home Forces are suitably organized to resist invasion, we should be able to carry on the war single handed for some time, if not indefinitely. But, if the Home Defence Force is drained away in desperate attempts to remedy the situation in France, defeat in France will involve the final, complete and irremediable defeat of this country.' There is little doubt that Britain's survival in 1940 owed much to Hugh Dowding.

After repelling the Allied counter-attack at Arras, Rommel pushed on despite reservations from the German High Command, that the panzers were too far ahead of the rest of Army Group A. But on 22 May, he was given permission to drive on to the coast and maybe, just maybe, the BEF could be cut off from the Channel ports, and the entire British force surrounded and destroyed.

It was, therefore, urgently necessary for a continuous series of defences to be formed to protect the south-western flank of the BEF along the canal line extending from the Escaut to La Bassée and from there to St Omer and the sea. To hold this extension, another Gort-improvised force was assembled – Palforce – under Major General Curtis. Bridges along the canal were prepared for demolition and stop lines were constructed to block the enemy's advance, but with no more than 10,000 men at his disposal, Curtis had scarcely enough men to cover all the crossing points.[15]

THE GUARDS' LAST STAND - BOULOGNE

Though the final details of the evacuation of the BEF were still being formulated, the only possible ports through which the BEF could be rescued were now confined to Boulogne, Calais and Dunkirk, but with the possibility that the Germans would advance up the coast, it was likely that Boulogne and Calais would be captured. This would leave just Dunkirk open. Nevertheless, if these two ports could be powerfully garrisoned, the BEF's western flank might be secured, or at least the German advance held whilst the main body of the British army was evacuated through Dunkirk. Though its water supply had been cut, the harbour facilities at Dunkirk were, at this stage, still intact.

So, two battalions of the Welsh and Irish Guards, commanded by Brigadier W. (Billy) Fox-Pitt, were ordered to sail immediately for Boulogne. The Guards were scattered across the south-east of England when the call came. The 2nd Battalion Irish Guards and the 2nd Welsh Guards had just returned from a gruelling night exercise and had ambled off to their tents on Old Dean Common near Camberley when they were roused again. They were told to be up, packed, and on their way to France by 15.30 hours. Their briefing gave them little indication of their mission.

They were issued with fifty rounds of rifle ammunition each and informed that the Guards brigade would be on its own and that they should expect no assistance from anyone else.[16]

Other elements of the Guards were on the south coast where they had been practising on the ranges at Lydd in Kent. They were ordered to meet up with the rest of the brigade at Dover. The Welsh and Irish Guards, departed for France on the evening of 21 May along with the 275th Battery (less one troop) of the 69th Anti-Tank Regiment.

The Guards arrived at Boulogne early the following morning. The port was packed with hordes of panic-stricken refugees desperate to rush on board the British ships. The Guardsmen had to fix bayonets to clear a path through the mob before they could disembark.

It had not been thought that Boulogne would come under attack and the port had not been provided with a garrison nor had its ancient defences been fortified. Only two days earlier, on 20 May, had the port been provided with any air defence with the deployment of eight 3.7-inch guns of the 2nd Heavy Anti-Aircraft Regiment and eight machine-guns of the 58th Light Anti-Aircraft Regiment. These two units were supported by a battery of the 2nd Searchlight Regiment. The only other British personnel at the port were 1,500 men of the Auxiliary Military Pioneer Corps (AMPC), none of whom were equipped as fighting soldiers.

There were a considerable number of young French and Belgian recruits in Boulogne but these had not yet been trained for combat. However, groups of stragglers from the defeated French forces had made their way to the coast and they had salvaged two 75mm guns, two 25mm anti-tank guns and two Renault tanks, one of which was broken down and could only be used on the spot where it stood.[17]

This then was the initial force available for the defence of Boulogne. Heading towards the port was the German 2nd Armoured Division – the Panzers were coming.

Rear General Headquarters of the British Expeditionary Force was located at Wimereux, some three miles further along the coast to the north of Boulogne. Immediately upon landing, Fox-Pitt made his way to RGHQ at 07.00 hours and reported the arrival of the Guards to the Adjutant-General of the BEF, Lieutenant General Douglas Brownrigg.

Brownrigg told Fox-Pitt that in addition to the above force the French 21st Division was on its way to take up a position to the south of Boulogne and that the British 3rd Battalion Royal Tank Regiment with a battalion of the Queen Victoria Rifles would soon be on their way from Calais. The odds had now been shortened and Fox-Pitt went off to examine the ground upon which he would give battle with a slightly better prospect of success.

Boulogne is cut in two by the River Liane. On either side of the river, hills overlook the town and the small port area. If the Germans were allowed to occupy the high ground they would dominate the battlefield. So, until the arrival of the promised reinforcements, Fox-Pitt ordered the Irish Guards to occupy the hills from the south of the river to the sea and the Welsh Guards, commanded by Lieutenant Colonel Alexander Stanier, the ground overlooking the northern half of the town.

Scarcely had the Guards taken up their positions when the sound of gunfire from the south was heard, prompting the men to start 'furiously' digging-in. By approximately 17.30 hours the Germans were within artillery range of the Irish Guards. After a short barrage the Panzers attacked but, when the leading tank had been knocked out by one of the Guards' anti-tank guns and the supporting German infantry had been pinned down, the assault petered out.

The Germans really needed a quick result at Boulogne so that they could press on up the coast to cut off the retreat of the BEF. But there was nothing they could do until dawn the following day.

At 07.30, with the Panzers in support, the Germans attacked the Irish once more. This time the Guards were pushed back and by 10.00 they had been forced to withdraw across the railway line that runs close to the Liane. Three hours later the Irish retreated towards the centre of the town.

Over to the east the French-held stronghold, the Fort de la Crèche, which defended the coast road about three-quarters of a mile to the north of Boulogne, was taken by the Germans and shortly afterwards the Welsh Guards came under heavy attack. This was the direction in which the reinforcements were supposed to arrive from Calais, so it was now clear to Fox-Pitt that no help would be coming his way. Nor was there much assistance from the French 21st Division, as a large part of this force was attacked and dispersed by Panzers whilst still entrained. Everything then, depended on the Guards.

Having reached the outskirts of the town, the Germans had come within sight of the port, and the ships standing a little way out to sea found themselves under bombardment. Instead of withdrawing, the ships of the Royal Navy began to engage targets on land. The destroyers *Whitshed*, *Vimiera*, *Vimy*, *Venomous*, *Wild Swan* and *Keith*, along with four French warships, shelled the German artillery and mortars, giving invaluable assistance to the Guards.

Despite the apparent success of the German advance, a little before 15.00 their gunfire ceased and the most advanced Panzers, seemingly fearing an ambush, pulled back. This decision was explained in the German XIX Corps War Diary: '1445. At about this time Corps Headquarters has the impression that in and around Boulogne the enemy is fighting tenaciously for every inch of ground in order to prevent the important harbour falling into German hands. *Luftwaffe* attacks on warships and transports lying off Boulogne are inadequate: it is not clear whether the latter are engaged in embarkation or disembarkation. 2nd Armoured Division's attacks therefore progress slowly."[18]

Though the Guards still held the town, and the French troops remained defiant in the citadel, at around 18.30 hours the War Office issued instructions for the Guards to be evacuated from Boulogne.

Accordingly, the Royal Navy destroyers moved into the harbour to begin the evacuation. Naval landing parties were sent ashore to help the Guards hold the streets around the harbour whilst the refugees, the wounded, and the men of the AMPC were embarked.

As the Guards gradually withdrew towards the harbour, No.3 Company of the Welsh Guards, commanded by Major Windsor-Lewes was left to hold two vital road blocks on the streets leading down to the harbour. Despite frequent attempts to communicate with battalion HQ, Windsor-Lewes, remained oblivious to the general movements of the rest of his regiment.

The rest of the brigade moved down to the harbour and the men were hurried across the bridge, the Pont Marguet, which led from the town across the Liane to the quay. Fox-Pitt checked each unit across – but there was no sign of No.3 Company. With the tanks rumbling ever closer, the brigadier had no choice. 'I can't wait any longer', he told Stanier, 'I'm going to blow the bridge'.[19]

The explosion failed to destroy the Pont Marguet, which was still passable with care. This mistake would actually save many British lives in the hours to come.

As the troops were waiting to be rescued from the quayside a heavy-calibre gun opened fire from Fort de la Crèche upon HMS *Venetia* as she was approaching the harbour entrance. The German engineers had managed to repair one of the French coastal guns which the defenders had damaged but failed to render unserviceable when the fort was captured. The first two shots missed their target but the third shot from the fort struck *Venetia* amidships. Two more rounds hit the destroyer. *Venetia* slumped low in the water and flames spread along her decks. Fortunately, she did not sink, as the destroyer would have blocked the entrance to the harbour. *Venetia* successfully backed out of the harbour but she had been unable to embark a single man.

By this time *Wild Swan* and *Venomous* had begun taking off the first of the Guards. The Germans could see that their prey was likely to escape and they redoubled their efforts to prevent the Guards from embarking. The German artillery, tanks and aircraft bombarded the quay and the harbour whilst the guns of the destroyers returned fire. Tanks verses ships at less than 1,000 yards!

Under cover of the *Wild Swan*'s 4.7-inch guns the Irish Guards moved down to the Quai Chancy, where they were able to find some degree of shelter from the German shells. With *Wild Swan* so tantalisingly close the men must have been sorely tempted to make a dash for the destroyer. But the Guards' discipline held and when the signal to embark was given it was conducted in good order.

The Welsh Guards then moved along the quay to embark upon *Venomous*. At that moment the Luftwaffe delivered another attack upon the harbour, many of their bombs hitting the quay. When the Stukas had passed, Stanier's men made their way to the end of the pier and, at a little after 21.30 hours, *Venomous* and *Wild Swan* pulled out of Boulogne, each carrying around 900 men. But a large part of No.2 and No.4 companies had clambered across the damaged Pont Marguet only to find that *Venomous* had gone.

Shortly after arriving in Dover later that night, Stanier realised that not only had No.3 Company failed to escape but also elements of No.1 and No.4 companies. It was evident that there were hundreds of men still at Boulogne.

Back at the French port, the Germans, tired and hungry, withdrew from the harbour precincts and a degree of quiet settled over Boulogne. They had failed to prevent the bulk of the Guards Brigade from evacuating, the harbour area was still in British hands and the French still held the Haute Ville. Victory it may have been for *Général der Panzertruppe* Rudolf Veiel, but it was a hollow and incomplete one.

Of those British troops still around the harbour, nos. 2 and 4 companies of the Welsh Guards, believing that there was now no hope of being saved, decided to try and fight their way through the German positions and escape up the coast.

At around midnight the Welsh Guards, along with the remaining men of the AMPC, made their way towards the town but were soon halted by German machine-gun positions. Frustrated, the men returned to the harbour and were amazed to see a destroyer moored by the quay. HMS *Windsor* had slipped into Boulogne in the dark unmolested by the Germans. Taking on board the naval demolition parties and various stragglers, as well as the Welshmen, *Windsor* left Boulogne with 600 very grateful soldiers.

Hundreds of men, however, remained at Boulogne. But the Royal Navy was not finished yet. In complete darkness, *Vimiera* backed up to the mole for a second time. There she waited for about an hour, in what was described as an eerie silence, as the last men of the AMPC and another 800 men from other units embarked. When she pulled quietly away from Boulogne at around 02.30, *Vimiera* had rescued some 1,400 men. The Germans never even noticed.

Incredibly, Windsor-Lewis' Welsh Guards were still holding the road blocks at the entrance to the harbour completely unaware that the rest of the brigade had been evacuated. Soon after daybreak on the 24th, however, one of his men brought Windsor-Lewis the shocking news that No.3 Company was now virtually alone in the French port.

Windsor-Lewes decided to retreat to the harbour, which, despite the surrounding presence of the German armour, his company achieved without loss. At the quayside Windsor-Lewes found a number of other stragglers, including a few French, the whole force amounting to around 500 men. With this band Windsor-Lewes prepared to hold the Gare Maritime for as long as possible.

In the station were two trains, one of which was a Belgian hospital train. Windsor-Lewis' men took up fire positions in and under the carriages of the trains and they established a breastwork of sandbags at the entrance of the station itself. For the remainder of the day, this tiny force held the Gare Maritime under an almost continuous fire from the attackers. The Germans even attempted to cross the harbour basin in a small boat, but the Guards held them off. Nevertheless, even in the better-sheltered parts of the station, the Guards were still taking casualties, though there was no obvious reason. Extra men were added to the look-out posts in the hope of spotting the suspected sniper, until the cause of the deaths was discovered. A fifth-columnist had infiltrated the ranks of the Guards dressed in British uniform. He had been shooting the men in the back of their heads whenever the opportunity arose. When the assassin was captured, Windsor-Lewis ordered him to be executed and thrown into the sea.[20]

The small British force held out at the station until dark, when the German fire died down for the night. With dawn on Saturday the 25th, came a renewed assault. Artillery pounded the station and the French troops in the Gare Maritime had already tried to put up a white flag but the Guards had torn it. Windsor-Lewis was driven back from the breastwork into the station building and it was clear that his brave little force could not hold out for much longer.

When, at around midday, Windsor-Lewis was presented with an ultimatum from the Germans to surrender by 14.00 hours or be wiped-out, he had little choice. Windsor-Lewis defied the Germans for another hour before finally bowing to the inevitable. There were only thirteen unwounded Welshmen; the men were almost out of food and ammunition and there was no water left. But Major Windsor-Lewis and his depleted little band had held the might of the German 2nd Armoured Division at bay for more than a day – one of the most important days of the war. Because that day was 25 May 1940, and the evacuation from Dunkirk began just twenty-four hours later.[21]

'HOLD CALAIS TO THE DEATH!'

Almost all the regular British regiments were with the BEF, but 30 Infantry Brigade was on anti-invasion duties across Suffolk and Kent when, at 18.30 hours on 21 May, instructions were issued for all ranks to report back to camp – immediately. Just as the Guards had been sent to Boulogne, so 30 Brigade was on its way to defend Calais.

Incredibly, by 23.00 hours, the entire brigade was entrained and on its way to Dover. Just a few hours later the 1st Battalion Queen Victoria Rifles arrived at Dover, followed by the 2nd Battalion King's Royal Rifles and the 1st Rifle Brigade. Armoured support took the form of the 3rd Battalion Royal Tank Regiment, equipped with Cruiser Mk. I tanks. The 229th Anti-Tank battery of the Royal Artillery completed the force, all of which would be under the command of Brigadier Claude Nicholson.

Nicholson had been instructed to keep communications open between Calais and Boulogne, but it was evident that if he moved any of his troops out of Calais towards Boulogne, then Calais itself would be undefended. So Nicholson decided to concentrate on defending Calais and passed on the message from London to his men. They were told to be prepared to hold Calais 'to the last'. The port was already under repeated attack from the *Luftwaffe* and much of the town was on fire and electricity and water supplies had been cut. Houses and cafés had been abandoned and food was scarce. Desperate times indeed.

With all the British units withdrawing towards the Channel ports, elements of the Royal Artillery – the 6th Heavy and the 172nd Light Batteries – were ordered from Arras to deploy around the outer perimeter of Calais. Other 'odds and sods' also made their way to the French port in hope of salvation, including some 800 French reservists and Marines.

A few hours after Nicholson had received the communication from the War Office to hold Calais to the last, the Germans were bearing down its outskirts. Gradually, the Green Jackets were forced back towards the Old Town by the sheer weight of the German regiments from the 10th Panzer Division. The fighting was fierce in the ruined alleyways and in the bombed buildings, with the Riflemen disputing every street and defending every house. The British tanks proved to be no match for the German armour and against the well-armed German regiments the British infantry had only rifles, Bren guns, the odd Lewis gun and the ineffective Boys anti-tank rifle.

As they withdrew to the inner perimeter, the Riflemen took up defensive positions along the old walls and, as the battle progressed, Nicholson moved his headquarters into the citadel. Calais was fortified during the Middle Ages and its ancient walls were still largely intact. A citadel, built in the sixteenth century but much improved since, formed the centre of the town's defences. Outside the perimeter wall was also a detached stronghold, Fort Nieulay, a mile to the west.

Nicholson ordered the King's Royal Rifles to hold the western sector of the walls and the Rifle Brigade the eastern walls. A contingent of the Queen

Victoria Rifles, along with a number of French troops, occupied Fort Nieulay, the rest being held in reserve to reinforce the battalions manning the walls.

The citadel had been held by French troops under *Chef du Bataillon* Raymond Le Tellier, but when he learnt that the BEF was to be evacuated he telephoned his commanding officer, who informed him there would be no evacuation for the French forces from Calais. After receiving this news most of the French troops 'drifted off'. Around eighty brave French soldiers stayed to do their duty even though, because of the failings of their comrades, they were roundly abused by the British troops.

Battling on virtually alone, the Riflemen fought for every inch of ground. Nicholson made numerous requests for supplies, food, ammunition and support but in the end all he received were messages: 'Defence of Calais to the utmost is of the highest importance to our country and our Army now,' read one of the signals from Lord Gort. 'First, it occupies a large part of the enemy's armoured forces, and keeps them from attacking our line of communications. Secondly, it preserves a sally-port from which portions of the British Army may make their way home ... The eyes of the Empire are upon you and the defence of Calais ... His Majesty's government is confident that your gallant Regiments will perform an exploit worthy of the British name.'[22]

Somehow, the Green Jackets hung on, and at 03.00 hours on 24 May, Nicholson received a signal from Major Dewing at the War Office: 'Evacuation [of the BEF] agreed in principal. When you have finished unloading vehicles, commence embarkation of all personnel except fighting personnel who will remain to cover final evacuation.' Nicholson was told that evacuation was 'probable' that night. When Churchill heard that Nicholson had been told that he would be rescued, he was furious and sent an angry note to General Hastings Ismay: 'Vice-Chief of the Naval Staff informs me that [an] order was sent at 2 a.m. to Calais saying that evacuation was decided on in principle, but this is surely madness. The only effect of evacuating Calais would be to transfer the forces now blocking it to Dunkirk. Calais must be held for many reasons but especially to hold the enemy on its front.'[23]

It was on this day – the 24th – that Hitler issued the above-mentioned instruction to General Guderian to halt his advance against the retreating British forces. 'By the *Führer*'s orders,' read the message from German Army Headquarters, the *Oberkommando des Heeres* (OKH), 'hold the favourable defensive line Lens-Béthune-Aire-Saint-Omer-Gravelines, and allow the enemy to attack it ... the principal thing is now to husband the armoured formations for later and more important tasks.'[24] Those more important tasks were the destruction of the French armies and the occupation of Paris. The operations around Dunkirk were now little more than a sideshow. Though Guderian had no choice but to comply with Hitler's orders in general terms, he pressed ahead with the attack upon Calais.

On the morning of the 25th, the 10th Panzers therefore renewed their attack, preceded by a heavy artillery bombardment. Every assault was repulsed but it was clear that 30 Brigade could not hold out much longer. So, in the afternoon, the German guns fell silent as General Schaal sent repeated demands into the town for Nicholson to surrender.

Nicholson would have none of it. 'If the Germans want Calais,' Nicholson is reported to have said, 'they will have to fight for it'. At 14.00 hours, another message was sent to Nicholson from London, on this occasion from Anthony Eden, who had recently taken over from Oliver Stanley as Secretary at State for War: 'Defence of Calais to the utmost is of the highest importance to our country as symbolising our continued co-operation with France.'

The Germans redoubled their efforts in the afternoon, again pounding the town with their artillery. As evening fell, the German infantry attacked, supported this time by the panzers. Somehow, despite mounting losses, the Riflemen held off the German assault.

At 21.00 hours on the 25th another message was received by Nicholson, this time from Churchill himself. The Prime Minister was acutely conscious of the consequences of the decision he was about to make. He was committing thousands of his countrymen to death or indeterminate incarceration. But it was a joint decision, made together by Ironside, Anthony Eden and the Prime Minister. Churchill recorded his feeling that evening: 'We three came out from dinner and at 9 p.m. did the deed. It involved Eden's own regiment, in which he had long served and fought in the previous struggle. One has to eat and drink in war, but I could not help feeling physically sick as we afterwards sat silent at the table.'

This is the message sent to Nicholson: 'Every hour you continue to exist is of the greatest help to the BEF. Government has therefore decided you must continue to fight. Have greatest possible admiration for your splendid stand. Evacuation will not (*repeat* not) take place and craft required for the purpose are to return to Dover.'

So now they knew for certain. 30 Brigade was to be sacrificed.

By the next morning, the Rifle battalions could count only about 250 men each still under arms. After a lull in the fighting overnight, Schaal took up the battle once again with some 200 Junkers Ju 87 Stuka dive-bombers joining the attack. At around 11.00 hours the walls of the town were breached when one of the bastions was overrun. It was the end for 30 Brigade. Soon most of the town was in German hands and at 15.00 hours the citadel was taken.

Nicholson had no choice but to surrender. His men were marched away that evening to spend the next five years in prisoner-of-war camps in Poland.

Just three hours after the fall of Calais the evacuation of the BEF at Dunkirk began.

The next day a signal was sent from Dover, from the Secretary of State to 'OC Troops Calais': 'Am filled with admiration for your magnificent fight which is worthy of the highest tradition of the British Army.'

The message was never received.

The contribution to the comparatively successful evacuation of the British Expeditionary Force at Dunkirk made by the Guards' last stand at Boulogne has never been quantified. Yet Boulogne is only twenty-three miles from Dunkirk and if that port had not delayed the 2nd Panzer Division, the Germans could have reached Dunkirk well-ahead of the bulk of the BEF. In theory, Boulogne could have been masked by a small German holding force, whilst the main body of the Panzer Division rushed on to Dunkirk. But the German High Command was extremely anxious about the Panzers' long, exposed flanks and to have left an open port in their rear, through which any number of reinforcements could have been sent from Britain, was a risk too far.

Calais, being closer to Dunkirk was, arguably, of even greater importance than Boulogne. That was certainly Churchill's opinion, 'Calais was the crux,' he later wrote. 'Many other causes might have prevented the deliverance of Dunkirk, but it is certain that the three days gained by the defence of Calais enabled the Gravelines waterline to be held and without this, even in spite of Hitler's vacillations and Rundstedt's orders, all would have been cut off and lost.'[25]

The defence of these two ports is an element of the Dunkirk story that receives relatively little attention and will probably always be overlooked in the momentous events that occurred just a few miles along the coast. That tale, one of the most remarkable ever related, now needs to be told.

Chapter 3

Operation *Dynamo*: Day 1, Sunday 26 May

It was Sunday 19 May when Vice Admiral Bertram Ramsay, Flag Officer Commanding Dover, had been summoned to the War Office in London for a meeting chaired by Major General Michael Riddell-Webster, Quartermaster-General to the Forces. The subject they were to discuss was 'the hazardous evacuation of very large forces' through Dunkirk, Calais and Boulogne. Ramsay was present because it was he who would be responsible for the evacuation, and all available shipping would be placed at his disposal.

It was envisaged that, starting on the 20th, the 'useless mouths', in other words the non-combatants, would be shipped back to the UK at the rate of 2,000 per day. Then, starting on the 22nd, the base personnel would be evacuated – some 15,000 in total. This would free the roads and the shipping for the vital third stage of the operation, the rescue of the fighting divisions of the BEF.

Just how many men would eventually be saved remained unknown, but even at this stage, the evacuation of tens of thousands of troops was seen as 'formidable' and was likely to be, as described by the Quartermaster-General's Department, 'on a scale unprecedented in the history of war'.[1]

Even at this preliminary stage, the difficulties that were likely to be experienced were understood, and proved all-too accurate:

a) It would only be possible to evacuate the personnel, and all the equipment not carried by hand would have to be abandoned.

b) That the organisation of units and formations could not be preserved, but that bodies of men would arrive haphazard, separated from their own officers and non-commissioned officers and without any knowledge of the whereabouts of others of the same unit.

c) That the normal machinery for providing the men with quarters, pay, clothing, blankets, and above all, food, would have ceased to exist. That no reliance could be placed on cooking equipment or on cooks and that no transport of any kind would be available.

With Ramsay being given complete control over the task he had been set, he called a meeting at Dover the following day. Ramsay's office at Dover was situated in the tunnels that had been excavated during the invasion threat from the French during the Napoleonic Wars. Though the tunnels had largely remained unoccupied since 1827, they were reopened following the outbreak of war in 1939. In the early months of the Second World War the tunnels were used as an air-raid shelter and then converted into an underground hospital.

The tunnels did not provide the most salubrious of working conditions, as Rosemary Keyes, a cypher staff officer, recalled, describing them as: 'a rabbit warren of dark, dreary, damp and airless passages and rooms. We worked all day in electric light, and the only time we saw daylight was when we went to the "heads" [toilet]. This was a small room with a noisome "thunder-box" but a beautiful view of Dover harbour, seen through a window cut out of the cliff face.'[2]

The tunnels also became the Naval headquarters at Dover. The nerve centre of the headquarters was a single gallery that ended in an embrasure at the cliff face. This was where Ramsay had his office.

A succession of small rooms leading deep into the chalk away from Ramsay's office housed the Secretary, the Flag Lieutenant, the Chief of Staff (Captain L.V. Morgan) and the Staff office itself. Beyond these was a large room used normally for meetings/conferences in connection with the operation of the Naval base. In the First World War, it had held an auxiliary electrical plant and was known as the 'Dynamo Room'.

It was in that room, on 20 May, where Ramsay called his staff together to discuss the evacuation of the BEF, along with Liaison Officers from the War Office Movement Control and the Ministry of Shipping. It was hoped that 10,000 men would be rescued every twenty-four hours from each of the three Continental ports still in Allied hands at that time – Dunkirk, Calais and Boulogne – with the thirty-or-so cross-Channel ferries, twelve steam-powered drifters and six coastal cargo ships that had been allocated to the task by the Admiralty. The ships would work the ports in pairs, with no more than two ships at any one time in the three French harbours. It was also understood that troops would also have to be lifted from the French beaches, and for this a large number of small boats would be required. Many more Navy personnel would also be needed to crew these vessels. It was agreed, even at this preliminary stage, that fighter cover would be essential to protect embarkations and sailings.

It was immediately obvious that a reorganisation of the base staff at Dover would be necessary to cope with the sudden rush of all the additional work. It was decided to set up this new body in the conference room itself. Thus, it was in this former Dynamo Room that the preparation, planning, and organisation of the evacuation of the British Expeditionary Force from France took place. It became known as Operation *Dynamo*.

Ramsay's office was normally in Dover Castle, and the Dynamo Room was hardly befitting a Royal Navy admiral, with a concrete floor partly covered by a thin strip of worn carpet, and a couple of charts to decorate its whitewashed walls. Its furniture consisted of a desk and a few chairs around a conference table. The improvised nature of the new operations room reflected, in a manner, the nature of the great flotilla of assorted vessels that would rescue the British Expeditionary Force.

As we know, Gort had already concluded that an evacuation was highly likely on 19 May. So, on the 20th, just as Ramsay on one side of the Channel was contemplating how to organise the evacuation of the BEF, on the other side of the Channel, Gort was considering just how he could withdraw his men safely to the coast. At 06.00 hours that morning, six of Gort's senior staff officers met to discuss just how such a retreat could be arranged.

The job of deciding exactly where the evacuation would be likely to take place, was handed to the BEF's acting Operations Officer, Lieutenant Colonel the Viscount Robert Bridgeman. Aware of the need for speed, Bridgeman set about his task immediately, and worked throughout the night, subsisting on chocolate and whiskey. He started on the premise that an evacuation could take place anywhere between Calais and Ostend, he had to find a stretch of coast that could easily be reached by the retreating troops, and easily defended by the three corps of the BEF.

Bridgeman had, therefore, to consider which port had the best approach roads and which might offer some degree of protection from the air, and which ports had the best facilities. He had to answer such questions as, were there canals or other features that could be held against the enemy, particularly on the flanks, were there towns that could be held as strong-points and were there dykes that could be opened to flood the ground and stop the German panzers?

After poring over maps of the French and Belgium coasts, Bridgeman decided that the twenty-seven-mile stretch between Ostend and Dunkirk was the most suitable. By the morning of 22 May, Bridgeman had covered every detail he could think of. Each corps was allocated the routes it would use to reach the coast, and which region of the coast each would hold. If the decision to evacuate was confirmed, there was now a plan in place.[3] In reality, there was little alternative, for when Bridgeman started his examination of the likely evacuation areas all the ports from Boulogne to Zeebrugge were open and in Allied hands, but by the time he had finished his study, only the stretch of coast from Gravelines to Nieuport remained available to the BEF, so rapidly was the strategic scene shifting.

Also on the 20th, Colonel G.H.P. Whitfeld, Assistant Adjutant General of the BEF was told that he would take command of the troops in the Dunkirk area. He was instructed to make his way immediately to Dunkirk, with his first task being to evacuate the non-combatant troops. 'The road from Boulogne to Dunkirk was crammed with refugees making progress difficult,' wrote Whitfeld as he headed for the coast, 'but I was in the town of Dunkirk by 13 hours. A general evacuation of the civilian population had been ordered and was in progress. There had been a certain amount of bombing but the town may have been said to be practically undamaged, and although the docks had received a certain amount of attention the locks were working and the civilian personnel were still working.'[4]

Whitfeld learnt that Dunkirk was under the direct orders of the *Amiral du Nord, le contre-amiral* Jean-Marie Charles Abrial and subordinate to him was *Général de Corps d'Armée* Marie-Bertrand-Alfred Fagalde who was in command of the French XVI Corps. Whitfeld therefore made his way to the French Naval Headquarters at Bastion 32 situated in the port itself.

The first of the 'useless mouths' were despatched to the UK on the 20th, and it was on the night of 20/21 May that the first shipping losses were incurred at Dunkirk. The tankers *Salome* and *Niger* were attacked by German aircraft as they attempted to leave the port. *Salome* failed to make it out of the harbour and *Niger* was sunk off Gravelines. The cargo ship *Pavon* was hit and was beached, and the French destroyer *L'Adroit*, which was covering the operation, was also damaged and abandoned.

Along with the lines of communication and base troops evacuated in the days before the fighting divisions marched into Dunkirk, the hospital carriers *Isle of Thanet* and *Worthing* transported hundreds of casualties back to Dover, and these vessels too were targeted by the *Luftwaffe* – a theme that would be repeated in the days to come.

The evacuation of these non-combatants ahead of the main operation resulted in 23,128 personnel returning to England. In addition to this, 4,368 fighting men had been evacuated from Boulogne and 440 from Calais. These numbers are often forgotten when the statistics for the Dunkirk evacuation are analysed.

The day after Whitfeld arrived, the French came across a German order of battle found on a dead German officer. When translated it revealed that Dunkirk was a definite objective of the enemy in the very near future. This information caused 'some alarm', as Whitfeld put it, amongst the French commanders who wanted to know what British troops were available to counter this intended attack upon Dunkirk – Abrial being kept in the dark at this stage about the decision to evacuate the BEF back to the UK.

Whitfeld asked if the numerous bridges around Dunkirk had been prepared for demolition and he was told to speak to Fagalde. But when he approached the general, 'His attitude to me was not even bordering on one of cordiality, and the atmosphere throughout the interview was far from pleasant,' wrote Whitfeld in his subsequent report. 'The General evidently resented such enquiries being made.' Fagalde probably resented such an enquiry as it transpired that none of the bridges had been prepared for demolition. Fortunately for Whifeld, that afternoon a large demolition party arrived from England with explosives with the aim of destroying the facilities of the main dock. As the *Luftwaffe* had started bombing the docks, the Germans were doing the job of the demolition team for them which, happily, meant that the explosives could be used on the bridges.

Because the French in and around Dunkirk were not made aware of the intention to evacuate the BEF, the behaviour of the British troops caused some offence, and Whitfeld had to deal with numerous complaints delivered with, as he put it, with 'some venom'. The complaints, Whitfeld found, were against British soldiers who were wandering about trying to find their way to the docks and were often in the last stages of exhaustion. In response, Whitfeld replied 'with some asperity' that 'the French soldiers were looting British lorries, stealing without question any car or motor bike they happened to see, and in fact taking away from the dumps all food supplies, intended for the British troops.' Clearly the entende was becoming less cordial.

There was also dismay that the attitude of the other Allied troops, the Belgians. Second Lieutenant David Smith, whose 101st (Royal Monmouthshire) Field Company, Royal Engineers, was attached to the 12th Royal Lancers, had moved west of the Yser Canal on 25 May and during the night settled in at Neuve Eglise. On the morning of the 26th, the Lancers were ordered to scout ahead of the canal line to locate the enemy. Contact was made with the Germans, and duly reported back to HQ. They then fell back across the canal to allow the bridges to be blown. 'Then,' David Smith pondered on 'another of those situations which made one wonder what really was the outlook of our Allies. A town the size of Ypres was not held at all by the Belgians and the only troops there were about twenty Belgian sappers and they had blown none of the bridges.' The 12th Lancers 'B' Squadron took over the defence of Ypres until the Belgian sappers, 'after a long period of complete stagnation, suddenly decided that they must immediately destroy all the bridges.' To Smith's dismay, it was found that the only bridges that had been prepared for demolition were those on the west of the town, whereas the Germans, obviously, were approaching from the east![5]

THE GRAVITY OF THE HOUR

With disaster on an unprecedented, almost unimaginable scale facing the British Army, Winston Churchill knew he had to prepare the nation for the bad news that would soon be coming out of France. On the 19th he made his first radio broadcast as Prime Minister:

A tremendous battle is raging in France and Flanders. The Germans, by a remarkable combination of air bombing and heavily armoured tanks, have broken through the French defences north of the Maginot Line, and strong columns of their armoured vehicles are ravaging the open country, which for the first day or two was without defenders. They have penetrated deeply and spread alarm and confusion in their track. Behind them there are now appearing infantry in lorries, and behind them, again, the large masses are moving forward. The re-groupment of the French armies to make head against, and also to strike at, this intruding wedge has been proceeding for several days, largely assisted by the magnificent efforts of the Royal Air Force.

It would be foolish, however, to disguise the gravity of the hour. It would be still more foolish to lose heart and courage or to suppose that well-trained, well-equipped armies numbering three or four millions of men can be overcome in the space of a few weeks, or even months, by a scoop, or raid of mechanized vehicles, however formidable. We may look with confidence to the stabilization of the Front in France, and to the general engagement of the masses, which will enable the qualities of the French and British soldiers to be matched squarely against those of their adversaries ... We must expect that as soon as stability is reached on the Western Front, the bulk of that hideous apparatus of aggression which gashed Holland into ruin and slavery in a few days will be turned upon us. I am sure I speak for all when I say we are ready to face it; to endure it; and to retaliate against it.

Churchill had not spelt out just how serious the situation in France really was or how precariously the BEF was placed. He had chosen his words carefully to be inspiring rather than factual – and to a large degree it worked. The Ministry of Information reported the following day people declaring it was 'a good fighting speech', and that they were 'encouraged and more determined' and noted that 'there was no talk of defeat; all they want is retaliation.'[6] The broadcast, which, despite the lack of specifics had been generally well received, bought Churchill a little time – time, maybe, to save at least a portion of the BEF.

Ramsay, meanwhile, had attended a further meeting in London on Tuesday 22nd, to determine the number of vessels and small craft that could be employed in the rescue mission. Over the course of the following two days the evacuation of troops from Boulogne was started, and completed on 24 May. The evacuation at Calais had been limited to lines of communications personnel; the fighting troops, as we have learned, having to remain at the port to prevent German forces moving up from the south to cut off the BEF from the coast. This meant that if the BEF was to be evacuated, it could only be from Dunkirk and its adjacent coast, much as Bridgeman had already concluded.

In the few days since the first meeting in the War Office, the military situation had deteriorated so sharply that Ramsay was advised by the Admiralty on 26 May that Operation *Dynamo* was to be implemented immediately 'with the greatest vigour'. Ramsay was told that it was expected that the evacuation was likely to last for just two days before it would be terminated by enemy action. He was advised that he would probably only be able to rescue 45,000 men.

Unfortunately, the instruction to evacuate the non-combatant troops spread rapidly and a 'somewhat alarming' movement towards Dunkirk soon began, as Whitfeld complained:

> At times, it was not a question of men coming into the town and slowly making their way to the report centre; on many occasions both officers and men hurried into the report centre at a speed which made one suppose the enemy were at least only a few yards behind them. It was clearly impossible for me to check up on the credentials of so many arrivals, as so many did, without an authority of any kind to support their application for embarkation. In many cases officers and men had become detached from their units for man days, and as the food and water shortage was acute in Dunkirk, I had no option but to send them onto the United Kingdom.

EVACUATION ORDERED

By 24 May, after a fortnight's desperate fighting, the area into which the BEF and Allied French units had withdrawn formed a rough triangle with sides about fifty miles in length. The base of the triangle ran along the French and Belgian coast from Gravelines to Zeebrugge with the apex near Douai. The eastern facing side of the triangle rested on the original Allied front line, and was held by the British 42nd, 1st, 3rd and 4th divisions as far as Halluin, where the Belgians took over, extending the line towards Ghent. The third side of the triangle ran from Douai, through St Omer and then along the River Aa to Gravelines and the sea; this latter sector being held by the French.

On the 25th, heavy attacks were launched against the Belgian front on the River Lys. Gort had been worried about the morale of the Belgians from the outset, and he now feared they would not hold out much longer under sustained pressure and he took steps to extend the British line if the Belgians gave way.

Vice-Chief of the Imperial General Staff, Sir John Dill, arrived at Gort's headquarters on the morning of the 25th, in response to a request from the

BEF's commander for Dill to see the state of affairs for himself. It did not take Dill long to appreciate the situation, and he sent a telegram to Anthony Eden outlining the seriousness of the BEF's predicament.[7]

This confirmed everyone's worst fears, and at around 10.30 hours on the morning of the 26th, Gort opened a telegram that had been sent from Secretary at State for War, Stanley. It was the news he had expected.

After informing Gort that the hoped-for French counter-offensive from the Somme would lack the strength to render any effective help to the armies fighting in the north, Stanley wrote: 'should this prove to be the case you will be faced with a situation in which the safety of the BEF will predominate. In such conditions [the] only course open to you may be to fight your way back to [the] West where all beaches and ports east of Gravelines will be used for embarkation. Navy will provide fleet of ships and small boats and RAF would give full support. As [the] withdrawal may have to begin very early, preliminary plans should be urgently prepared.'[8]

Throughout the four terrible years of the First World War the BEF had dug-in and held its ground. It was what the stubborn British Tommy did best. In this current conflict, it was expected that the British Army would have to face another long slog on the Continent. Yet, after just two weeks, the British Government had already concluded that the situation in France was beyond redemption. Gort had been told to try and save the army, but with French resistance, and morale, collapsing, and the German panzer divisions speeding round the British flank, there seemed little prospect of the BEF being able to escape.

Gort replied solemnly that: 'I must not conceal from you that a great part of the BEF and its equipment will inevitably be lost even in the best circumstance.'

Lieutenant General Alan Brooke, who commanded II Corps, concurred with Gort's pessimistic assessment of the BEF's predicament: 'Nothing but a miracle can save the BEF now and the end cannot be far off,' he had written in his diary on 23 May. Three days later, after being briefed by Gort on the decision to evacuate, he calculated that, 'It is going to be a very hazardous enterprise and we shall be lucky if we save 25% of the BEF!'[9] The official historian of the Flanders' campaign, Major L.F. Ellis, declared that, 'The British Expeditionary Force was indeed in a desperate situation, more desperate even than bare facts revealed.'[10]

Ironside, who was to stand down from his position of Chief of the Imperial General Staff to concentrate on Home Defence, expressed similar views: 'We shall have lost practically all our trained soldiers by the next few days – unless a miracle appears to help us.'[11]

Britain, it seemed, was about to lose its army and was heading for a catastrophic defeat, unparalleled in its once-proud history.

THE DUNKIRK DEFENCES

Early on the morning of the 26th, Gort went to see *Général* Georges Blanchard, who that just been promoted to General Officer Commanding the French 1st Army,[12] at his headquarters at Attiches. Gort voiced his concerns about the state of the Belgian Army and Blanchard conceded that he feared the Belgians would soon capitulate and that the situation on the eastern flank was equally perilous. After an hour, the two commanders agreed on a joint plan for the withdrawal of the main bodies of the BEF and the French 1st Army to behind the line of the Lys. 'The layout of the BEF was now beginning to take its final shape,' wrote Gort. 'Starting from what could be described as a normal situation with Allied troops on the right and left, there had developed an ever-lengthening defensive right flank. This had then become a semi-circular line, with both flanks resting on the sea, manned by British, French and Belgians. Later the position became a corridor in shape. The southern end of this corridor was blocked by the French 1st Army; and each side was manned, for the greater part of its length, by British troops. Next to the sea were French troops on the west, and French and Belgian troops on the eastern flank.'

Gort then had to plan the withdrawal, and by the evening of the 26th he had drawn up his arrangements for the retreat to the coast in and around the port of Dunkirk. At this stage, the front held by the BEF extended for some 128 miles. Though sections of this front were held by French forces, the BEF occupied ninety-seven miles, an area far too large to be defended. This area had to be progressively shrunk. It had been agreed with Blanchard that the front would be reduced by fifty-eight miles, this reduction to take place over the course of the following three days, ending on 29 May. 'The difficulties of execution were great,' wrote Ian Hay in a government publication of what was termed *The Battle of Flanders*, 'for the corridor of withdrawal was growing narrower ... especially the south side, where the canal line had been forced at several points

– and the troops were invariably getting into one another's way. The roads were few and narrow, and the French troops added to the difficulties of the situation by bringing into the area considerable quantities of horse-transport. Pitiful crowds of refugees added to the congestion and tragedy of the scene.'[13]

Attempting to withdraw with the BEF on 26 May was Leading Aircraftsman Ken Anderson, who was part of a seven-strong meteorological team attached to the Royal Artillery's 2nd Survey Regiment:

> The sun shines; the sky is a cloudless blue. The Luftwaffe is everywhere, smashing everything that moves. We are surrounded by field guns, and we share with the gunners ninety minutes of dive bombing Stukas – the terror weapon. Helpless, we cower in the ditches and pray. Hedge-hopping fighters machine-gun us – spurts of dust in the road – whoosh of flame and smoke from stricken vehicles. Noise. Smoke. Flame Helpless, we cower in the ditches and pray. How did we reach this place? … As a unit, we are now valueless except as individuals with rifles [and] any time now we may find a desperate use for those. The day wears slowly on; we wait for we know not what. We are very frightened.[14]

Alan Brooke's diary, which he had considered destroying for fear that it would fall into the hands of the enemy if he was captured, reveals his anger at the situation the BEF found itself in. He was particularly annoyed at the lack of control by the local French authorities. The town of Armentières had been badly bombed and half the buildings in the town had been demolished, which included the mental institution and the inmates had been left to wander free:

> These lunatics let loose at that time were the last straw! With catastrophe on all sides, bombarded by rumours of every description, flooded by refugees and a demoralized French army, bombed from low altitude, and now on top of it all lunatics in brown corduroy suits standing at the side of the road grinning at one with an inane smile, a flow of saliva running from the corner of their mouths, and dripping noses![15]

After planning the withdrawal, Gort's next consideration was for a bridgehead around Dunkirk to protect the port as the troops were embarking. The task of establishing the bridgehead was handed to Lieutenant General Sir Ronald Adam. Gort asked the War Office if he could be sent a brigade of the 1st Canadian Division from England to provide him with a 'nucleus' of fresh and well-trained troops to help hold the bridgehead. At first this was agreed and orders were issued to ship the brigade to Dunkirk on the night of 26/7th, but then these orders were cancelled. It would be difficult enough to rescue the troops already in France without adding to those numbers.

Adam immediately took command of all the troops in the Dunkirk area and began making arrangements to receive the three corps of the BEF and prepare lines of defence. He was told to 'act in conformity' with the French forces in the area, but only if this did not in any way endanger the British troops or impede their withdrawal.

As the troops fell back, the lines of communication between the coast and the frontline were being shortened by the hour. This meant that the remainder of the rearward troops, who were no longer required, could be evacuated without delay, and with these men out of the way, the port could be left clear for the fighting troops – the ones who would have the enemy on their heels as they tried to escape.

In conjunction with Fagalde, Adam quickly set out his ideas for the defence of Dunkirk and the flat beaches to the north of the port. These beaches stretch to the Belgium border, eight miles away, and from there to Nieuport, nine and a half miles farther still. For the whole seventeen and a half miles the shore is a wide belt of shelving sand behind which are mile after mile of sand dunes, partially clothed in long, sharp spouts of grass and patches of sea thistle. Set amid the dunes are the little resorts of Malo-les-Bains, Bray-Dunes and La Panne (or De Panne to the Belgians). Away from the coast beyond the dunes was, in 1940, a wide strip of open land – common and meadow – leading to the Dunkirk to Furnes canal.[16]

The French defences of Dunkirk were based on the peacetime organisation of the Secteur Fortifié des Flandres. These comprised two sectors. The inner one, under the command of *Général* Beaufrère, ran along the line of the Mardyck Canal to Spyker, then by Bergues to the frontier and so to the sea. The outer sector, which was the responsibility of *Général* Barthélemy, lay on the line of the river Aa to St. Omer and from there by Cassel and Steenvoorde to the frontier.[17]

To man these defences *Général* Fagalde had a collection of local troops, equivalent to a weak division, plus the French 68th Division which had just withdrawn from Belgium. The local troops were deployed on the outer line and the 68th Division was handed the task of holding the French part of the inner sector.

A key part of the Dunkirk defensive scheme was the inundation of the ground to the west of the port as far as Bergues. Fagalde immediately put this in hand, opening the sluices on the River Aa. It was this western side of the inner perimeter that Fagalde and Gort would later agree the French should be responsible for, with the British being responsible for the eastern half which reached as far as Nieuport.

THE WITHDRAWAL TO DUNKIRK

The retreat was undertaken amid chaotic conditions, with abandoned vehicles and a flood of fleeing civilians blocking the roads. 'The refugees continued to present a sorry picture indeed,' Lance Corporal Kenneth Carver, 5th Motor Ambulance Convoy, RASC, later remembered. 'It was heart-rending to see the people with all their worldly belongings on their carts, shoulders, wheelbarrows, perambulators ... You had to push these people aside while trying hard not to cause casualties, but invariably you pushed a cart or wheelbarrow into a hedge, and your instructions were to keep going and not to help people at all ... These people were travelling for miles and miles with no food or water or accommodation.'[18]

The orders to retreat were also puzzling to the British troops who had, in many cases, not been heavily engaged, and certainly had not been beaten. Second Lieutenant Peter Martin was with the 2nd Battalion, Cheshire Regiment: 'We went from river to canal to river all the way back until we were told we were heading for Dunkirk and evacuation. As my battalion hadn't been troubled desperately by the Germans at all, it was incomprehensible.'

Les Clarke, with the 6th Battalion, Durham Light Infantry, holding the line of the Yser Canal, was as baffled as Peter Martin with the instructions his battalion received to disengage with the enemy: 'Rumours spread like flames in a cornfield that they were due to head out shortly. The troops on their flank, the Northumberland Fusiliers, appeared to be pulling back and word went round that the army was pulling out from Dunkirk. Morale was poor. Les was ordered to help with the destruction of the 2in and 3in mortars, which was apparently part of the process of getting rid of equipment prior to leaving for the coast. They were collected together and dropped down a well in the grounds of a chateau. It seemed a bit foolhardy, given that they were in the middle of a battle.'[19]

Some men, though, had to fight their way to the coast, and many became isolated from their parent units, struggling along in small groups, or joining others who seemed to know where they were going. Many men marched into the perimeter after moving all night on the packed roads. In the darkness, some had lost their officers and had just made their way along with others heading for the coast. This disorganisation was later commented on by the man who became the Senior Naval Officer at Dunkirk, but it must be remembered that the BEF had not trained its men for such a circumstance as the soldiers now found themselves in. No general trains his troops to retreat.

But if the BEF had not planned or prepared for the situation it now found itself in, neither had the Germans. With no-one at the German High Command quite sure what to do, the enthusiastic statement by a Chief of the *Luftwaffe* General Staff *Général der Flieger* Hans Jeschonnek that he could destroy the British from the air, was quickly seized upon, and were reflected in Hitler's Directive No.13 issued on 24 May, in which he declared: 'Next goal of operations is the annihilation of the French, British and Belgian forces … During this operation, the task of the Luftwaffe is to break all enemy resistance in the encircled parts and to prevent the escape of the British forces across the Channel.'[20]

But the commanders of the *Fliegerkorps*, the air groups that would have to carry out the bombing, were less enthusiastic whilst there was a far bigger prize – the capture of Paris and the rest of France – in the offing. So, while the operations against the BEF were considerable, much of the *Luftwaffe*'s effort towards the end of May was focussed elsewhere.

The Germans believed that the BEF was trapped and stood little chance of getting away. This was, in large measure, due to the calculations of *Generaladmiral* Otto Schniewind, who told the chief of the *Luftwaffe* Göring on 26 May that:

A regular and orderly transport of large numbers of troops with equipment cannot take place in the hurried and difficult conditions prevailing ... Evacuation of troops without equipment, however, is conceivable by means of large numbers of smaller vessels, coastal and ferry steamers, fishing trawlers, drifters, and other small craft, in good weather, even from the open coast. The [Royal] Navy, however, is not in a position to take part successfully in this with the means at its disposal. There are no signs yet of such transport being carried out or prepared.

How wrong he was.

OPERATION DYNAMO: DAY 1

Dynamo was set to commence at 18.57 hours on the evening of 26 May. One of the first tasks that had to be undertaken was that of establishing a secure route across the Channel. There was little point in rescuing the soldiers from the panzers for them to be sunk by the U-boats or the Stukas. So, Ramsay had to form a protective screen to the eastwards of the evacuation area and provide anti-aircraft defences. Ramsay also sent his minesweepers to clear the seas around Dunkirk. The defence of Dunkirk port and its beaches would be the responsibility of Fighter Command. Now, though, came Ramsay's greatest task – that of finding enough vessels to rescue the BEF.

On the 26th, the only vessels immediately available were fifteen 'Personnel' ships, which were mainly cross-Channel or Irish Sea ferries, or packets, which were at Dover or in the Downs and a further seventeen which were at Southampton. Also at Southampton were three Dutch and Belgium ferries. In addition, there were six coastal ships and sixteen wooden and steel barges in the Downs. Thirty-nine or forty self-propelled, flat-bottomed, Dutch barges, known as *schuits* (universally Anglicised as 'skoots' by the British), had escaped across the North Sea to British ports and were made available as well as thirty-two motor transport ships, stores ships and tankers.[21]

As it was expected that most of the British troops would have to be lifted off the beaches, small craft would be needed for the inshore work. For this, Dover Command had seventy-six small vessels, to which were added four Belgian passenger launches, and the motorboats of the Contraband Control Base at Ramsgate. Many more small boats than this would be required and finding these was the responsibility of the Director of the Small Vessels Pool, Vice Admiral Sir Lionel Preston. How successful he would be might well determine the fate of many thousands of British soldiers.

Before the official start of *Dynamo*, the hospital carrier *Isle of Thanet* had taken a shipload of casualties from Dunkirk early on the morning of the 26th, and her sister ship *Isle of Guernsey*, accompanied by *Worthing*, had left for France later that forenoon, coming under aerial attack when off Calais. Nevertheless, they both reached Dunkirk that night, their passage into the harbour being illuminated by the fires that raged along the docks and across the town. 'Arriving off Dunkirk, which was under an even heavier pall of thick black smoke than Calais,' wrote *Isle of Guernsey*'s skipper, Captain E.L. Hill, 'we manoeuvred our way inside through the various wrecks of vessels which had been struck by bombs and the *Worthing* having been made fast to the Quay we moored alongside her. A few moments after our arrival streams of motor ambulances arrived threading their way through the columns of troops who were not so seriously wounded and were able to walk. Loading was commenced immediately and every member of the ship's crew assisted in stretcher bearing so as to facilitate loading.'[22]

The ships each embarked about 300 stretcher cases, using every bit of available space, even placing stretchers in corridors and between cots on the deck. Two other hospital carriers, *St Julien* and *St Andrew* failed to reach Dunkirk, being shelled by enemy-controlled guns at Gravelines.

Nor was it only westbound ships that carried personnel across the Channel, for *Maid of Orleans* sailed for Dunkirk with 250 men of the Royal Corps of Signals and the Royal Army Service Corps to help supervise and control operations in and around the harbour. She also carried 1,200 gallons of much-needed water, other stores, cases of maps, etc., the men of the BEF having been on half-rations since the 23rd. On her first attempt at entering Dunkirk, *Maid of Orleans* came under aerial attack and returned to Dover in the company of *St Julien* and *St Andrew*. But she tried again and reached the French port, escorted much of the way by the destroyer *Wild Swan*.[23]

Except for the destroyer HMS *Wolsey*, which left Dover at 19.30 hours, the steamer *Mona's Isle* was officially the first ship to sail on the great mission to rescue the BEF. On the outbreak of war *Mona's Isle*, which used to operate passenger services between the Isle of Man and Belfast and Dublin, had been requisitioned by the Admiralty and fitted out as an Armed Boarding Vessel. She reached Dunkirk around midnight, berthing at the Quai Félix Faure as the *Luftwaffe* were bombing the harbour, the ship firing all its guns at the enemy aircraft. She collected 1,420 troops and set off back to the UK. On her return, she was shelled by German artillery off Gravelines shortly after which, at 08.25 hours on the 27th, she was machine-gunned from the air. Her captain, Commander J.C.K. Dowding, submitted a report on the attack:

> Six Messerschmitts appeared. Opened fire with [the] 4-inch and 2 Lewis guns and 12 pdr. Aircraft carried out about four attacks, from the sun, invisible to us. From astern. Terrific machine gun fire, a great deal of which missed ahead, but many direct hits with cannon, especially round 12 pdr. whose crew under Sub Lt A.E. Neave R.N.R. stood up to it extremely well, but sustained casualties, including the sub lieutenant. The packed troops on the open deck suffered badly; had the shooting been accurate the losses would have been very much greater.[24]

The enemy planes only disengaged when they were out of ammunition. Nevertheless, *Mona's Isle* reached Dover escorted by the destroyer *Windsor* (which transferred its medical officer to the steamer to help attend to the wounded) at midday on the 27th, becoming the first ship of Operation *Dynamo* to make the complete round trip from Dover to Dunkirk. The attacks the steamer had endured resulted, unfortunately, in eighty-three casualties, of which twenty-three had been killed.[25]

She was not, however, the first ship back from Dunkirk. That honour went to her sister ship, *Mona's Queen*, which reached Dover with 1,200 men shortly after midnight on 26th/27th, having set off before the official start of *Dynamo*.

Another of those personnel ships that arrived at Dunkirk on that first day of the evacuation was the Southern Railway Company's *Maid of Orleans*. Acting as Chief Engineer on the ferry was George Frederick Tooley:

> The harbour and port made a depressing sight. Burning oil tanks and dense clouds of smoke spread a pall of gloom, which to some extent

prevented exact detection by hostile aircraft and gave some cover to those sorely in need of it. A considerable number of wrecks in the vicinity and approaches made navigation a nightmare. All this came as a profound shock to those of us who had previously been engaged in trooping from Southampton to Cherbourg in orderly convoys with no more excitement than an occasional U-boat or E-boat scare or a German plane reconnaissance.[26]

The Armoured Boarding Vessel, and previously Isle of Man Steam Packet Company SS *King Orry*, also managed to sail into Dunkirk harbour, where she embarked 1,131 soldiers. Commander J. Elliot RNR cast off and in the early hours of 27 May, *King Orry* reached Dover. She ran the gauntlet of fire from the batteries as she passed Calais, being hit, resulting in a number of casualties on board, but the steamer reached Dover, docking just before midday.

The only small boats available at this stage of the operation that could get close inshore to take men directly off the beaches were the cutters and whalers, i.e. the rowing boats carried by Royal Navy ships. Ramsay was made aware of this potentially grave deficiency and at 20.28 hours, he sent a signal to the Admiralty: 'Investigate and report how many cutters and whalers can be made available for immediate service under V.A. Dover.'[27]

It would take days for the Admiralty to gather such boats and ship them across the Channel. This meant that most of the troops would have to be collected from the harbour itself. But Dunkirk was a forbidding place, of which the historian David Divine, writing in the 1950s, painted a graphic, if grim, picture, portraying the last hours of the first day of the evacuation:

The port of Dunkirk as darkness fell this Sunday was a place of horror. To the west of the great basin enclosed by the outer moles the oil-tank farm was blazing. Flames silhouetted the moles and lit the underside of the bascule bridge that was jammed open at the entrance to the main basin, and the high, white column of the lighthouse. Warehouses up and down the 115 acres of the basin were burning. The wrecked cranes were outlined against their brilliance. Smoke lifted intermittently to show the fires of the town itself. And endlessly through the night the thunder of the bombs and the lightning flash of their explosions marked the progress of destruction.[28]

On this first day, only 7,669 men had been evacuated, all of whom arrived in England on the 27th, and it must have appeared that the Admiralty's estimate of only being able to rescue 45,000 men was probably reasonably accurate. There is no doubt that as day broke on 27 May, it appeared that the British Army was soon to experience a disaster on monumental scale.

Chapter 4

Operation *Dynamo*: Day 2, Monday 27 May

While the first troops were landing in England, those holding the line of La Bassée Canal were coming under increasing pressure. This included the 2nd Battalion, Royal Norfolk Regiment, which, along with the 8th Battalion, Lancashire Fusiliers, was holding the Allied line at the villages of Riez du Vinage, Le Cornet Malo and Le Paradis with the battalion headquarters at Le Paradis. The instruction the troops were given was simple – hold out as long as you can.

Hold out they did, but eventually, through sheer weight of numbers, and with their ammunition all-but consumed, the Norfolks were overrun by the S.S. Totenkopf Division. Around 100 of the Norfolks surrendered, many of who had been wounded in the fighting. What happened next was related Private Stanley Priest, one of only two men who lived to tell the tale of the massacre at Le Paradis. He takes up the story after the Norfolks had surrendered:

> They were taken to a field besides the barn. They were stripped to the waist and one fellow got a rifle butt in his face and his teeth were knocked out. Then they were marched 400 or 500 yards down a country lane into a meadow. Bill noticed that as they filed into the meadow, there was an officer standing by the gate and he saw two machine-guns had been set up pointing towards a little barn. They were taken to this barn, and made to stand outside it … and then the machine-guns opened up … Luckily, Bill, and a man named Bert Pooley, were standing near a little dip in the ground. They dived into the dip, and the bodies of their comrades saved them.[1]

The Germans wandered through the fallen Norfolks, finishing off anyone who appeared to still be alive. Both Priest and Pooley were badly wounded – Priest in the arm and Private Albert Pooley in the right leg – but they kept quiet and played dead. Priest lay next to a man whose brains were blown out, covering Priest's face.

Priest lay there all day, believing he was the only one who had not died, until he heard someone snoring! Private Pooley was also still alive. Though there were still German troops in the vicinity, the men knew that with their wounds they would die if they remained there. So, when it was dark, Priest picked up Pooley and carried him across the fields until they reached a farm, finding shelter in a pigsty along with two pigs that had been killed in the earlier fighting. The two men hid in the pigsty for three days, surviving on raw potatoes and water in filthy puddles. They were eventually spotted by the owner of the farmhouse and they received help from the locals. Pooley's leg, however, was becoming gangrenous, and a doctor who had been summoned from Béthune told them that Pooley needed hospital treatment. There was no choice but for the two soldiers to give themselves up – into the hands of the *Heer*, the regular German Army, not the SS. Both became prisoners-of-war, though Pooley was repatriated in 1943 due to the severity of his injuries.

After the war, the two survivors set about gathering evidence of the massacre at Le Paradis, which led to the trial of the German officer who ordered the killings, *Obersturmbannführer* Fritz Knöchlein. In October 1948, Knöchlein was found guilty of war crimes and was sentenced to death. He was hanged on 21 January 1949.

Some twenty miles to the south-east of Dunkirk, near the village of l'Épinette, eighty men of 'D' Company, 2nd Battalion Manchester Regiment, were preparing to ambush a German patrol that was approaching the British positions. In command of the Manchesters was Captain Jack Churchill, who had represented Great Britain in the 1939 World Archery Championships in Oslo. Churchill had taken his beloved longbow with him to France (as well as his Scottish broadsword) and even though the 2nd Manchester was a machine-gun battalion, he was keen to use the bow against the enemy. Taking up a position in the loft of a granary, he saw a German NCO as an inviting target. He told his men that he would shoot the German *Feldwebel* which would be the signal for them to attack. Churchill loosed his arrow, which hit the German in the chest, launching the attack. With that shot, 'Mad' Jack Churchill, became the only British soldier in the Second World War known to have felled an enemy with a longbow.[2] Churchill held l'Épinette throughout the day, repelling a probe by four German tanks as late as the morning of the 28th, until he received orders to withdraw to Dunkirk.

It was on the afternoon of the 27th, that the men of the 1st Division were ordered to move to Dunkirk to establish a base around which the other divisions could be organised into a defensive perimeter to cover the evacuation. After the unexplained movements of the previous few days, the instructions to move to Dunkirk, according to an officer in the Coldstream Guards, was an undoubted shock, but also something of a relief:

> No one had expected this. We had vague ideas of falling back, as the armies of 1914 had fallen back, until, somehow, sometime, we too should stand and fight our victorious Battle of the Marne. But this! There was a sudden loosening of the tenseness we had been living in for so long. We felt a surge of contentment beneath our anxiety about the war news in general and our own immediate prospects in particular.[3]

Soon after receiving the instructions to withdraw, many units of the BEF were in headlong retreat, including that of a young Royal Artillery gunner from the garrison town of Tidworth in Wiltshire, whose details were subject to wartime censorship:

> I was forty miles from Dunkirk when the order came to save ourselves. I scrounged a lift in a tank.
>
> For two days, we ran in and out of the German columns. Once we came right on them, but we just laid low and they passed us by. Once we struck a small unit and opened fire on them. We cleaned them up and then moved quick.
>
> We steered by compass. We had no water and precious little food. But we meant to get that tank to Dunkirk somehow, and we did it.
>
> Before we broke up our unit to make for the coast, we blew up our guns – that had demolished in five minutes a village in Belgium where a German battery had been set up.[4]

Though the British were in the throes of abandoning France, (Gort having been told by Eden in a telegram of the 27th that his 'sole' task was now 'to evacuate to England maximum of your force possible')[5] the French, in the form of *Général* Georges Blanchard, continued to cooperate with the fleeing Allies, agreeing to leave specified roads for the BEF's sole use. The roads, though, were narrow and still badly congested with refugees. The arrangements for the withdrawal, as agreed with the French, were issued to divisional commanders from British corps headquarters on the 27th:

> The BEF in conjunction with the French First Army is withdrawing to the line of the River Lys in three stages.
>
> First Stage: 1 and 2 Corps thinned out on the night 26/27 May.
>
> Second Stage: 1 and 2 Corps withdraw behind the River Lys on night of 27/28 May with Rear Guards on line of Deule Canal – Deulemont.
>
> Third Stage: Rear Guards to River Lys on night 28/29 May.
>
> The French First Army is conforming on the west of 1 and 2 Corps. Roads Lille – Armentieres to the west inclusive [are allocated] to French First Army. The French right on the Canal de Lys will be Merville. Not yet known whether inclusive or exclusive.
>
> 2 Div and subsequently 44 Div will act as flank guards to the withdrawal, covering the French First Army which is withdrawing on the west of 1 and 2 Corps. They will withdraw in close cooperation with French 5 Corps ... 2 and 44 Div must use roads allotted to the French and as far as possible avoid the main routes...
>
> All transport not required for the conveyance of supplies, petrol or ammunition will be used to convey personnel and when required no longer for this purpose will be parked off roads and abandoned. All water trailers will be taken with units.[6]

These arrangements were explained to Major General S.R. Wason, who had been summoned to GHQ to be informed that he was to take over III Corps from Adam who, as we know, had already made his way to Dunkirk to organise the evacuation. In addition to being given details of the process of withdrawal, Wason was told that enemy pressure could become so severe that his divisions might have to fight their way back to the coast individually.

After digesting this information and examining the relevant maps, he saw a potential problem. The French were to fall back on an area west of Dunkirk and III Corps to an area east of Dunkirk. From their starting points, it was therefore inevitable that the two bodies would cross each other's path, with the confusion and delay that would obviously occur.

Wason was consequently advised to go to the French headquarters and resolve this potentially dangerous situation. He set off at around 20.30 hours, but found the road seriously congested, and it was not until after 23.00 hours that he arrived. There he found that already the French were behind schedule and that the Germans were pressing hard on the French headquarters and he had some difficulty in extricating himself the next day. On the return trip, the road was blocked with retreating troops and fleeing civilians, and, astonishingly, he had still not reached III Corps headquarters when night fell. 'My driver was too tired to drive a second night running,' Wason wrote, 'having had virtually no chance of sleep during the day, so I decided to wait a couple of hours or so and go on at first light.'[7] By the time Wason reached his headquarters, III Corps had been without a leader for more than twenty-four hours.

During the afternoon of the 27th, Second Lieutenant Anthony Rhodes of the Royal Engineers, was amongst officers told to report at 18.30 hours to his headquarters where they would be informed about a very important plan. The colonel addressed the assembled officers:

> Lord Gort has been ordered by Whitehall to withdraw the Army before it is too late. The French and Belgians have let us down; we cannot be certain who is to blame for it. What *is* certain is that it is no fault of ours ... The evacuation, gentlemen, is to take place from Calais and Dunkirk, the only two ports left in our hands [*sic*].
>
> We are going to attempt something essentially British; I venture to say that only the British would dare to attempt such a hare-brained scheme ... I can't tell you much about it, because no plans have been made. We cannot be certain that there will be boats at the coast to take us off. We have simply got to chance it. All I can tell you for certain that we shall be fighting a hard rearguard action all the time.[8]

If the Royal Navy was going to be able to continue crossing the Channel to rescue at least a portion of the BEF, much would depend on the RAF providing protection from the air. Well aware of the burden of responsibility that would weigh upon the RAF, the Chief of the Air Staff, Sir Cyril

Newall, issued the following signal to the chiefs of all RAF commands early on the 27th:

> Today is likely to be the most critical day ever experienced by the British Army. The extreme gravity of the situation should be explained to all units. I am confident that all ranks will appreciate that it is the duty of the R.A.F. to make their greatest effort today to assist their comrades of both the Army and the Navy …
>
> [Fighter Command shall] ensure the protection of Dunkirk beaches (three miles on either side) from first light until darkness by continuous fighter patrols in strength and have due regard to the protection of bomber sorties and the provision of support of the B.E.F. area.

It was to be Air Vice Marshal Keith Parks' 11 Group that would bear the greatest responsibility for protecting the ships and the evacuation beaches, particularly the squadrons at the key Sector Station of Biggin Hill. The Spitfires and Hurricanes were to operate in alternating waves at squadron strength, at fifty-minute intervals, from 04.30 to 19.30 hours each day.[9]

The following combat report from 27 May, typifies the mixed fortunes Fighter Command experienced on that first full day of Operation *Dynamo*:

> On their first sortie the pilots of 610 Squadron, flying in their Spitfires at 18,000 feet, sighted a twin-engined [*sic*] Heinkel 111 bomber some 3,000 feet below. Anxious, in this his first combat, to make certain it was a Hun, Squadron Leader Franks dived down and calmly flew alongside taking a good look; the swastika on the tail, the black crosses on the wings were plain to see.
>
> Franks ordered Red Two and Red Three to attack. Flying Officer Smith poured all his ammunition into the Heinkel, only breaking off when the starboard engine was enveloped in flames. Sergeant Medway followed him up with a five-second burst.

The three Spitfires of Yellow Section joined in on the attack, followed swiftly by Blue Section, but with the German bomber clearly doomed, Franks called them off.

The pilot of the Heinkel managed to fire off Very flares which attracted the attention of an estimated forty Bf 109s that rushed onto the scene:

Undismayed by odds of over three to one, the Spitfire pilots went straight in to attack and sent three Messerschmitts spinning down in flames, with another three 'probables'. From this brief but hectic party Flying Officer Metcalf and Sergeant Medway failed to return.[10]

It was not just Fighter Command that would play a vital role in the evacuation. On the 27th, Wing Commander Frank Linden Hopps considered what help Coastal Command could give to the BEF. At a meeting with Air Vice Marshal Charles Blount of the BEF's Air Component at 22.00 hours at RAF Hawkinge, Hopps was told the situation was 'so serious that the enemy were expected to occupy Dunkirk within forty-eight hours'. Naturally, Hopps was willing to provide what assistance Coastal Command could offer. It was agreed that in the time available, and because of the highly fluid nature of the operations in France and Belgium, it was not possible to plan strikes on German columns, instead two Coastal Command squadrons would engage in 'roving commissions', attacking targets of opportunity. These were in addition to the usual daily Coastal Command patrols along the English Channel. The only proviso that Hopps insisted on was that the bombing missions mounted by his aircraft (which became known as the Coastal Command Striking Force) would take place on or close to the coast. It was agreed that each day, the sorties of the previous night would be analysed at 08.00 hours each morning, and a plan put in place for the next phase of operations.[11]

The exact situation at Dunkirk, however, was unknown in England, so Captain William Tennant, chief staff officer to the First Sea Lord, volunteered to cross the Channel on the afternoon of 27 May and report his findings back to the Admiralty. With a naval beach and pier party of twelve officers and 160 ratings, plus communication staff, to help organise the embarkation, Tennant left Dover on HMS *Wolfhound* at 13.45 hours. The destroyer was attacked by dive-bombers on the way to France every thirty minutes between 16.00 and 18.00 but arrived unscathed.

It was four Ju 87s that *Wolfhound* had encountered on its way across the Channel, with two bombs hitting the water close to its starboard bow. 'Splinters came on board,' reported Lieutenant Commander J.W. McCoy, 'the remaining salvoes were not close. *Wolfhound* opened fire and it is considered that two aircraft were hit. One aircraft emitting heavy smoke and another jettisoning its bombs about two miles away.'

Wolfhound pulled into Dunkirk, just as the port was under attack from a larger force of Stukas. The author Robert Jackson described the scene faced by Tennant and his team:

> As *Wolfhound* approached Dunkirk … the pall of smoke assumed frightening proportions as it coiled and billowed in the summer air, and at its foot the whole waterfront seemed to be ablaze. Rivers of flame seethe along the quay from lines of burning warehouses, and as the destroyer approached the harbour a carpet of soot descended on her like black rain. The *Wolfhound* berthed to the screech and crump of bombs.[12]

Into the midst of that dense smoke from the burning oil depots and refineries, Tennant disembarked his party, divided them up into sections and told the officers in charge of each section to 'scatter' their men around the port to make them less vulnerable to bombing attacks, whilst he made his way to Bastion 32. 'The sight of Dunkirk and nearby districts gave one a hollow feeling in the pit of the stomach,' he wrote in his report. 'The Boche had been going for it really hard, and there was not a pane of glass left anywhere – most of it was still lying in the streets. There were also "unremoved" dead lying about from the last air raid.'[13]

He immediately realised that the port was untenable and that he could not maintain *Wolfhound* in Dunkirk to act as a radio link with Dover as had been hoped. *Wolfhound*, along with her sister ship *Wolsey*, were ordered to pick up some of the waiting troops and return to Dover. Tennant assumed the position of Senior Naval Officer, meeting with senior Army officers to discuss the situation in Dunkirk. With the town having been heavily bombed, fires raged through the streets and, as Private William Ridley, 9th Battalion, Durham Light Infantry, graphically described, Dunkirk, 'had the stink of death. It was the stink of blood and cordite.'

One of the men that sailed with Tennant in *Wolfhound* as part of the naval beach party was Yeoman/Signaller Victor Chanter:

> On the approach to Dunkirk we turned east along the coast; and along with several seamen, I was taken inshore by launch. At a point now too

shallow for the launch, we scrambled over the side with our gear ...
A pall of smoke hung over Dunkirk, and we were to discover that La
Panne was to be evacuation headquarters. Our home for the next few
days was to be the beach ...

We commenced organising orderly queues, lines of soldiers for embarkation into small rowing boats and floats, lines which often dispersed
quickly into the dunes behind the beach with the arrival of bombs and
bursts of machine-gun fire from German aircraft strafing the sands.[14]

It was also on this day that Anthony Rhodes, whose unit formed part of the 3rd
Division, had his first glimpse of war-torn Dunkirk:

It must have been very nearly six o'clock on the morning of Monday
the 27th of May when we passed over the hill that hides Dunkirk and
saw the town in the distance; the pall of smoke above it came from
burning oil tanks on the southern outskirts.

I was to have good cause to be thankful for those oil tanks later [for
the smoke helped hide the men from the attacks by the *Luftwaffe*],
but at the time I deplored the smoke and the flame above them as a
horrible sign, an omen that our reception and departure would not be
the quite the orderly affair that I, at any rate, had hoped for.[15]

Tennant, meanwhile, had made his assessment. The wrecked and burning port
was no longer a safe or practical point for the ships to load up with men. This
left just the soft, sandy beaches that stretched for sixteen miles eastwards from
Dunkirk to Nieuport. So, he sent the following signal to Dover, timed at 19.58
hours, though not received at Dover until almost an hour later: 'Port continuously
bombed all day and on fire. Please send every available craft to beaches East of
Dunkirk immediately. Evacuation tomorrow night is problematical'.[16]

Just seven minutes after his 19.58 signal, Tennant sent a 'Most Immediate'
message which was received by Ramsay at 20.25 hours, some thirty minutes
ahead of the first signal: 'Port consistently bombed all day, and on fire.
Embarkation possible only from beaches East of harbour A.B.C.D. Send all
ships and passenger ships there to anchor.'

What Tennant was referring to was that the beach from Malo-les-Bains
through Bray-Dunes to La Panne had been divided to four zones A B C D

(though this was later reduced to just three). So Tennant then sent parties along the shore towards La Panne to organise the beaches to allow for the orderly passage of the troops through the beaches onto the boats.

In response to Tennant's signals, at 21.42 hours, Ramsay sent the following instructions to the warships under his command: 'Close beaches one to three miles east of Dunkirk with utmost despatch and embark all possible British troops using your own boats. This is our last chance of saving them.' As a result, the destroyers *Gallant*, *Vivacious*, *Windsor*, *Anthony*, *Vimy*, *Impulsive* and the cruiser *Calcutta* made for the beaches at Bray and Malo, whilst *Grafton* and *Greyhound* headed for La Panne. Other similar messages went out from Dover over the course of the following hour-and-a-half: 'Last chance of saving the BEF is tonight,' Ramsay told the captain of HMS *Sabre*'; 'This is our last chance,' he told HMS *Vimy*.[17] All the ships that subsequently reached Dunkirk were rushed to the beaches.

Lifting the men from the beaches, however, would be a slow and laborious task. The gently shelving beaches could not be approached by the larger ships, which meant that only small boats could go inshore to collect the soldiers and transport them to the ships anchored in deeper water.

Tennant looked around for a solution. He saw that whilst the port had been hit repeatedly by the German bombers the two wood and concrete breakwaters, or moles, on either side of the harbour were still intact. Of these the short West Mole was only 152 metres long and was surrounded mostly by shallow water, however the East Mole stretched for more than a kilometre out into the Channel, and the water on either side, particularly at high tide, was deep enough for ships to berth against. It was, though, only five feet wide and had not been designed for embarking personnel. This was not a stout stone wall with berthing places along its length, as might be imagined around a harbour. It was a narrow plank-way with, on either side a protective railing made of strong timbers with, at intervals, taller posts that could be used by ships to secure themselves in emergencies. At the far end of the Mole was a concrete 'nose' upon which stood a short lighthouse. The Mole was built in this fashion to allow the tides to roll in and out and to put less strain upon its structure.

If this mole could be used by the ships, it might prove to be the solution Tennant sought. To test his idea, he asked the General Steam Navigation

Company motor vessel *Queen of the Channel* to try and berth against the East Mole. Captain W. J. Odell skilfully eased his 250-foot passenger ship cautiously against the slim structure and safely secured the motor vessel. Tennant had found his answer. By using both sides of the East Mole, as many as eight ships could be accommodated at a time. Maybe, just maybe, a larger portion of the BEF could be saved than anyone imagined.

Just after *Queen of the Channel* had berthed against the East Mole and begun embarking troops, the *Luftwaffe* mounted another attack upon the harbour. Odell was immediately ordered to leave Dunkirk and make his way to the beaches. *Queen of the Channel* had only taken fifty soldiers off the Mole. Nevertheless, having moved eastwards, she lifted about 150 men from the beaches using her own boats before being ordered back to the harbour, where she collected a further 700 men. In the early hours of the 28th *Queen of the Channel* set off for England.

Queen of the Channel had been one of two passenger ships – the other being *St Seiriol* – and two hospital carriers, *Maid of Orleans* and *Isle of Thanet*, which had left Dover at 13.30 hours. When *St Seiriol* arrived at Dunkirk she tied up on the East Mole to await instructions. This Liverpool and North Wales Steamship Company ship operated between Liverpool and Llandudno around Anglesey. She also undertook trips to Douglas, Isle of Man. Her Chief Engineer was J. McNamee:

There was an air raid in progress as we arrived alongside. Our guns with others were in action. We landed a man on the pier [Mole] to hang on to our ropes. About 8 P.M. Lieutenant Commander Williams, R.N., came on board and told the captain to proceed out of the harbour, lower his boats, and get the men on board from the beach.

We got to the anchorage. I lowered the first boat in charge of the second officer and the second boat in charge of R. Thomas, A.B. The third boat was taken by the crew of a trawler.

When I was about to lower the fourth boat we received information that there were a number of troops arriving at the pier. With the remainder of the crew we still had on board we proceeded alongside the pier We got about 600 men on board, they were arriving in batches, about 11 p.m. we were told that there were no more men in the vicinity, so we cut our mooring ropes. On hearing more men running along the pier we got the ship alongside the pier again and got about 80 more on board.

During its stay by the Mole, the harbour was bombed in four separate raids, and as *St Seiriol* was moving off from the Mole, the German aircraft dropped illuminated parachutes that lit up the whole scene. The ferry then went back towards La Panne to pick up the boats it had dropped off, but Captain R.D. Dobb was ordered to make his way to Dover via Calais.

The attack German attack upon the harbour was seen by the crew of HMS *Vivacious* as the destroyer approached Dunkirk on its second trip of the 27th:

> Intense aircraft attack by about twenty-five enemy machines was encountered off the Eastern Entrance with about 100 bombs being dropped on the ships and three enemy machines were shot down (Two Junkers 88 and one Heinkel 111). One burst into flames and crashed on the beach, and another with the port engine on fire crashed into the sea. The third was not seen to crash but the pilot was seen to leave the plane by parachute.

The *Luftwaffe* mounted 225 conventional bomber and seventy-five dive-bomber attacks on Dunkirk during the day, dropping more than 350 tons of ordnance – 15,000 high explosive bombs and 30,000 incendiaries.[18] The first of these raids, delivered by the Heinkel 111s of KG 1 and KG 4, struck the harbour, destroying seven docking basins, five miles of quays and 115 acres of docks and warehouses. The second wave that day, from KG 54, hit and sank the French steamer *Aden* near the East Mole.

This was followed by an attack from StG, its Ju 87s sinking the French steamer *Côte d'Azur* and an auxiliary mine-sweeper. The Stukas also sank the small British coaster, *Worthtown*. The last raid was by Do 17Z Dorniers of KG 2 and KG 3, which wrecked the railway yards and struck the Saint-Pol refinery.

The RAF did respond, mounting 287 sorties along the coast from Gravelines as far as Ostend, claiming to have shot down twenty-one German bombers, with the loss of fourteen Hurricanes and five Spitfires.[19] Fighter Command's aircraft had, of course, limited time over the French and Belgian coasts, and it was not possible to predict when the next German raid was to be delivered. This meant that often the *Luftwaffe* could fly unimpeded over Dunkirk and the adjacent beaches, leading, as we shall see, to many complaints from the soldiers that they had been abandoned by the RAF. It was not true. Sixteen squadrons of Air Vice Marshal Keith Park's No.11 Group provided cover for the beaches. After day upon day of fighting, the exhausted pilots were withdrawn to be replaced by those from nos. 12 and 13 groups. During the course of Operation *Dynamo*, thirty-two squadrons were employed in covering the evacuation.

'DUNKIRK HAD FALLEN'

The Dutch skoots *Lena*, *Hebe II* and *Oranje*, also reached France on the 27th, and anchored off the beaches and embarked troops during the night, setting off on their return trips in the early hours of the 28th. Some of the others (*Bernrif*, *Brandaris*, *Hondsrug*, *Jutland*, *Patria*, *Tilly* and *Twente*) were within sight of Dunkirk when, due to a miscommunication, they returned to the Downs. What actually happened was that following Tennant's instruction to send the ships to the beaches, a signal was sent by the Sea Transport Officer to 'turn back ships attempting to enter Dunkirk'. This was supposed to have directed the ships to the beaches but, quite understandably, it was interpreted as meaning that the ships should return to the UK. This message was received by the passenger vessel *Canterbury*, which had entered Dunkirk harbour at 20.00 hours, and left at 20.58 hours with 457 troops, including 140 stretcher cases. When *Canterbury* was about six or seven miles from Dunkirk she met the skoots and relayed the message, whereupon they turned back to England, reporting that 'Dunkirk had fallen'. This false information was passed to the passenger vessel *Dorrien Rose* but, to her captain's great credit, he pressed on and reached Dunkirk.

One of the ships that reached Dunkirk, did so without its captain. Lieutenant Commander Richard George Kirby Knowling, was the skipper of the destroyer HMS *Vimy* which was heading across the Channel on the night of 27/28 May, when he disappeared. Just before midnight on the 27th, he left the bridge with the intention of going below. When, after a while, he did not return to the bridge, a search was undertaken, but there was no sign of *Vimy*'s skipper.

The rails and life-lines were all secure and undisturbed and there was no obvious explanation for the officer's disappearance. The only one that was offered was that Lieutenant Commander Knowling, who had been suffering from a sprained ankle at the time, might have been thrown off balance – and overboard – when the warship made a turn at speed.[20]

HMS *Vivacious*, with other destroyers including the Polish warship *Blyskawica*, was ordered to take up a position one mile east of Dunkirk and she arrived there at 00.30 on the 28th. 'The town was undergoing continual bombardment and flames from ammunition dumps and oil fuel depots reached two to three thousand feet,' reported its skipper, Commander E.F.V. Dechaineux of the Royal Australian Navy. 'During these raids "whistling" bombs were heard, their noise being similar to that of a siren. Two enemy aircraft came through the thick smoke cloud and attacked the ships with machine guns. The *Blyskawica* shot down one of these in the harbour.'[21]

Using its whaler and with the help of a number of drifters, by 03.30 the section of beach allocated to *Vivacious* was cleared of troops, the destroyer having taken on board 353 men. Commander Dechaineux received a message from one of the personnel ships that Dunkirk was also clear of troops, so *Vivacious* returned to Dover only half-full.

Meanwhile, the Admiralty endeavoured to comply with Tennant's request for more vessels to be sent to Dover, especially small craft that could be used to take the troops directly from the beaches. Because of the Small Craft Registration Order, the Admiralty held full details of all the boats that might be available within a reasonable sailing distance of Dover. This order had gone out on 14 May, being broadcast by the BBC in the nine o'clock news. Its timing was quite coincidental, being a step taken by the Admiralty because of the increasing demand for vessels due to the general war situation, and was not a direct consequence of the Dunkirk evacuation. In particular, the adoption of magnetic mines by the Germans had led to the building of wooden minesweepers and the country's boatyards were fully occupied meeting the Admiralty's requirements, which led to a shortage of other small craft. The order read as follows: 'The Admiralty have made an order requesting all owners of self-propelled pleasure craft between 30 and 100 feet in length, to send all particulars to the Admiralty within fourteen days from today, if they have not already offered or requisitioned.'

Soon all the owners or operators of tugs, ferries, barges, motor-launches, lighters, fishing boats and schooners, as well as boat-yards, boat-builders and yacht clubs up and down the Thames and along the south and south-eastern coasts, were being contacted by the Ministry of Shipping. Early on the morning of the 27th, the Admiralty had already asked the Ministry of Sea Transport to find between forty and fifty such small craft to assemble at Sheerness for 'a special requirement'. Vice Admiral Sir Lionel Preston, Director of the Small Vessels Pool, provided a list of those vessels from the Small Craft Register that he thought would be able to assist with the evacuation, but it was soon found that many were not suitable.

A meeting was hurriedly arranged with the Director of Sea Transport, H. C. Riggs, in which it was agreed that Preston would despatch some of his officers to examine the boat-yards from Burnham and Brightlingsea round to Shoreham-by-Sea, and to send all vessels that they thought fit for service round to Sheerness.

While those officers set off to search the coast, Riggs phoned Douglas Tough of Tough's Boatyard at Teddington on the River Thames. Taking Tough into his confidence, Riggs briefly outlined Operation *Dynamo*, the kind of boats needed and, most importantly, the urgency of the situation. The results were dramatic. Assisted by individuals such as Ron Lenthall and Chief Foreman Harry Day, Douglas Tough, along with a naval officer, set about gathering the small craft asked for, starting with fourteen in his yard opposite Teddington Lock. They then set off along the river. If they saw what they considered to be a suitable craft, efforts were made to contact the owner; often with the result that the owners volunteered to sail the boats themselves. If no contact could be made with an owner, the boat was simply requisitioned.

Once a boat had been secured, voluntarily or otherwise, a crew was put on board and eventually, more than 100 vessels were assembled at the Ferry Road Yard. There were not enough men regarded as competent enough to take all the boats down to Sheerness, so the available crews had to work in rotation to get the boats down to the coast.

Until these vessels could be collected and organised, there remained very few small boats available to take men off the beaches. The main effort of the 27th, therefore, was focussed on pressing the ferries to undertake as many trips to Dunkirk as possible. This was maintained at a rate of two every three and a half hours throughout the day, but this came at a heavy cost. Between sailings timed 03.00 hours and 15.00, no less than five transports were shelled and returned to the UK without making the trip, and another, *Mona's Isle*, was damaged by shellfire.

Returning by what was designated Route Z, which took the Isle of Man Steam Packet Company vessel southwards passed Gravelines and Cap Gris Nez before heading out for Dover, *Mona's Isle* came under fire from German batteries on the beach and from coastal batteries taken over by the invaders. Shells fell all around, sending plumes of water high into the air and at least two hit the boat. *Mona's Isle* was then attacked by approximately eight Bf 109s. On board *Mona's Isle* was Denys Thorp RNVR, who later reached the rank of Lieutenant Commander:

> Four or five ratings were wounded. Petty Officer Pope RNR though badly wounded in the wrist closed some ready use lockers in the 12-pounder enclosure after the 12-pounder crew were knocked out, in the face of heavy machine-gun and cannon fire and afterwards received the DSC. The plight of the soldiers wounded was more tragic as after what they had endured in France they came aboard this ship thankful to be in the Navy's care and bound for home with the feeling that their troubles were for the moment at an end. I was very upset by this aspect at the time and it took me a long time to forget that no doctor was carried and no sick bay attendant, but their mates came to their help and did what they could for them. The ship was in a sorry state and when the damage was assessed the situation did not look too bright. It was found that the tele-motor pipes were severed and the ship could not be steered as the hand steering gear had been removed when the ship was converted. All the boats were shot up and rendered useless and the wireless aerial had carried away, the W/T set out of action. Many steam pipes were leaking and steam and hot water were issuing from unexpected places.[22]

Luckily, the white cliffs of Dover were in sight, and so by careful use of port and starboard engines, the packet was able to reach the safety of the port. Twenty-three men on board had been killed and a further sixty wounded. It was the last effort by the steamer which, in her two trips, had taken 2,634 men from Dunkirk.

The cargo ship MV *Sequacity* did not even reach Dunkirk. Her loss was reported by her skipper Captain J. MacDonald:

> All went well until we arrived off Calais, then I noticed some shells falling in the water ahead of us. I thought it was land batteries ashore firing at some mines, but soon after the shells started dropping all around my ship, and one came through the port side, at the water line in the main hold and went out the starboard side.
>
> I sent my mate down into the hold with some of the crew to try and patch the hole up. The next shot came through the port side of the engine room and smashed up the auxiliary engines that drove our dynamo, etc., put our switchboard out of action, and went out the starboard side.
>
> This put our pumps entirely out of action for pumping water out of the hold.
>
> Another shot came through the wheelhouse and went through the hatches, down the forehold, and right through the ship's bottom.[23]

If this was not bad enough, the *Luftwaffe* then appeared overhead, and its bombers attacked both *Sequacity* and the accompanying collier *Yewdale*. More shells rained in on the stricken coaster and to make matters even worse the wind increased, causing a 'nasty' swell which caused water to lap into the hole in *Sequacity*'s side. The coaster began to list. *Sequacity* was clearly going down, and rapidly.

Captain MacDonald blew on the ship's horn to attract *Yewdale*'s attention, but amid the noise and confusion of battle this was not noticed. An RAF fighter happened to be flying over the two ships and saw that *Sequacity* was in trouble. The aircraft dropped red flares ahead of *Yewdale*, and the crew on board the collier looked back to see *Sequacity* stationary in the water and listing severely. MacDonald launched *Sequacity*'s lifeboat and his crew made it safely to *Yewdale* as the coaster went down by the head.

The Southern Railway steamer *Biarritz* was also shelled and damaged off Calais, as was the LNER passenger ship SS *Archangel* and the former Isle of Man packet steamer, converted to an Armed Boarding Vessel, HMS *King Orry*.

As a result of the damage inflicted on these ships, and with the loss of *Sequacity*, Ramsay, reported to the Admiralty that the normal Dover to Dunkirk passage (Route Z), was impracticable in daylight owing to fire from shore batteries extending from Les Hemmes to Gravelines. This meant using the route through the Zuydecoote Pass to the north of Dunkirk, which extended the distance of the round trip from eighty miles to 172 resulting in a general slowing up of traffic. This route, classified as Route Y, had to be swept before it could be used. Work was also commenced to sweep a channel from the North Goodwin to the Ruytingen Pass and thence into the Dunkirk Roads (Route X), thus shortening the round trip from 172 miles to 108.

The situation was equally perilous in Dunkirk itself, which was under almost continual bombardment, and every cellar or possible bomb-proof shelter was crammed with soldiers. With the passage of every hour increasing numbers of men filed into the town, many having lost touch with their parent units, and, wandering through the rubble-strewn streets, they were inviting targets for the *Luftwaffe*. The bombing resulted in the complete breakdown of communications, with streets rendered impassable and Army units being dispersed.

This made Colonel Whitfeld's task of organising the evacuation areas even harder, particularly with regards to the wounded. Though he would have wished to have been able to house the wounded as close to the port as possible, the bombing of Dunkirk made this impractical and he was obliged to set up the main base hospital in a large house called Chateau Rouge in Rosendaele near La Panne. 'My intention was to use this hospital for local wounded pending embarkation,' Whitfeld wrote, 'and also as a lying up place for ambulance convoys pending the arrival of hospital ships or carriers.' Whitfeld appointed Lieutenant Colonel Rose from the GHQ staff to act as senior medical officer and then attempted to control the evacuation of the wounded as follows, working on the assumption that two hospital carriers per day would reach Dunkirk:

At the Chapeau Rouge the ambulance convoys were collected and kept as far as possible under cover from air observation. Immediately the carriers arrived near Dunkirk a Despatch Rider was sent to the hospital warning them to be ready to move ... The Monitor Dock was the best place the evacuate the wounded from if it was possible to do so, and generally speaking the carriers made an attempt to tie up there. To reach the Monitor Dock entailed a drive through the town of Dunkirk and dockland. As the town and docks were a shambles and highly dangerous, the chance of getting the ambulances to the ships was often very slight. It often happened that as the ambulances were in sight of the ships a heavy bombing raid was made and the ships had to push out as soon as possible. The ensuing confusion of attempting to turn the ambulance convoy among broken and burning motors, stores, sheds, etc., may be imagined.[24]

The ambulances could not remain in Dunkirk and had to drive back to the comparative safety of La Panne and wait for the next opportunity to try and reach the docks. These operations were so difficult and dangerous that Whifeld believed Lieutenant Colonel Rose had been killed in the bombing on the 27th and was surprised when he later discovered that he had made it safely back to the UK. A few hospital trains managed to get through to Dunkirk but the line was soon smashed by the bombs of the *Luftwaffe*. Later in the evacuation many of the stretcher cases were embarked, with some degree of success, from the East Mole.

Whitfeld also saw that Bastion 32 was becoming over-crowded, and whilst the French had gracefully accommodated the colonel and his small staff when he first arrived, they were now becoming increasingly resentful of the British officers who were moving into the Naval Headquarters and, evidently, taking over the building. So Whitfeld organised a 'Town Mayor's Office' in Dunkirk and a small Movement Control staff to help ease the flow of troops through the town. The office was blown up and burnt later on the 27th, after which Whitfeld ordered the evacuation of the town.

The evacuation of Dunkirk meant that all those British troops who had been sheltering in the town had to move east to the beaches, though not everyone complied. As the soldiers left Dunkirk, the *Luftwaffe* delivered another attack upon the port. Lieutenant Rhodes was one of those soldiers:

The German pilots must have observed the long line of men coming from the town because, after dropping their bombs, they turned about, and made a low-level machine-gunning attack on us as we crouched in our holes. The officially advocated behaviour of standing up and firing a Bren gun at the aeroplane, even when it is on top of you, was put into practice by two of our men who were both promptly riddled with bullets.[25]

Though the lack of organisation by the Army during the evacuation was commented on many times by both naval and military personnel, Lieutenant Colonel T.J.W. Winterton, the BEF's Assistant Quartermaster-General, did actually put in place a team at each of the three beaches, consisting of two lieutenant colonels assisted by eight majors or captains. Their roles were as follows:

a)   To select routes to the beaches and to provide guides along those routes.
b)   To select areas in which to hold the troops under cover prior to evacuation.
c)   To arrange for small parties to be available at all times at loading points when boats were working.
d)   To call forward troops as required from assembly areas.
e)   To liaise with Naval personnel on the beaches, and to see that the correct number of men were allocated to each boat, this number to be laid down by the Navy.
f)   To see that no unnecessary kit was taken on board.[26]

This system broke down due to troops arriving in vast numbers and in many cases without their officers.

CASSEL COFERENCE

Beyond Dunkirk, the first rounds in a savage contest for one of the key locations on the approach to Dunkirk was being fought. It had been four days earlier, on 23 May, that the Germans had pushed into St Omer and it quickly became apparent to Major General Mason-MacFarlane that once the enemy were across the canalised stretch of the River Aa there was nothing to stop them moving on to Cassel. The town of Cassel sits on the highest point in French Flanders, occupying a position above the junction of five important roads, including the main route to Dunkirk on this flank of the BEF's line. He quickly organised a force to hold Cassel which was added to on the 24th and placed under the command of Brigadier Nigel Somerset. What was named 'Somer Force', consisting of two battalions of Somerset's own 145 Brigade (the 2nd Battalion, Gloucestershire Regiment and the 4th Battalion, Oxfordshire and Buckinghamshire Light Infantry) supported by tanks and Bren gun carriers from the 1st Light Armoured Reconnaissance Brigade, arrived in the town on the morning of the 25th. Two days later, the Germans attacked.

With four tanks spearheading their advance, German infantry assaulted the foot of the south and south-east sides of the town where 'C' and 'D' companies of the Glosters and the 4th Ox and Bucks were posted. Major Gilmore, in command of the Glosters received a report that the enemy was attempting to establish themselves in some cottages dangerously close to the south of their position:

> I ordered the company to dislodge them with the bayonet. [Captain] Cholmondely, taking a party of six men, managed to work up to their cottages, which had been originally occupied by our machine gunners the previous day, but who had either put out of action or had evacuated their position without informing anyone. The party got into the cottages, killed one man while the others cleared off.[27]

The defenders had repulsed the German attack; but it was only the start and, as more enemy troops gathered below Cassel, the fighting took on the nature of a siege.

It was on the morning of the 27th that Lord Gort and General Adam arranged a meeting with Général Fagalde and Admiral Abrial at Cassel to discuss the evacuation of the BEF and the establishment of the defensive perimeter around the embarkation areas. However, neither Abrial nor Fagalde had been informed by the French Government that the BEF was to be evacuated back to the UK. Indeed, it was as Fagalde was driving up from Dunkirk for the meeting at Cassel that he became aware that something was horribly wrong. The road from Dunkirk had been choked with abandoned British Army vehicles and, when he stopped to ask a British officer why so many large lorries had seemingly been left by the roadside by their drivers, he was told that they had been ordered to leave their vehicles and move to Dunkirk.

To their immense credit, the two French officers acted with great professionalism and agreement was reached on the nature and extent of the Dunkirk defences. It was decided that the perimeter would run from the coast at Nieuport in the east to Furnes then westwards to Bergues along the line of the Furnes-Bergues Canal, before cutting back towards the coast at

Mardyck. This meant that the perimeter, into which the BEF would withdraw, was twenty-three miles east to west and seven miles wide at its deepest point (between Dunkirk and Bergues). As we have already learned, the British troops were to hold the perimeter from Nieuport round to Bergues, with the French occupying the western sector down to Mardyck. These positions would come under increasing pressure as Hitler, finally realising that by focussing on destroying the other French armies he was allowing the British to slip from his grasp, issued instructions to the 19th Division to close within artillery range of Dunkirk, 'in order to cut off, from the land side, the continuous flow of transport (evacuations and arrivals)'.[28]

That flow of transport, particularly the personnel ships, continued well throughout the 27th. Amongst these was the paddle-minesweeper *Brighton Belle* which was loaded up with 800 men as it set off back to the UK, one of whom was Major C. R. Wampach of the Royal Engineers:

> The long march to the coast was a nightmare! Towns were in ruins and burning, civilians lying dead in the streets, roads packed with refugees and all the while we were under constant air attack. In spite of this we managed to wash, shave, obtain rations and get some sleep. We were all incredibly tired but it is amazing what can be tolerated when needs must. We were fortunate that the weather was wonderful. I always remember taking a break in a field not far from Dunkirk. We lay down totally exhausted, near to despair but in the distance we could hear the skirl of the pipes. The Black Watch Pipers came marching along the road-heads held high and erect. The effect this had on all of us was remarkable. It seemed to give us all an injection of morale and we rose as one man and followed the pipers on the way to the beach. Eventually we found ourselves with thousands of others at Malo-les-Bains, a seaside resort near Dunkirk. Here there was some semblance of order with officers trying to re-organise units.[29]

To help speed up the turnaround rate of the ships, five UK ports were to be used to disembark the troops. The destroyers were to use Dover; drifters, skoots, coasters and minesweepers were to sail into Margate or Ramsgate, as directed, the personnel ships were to go to Folkestone and, lastly, the cruiser *Calcutta* was to disembark at Sheerness.

The general strategic situation, though, remained grave, with the French Army in a state of near anarchy and the Belgian Army close to collapse. Arriving at his headquarters in Lomme, Alan Brooke, in command of II Corps, was addressed by his aide, Lieutenant Colonel Ronald Stanyford, who pointed to a body lying in the gutter on the opposite side of the road. 'They have just shot that chap.' Brooke asked who it was that had shot the man? 'Oh! Some of these retiring French soldiers, they said he was a spy, but I think the real reason was that he refused to give them any cognac.'[30]

Back in the UK, the priority was to despatch as many small vessels as possible to help lift the troops from the beaches. The Naval Officer in Charge, Ramsgate, had the job of arranging the fuelling and despatching of all small power boats and the larger boats that would tow the smaller vessels across the Channel. Rear Admiral A.H. Taylor became 'Dynamo Maintenance Officer' at Sheerness, tasked with making sure the boats, particularly the towing vessels, were in a suitable condition for the stresses they would be under on the long trip to Dunkirk.

Once out at sea, it was not possible for most of these boats to be contacted by wireless and during the crossing some became detached from their tows. Much time was lost trying to gather up the lost boats.

Over in Dunkirk, Tennant was unimpressed with the chaotic state of the army as the first troops gathered on the beaches: 'As regards the behaviour and bearing of the troops, both British and French, prior to and during the embarkation, it must be recorded that the earlier parties were embarked off the beaches in a condition of complete disorganisation. There appeared to be no military officers in charge of the troops, and the impression was undoubtedly enhanced by the difficulty in distinguishing between the uniforms of such officers as were present and those of other ranks. It was soon realised that it was vitally necessary to dispatch naval officers in their unmistakable uniforms, with armed beach parties to take charge of the soldiers on shore immediately prior to embarkation.'[31] Before the arrival of these naval officers, Tennant's party was sent to the beaches to 'police' the troops and keep some kind of order, where each of the three corps of the BEF had been allocated a section of beach.

Only two of the personnel ships actually made the round trip during the 27th. The first of these was General Steam Navigation Company's MV *Royal Daffodi*, which normally took passengers from London to Ostend. It left Dover at 10.54 hours under escort of the destroyer *Vimy*. They formed convoy with HMS *Anthony*, which was escorting the cargo ship SS *Kyno*, though these latter two were called back in mid-Channel. *Anthony* and *Royal Daffodi* were then joined by the hospital ships *St Andrew* and *St Julien*. *Royal Daffodi* succeeded in recovered 840 men and headed back to the UK.

The second to make the round trip on the 27th, was the Great Western Railway Steamer *St Helier*, though she was ordered back before she could embark any troops. *Wolfhound* and *Wolsey* recovered 206 and 130 men respectively from the beach at Marlo, but these destroyers did not depart for Dover until after midnight.[32]

In addition, seventeen flare-burning drifters of the Dover Auxiliary Patrol sailed from Dover for Malo Beach, and during the night lifted 2,000 troops from the beach by ships' dinghies. With more than 200,000 men waiting on the beaches, or fighting their way through to Dunkirk, the number of troops rescued so far was alarmingly small.

It was disappointing to all concerned that after two days so few men had been rescued. There was not much time left to save the BEF, and the continuing success of the entire operation depended on how long the Germans could be kept at bay. On the night of 26/27 May, I and II Corps had swung back with their right resting on Fort Sainghin to the south-east of Lille and had held fast throughout the 27th. This meant that the Navy would get at least one more day to try and save the army.

Chapter 5

Operation *Dynamo*: Day 3, Tuesday 28 May

By the night of 27/28 May, the main bodies of I and II Corps had withdrawn behind the River Lys, leaving a strong rearguard holding the line of the river. The rearguard followed the main columns on the night of 28/29 May.

However, on 28 May, the Belgian Army, trapped by the Germans in what remained of unoccupied Belgium, surrendered. This opened a twenty-mile gap on Gort's eastern front between the British and the sea. At a time when Gort was seeking to reduce the area held by the BEF he had to send the 3rd, 4th and 50th Divisions to plug this gap.

This sudden, though hardly unexpected, capitulation, prompted King George to send a supportive telegram to Gort: 'All your countrymen have been following with pride and admiration the courageous resistance of the British Expeditionary Force during the continuing fighting of the last fortnight. Faced by circumstances outside their control in a position of extreme difficulty, they are displaying a gallantry which has never been surpassed in the annals of the British Army. The hearts of everyone of us at home are with you and your magnificent troops in this hour of peril.'[1]

Facing eight German divisions along this eastern perimeter from Nieuport to Ploegsteert ('Plugstreet') were just five British divisions, but the most important sector was in the centre which ran from La Motte through Plugstreet to Comines which linked the western and eastern fronts. Here the French III Corps and the remains of the 1st Army's Cavalry Corps, held the middle of this central sector from Estaires to Plugstreet with the 42nd and 4th divisions of the BEF occupying the left which touched the eastern front. It was to the south of this central front, however, that the most pressure was being exerted by a combined German force of Rommel's 7th Panzers and Bock's 7th Infantry Division.

The situation on the western side of the pocket was a confused one, the Germans having broken through the British line at a number of points, forcing the 2nd and 44th Divisions to pull back closer to Dunkirk. The 44th Division had lost heavily as it withdrew to Mont des Cats, and the 2nd Division was so badly mauled that its survivors were sent back past Poperinghe to the coast. To add to the confusion, the still only partially-formed III Corps found its component parts cut off from each other by the German advance.

These developments left the hill-top town of Cassel standing isolated and seemingly forgotten – for the despatch rider carrying the order for Somerset to retreat had got lost. As the Germans were now able to push on along the road to Bergues, the defenders could see that they were cut off from the rest of the BEF. All they could do was watch the enemy columns driving by and wonder at the fate that awaited them. They did not have to ponder on this for long, as the Germans renewed their assault in the morning, with aircraft, artillery, tanks and infantry, driving the outlying companies of the Glosters and the Ox and Bucks from the foot of the hill. The defenders retired up the slopes to the town where Lieutenant General Henry Pownall, the BEF's Chief of General Staff, encouraged by the successes of the 27th in holding off the Germans, had set up his Command Post.

Under the cover of a heavy and continuous artillery barrage, the Germans stormed up the heavily-wooded slopes, which provided the attackers with excellent cover as they pressed up towards the hill-top town. The attack lasted all morning, but the town remained firmly in British hands.

One of the places where the Germans had already broken through the British line was five miles or so to the north of Cassel at the important road junction at the town of Wormhoudt. This was occupied on the 26th by the 2nd Battalion, Royal Warwickshire Regiment, being joined by the 8th Battalion, Worcestershire Regiment, and later the 4th Battalion, Cheshire Regiment and some artillery. It was a little after midday on the 27th when Wormhoudt first came under attack, with German aircraft dropping around ten bombs on the town, but it was not until the following day that the battle for Wormhoudt began in earnest.

At 09.40 hours on the 28th, convoys of German lorries arrived, out of which poured large numbers of infantry. They took up battle positions and opened fire on the Warwicks holding the west and south-west perimeter. German artillery then began shelling the town. The defenders held their ground staunchly until an incident in the late morning changed the entire nature of the battle for Wormhoudt and led to the most shameful episode in the entire Dunkirk story.

The commander of the German regiment spearheading the attack upon Wormhoudt, *Obergruppenführer* Josef Dietrich of the SS Leibstandarte Adolf Hitler, became trapped in a ditch when his car was ambushed by the Worcesters. To extricate him the Germans sent for the panzers.

The tanks of the 3rd Panzer Regiment soon rumbled up, and though the British Boys anti-tank guns crippled four of the panzers, it was an uneven fight. Even so, the defenders held out until all their ammunition had been used, and the Germans overran their positions. They dropped their weapons and surrendered to the SS.

At this point both sides could be proud of what they had achieved. The Germans had captured a position of strategic importance and the British had held up the Germans for the best part of a day, giving the men crowding into the evacuation area an increased chance of escaping. But, sadly, the Wormhoudt account did not end there.

A number of the survivors from the Warwickshire and Cheshire regiments and a few from the Royal Artillery, amounting to around eighty to ninety men, were rounded up by the SS and forced to strip and march into a barn. Amongst those men was Gunner Brian Fahey of 208 Battery, Anti-Tank Regiment, RA, who had been wounded earlier in the day:

> There must have been about 100 men in the barn, and then the Germans surrounded it, and threw in hand grenades. It was apparent that they were going to murder us all. I suppose the men in front took the full force of the blast, but we all went down like a pack of cards. I heard the noise of the explosion, and it hadn't damaged me, but we were terrified.[2]

When the officer commanding the SS troops saw that not all the men had been killed by the grenades, he ordered the survivors out in batches of five, where they were shot. Brian Fahey had only been wounded by the grenades and was part of the second batch of five:

> We went outside and took our positions. I was number five, and they turned us all around and I was shot in the back. It was like a punch, like a severe blow, and it knocked me over, and I suppose I passed out.

When I finally came to, it had all gone quiet in the barn, and I could feel this bubbling in my lung but I realised that I wasn't dead … I was about twenty yards from the barn and blood had pumped all over my jacket and my shirt was soaked, and I could only use my left elbow and right knee. I crawled back into the barn and there were men in there. Most were dead and some were dying.

Fahey and the handful that had survived the massacre lay wounded and abandoned without food or water throughout the 28th and for the next two days, and at least one of those badly wounded men died after regular German Army soldiers arrived at Wormhoudt and took the British soldiers into their care. It is a disgrace that, unlike the slaughter at Le Paradis, and despite a number of investigations, no one was ever held to account for the murder of the unarmed British prisoners.

The German breakthrough at Wormhoudt and Cassel meant that the troops defending the little village of Socx then came under heavy attack and were forced to withdraw to Bergues, held by the weakened 46th Division, under the command of Major General Curtis. Bergues was an old country town built on the side of a low hill at the junction of three canals. It was encompassed by its seventeenth century ramparts.[3] Occupying a pivotal point in the perimeter, it had to be held at all costs and would shortly come under intense attack.

THE NET TIGHTENS

By early morning of the 28th, the leading units of the 1st Panzer Division were only eight miles from Dunkirk and later in the morning Guderian toured round the western front of the perimeter to examine the strength of the Allied positions. He concluded that, 'Further tank attacks would involve useless sacrifice of our best troops.'

Though the troops holding this sector would not have to contend with the German tanks, later in the day to the east the Germans reached Nieuport on the coast just to the north of La Panne, and the German capture of Ostend was confirmed. The net was tightening around the BEF.

It was at Nieuport that on the morning of the 28th, Brigadier A.J. Clifton, in command of the 2nd Armoured Reconnaissance Brigade was told to take command of the troops in the vicinity of Nieuport to block the gap in the perimeter caused by the collapse of the Belgian army. He was told that, in addition to his own force, the only troops immediately available to him were odd parties that had either been collected in the Furnes/Nieuport area or were in the course of being assembled and sent there. His general instructions were: 'To organise a defensive line from the sea near Nieuport and along the line of the canal to Furnes, and to hold onto that line until relieved by other troops which might be expected in the course of the next day.'[4]

Shortly after digesting this information, he received a message from Brigadier Edward Lawson saying that he had taken charge of the defences in and around Furnes. The two brigadiers then agreed that Clifton should take responsibility for the canal line from Wulpen, through Nieuport to the sea.

Clifton's force included the 12th Lancers, which undertook a patrol around the Nieuport area, reporting back that the main road bridge over the canal at Nieuport was still intact and that enemy motorcyclists and motorised infantry, along with a few 'large' tanks, was immediately north of the canal and it was impossible either to cross the bridge or blow it up. In what was becoming a familiar story, the bridge had been prepared for demolition, but the electrical leads were on the wrong side of the water.

Lieutenant Colonel Edward Brazier of the 53rd Medium Regiment Royal Artillery who, having destroyed his guns as ordered, deployed his gunners into defensive positions but warned Clifton that he lacked the weapons to challenge the tanks and that so far they had only been prevented from advancing by the 12th Lancers 'making ugly faces at them'! Clifton was able to provide Brazier with four 18-pounders, which were sighted in gunpits commanding the exits from the bridge, and his brigade's light tank troop, which had been delayed on the road to Wulpen, arrived to help bolster the defenders.

At around 15.00 hours, Clifton was made aware that the Germans had engaged the troops holding Furnes and that the enemy was showing 'considerable interest' in the unblown Nieuport bridge. Clifton asked for help and French and British engineers with sappers and a truck–load of explosives duly arrived. But it was too late. Despite heroic efforts to mine the bridge, fire from the Germans was too intense and the engineers had to accept defeat. This meant that the Germans had a route across the canal and from there directly to the evacuation beaches. If Clifton's small force could not hold the bridge there would be slaughter on the beaches.

Clifton received reinforcements in the early evening from a Base Depot camp, but they were a mixture of men from various regiments placed under officers they had never seen before, and around a third of them had no rifles. Even with this augmentation to his force, Clifton accepted that he could not hold the entire length of the canal in anything like sufficient strength. So, he established a strongpoint at Wulpen, sending patrols along the canal to Nieuport.

From Wulpen to Furnes was the 8th Brigade of what was Montgomery's 3rd Division with the 9th Brigade holding the eastern end of the Furnes-Bergues Canal. In between these two, in Furnes itself, was the 7th Guards Brigade, of the 1st and 2nd Battalions Grenadier Guards and the 1st Battalion Coldstream Guards. The Guards settled in on the 28th, but the next day they would find themselves fighting for their lives and those of the troops on the beaches.

Within the wider Allied pocket, the troops were trying to make their way to Dunkirk as quickly as they could but the traffic on the roads had assumed 'formidable proportions'. Ever since the start of the German offensive on 10 May the French and Belgian civilians had taken to the roads. In the first few days of the fighting, the British troops had been moving in the opposite direction – towards the enemy. But when the BEF withdrew to the Dyle, the traffic problem became acute, as Gort explained in his dispatch of the 28th:

Refugees began to leave their homes in northern France before the French Government put into operation the plans they had made. The French organisations were not available and no British troops could be spared to control the traffic. The refugee problem had therefore become increasingly acute, and the tide which at first set westwards from Belgium had now met the enemy again in the Somme area and had begun to turn back on itself. Scenes of misery were everywhere, and the distress of women, children and aged people was pitiable. Fortunately, the fine weather and warm nights mitigated their plight to some degree and though the outbreak of famine was expected at any moment it did not actually occur in the area of the B.E.F. Little, unfortunately, could be done to help the refugees, since supplies for the troops were still seriously short. Moreover, their presence on the roads was often a grave menace to our movement. It had been necessary to give Corps a free hand in handling them: on occasions, it had been necessary to turn vehicles into the fields in order to keep the roads clear.

Amongst those that did manage to push his way through the fleeing crowds to reach Dunkirk was Lieutenant Anthony Rhodes of 253 Field Company, Royal Engineers:

> We arrived at Dunkirk on the night of the 27/28 May, and the first sign we had of the town was in the early hours, looking north-west, where we saw an enormous column of black smoke ... We picked our way through the centre of Dunkirk, which was under a pall of smoke, with the stink of burning buildings, and vehicles falling to pieces everywhere.[5]

Aubrey P. Lamplough-Lamplugh, a captain in the RASC in charge of a supplies convoy in Belgium, told the *North Devon Journal* of his experiences during the retreat to Dunkirk. When he was re-routed after the advance to the Dyle, 'we had no sort of idea why we were changing our course, and we really had little idea whether we were retreating or advancing in some new direction.' His new course passed through Lille, Popperinghe, and Menin, on the way to Ghent or Bruges, as directed. At one point on his route he passed through a burning town: 'Our course lay through this town, and since our cargo was petrol, ammunition and other supplies, we knew we would be running a great risk from the heat. However, our orders were to get through with all speed, and through we went. The driver of our final lorry told us later that his vehicle just missed the debris of two houses that collapsed across the street immediately behind him.'[6]

Lamplough-Lamplugh's convoy was twenty-five miles from Dunkirk when the men were ordered to disable all their vehicles and put them across the road to act as a barrier to block the advancing enemy:

> With 25 miles to walk to the coast we set off and did the journey in seven hours – about 110 of us. We did not pause until the coast was reached. Our orders were to get to a point N.E. of Dunkirk by the compass. We got to headquarters in a village [La Panne], where we

were told to commandeer any vehicles we could lay our hands on and get our men to Bray-Dunes. We were there in half an hour but we were followed by bombs all the way. We spent two nights at Bray. In view of the situation I gave the men liberty to make their own way to attach themselves to a larger body of men than our own.

The remarkable story of Lamplough-Lamplugh's eventual escape back to England will be told later in this narrative.

Already at Dunkirk was Anthony Rhodes, who had taken refuge in the cellar of one of the damaged buildings:

By midday the cellar was becoming rather smelly, it held sixty men only with difficulty. Many of them did not bother to come up for air during the intervals (between air raids), and it soon took on that musty, military smell, so much part of an army ... By four in the afternoon our nerves were becoming a little frayed. One of the NCOs (wearing last-war ribbons) was crying quietly in the corner and several men began to make queer little animal noises – rather like homesick dogs.[7]

THE CONTINUING EVACUATION

The evacuation was slowly speeding up as more vessels became available. But during the early hours of the 28th, disaster struck out at sea. *Queen of the Channel*, the first ship to have used the East Mole, had set off from Dunkirk at around 04.00 hours with approximately 900 troops on board. Shortly after leaving the French port, as dawn was breaking, she was attacked by dive bombers.

The bombs fell abaft of the main mast damaging the rudder, smashing the starboard propeller shaft and breaking the ship's back as it lifted out of the water. With the *Queen of the Channel* in serious distress the nearby coaster *Dorrien Rose* under Captain W. Thompson, and carrying military stores to the Dunkirk beaches, approached bow to bow and within thirty-five minutes had taken off the troops from the sinking ship. Also taken in tow were four of the *Queen of the Channel*'s lifeboats, though two would later come adrift. The *Dorrien Rose* reached Dover at around 14.00 hours.[8]

The damage sustained by *Queen of the Channel* proved fatal and the ship sank later that day. The loss of this ship saw daylight operations restricted after the 28th to naval vessels and small boats. The larger unarmed vessels were from that time onwards only permitted to operate at night. It was the naval vessels, and in particular the destroyers, that were from the 29th to play the lead role in the evacuation.

With his plan to use the East Mole, the destroyers *Mackay*, *Montrose*, *Verity*, *Sabre*, *Worcester* and *Anthony* berthed alongside, where Tennant had organised the rapid flow of men and arranged for berthing parties to help the ships tie up. Once loaded, the destroyers pulled out stern first and then turned for Dover.

HMS *Mackay* had reached Dunkirk at 09.55 hours from the Irish Sea and in the space of just an hour had picked up 600 men from the far end of the Mole. As *Mackay* backed away from the Mole, her berth was taken by *Montrose*.

The destroyer *Montrose* had travelled down from Milford Haven on 27 May at a comparatively leisurely twenty knots and when off Dover had been instructed to make its way to Dunkirk, and speed was increased to twenty-eight knots. 'The weather was fine and calm on the way across with fairly high clouds,' recalled her skipper. 'At one period a tremendous air battle was heard going on above the clouds but none of the actual fighting was seen.'[9] At 10.15 *Montrose* berthed alongside the seaward end of the East Mole. As well as taking on board the soldiers that shuffled along the Mole, *Montrose* took all the stretcher cases she could as she was the only ship berthed at that time with a doctor on board. An hour later *Worcester* and *Anthony* arrived and berthed ahead of *Montrose*.

The hospital carriers were also instructed to operate from the East Mole, where lifting the stretcher cases on board meant all hands were needed. 'We moored alongside the north-east side of the Breakwater mole,' recalled an anonymous nurse of the Queen Alexandra's Royal Naval Nursing Service:

The quay was broken and on fire in places; the patients were embarked with no gangway, just lifted over the ship's side. The ship's officers and crew, stewards and RAMC personnel all acted as stretcher bearers and carried the patients up the length of the quay under machine gun fire from the air. The Naval Officer in charge on shore was so calm that one literally did not realise the aerial battle that was going on all the time. The quiet, when the firing ceased, was more noticeable than the continuous noise had been.[10]

Isle of Thanet, formerly a cross-Channel ferry for Southern Railways serving the Folkestone to Boulogne route and then the Southampton–St Marlo service, was commissioned as Hospital Carrier No. 22 on 5 September – just two days after the declaration of war – and was based at Newhaven. One of her engineers was Brian Murray:

> I stood on the deck of our fast-moving ship wondering why we were heading east into the rising sun and not as usual south towards Dieppe. We arrived into Dunkirk about lunchtime. All was quiet, extremely quiet. The quayside was deserted, so unlike what we would expect to see. A British destroyer followed us in and moored up alongside. I remember the lettering on her bows. It was L.20.[11]
>
> Within half an hour the war really began – the banging and shooting war that was to go on for five long years. Several German planes arrived and as they proceeded to drop bombs, our friends in the destroyer opened up and engaged them with her 4in. guns to the detriment of the chief steward's crockery and my nerves. As you can imagine, that complacency of ours that had taken seven long months to develop was dispelled in almost one bang – I know that mine was.
>
> During that small battle between our navy and the *Luftwaffe* a hospital train ran on to the dockside and immediately the ship came to life. All the ship's company not on duty turned to and assisted the hospital staff, which consisted of some 40 men and officers with 6 Queen Alexandra's Army Nursing Service sisters, to load on the wounded. Later that evening, having experienced almost continuous hostile air attack during our stay, we got underway and steamed for Newhaven.

On its way to Newhaven, *Isle of Thanet* collided with the Examination Service Vessel *Ocean Reward*, which sank immediately. A search was made for survivors, but none was found. *Isle of Thanet* was too badly damaged to play any further part in *Dynamo*.

The flow of destroyers, the ships that would eventually become the unsung heroes of the Dunkirk operation, continued throughout the day and night. Of these HMS *Sabre*, was already on her second trip. She had set off from Dover at 23.00 hours on the 27th and, racing across the Channel at twenty-seven knots, had arrived off Marlo at 01.20 and taken on board six boat-loads (two trips for three boats), amounting to about 100 troops. While waiting, *Sabre* was machine-gunned by a lone aircraft but sustained only one slight casualty. Two drifters also went alongside *Sabre* and transferred their troops. *Sabre* returned to Dover in time to follow *Montrose* back over to Dunkirk.

Whilst waiting for *Montrose* to berth against the East Mole a Hurricane was seen making a forced landing on the beach west of Dunkirk. The destroyer's motor boat was sent in to rescue the pilot. In so doing she grounded on a falling tide and got sand in the engine. The boat had to be left behind, as at 11.00 hours, *Sabre* berthed alongside *Montrose* and began taking on troops from the Mole.

Everything was proceeding satisfactorily, until just after 11.30, *Montrose*'s captain related:

> Several enemy aircraft attempted to bomb and machine gun the pier and ships were driven by gun fire from *Montrose* and shore batteries. Vast columns of smoke were drifting westwards from the burning oil tanks ashore and houses on the sea front burst into flames from time to time. The crash of exploding bombs and the thudding noise of anti-aircraft weapons was continuous and frequent air combats were seen during the forenoon. The long pier jammed with troops made a particularly selectable target for enemy aircraft and it was very fortunate that they were prevented from machine gunning the soldiers as the latter awaited embarkation.[12]

By 12.40 there was no further accommodation left on board either *Montrose* or *Sabre* and the two destroyers set off for Dover together at twenty-six knots. At 14.30 these two warships, along with HMS *Anthony*, were spotted by what was estimated to be at least forty-five enemy aircraft. *Montrose*'s captain described the attack:

> Early in the battle one aircraft attacked *Montrose* from about five thousand feet and when his bombs were seen to be released, the wheel was put hard over and emergency full speed ordered. Five bombs

fell close together abreast X gun, the nearest being 20 feet away, avoiding action was rather cramped owing to proximity of sand banks to starboard and other Destroyers to port. Persistent machine-gun attacks were made on the ship but by frequent alteration of course no hits were obtained. Steady and constant fire from the ship's two pom-poms and 3-inch H.A. gun kept the attackers from coming low, the average height being about eight thousand feet. 250 rounds of pom-pom and 45 rounds of 3-inch H.A. ammunition were expended. All guns functioned perfectly and in the last attack one hit was scored on an enemy bomber which was subsequently seen to crash and burst into flames on the shore.

During the battle, the soldiers helped maintain a rapid rate of fire from *Montrose* by assisting with passing ammunition to the ship's guns.

The destroyer disembarked its human cargo – 1,200 soldiers and twenty-eight stretcher cases – on Dover's Admiralty Pier at 18.17 hours. Likewise, *Sabre* reached Dover unscathed from the attack, having avoided the German bombs by zig-zagging at high speed, though some of the bombs landed close enough to shake the ship and shower the deck with water.

The destroyers *Javelin* and *Jaguar* were ordered to embark troops from Bray Beach at 13.30 hours. *Javelin* had only her motor cutter and her whaler and when both boats went close inshore they were surrounded and swamped by the anxious soldiers. Sub Lieutenant J.I.A. Mitchell, in charge of the boats, managed to bail out both of them and restart the cutter's engine. Gradually, Mitchell began transferring the troops out to *Javelin* and, despite several bombing attacks had, by 18.30 hours, loaded 700 men onto the destroyer. *Javelin* reached Dover at 22.30 hours.[13]

Meanwhile to the west, the Eastern Mole was, by this time, crammed with troops, and several German aircraft attempted to bomb the narrow breakwater. But the ships berthed alongside the Mole were no ordinary transports, they were fighting ships, and the destroyers opened up with their light armament, and the enemy planes were driven off. The aim of the German aircrew was also hampered by the smoke from the burning oil tanks to the east of Dunkirk which drifted over the town and the harbour. To this was added the dazzling flames and air-borne debris from houses that had been bombed along the sea front.

The Anti-Aircraft cruiser HMS *Calcutta* was attacked on its way over to France by a German E-boat, a torpedo flashing just 100 yards past the ship's stern at 01.25 hours as the cruiser made its way to anchor off La Panne, at around 02.30 hours.

The first supplies of food, water and ammunition from England reached the beaches during the 28th, and were landed at La Panne. Already off the beaches were the paddle-minesweepers, *Sandown* and *Gracie Fields*, as well as the destroyers *Grafton*, *Greyhound* and *Impulsive*. The skoot, *Hebe II*, unable to find any troops to collect from the beaches, went back to Dunkirk and collected 150 men from the East Mole. Clearly there was still a considerable degree of confusion and lack of coordination between ship and shore. In all fairness, as the Admiralty accounts make clear, the flow of troops to any one point could not be known at this early stage in the operation with the various units arriving in piecemeal fashion. It was, therefore, impossible to regulate the movement of the ships to meet the fluctuating, and unpredictable demand.

At 03.20 hours, HMS *Vimy* arrived off the beach at Zuydcoote, some three miles east of Dunkirk and sent her boats to assist in filling up the minesweeper *Brighton Belle*, whilst the destroyer went to the East Mole and collected 613 soldiers.

Brighton Belle set off for Ramsgate with 350 troops (variously given as 800)[14] she had plucked off the beach at Zuydcoote, but she came under aerial attack and, in the confusion of trying to avoid the enemy aircraft, at 13.30 she struck a submerged wreck off the Gull Light buoy. Sapper Eric Reader had been rescued from the beach and was huddled in the ship's boiler room drying off when the ship rammed into the wreck with a fierce jolt: 'Never touched us,' an old cockney stoker called out cheerfully, Reader recalled. But soon the water started to gurgle into the boat and the *Brighton Belle* began to sink. The fearful troops began tumbling up onto the main deck as the boat's hooter blasted out the dots and dashes that signalled SOS. Luckily, *Sandown*, *Medway Queen* and the ex-Belgian canal boat *Yser*, were close by.

On 28 May, as part of the Dover Patrol, HMS *Medway Queen* was anchored off the south coast watching out for German aircraft laying mines when she was ordered to make for Dunkirk. *Medway Queen*'s cook was Thomas Russell: 'One afternoon in May 1940 the *Medway Queen* left Dover for the Continent where our forces were in trouble. A long time before we got there we saw the flames,

and soon we smelled the fuel oil. No person who was there will forget it ...
We had a motor boat which towed another one to and fro from the beach. The
army lined up on the shore – I did not see anyone panic or jump the queue ...
On one trip we came back in company with the *Brighton Belle*; she hit a wreck
... we went alongside and they all came aboard before she sank. Fortunately, it
was a calm day as we were very overloaded, but we got home okay.'[15] Everyone
on board was taken off – even the captain's dog.[16]

Thomas Russell also wrote of what happened when the paddle steamer
reached the UK: 'When the ship returned to Ramsgate, ladies were waiting
with tea and sandwiches and our passengers were whisked away. We refuelled,
stored, tided up and it was time to go again.'

There was, though, a growing number of men waiting to be evacuated,
and at 09.35 hours Tennant sent a signal to Dover: 'There are 2000 men on
Dunkirk beach and 7000 men in sand dunes for whom I have had no ships.
They are now in need of water and Army cannot supply. Unlimited numbers
are falling back on this area and situation will shortly be desperate.'[17] Luckily,
as Tennant repeatedly reported, intervention by the *Luftwaffe* was limited, the
only attacks that occurred, he wrote, 'were those when our aircraft were some
distance off at the further points of their patrol.' At the end of his report on
the 28th, he concluded with further praise for the RAF, 'Fighter protection has
been invaluable and bombing only sporadic.'[18]

Flight Lieutenant Tom Vigors of 222 Squadron was one of those RAF
pilots in action on the 28th. 'The sea below us,' he wrote in his memoirs, 'was
dotted with craft of every variety, from small motor boats to large steamers and
warships, all plying their way either to or from the Dunkirk beaches.' But, as he
studied this inspiring scene, the warning of, 'Bandits at six o'clock below us',
sounded in his headphones. Vigors dived with the rest of 'B' Flight, to engage
in his first ever combat:

The enemy were now diving and trying to turn to face us. With sticks
hard back we were trying to cut inside their turn. Suddenly I saw a
line of white tracers flying past my port wing tip and at the same time
heard a yell in my headphones, 'Look out! More bandits behind us!'[19]

Vigors looked over his shoulder to see a Bf 109 alarmingly close on his tail:

My first reaction was extreme fear which temporarily froze my ability to think. This was quickly replaced by my overwhelming desire for self-preservation ... I pushed violently forward and sideways on the stick, which flung my Spitfire into a sudden and violent dive. My whole weight came unpleasantly hard against my shoulder harness. But thankfully the tracer disappeared ... The enemy fighters had apparently passed clean over my head as I could see a wide circling mass of Spitfires and 109s interlaced with many white lines of tracer.

Tom Vigors lived through that first day to fight again. He shot down a BF 109 on 30 May and a Heinkel 111 two days later.

Driver Benjamin Nickholds of the Royal Army Service Corps reached the Dunkirk area on the 28th, where he was to spend two days and two nights:

I joined the queue which seemed to go on for ever. In it were servicemen from many different units. Most had abandoned almost their entire kit. I still had my rifle, ammo, a full water-bottle and some emergency rations. There was no water in town and very little on the beach. I had to survive with what I had.

It was an orderly queue of very tired men who waited patiently to be rescued. They hoped to get a ship from the dock to take them to England. Dunkirk was in flames and a cloud of smoke hung over the dock. Periodically, a Stuka dive bomber would appear from behind this cloud. It was a terrifying experience as we saw them dive with screaming engines straight for us. They released a bomb which also screamed louder and louder until impact. We scattered as soon as we saw the approach of a bomber but took the same places in the queue when the raid was over ...

The bombs tended to penetrate a little into the sand and some of the blast was deflected upward by the sand. Some shrapnel did take a little flesh from my hand and dent my helmet. I may owe my life to my helmet ... When the bombs landed on the beach or in the sea, the shockwave knocked the breath right out of us. Now and again one of the lads could stand it no more so he would dash into the town but it was no safer there. Some of them did not come back.[20]

The orderliness of the queues at this stage of the embarkation was also remarked upon by another of the soldiers, a Royal Artillery officer, Captain Richard Campion Austin:

> We tacked ourselves onto the rear of the smallest of the three queues, the head of it was already standing in water up to the waist. Half an hour passed. Suddenly a small rowing boat appeared. The head of the queue clambered in and were rowed away into the blackness. We moved forward, and the water rose to our waists.
>
> Our only thoughts now were to get to a boat. Along the entire queue not a word was spoken. The men just stood there silently staring into the darkness, praying that a boat would appear and fearing that it would not. Heads and shoulders only showing above the water.[21]

The Hunt-class minesweeper HMS *Pangbourne* made its first trip to Dunkirk on 28 May. The vessel's approach to Dunkirk was recorded by an unnamed sub lieutenant, who was *Pangbourne*'s Duty Officer:

> A peculiar smell is in the air. I know it from my days in the Merchant Service. It's burning oil fuel and there on the horizon ahead is a black cloud – smoke from the burning tanks of Dunkirk. It is flat calm now, and the wind has dropped, and as we draw nearer the eastern sky glows from a million fires.
>
> 'We round Nieuport buoy and turn to the southward; I turn my glasses on the beaches. The silver sands are stained with black. I look again. The stain is a packed mass of people. Thousands upon thousands of them, looking to seaward to watch the flotilla arrive. And now I can see something more – something which my bewildered mind is unwilling to believe. The people are soldiers in British khaki! Can things be going so badly for us that we are evacuating our army?

Indeed, the British were evacuating their army and this had to be explained to *Général* Blanchard when, at 11.00 hours, he went to Gort's headquarters at Houtkerque. There Gort read out his orders to evacuate the BEF. Like Fagalde and Abrial the day before, Blanchard had not been informed by his government of the British decision and he was mortified to hear that the British were abandoning him. He was even more upset to learn that Weygand had known of the British evacuation two days earlier and had not told Blanchard of this, or of the agreement with the French Government that French 1st Army would withdraw to Dunkirk to both help defend the perimeter and to evacuate as many French troops as possible.

Blanchard protested that his men were too worn out to withdraw any further and that, in any case, he would never abandon France. Gort wrote in his despatch to London, how he tried to persuade the French general:

> I then begged *Général* Blanchard, for the sake of France, the French
> Army and the Allied Cause to order *Général* Prioux [who commanded
> the French 1st Army's Cavalry Corps] back. Surely, I said, his troops
> were not so tired as to be incapable of moving. The French Government
> would be able to provide ships for at least some of his troops, and that
> the chance of saving part of his trained soldiers was preferable to the
> certainty of losing them all.

Blanchard would have none of it. Evacuation from open beaches was impossible and would only lead to an even greater disaster than trying to stand and fight the enemy. Gort concluded his despatch with the terse sentence' 'I could not move him.'

Be that as it may, some French troops were already trying to get away on British ships. This was experienced by Lieutenant Commander T.G.P. Crick who had sailed across to France to assist with the embarkation, but was wounded in the foot in an air attack and could not continue his duties. He was carried onto HMS *Calcutta* and taken back to England. However, during his short time on the beaches he was 'besieged' by French and Belgian officers begging to be taken to the UK or another part of France: 'These officers all stated that their desire was to reform and fight again,' Crick told Ramsay upon his return to Dover. 'I informed them all sympathetically that I could not give them a passage without approval of General Adam. As this was not forthcoming in the majority of cases, about twenty of them got a diesel engine boat from the beach and requested that they might come across to England in company with me.' This was something Crick felt he could agree to, allowing the French officers to be towed across the Channel.[22]

Gort shifted his headquarters to La Panne in the afternoon of the 28th, to be close to the evacuation beaches and where there was a direct telephone link with London. It was there where King Albert of Belgium had his headquarters during the First World War. Gort received a briefing on the current state of affairs from General Adam and the Quartermaster General, Lieutenant General W. G. Laidsell: 'No ships could be unloaded at the docks at Dunkirk, and few wounded could be evacuated. There was no water in Dunkirk and very little on the beaches, 10,000 [men] having been taken off in the last two days, chiefly from Dunkirk.' Adam, though, remained positive, saying that 'given a reasonable measure of immunity from air attack, troops could gradually be evacuated ... If, however, intensive air attacks continued the beaches might easily become a shambles within the next forty-eight hours.'[23]

Gort duly passed this information onto London, asking what course of action should he take if indeed the beaches became a killing ground. He received the following reply from the Chief of the Imperial General Staff, General Edmund Ironside:

> H. M. Govt. fully approve your withdrawal to extricate your force in order to embark maximum possible of B.E.F. If you are cut from all communication with us, and all evacuation from Dunkirk and beaches had, in your judgement, been finally prevented after every attempt to re-open it had failed you would become sole judge of when it was impossible to inflict further damage to the enemy.

The wording of this message could have only one meaning; that Gort had been given permission to surrender, but the decision if and when the BEF should put down its arms rested solely with him. Such is the burden of leadership.

It was on the afternoon of the 28th that Blanchard went to Gort's new headquarters. He had evidently spent the day pondering over Gort's appeal to him earlier in the day, and had seen the wisdom of the British commander's words. It was hard for him to accept not just that the French Army was collapsing but that its defeat was so complete that there was no alternative but to leave the country. Blanchard consented, agreeing that part of the French 1st Army would withdraw to within the Dunkirk perimeter on 30 May.

Those troops who had reached Dunkirk were, in many cases, in poor condition, as the young anonymous officer onboard HMS *Pangbourne* detailed in his graphic account:

> We tie up [alongside the Mole] and they swarm aboard us. Dirty, ragged, weary soldiers, with a forced smile on their white faces and a cheery word for the sailors although they are dead on their feet. They come without coats, some without shoes or socks – but few without some sign of an unbeatable spirit. We stow them wherever there is an inch of space, and they flop down as they are and relax. They seem to think because they are aboard a ship danger is past. And now we have received a message that we must shift berth into the inner harbour, where an ambulance convoy is waiting with stretcher cases.

Pangbourne found its way into Dunkirk's inner harbour with great difficulty, and was secured to the dock wall, at which point the stretcher cases were brought aboard, being deposited wherever space could be found. Fully loaded, the minesweeper headed back out to sea, bound for Ramsgate.

The destroyer HMS *Impulsive* had arrived off La Panne at 03.45 and anchored as close inshore as possible. Her two whalers were sent inshore to embark troops, ferrying men from the beach to large motor boats which were lying further off the shore. Progress was slow, and *Impulsive* was ordered to sail to the East Mole.

At 06.20 the destroyer secured alongside the outer end of the Mole and started embarking troops that were waiting there. She very quickly filled up with around 750 soldiers and sailed for Dover along Route Y.

After a quick turnaround, *Impulsive* headed back to Dunkirk at 12.35. It was during this passage that she was spotted by six Heinkels, that lined up to attack. Lieutenant Commander W.S. Thomas recorded the following:

> By proceeding at full speed and making frequent and violent alterations of course, the bombs, which could be seen falling, were successfully avoided and no hits were scored. Aircraft were bombing from approximately 1000 feet. On completion of the bombing three

aircraft remained behind and attacked with machine guns. A northerly course was steered during these attacks in order to avoid the narrow channels, and it was during these attacks that the ship was damaged and the casualties occurred. B gun was put out of action by an armour piercing bullet which penetrated the gun shield, wounded the trainer and lodged in the air pipe to the run out cylinder, causing the gun to remain in the recoil position … On the first attack developing I cleared the bridge of lookouts and signalmen remaining up there by myself. The last lookout to leave the bridge was seriously wounded in the chest.[24]

Six men were wounded, two seriously, all by machine-guns. The possible use of armour-piercing bullets would be mentioned again by other captains. After expending all their ammunition, the Heinkels disappeared and *Impulsive* continued to Dunkirk in the company of the other destroyers *Greyhound* and *Verity*, which had just arrived on the scene.

Luck, as in all aspects of life, played a part in the evacuation. Numerous ships were damaged by bombs that dropped not directly on a ship, but close by. HMS *Vimy*, though, came through all the aerial attacks unscathed:

At 14.15 about 20 Heinkel bombers attacked, in groups of two and three, *Vimy* and four other destroyers in the vicinity. Avoiding action as far as possible was taken and anti-aircraft fire opened. All attacks were high level with salvoes of five heavy bombs from each aircraft. Aircraft endeavoured to attack from astern. No hits were received but two salvoes burst within 20 yards of the ship one off the bow and one off the quarter, no damage resulted.[25]

The Halcyon-class minesweeper HMS *Gossamer* arrived at Dunkirk at 21.15 hours on the 28th, having sailed from Harwich shortly after midday. As the minesweeper moved in towards Bray beach, her skipper, Commander Richard Cyril Vesey Ross, saw what he thought was 'a large wood close to the shore', but as the ship got closer 'this was seen to be a mass of troops on the sand'. A young officer on *Gossamer*, Lieutenant Peter Hadley, also recorded his first sighting of the sands at Bray:

The beach was an extraordinary sight. As far as the eye could see it stretched away into the distance, the firm sand of the shore stretching farther back into dunes where the surface was no more than a thin yellow powder interspersed with parched tussocks of course grass. And covering this vast expanse, like some mighty antheap upturned by a giant's foot, were the remains of the British Expeditionary Force, some standing in black clusters at the water's edge, waiting for the boats that were to take them to the two or three ships lying off-shore, while others, whose turn had not yet come, or who were too tired to care whether it was their turn or not, lay huddled together in a disorderly and exhausted multitude.[26]

It was on the 28th, that the first of the 'Little Ships' reached Dunkirk. The various boatyards that had been searched by the men from the Admiralty had yielded upwards of forty serviceable motor-boats or launches, which were assembled at Sheerness. At the same time lifeboats from liners in the London docks, yachts, fishing-craft, lighters, barges and pleasure-boats, coasting vessels, skoots, motor boats and other small craft – including rowing boats for inshore work off the beaches – were called into service. The final total of these Little Ships amounted to some 700-850, though the exact number is not known.

Lieutenant Dann RN sailed with the first convoy of this motley collection of boats:

The first assembly was typical of the whole of this miniature armada. A dozen or so motor yachts from 20 to fifty feet in length, nicely equipped and smartly maintained by proud individual owners, a cluster of cheap 'conversion jobs', mainly the work of amateur craftsmen, who had set to work in their spare time to convert a ship's lifeboat or any old half discarded hull into a cabin cruiser of sorts ...[and] half a dozen Thames river launches resembling nothing so much as the upper decks of elongated motorbuses with their rows of slatted seats ... The very names of these latter craft are redolent of the quiet of Richmond, Teddington and Hampton Court: *Skylark*, *Elizabeth* and *Queen Boadicea*. A strange flotilla indeed to be taking an active part in what has been described as the greatest naval epic in history.[27]

In the very first flotilla was a black motor launch *Advance*, manned only by three bearded civilian yachtsmen. They made the crossing successfully and after the first machine-gun attack by the *Luftwaffe* 'three cheerful bearded faces appeared above the fore cabin roof and three pairs of hands were clasped and shaken overhead as a signal all was well.'

Once they arrived off the beaches many of the boats remained there to transport the troops from the shore to the waiting ships anchored in deeper water. Harry Brown and Fred Hook were the crew of one of those vessels, a small motor-boat from Deal called *Gypsy King*. Its skipper A. Betts, submitted the following report:

> We went to Dunkirk on May 28th. We stayed there about forty-eight hours. We were under shell-fire and machine-gun fire. We stayed there till every British soldier was off the beach. I would like to mention Harry Brown who did a brave action. We just loaded [the] boat with troops. We saw a pontoon with soldiers in, being swamped with waves. Brown, being the swimmer, decided to go over the side with a rope, he tied it to the pontoon and saved the soldiers from being drowned.

As the day progressed, the build-up off troops on the beaches exceeded the capacity of the ships, large and small, to recover them, and long lines of desperate, but patient soldiers, began to form:

> There they stood, lined up like a bus queue, right from the dunes, down the shore, to the water's edge, and sometimes up to their waists beyond. They were as patient and orderly, too, as people in an ordinary bus queue. There were bombers overhead and artillery fire all around them. They were hungry and thirsty and dead-beat; yet they kept in line, and no-one tried to steal a march on anyone else. Most of them even managed to summon up an occasional joke or wisecrack.

A somewhat different picture of the situation on the beaches was given by Reg Rymer, Private, 2nd Battalion, the Cheshire Regiment:

Obviously, the main job was to get out to the boats. Because when we finally decided to come down out of the ... sand dunes ... you've got to remember, we're running across the beach, and you're jumping over blokes, you know, that are no longer with us, sort of thing. And dodging and diving, because they're [the *Luftwaffe*] coming down, machine gunning you, and everything else. You're trying to keep an eye on there, and there's another one coming that way.[28]

All available destroyers were working off the La Panne to Malo beaches using their own boats as most of the Little Ships were still en route. A moderate surf on the beaches reduced the rate of embarkation and exhausted the boats' crews, the majority of whom were 'hostility only' ratings, rendering the whole operation slow and difficult.

The heavy surf caused problems even for the skoots, commanding three of which from the bridge of *Abel Tasman* was Lieutenant C.H. Beal. The Dutch coaster had arrived at 08.00 hours with a cargo of ammunition, and the skoot was beached broadside on, at low tide on the sand at La Panne. After unloading the ammunition, Beal waited for the tide to turn, but at 14.00 hours the three ships as well as the troops on the beach were attacked by twenty German bombers. Only one bomb, an incendiary, hit the skoots which fell into the, fortunately by then, empty hold of *Abel Tasman* without causing any damage. They were also machine-gunned, with one man being killed and another fatally wounded (this was the attack that also wounded Commander Crick). At 15.30 hours, Beal began to take troops on board on a rapidly rising tide. The two other skoots under Beal's command began to float, but *Abel Tasman* remained firmly grounded. A rope was passed to one of the other skoots, *Alice*, but this ship's engines failed. *Alice*'s crew took to its boat and rowed over to the other skoot, *Kaap-Falga* – which then sailed off leaving *Abel Tasman* still stranded! 'The ship was by now, 17.45 afloat,' wrote Beal, 'but bumping and being driven inshore by the offshore wind. I managed to get the stern clear by putting the troops forward and then the bows by moving them aft. We then went ahead and after grounding heavily twice, we got into deep water. As the German aircraft were still present, we took advantage of a rain squall and sailed immediately.' *Abel Tasman* reached Dover safely at 07.00 hours on the 29th, with 200 men of the RASC and about twenty French staff officers.[29] One can only wonder if these were the same French officers that had earlier approached Commander Crick?

MORE SHIPS REQUIRED

There could only be a matter of another day or so before the Germans broke through and the embarkation had to be speeded up if even the estimate of 45,000 men were to be saved. Ramsay approached the Admiralty to see what could be done, and, accordingly, the Commander-in-Chief, Western Approaches and Commander-in-Chief, Portsmouth, were instructed to sail every available destroyer to Dover. In addition, the 7th and 8th Minesweeper Flotillas were ordered to Harwich and placed under Ramsay's orders, though it would be another two days before these reached Dunkirk, and patrols of all available Motor Torpedo Boats and Anti-submarine trawlers were ordered to cover the north-east flank of the evacuation area against attack by enemy surface craft from the north. It seemed as if the Admiralty had suddenly woken to the plight Britain was in, with its only army stranded on the Continent, and at last every effort was being made to rescue the BEF.

With many more ships becoming available, Ramsay signaled his evacuation plan for the coming night to Tennant at 15.55 hours. As civilian ships were to be restricted to the hours of darkness, seven personnel vessels set off from England late afternoon/early evening, aiming to arrive at Dunkirk at or around 22.00 hours. With them were three hospital ships and two destroyers, all twelve craft being instructed to embark troops from the East Mole. In addition, there were no less than twenty other destroyers, nineteen minesweepers (both paddle and fleet minesweepers), seventeen drifters, upwards of forty skoots, five coasters, twelve motor boats, two tugs, twenty-eight cutters and lifeboats, which were to operate the full length of the beaches from Dunkirk to La Panne.

By 21.30 five of the minesweepers had arrived off the beaches, and later four more, including HMS *Sharpshooter*, on board which was Seaman Thomas King:

> On our first crossing the weather wasn't very pleasant, it was what we call 'crinkly' in the Navy. We could do fifteen knots, so it took us two

and a half hours to get from Dover to La Panne. We went as a fighting ship, which we always were, and we just didn't know what to expect. We didn't know if we were going to anchor off or just steam around. Eventually we did anchor ... There was no order on the first occasion; it was a free-for-all. Soldiers didn't know the life-saving capacity of boats and we could only take ten to twelve in a twenty-two-foot whaler. We kept our distance from the water's edge [as] we needed to get seaborne again.[30]

It was also on the evening of the 28th that George Hogg, a member of a thirty-man Field Hygiene Section RAMC, was ordered to make his way to Dunkirk, being told to head for the beach and to try and keep to the firm sand and not go into the sand dunes:

We started off after taking the plugs out of the lorry oil sumps and left the engines running until they seized up. We passed through the village and empty trucks till we came on to the road which was elevated like a railway embankment ... We cut across fields being flooded and onto roads before reaching the beach. The sky was covered with smoke from oil tanks burning at Dunkirk and everything was very dismal ... A very welcome sight was a flight of Spits or Harriers patrolling the beach. These were the first British planes we had seen since the fun started. We had seen French planes at an airfield all mangled on the ground before taking off. There was, at this time, no German planes to be seen. We had thought it was the thunderstorms which had kept them off. As we neared Dunkirk it was dark. All the large buildings on the left of us on what must have been a promenade were burning, lighting up the sands.

The Mole was of stone and rounded on the sands side. A commanding voice shouted (quietly) another ten quickly. We scrambled up and no one told us in the dark that there was an eight to ten foot drop on the other side. We were cleared away quickly for the next "drop". We lay on the concrete pier. Smoking and lighting up was forbidden. Occasional shells came over but did not land near us. We had to keep quiet. Every now and then the oil tanks erupted in flames on the other side of the harbour, lighting everything like daylight.

It was beginning to get light and we were told to hurry to the end of the Mole. All the troops we thought were lying there were gone! The mole turned from stone to wood and planks were laid over holes with the water swirling below. At the end of the pier was the *Scotia* an LMS ferry … On the deck of the *Scotia* we were standing packed tight. We were the last on. On her next trip she was sunk.[31]

This day saw the loss of seven ships. As well as *Isle of Thanet* being put out of service, *Queen of the Channel*, *Brighton Belle*, the skoot *Alice*, the drifter *Ocean Reward*, the anti-submarine trawler *Thuringia* and the mine-sweeping trawler *Thomas Bartlett* were all sunk. HMS *Windsor* had also been damaged, having been attacked by fifteen Stukas supported by ten fighters when close to No.1. Buoy near the South Goodwin Lightship. The German bombers failed to hit the destroyer, but near misses and machine-gun fire caused extensive damage, with the radio, the degaussing gear and the ship's ASIC being put out of action. The starboard side of the boat was 'riddled like a pepper pot', according to Commander Peter Pelly, and thirty men were wounded.

These seemed like heavy losses for the comparatively few soldiers that had been rescued. With time running out, it seemed that the evacuation of the BEF was going as badly as feared.

Chapter 6

Operation *Dynamo*: Day 4, Wednesday 29 May

Throughout the course of the 28th, 5,390 men were landed in the UK from the beaches to the east of Dunkirk and 11,874 from the harbour (stretcher cases) and the East Mole. With the 7,669 landed on the 27th, it meant that just 24,933 men had been rescued so far, little more than half of the total the Admiralty had estimated the Royal Navy could save. But the perimeter was holding, offering the prospect of extending the operation and, at last, the Admiralty was committing every available resource to *Dynamo*.

With agreement having been reached with *Général* Blanchard, the French 1st Army was also withdrawing towards Dunkirk and participating in holding back the Germans. This enabled the BEF's I and II Corps to disengage from the enemy and withdraw into the Dunkirk perimeter, III Corps, being the least advanced, having already reached La Panne.

Large numbers of Blanchard's troops were also entering the perimeter, bringing with them a great deal of their transport. 'The congestion created within the perimeter was well-nigh unbearable,' complained Gort, 'and for two days the main road between La Panne and Dunkirk became totally blocked with vehicles three deep.'

The arrival of the French troops presented a real problem for Admiral Abrial who had only learnt of the decision to evacuate at the meeting with Gort at Cassel on the 27th, which meant that no evacuation plan had been drawn up for the French and there were no French ships waiting to receive the troops. Naturally, the French that were now piling into the already crowded beaches expected to be taken off in the same proportion as their British allies. The potential for trouble was obvious, and so until Abrial could arrange for transport, Gort allocated two ships to the French troops, so that they could see they were not being willfully left behind.

Amongst those French troops was Marceau Lantenois of the 2nd Company, 43rd Battalion, First Regiment of Engineers:

We left for Dunkirk and Malot. We rode either by car or on foot. There were scores of bombing raids there as well, all along the road. It was terrible. We were shelled heavily. I lost some comrades and even cried there. Good comrades who were left by the road.

Well, after that, I think I arrived in Dunkirk. No, it was not Dunkirk, it was Malot, Malot-les-Bains. I remember it was Malot because we hid ourselves in a casino when the bombs were falling. It was a sad place, Dunkirk. Everything had been devastated; there was smoke and all that. There was even a woman crying – she had lost her mind because of the bombing.

We got into the Casino, to protect ourselves from the bombs as well, but we didn't know where to go. And, on the beach, there were the dead. Some of them had holes in their heads. And on the sea, it was horrible. Boats were sinking all around. There were some of which we could see only the mast. And planes were falling into the water.[1]

As the British withdrew to Dunkirk, they were ordered not to allow equipment to fall into enemy hands, which astonished Corporal George Ledger of the 8th Battalion, Durham Light Infantry:

When we got to the outskirts of Dunkirk, we came upon a whole consignment of dumped arms, lorries and equipment; miles and miles of it. Wherever you looked, the whole place was engulfed with abandoned weapons and machines. A lot of us were sent out to immobilize some of the vehicles. We'd put things into the radiators, or drop a grenade in and smash it.[2]

Troop Sergeant Bernard Kaye, of the Royal Engineers 16th Assault Squadron, also remarked on the mass of abandoned and destroyed equipment:

The road to Dunkirk was littered with the cast-off equipment of a modern army. Nothing too big, nothing too small, it was all there. The army vehicles, which we had left behind, were to be burned to deny their use to the enemy. There was sufficient equipment to keep an army and navy store supplied for hundred years or more! There were vehicles of all kinds, large artillery pieces, with their barrels spiked, to lightweight tanks sticking up out of the waterways. The sight of all these valuable military pieces was depressing to us, and told the story of an army routed and defeated.

Soon we were entering the main port of Dunkirk, which appeared to be largely in flames and the dismal sound of collapsing buildings reverberated through the empty streets. It appeared there had just been an air raid. Dunkirk was in ruins. The roads were cratered everywhere and tram lines stood on end where the many bombs had landed. The corpses of mutilated soldiers lay everywhere and the smell of burning flesh was nauseating.[3]

It was evident that the British were abandoning France, but the German Army was not prepared to just sit and let the *Luftwaffe* finish off the BEF, and throughout the 29th German troops attempted to cross the canal between the French-Belgian frontier and Nieuport. At the latter place, where, it may be recalled, the bridge had not been blown, the Germans attempted to cross over the bridge by means of subterfuge: 'machine gunners advanced between horses and cattle, and adopted various disguises, even dressing as nuns,' Brigadier Clifton reported.[4] These, though, were all detected and driven back with loss, as were parties that attempted to cross the canal in rubber boats.

With the Germans being held at the perimeter, the evacuation was progressing much faster than at any previous time. At 10.01 hours, Tennant sent one of his frequent situation reports to Ramsay:

> Embarkation proceeded at rate of 3 to 4,000 an hour. Troops were now consisting mainly of the Fighting Corps, all the non-combatant troops in the area having been evacuated. The display of this Corps Troops was noticeably superior – previous detachments had reached the embarkation point in a straggling manner with scarcely any semblance of order. The Corps Troops marched in formation along the beaches, quickly scattering during an air raid, and reforming and continuing afterwards. It was this order which enabled such a high rate of embarkation to be maintained.[5]

Disaster, though, had earlier befallen HMS *Grafton*. The destroyer had left Dunkirk fully loaded with approximately 800 troops at 00.15 hours with all its lights on. This attracted the attention of German aircraft, which were heard to pass overhead and several bombs were dropped close by the ship, one of which struck a small vessel about 1,200 feet astern.

Grafton continued on her voyage until, at around 02.30 hours, Commander C.E.C. Robinson, who was sleeping in his cabin, was woken with the news that a nearby ship had been torpedoed. The captain quickly reached the bridge and ordered the ship to be stopped and both whalers lowered. Also on the bridge was a young Lieutenant, who would be the most senior officer to survive the following few minutes: 'I then saw close on the starboard bow, the bows of a ship standing out of the water. There appeared to be a number of men clinging to the bows and also judging by the shouts for help, men in the water as well. While I was superintending the lowering of the whalers a signal was made to a darkened ship, which I afterwards learned was HMS *Lydd*, asking for information. She replied that she thought HMS *Wakeful* had been torpedoed by a submarine.'

The information from *Lydd* was accurate, and *Wakefield* had indeed been struck by a torpedo, though fired not from a submarine but the *Schnellboot S-30*. She was returning to Dover with approximately 650 troops when a torpedo hit her forward of the boiler room. She broke in half and went down in fifteen seconds. All the troops were asleep below and went down with the ship except one, and all of those in the engine room department except one or two also went to the bottom with her.

A few others had also survived, but their ordeal was far from over. Being on deck, most of the guncrew had floated clear of the sinking destroyer and an additional thirty men and an officer remained on the stern portion of the warship. After about thirty minutes, the Admiralty motor drifters HMT *Nautilus* and HMT *Comfort* came on the scene and started to pick up those still swimming in the sea. *Nautilus* picked up six and *Comfort* sixteen, including *Wakeful*'s skipper, Commander R.L. Fisher. HMS *Gossamer* was the next to arrive, lowering its boats which picked up a further fifteen men. Those still in the water and the boats that were trying to rescue them had drifted some distance apart with the tide. Though *Comfort* cruised round the area for a further thirty minutes, with those on board shouting as loud as they could, no more men were found in the sea, so Fisher directed the drifter to return to the wreck of *Wakeful* to rescue the survivors still clinging onto the stern of the destroyer:

When we got there the stern had fallen over and many men were shouting in the water. HM Ships *Grafton* and *Lydd* were close to the wreck and I went alongside the former's starboard quarter to warn her that she was in danger of being torpedoed. At that moment (02.50) a torpedo hit her in the wardroom and the *Comfort* was lifted in the air, then momentarily swamped and as she bobbed to the surface again I was washed overboard. I was able to grab a rope's end, but as the *Comfort* was going full speed ahead with no-one on deck I soon had to let go.

The *Comfort* then came round in a wide circle and suddenly both HMS *Lydd* and HMS *Grafton* opened a heavy fire on her with Lewis guns and, I think, four inch. I realised that they very naturally thought she was enemy and kept under water as much as possible when the bullets were coming near me.

This unfortunate incident saw all the *Comfort*'s crew except one and all *Wakeful*'s survivors onboard her, except four, which included Fisher, being killed. When the firing had stopped, Fisher began to swim towards *Comfort*, which was still afloat but drifting:

As I reached her bow and was feeling for a rope's end, HMS *Lydd* bore down on her at full speed and rammed her amidships on the opposite side, cutting her in half. I was submerged but came to the surface after an interval and swam about till about 05.15 when I was picked up by a boat from the Norwegian ship *Hird* carrying 3,000 troops from Dunkirk.

Fisher's ordeal was finally over, only for him to later be told that of almost 700 crew and soldiers on *Wakeful*, he was the sole survivor. As it happened there was at least one other survivor. Of those 700 men, approximately 640 were soldiers, one of whom was Private Stanley Mewis of the 658th General Construction Company, Royal Engineers. His initial effort at getting off the beaches saw him join around 150 others in climbing on a large boat that had moved inshore – but as it transpired, too far inshore, as it grounded with the added weight of the soldiers. The skipper ordered the men to run from one side to the other to rock the boat whilst he reversed engines but it was to no avail. When the tide came in the boat was swamped and abandoned. 'That was my first attempt,' recounted Mewis:

> At the second attempt, we got on an old British destroyer it was HMS *Wakeful*, luckily I was one of the last on board and we hadn't got hit up to that time. We were just pulling up anchor, I remember the sun was going down and there was a great cheer went up from the troops on board. We went out about three miles and when we were hit by a torpedo in the middle of the ship. The ship didn't sink immediately it just folded up ... I was thrown into the sea and was picked up by a small powerboat and put back on the beach. It was the lowest day of my life I was so depressed to be back where I started on the beach.[6]

Grafton's surviving senior lieutenant continued with his report:

> After *Grafton*'s boats had been in the water about ten minutes, the Captain observed a small darkened vessel on the port quarter at about three cables. Believing this to be a drifter he signaled it to close and pick up survivors. I did not observe this ship closing, as my attention was concentrated on the whalers in the water. Within a few seconds, one of the lookouts on the port side of the bridge reported 'Torpedo port side'. This was followed almost immediately by a violent explosion. A second explosion which seemed of the same intensity followed a few seconds later. I rushed to the after end of the bridge to try and find out what damage had been done. I sent a messenger down to the Engineer Officer to make a report to the bridge as to the extent of the damage, and tried to get as many seamen as possible to keep the soldiers quiet and stationary.[7]
>
> After about five minutes I went back to the compass platform to report to the Captain. I found that the compass platform had been wrecked. The whole of the fore screen had been blown in, and the Asdic Control and both binnacles smashed. The sides of the bridge were left standing. The bodies of Commander C.E.C. Robinson and Lieutenant H.C.C. Tanner (2nd Lieutenant) and a signalman, were buried under the wreckage and a leading signalman had been blown onto B gun deck. All four must have been killed instantaneously.

Captain Sir Basil Bartlet was one of the soldiers who had been taken on board *Grafton*:

> There was a terrific explosion as the torpedo hit the destroyer. I suppose the force of it must have knocked me unconscious. First thing I knew I was stumbling around in the dark trying to find the door of the cabin. The whole ship was trembling violently, the furniture appeared to be dancing about. There was a strong smell of petrol. I heard someone scuffling in a corner and just had the good sense to shout: 'For God's sake don't light a match.' With the greatest of difficulty, I found the door and managed to get it open it ...
>
> The deck was a mass of twisted steel and mangled bodies. The Captain had been machine-gunned and killed on the bridge. The destroyer had stopped two torpedoes. She'd been hit while hanging about to pick up survivors from another ship, which had been sunk a few minutes before. She was a very gruesome sight.[8]

Another of the soldiers on *Grafton* was Tom Perrin, who was with the 9th Army Field Workshop, Royal Army Ordnance Corps:

> I was standing by a fan inlet which had a high-pitched whine, and in the silence after the noise of the explosions I remember the fan running down and the pitch of the sound getting lower. We lay, wallowing in the Channel swell praying that the bulkheads would hold. If they had gone there would have been few survivors for there were no life jackets and most of the lifeboats and rafts had been damaged in the explosions. Everyone was ordered to keep still and to keep silent. I still remember the eerie silence, 1400 men [*sic*] making no sound, only the slap, slap as small waves lapped against the ship. There seemed to be two options now, either the E boats came back and finished us off, or rescue. Which would be first?[9]

Grafton had been attacked by the German submarine *U-62*. HMS *Lydd* tried to go alongside *Grafton* but in the confusion caused by the attack, *Lydd* hit *Grafton*'s starboard side. *Lydd* then saw a vessel in the darkness, which her skipper took to be a German E-boat, that, it was thought erroneously, was the vessel that had just torpedoed *Grafton*. In fact, it was *Comfort* that *Lydd* rammed and which sank immediately.

The crew on both *Grafton* and *Lydd* believed that there were E-boats in the area and when another vessel was seen in the distance, Lieutenant Blackmore and Chief Petty Officer Chappell, who manned one of *Lydd*'s Lewis guns, opened fire and later reported that this vessel had 'blown up, with a bright flash'.

Realising that he was now in command, Robinson set about determining the extent of the damage to *Grafton*:

> Finding it impossible to get hold of the Engineer Officer, due to the crush of soldiers and realising the ship was not sinking rapidly, I went down to inspect the damage. It was impossible to get clear of the bridge until the soldiers had been quietened down. With the assistance of Lieutenant Blackmore, I was able to do this and pass the word for the Engineer Officer. He reported that the stern of the ship from the after magazine bulkhead, aft, had been blown off, and that the upper deck abaft the after tubes had been buckled across its entire width as though the ship's back had been broken there. The ship was still on an even keel though down by the stern.

By this time there were no other ships in sight and no immediate hope of rescue. Robinson sought to lighten the ship and was able to discharge the forward torpedoes, but the rear tubes had been buckled in the explosion. Everything that could float, the ship's life rafts, Carley floats and even wooden fittings that could be removed, were made ready in case the destroyer had to be abandoned before help arrived. Both *Grafton*'s whalers were manned and waited off the ship. All compartments below decks were evacuated, and auxiliary steam was being maintained. But wind and sea started to freshen from the north-west, and the ship started to roll rather slowly and unsteadily.

Help, however, was at hand. At around 03.35 hours two merchant ships were spotted approaching from the direction of Dunkirk. A signal was made asking them to take off the soldiers. They stopped about a mile off *Grafton*'s port beam and lowered boats. But *Grafton*'s adventures were not over, for at that moment an E-boat was seen approaching at high speed on the starboard bow at about 4,000 yards. The destroyer opened fire with its upper pair of 4.7-inch guns and, as the range closed to 1,500 yards the starboard machine-guns joined in. The E-boat veered away and was not seen again. It is not known if the E-boat fired a torpedo, but none was spotted.

Shortly after this help arrived, as Tom Perrin remembered:

> Out of the morning mist appeared a destroyer escorting a cross channel steamer the S.S. *Malines* which tied up alongside the *Grafton* and in single file we crossed from the bridge of the helpless Royal Navy ship to the deck of the steamer. It took quite some time before everyone was off the *Grafton* as there was a considerable number of wounded, some of them stretcher cases, but eventually the last person left the *Grafton* and we pulled away on what we sincerely hoped was the last part of our channel crossing. When we were well clear HMS *Ivanhoe* torpedoed the hulk of the *Grafton*, which disappeared quickly below the waves.

THE BEACHES

Operating early off the beaches on the 29th, was the paddle steamer *Medway Queen*. As might be gathered from her name, *Medway Queen* had been employed on the River Medway and the Thames Estuary before being requisitioned by the Admiralty and fitted out as a minesweeper. She was ordered to take station off La Panne, having towed some small motor boats over from England, to collect men from the beach. As dawn broke on the 29th, the crew sent in the boats, time and time again to load up as many men as they could carry. By 07.00 hours, the *Medway Queen* had taken on board around 1,000 men and she set off back across the Channel.

On being informed by Lord Gort that III Corps had reached La Panne, Ramsay ordered all destroyers and light craft to that end of the beach to make a concerted effort to lift off these troops. The cruiser *Calcutta* was off La Panne and she used her boats to lift 1,200 troops off the beach before, at close to 14.00 hours, she set off for Sheerness. The captain of *Calcutta* had sent a boat to pick up Lord Gort, but the general 'courteously refused' to leave his men.

As well as the destroyers, also operating off La Panne were five drifters, three motor launches, the minesweepers *Sutton* and *Salamanca* and the tug *Java*. Together these vessels saved 6,652 men, thanks to a large degree, to the paddle steamer *Oriole* that beached herself at La Panne to act as a form of pier to which the other vessels could go alongside. The soldiers were able to climb onto *Oriole*, and move across its decks to the waiting ships, though it seems that the paddle steamer went just a bit too close inshore, as Lieutenant I.G.N. Lindsay explained:

Ships boats were lowered since the heavy swell prevented the larger ships getting close enough to the shore to pick up the soldiers. This was becoming a very slow job as the same swell was turning the ships' boats over so Lieut. Davies, C.O. of HMS *Oriole* decided that, since we were shallow draughted and flat bottomed, he would take her in until she just touched the bottom and use her as floating jetty, gradually creeping out so that soldiers could climb over the bow and pass aft to join ships with deeper drafts. This plan lasted for some time but eventually the edging astern was just a little too late and we found ourselves stuck. Before long the tide had left us high and dry and we were at least half a mile inland with a Dutch coaster, *Oranje*, between us and the sea.[10]

On board *Oriole* was a Pathé News cameraman, Charles Martin:

All round us were craft of every size and shape and as we were a paddle steamer we could run aground, which we did and immediately the fellows began to swim out towards us. Suddenly, we heard the noise of aircraft and within a few seconds out of the sky came droves of German machines, power-diving.

I was on the bridge when they came straight for our ship and sprayed it with tracer bullets. A few seconds previously I had seen tens of thousands of men on the shore. When I looked again, the beach was like a place of dead men, for the troops had thrown themselves flat on the sand. I waited and they all stood up again, unharmed and still in line.

The destroyer *Harvester* had anchored off the beach at Braye in the early hours of the 29th, and had sent her motor-boat to collect soldiers but not with much success, as Leading Seaman Ernest Eldred observed:

> I saw several small boats capsize, but I don't think it was due to indiscipline, I just think there weren't enough naval or seafaring personnel to supervise the operation. Troops were getting into boats probably meant to carry ten and there'd be fifteen trying to get in. They would only have two or three inches' freeboard between the top of the boat and the water. As soon as they started moving the slightest swell would swamp them … Quite a few men were carrying rifles and some had their packs, tin helmets and such. Equipment shouldn't have been carried. It should have been personnel or equipment, but not both.[11]

Loading was therefore very slow and even when *Harvester* started to use her Carley floats, it was taking hours to load just small numbers of men. But after *Oriole* had been beached the rate of embarkation increased considerably. It had taken almost twelve hours for Lieutenant Commander Mark Thornton to embark 600 men and when the tide fell, leaving *Oriole* high and dry, he decided there was no point in trying to take on any more soldiers. *Harvester*, which had begun its operations off Braye at 00.50 hours, departed at 12.35 hours.

Commander Thornton also tried to get the troops on the shore to build a pier and he sent Sub Lieutenant E.C. Crosswell to arrange this. As will be seen later, this proved to be a brilliant idea.

The destroyer HMS *Icarus* anchored off Zuydcoote at 15.15 hours. On her first round trip she had embarked men from the East Mole with little difficulty, but found lifting men from the beaches a quite different and frustrating operation, as can be gleaned from Lieutenant Commander C.D. Maud's report:

> I anchored as close as possible inshore to cut down the length of the boats trip but later grounded with the turn of the tide: no damage occurred and later on the Schoot *Doggers Bank* towed my stern clear without difficulty.
>
> On anchoring, I had lowered all boats, motor boat and both whalers and also four Carley floats, two large and two small. It had been my

intention to try to get close enough to the shore to be able to float the Carley floats ashore on the end of a line and then haul them back to the ship, leaving the motor boat to do the towing of the whalers. It was unfortunate that the shelving beach did not allow me to get close enough to carry out this in practice. I found that actually the Carley floats were little used by the troops who were unhandy in the floats.[12]

The soldiers' inexperience with small boats was a problem many other sailors would encounter over the following days.

Attacks by the *Luftwaffe*, which began at 16.00 hours, forced *Icarus* to weigh anchor and move away from the shore. At around 17.30, the schoot *Doggers Bank* went alongside *Icarus* and transferred her full load of 470 troops. This was a smart move made by the respective skippers, as the schoot had a shallower draft than the destroyer and so could get closer into shore, whilst the destroyer could travel back to England with the soldiers much quicker than the Dutch coaster. The transfer of the troops was interrupted by German air attacks, but was completed by 18.30, and *Icarus* set off back to Dover by Route X which had finally been swept of mines and was now available.

As she pulled *Icarus* was targeted by the enemy bombers:

Shortly after getting under way ... a cloud of enemy machines was sighted above us. A.A. fire was once opened as soon as suitable targets came in line. It is difficult to estimate the number of planes that were in this raid but I would say that there were at least forty. In an incredibly short time dive bombing attacks developed on all ships in sight. A paddle minesweeper just ahead of *Icarus* and approaching on opposite courses was attacked and sunk: the harbour looked as if it was being attacked by many planes at once and then the dive bombing attack developed on *Icarus*. The channel restricted my movements considerably and it was not possible to make any alteration of course and so I did the best I could by making violent alterations of speed from 'Pull Ahead Both' to 'Stop Both' as the attacks developed. The engine room department, realising what was required, worked the throttle valves as fast as humanly possible, and it is no doubt that largely due to their efforts the ship was not hit.

I think that at least ten planes attacked us, some together, and some shortly after one another: there were close misses ahead which had we not stopped engines a few seconds before must have hit us, and there were close misses astern shortly after we had increased to full speed again ... There was one salvo of three bombs which I was certain was going to hit at 'B' Gun and which actually landed in the water abreast 'B' Gun three feet from the ships side and which miraculously did not explode.

The ship was also machine-gunned during these attacks and it was this which caused the casualties which amounted to one killed, five seriously injured and about twenty slightly injured, all with the exception of two being soldiers.[13]

The Germans appeared to be using a semi-armour piercing bullet inside the ordinary machine gun bullet. It was one of the small calibre bullets that penetrated the forecastle deck and killed a soldier even though he was wearing his tin helmet at the time.

The shock from the two near misses damaged *Icarus*' steering mechanism but the destroyer suffered no other harm and was able to continue towards Dover, but the danger was not past:

We sighted another German bomber and opened fire. This machine circled round and then lined up astern on the port quarter to make a low-level bombing attack at about 1500 to 2000 feet. I made both funnel and C.S. smoke at once and as soon as the bomber was lined up to start his attack I increased to full speed. There were not so many navigational hazards and I therefore kept my alteration until the end of his attack.

The attack developed slowly, both our guns firing but apparently not deterring him much. At the moment, I judged that he was about to drop his bombs I made a very large alteration of course to port and this salvo missed. The enemy plane then circled ahead and round again to the port quarter for his second attack. This time I reduced speed slightly and waited until he was about to drop his salvo. In this attack, I am certain that my smoke screen caused the pilot to make a bad estimation of my course because as he was nearly in the bomb release position I saw him give quite a considerable alteration of course to port and I therefore increased to full speed again and put the rudder hard a' starboard and the second salvo fell clear to port.

The German bomber then circled round again for another attack. As the aircraft raced in from ahead and slightly to port, *Icarus'* guns hammered at the rapidly-closing target, and the bomber veered away. For a third time, the bomber attacked the destroyer, releasing a salvo of bombs, all of which landed in the sea to port of *Icarus*. On each pass, the aircraft had machine-gunned the warship, but failed to hit any of the crew or passengers. Having expended all its bombs, the aircraft flew off. There were no further incidents and *Icarus* reached Dover at 20.50 hours and disembarked its troops.

The attacks by the *Luftwaffe* had changed the situation drastically, as a clearly anxious Tennant reported:

> Bombing of beaches and Dunkirk pier has now commenced without opposition from fighters. If they hit Dunkirk pier embarkation will become very jammed. Beach at La Panne covered with troops congregating in large numbers. Very slow embarkation taking place from Eastern Beach. The French Staff at Dunkirk feel strongly that they are defending Dunkirk for us to evacuate, which is largely true. To continue evacuation my appreciation is as follows: The perimeter must be strongly held, food and stores immediately provided, and bombing of Dunkirk pier must be prevented. There is no other alternative evacuation to take off more than a tithe of men now on each beach before they are bombed continuously.[14]

THE DAY OF THE DEFIANTS

It was towards the end of the aerial bombardment that the destroyer *Greyhound*, which was also anchored off La Panne, was severely damaged by two near-misses. Her captain, W.R. Marshall A'Deane, takes up the story:

> Embarkation by whaler and motor boat was carried out steadily until 1600 when an attack was. made by bombers the fourth salvo of which

scored two near misses, the splinters killing 20 men and wounding 70 and causing the following damage. In the engine room one air ejector and one forced lubrication pump were put out of action. In No.3 boiler room main feed pipe was pierced resulting in complete loss of feed water, and an exhaust pipe from a feed heater punctured which caused the boiler room to fill with steam.[15]

Greyhound weighed anchor but because of the number of wounded on deck, she could not haul her boats in and these were ordered to go to one of the two minesweepers *Sutton* and *Salamander,* which were still at anchor. *Greyhound* was able to return to Dover under her own steam and discharged 432 fit soldiers as well as its casualties but was too badly damaged to play any further part in *Dynamo.*

HMS *Saladin* also survived a bombing attack. The destroyer approached Dunkirk at around 18.45 hours as the *Luftwaffe* was raiding the port. As *Saladin* entered the channel towards the harbour she also came under attack, the first of ten she was about to endure. The destroyer took avoiding action by 'swinging' the ship and increasing speed as the bombers dived to attack, and all bombs missed, though the nearest fell only about five feet away from the warship. *Saladin* carried only one 2lb Pom Pom and two Lewis guns for anti-aircraft defence and so felt particularly vulnerable. Lieutenant Commander L. J. Dover decided to continue along the coast where other destroyers could be seen, hoping to benefit from their greater anti-aircraft armament. 'In one of the early attacks,' reported Lieutenant Commander Dover, 'splinters which penetrated the Engine Room fractured the Starboard dynamo exhaust pipe and the throttle to the Port dynamo, thereby putting both dynamos out of action, and filling the Engine Room with steam.'[16]

After hurried running repairs, *Saladin* was able to make steam again, but then she was hit and a fire broke out aft. Dover sent Lieutenant J.H. Edwards to deal with the problem. 'He found the ready use cordite in the after gun position burning; after having to lie down twice when attacks were made he, with two Able Seaman, threw the burning charges from one box and the other box which was alight over the side.' Edwards saved the ship from a very dangerous fire.

Tennant had reported that the *Luftwaffe* had delivered their attacks without opposition from the RAF and, no doubt, that is how it must have appeared to him at the time. Yet 29 May was one of the most remarkable in the history of Fighter Command. For this was the day of the Defiants. The Boulton Paul Defiant was uniquely designed with four Browning machine-guns in a rear rotating turret but with no forward-facing guns. Due to production delays, the Defiant did not enter service until after the start of the Battle of France, on 12 May. By this time, the pilots of the *Luftwaffe* had become accustomed to encountering Spitfires and Hurricanes, and the Defiant looked very similar to the Hurricane. As a result, to start with, a number of German pilots mistook the Defiants for Hurricanes and attacked from the rear only to find themselves flying into the muzzles of the Defiants' machine-guns.

The first squadron to be equipped with Defiants was 264 which, on the 29th, undertook two sweeps over the Dunkirk area, and was able to claim an astonishing tally of victims. They claimed to have destroyed two Bf 109s, fifteen Bf 110s, nineteen Ju 87s and one Ju 88, making a total of thirty-seven enemy aircraft brought down. Not a single Defiant was lost. It was the best day a British fighter squadron ever had.[17] That evening, the Air Ministry sent a telegram to the squadron: 'The Air Officer Commanding in Chief sends sincere congratulations to No. 264 Squadron on their magnificent performance in shooting down over 30 enemy aircraft to-day without losing a single pilot, one of whom brought his aeroplane back minus both elevators and one aileron.'[18] The German pilots quickly discovered their mistake and the Defiants would never again experience a day like that memorable one at the end of May 1940.

THE PERIMETER

Beyond the evacuation area, at Cassel, the infantry of the Glosters and the Ox and Bucks still held out amid the ruins of the hill-top town. To the surprise of the defenders, who had come to the conclusion that they were completely surrounded, a British dispatch rider rode into the town. The men were equally amazed by the message the rider carried with him – to abandon Cassel and make for Dunkirk. 'We had been ordered to hold Cassel to the last round and last man, to cover the withdrawal to Dunkirk, so we did not expect the order to withdraw,' recalled Second Lieutenant Julian Fane. 'By this time, the

Germans were all round us and we were prepared to settle down to a good fight. Imagine our surprise when we received the message to break for it!'[19] Accordingly, plans were drawn up to slip down from Cassel that night under the cover of darkness.

Gunner Harry Munn was with the 209/53 Anti-Tank Regiment Royal Artillery at Cassel:

On the evening of the 29th May orders were given for the destruction of our guns and vehicles and with heavy hearts we went to Major Cartland's H.Q. Major Cartland made a speech in which he explained our position and said the Brigade would leave Cassel on foot and attempt to reach our lines. No mention was made that the evacuation was already taking place at Dunkirk. He also said it was an 'every man for himself' situation and any man who wished to make his own way was free to do so. All elected to follow the Major and armed with rifles, Brens and Mills bombs we set off through the burning town of Cassel.[20]

The men of Somerforce at Cassel started from the hill-top town at 21.30 hours on the 29th, with the 4th Ox and Bucks leading the way and the remnants of the Glosters taking up the rear. Moving rapidly through the trees down the slope, they avoided contact with the enemy and pressed on through the dark towards Dunkirk. They continued to slip through the German positions undetected until, at around 03.30 hours, as the first rays of dawn spread across northern France, they stumbled into the enemy.

The men of the Ox and Bucks, with only their rifles for protection, began battling with the German infantry they had blundered into. But soon six tanks swung into view. It was the end of their bid to reach Dunkirk, and their lieutenant colonel ordered his men to lay down their weapons. Most of the Glosters met a similar fate, as did Harry Munn.

Small groups of both battalions did manage to escape to Dunkirk during the night of the 29th, after spending all day hiding from the Germans. It was a sad anti-climax to the valiant defence of Cassel.

So far, the perimeter around the beaches and Dunkirk had held, but the Army was coming under increasing pressure and Coastal Command was asked to assist. Although it had been agreed on the 27th, that the aircraft would engage in roaming patrols seeking out their own targets, on the 29th they were asked to try and eliminate a definite enemy battery position situated about three miles south-west of Bergues. Wing Commander Frank Hopps later reported on the operation undertaken by 825 Squadron:

> In the area around the reported position of the battery there were known to be very little anti-aircraft opposition and very little report of enemy fighter activity. Whilst it is appreciated that a battery is not a really suitable target for any aircraft, the importance of at least producing distraction of the personnel of the battery was so great that it was considered justifiable to make the attack. In point of fact the squadron became divided in the thick smoke near Dunkirk and six of them eventually went to the Calais area in search of a target. Although this was a very gallant attempt to strike at the enemy, it was definitely contrary to the orders which were given out and, unfortunately, it involved the aircraft in considerable opposition in which five aircraft were lost.[21]

Amongst the men lost was the squadron commander, Lieutenant Commander J.B. Buckle. It was the last time Coastal Command attempted to bomb an artillery battery during *Dynamo*, its lumbering Swordfish being easy victims for the Messerschmitts. By the end of the evacuation of the BEF, 825 Squadron had lost eight of its twelve planes.

There were equally serious problems for HMS *Montrose*. In the early hours of the 29th, at 00.13 hours to be precise, she ran into a patch of fog on her way over to Dover. She also ran into something far more solid – the tug *Sun V*. With her bows badly damaged, she had to be towed back to Dover stern first by the tug *Lady Brassy*. *Montrose* did not reach the UK until 15.50 hours. She was moved to the inner basin at Dover where temporary repairs enabled her to sail under her own steam to Sheerness early the following morning. *Montrose* was joined on that final trip by the destroyer *Makay* which had also run into trouble shortly after 00.00 hours on the 29th. In this instance, it was the ground that the destroyer ran into off Zuydcoote. Like *Montrose*, *Mackay* was too badly damaged to take any further part in Operation *Dynamo*.

MORE LITTLE SHIPS

It was on the 29th that the Little Ships began to arrive off the beaches in greater numbers. This included six Assault Landing Craft which had been carried across the Channel on the SS *Clan Macalister*. Three of these, *ALC 5, 16* and *17*, were swamped by desperate French troops. As soon as *ALC 5* reached the shore it was 'rushed on all sides by French soldiers, so many of them got on board that the boat grounded'. It was only when some of them had been pushed off that the boat could be refloated. Sub Lieutenant R.O. Wilcoxon RNVR, in command of *ALC 15*, had an even worse experience, 'she was boarded by French soldiers, who overwhelmed the boat to such an extent that she became partially swamped, and the starboard battery was flooded and both engines failed.' Again, it was only by evicting some of the Frenchmen that one of the engines could be started. But the boat was damaged when going astern and water poured into the landing craft. *ALC 15* was kept afloat only by constant pumping and bailing but she continued to operate, taking off some 600 men. *ALC 17* likewise was grounded by French troops and remained stuck on the beach for three hours. When the tide flooded in and the boat began to float, the French troops made another rush for her, and it was only thanks to some British soldiers who drove the French away, that the landing craft was able to get off the beach. *ALC 17* then ferried troops to the waiting ships all day and throughout the night until her engines broke down.

The story was the same for one of the first motor-boats to reach France, *Scenceshifter*. She too was rushed by French troops, was swamped and sunk, becoming a total loss.

Six motor yachts also reached La Panne and began towing the ships' whalers out to the anchored ships. Amongst the latter was the yacht *Viewfinder*, which was dragged around by Belgian solders and it too became a total loss. As other motor boats arrived they began to play an increasingly important part in the operation, travelling forwards and backwards between ship and shore.

The reason why so many smaller boats were reaching Dunkirk was because an appeal had at last gone out on the BBC for, what was termed, recruits to man the Little Ships. But even at this quite late stage of *Dynamo*, the true reason for the call for experienced seamen was not revealed, but many must have guessed.

> The Admiralty want men experienced in marine internal combustion engines for services as enginemen in yachts and motorboats. Others who had had charge of boats and have good knowledge of coastal navigation, are needed as uncertified second hands. Applications should be made to the nearest registrar, Royal Naval Reserve, or to the Fisheries Officer.[22]

What this did show, was that the Admiralty was becoming increasingly confident that the perimeter would hold long enough for such recruits to be registered and employed effectively.

The General Steam Navigation Company Motor Vessel *Bullfinch*, a small (432-ton gross) coaster, was deployed at La Panne on the 29th. One of its crewmen was a gunner, Albert Atkinson of 237 Battery, 60th Field Regiment, Royal Artillery: 'As the troops had come on board they were asked to empty their .303 ammunition out of their pouches into a six-foot galvanized bath, before being sent below for shelter, as the Germans were attacking almost non-stop.' The only people allowed to remain on deck were Albert with a Bren gun and his two magazine-loaders. Once these two had prepared around fifty magazines for the gun, Albert sent them below. When the *Luftwaffe* flew in, Albert rested his Bren on the ship's lifeboat davits – and fired. He claimed two Stukas, which crashed into the sea, and a third which was seen flying away trailing smoke and losing altitude.[23]

Arriving overnight, the situation on the beaches on the 29th shocked Norman Wickman of 62nd Chemical Warfare Company:

> With twilight approaching, our small group of four stepped onto the beach at Bray-Dunes. Tens of thousands of exhausted troops congregated on the golden sands with not a spark of fight left in them. Other soldiers formed long lines out to sea. Only their determination to reach home, a mere 22 miles across the English Channel, kept them waiting patiently for rescue boats. They stood

chest deep in water, oily and slick from the shipwrecks offshore. Here and there, a body floated, a remnant of the human cargo lost to German bombs. An occasional victim of strafing and shelling littered the sand. The sickly-sweet stench of death lingered in the still air.

I surveyed the beach, trying to make sense of the scenario before me. Slowly, understanding dawned. Disbelief, horror, then anger welled up, followed by intense shame. Until that moment, I had believed we were an Army in retreat. Now, I realized, I belonged to a defeated army. My pride fought against accepting this fact. I still had plenty of fight left, but looking again at the thousands of dejected men, I could see these soldiers had had it. I was filled with confusion and despair.[24]

Norman Wickman did not need to despair, for by early afternoon there were fourteen ships lying off Dunkirk. This included six trawlers from the Dover Minesweeping Command, which were sent to the East Mole. The number of ships now involved in Operation *Dynamo* meant that as soon as one ship cast off another swept in to take its berth. When the SS *Lochgarry* pulled away for England with 1,000 men on board, her place was immediately taken by the six trawlers which triple-banked against the Mole.

By 17.00 hours on the 29th, what was left of the flotilla of paddle steamers that had made the round trip from France, lined up to cross the Channel once again for the night-time lift. This time Lieutenant Thomas Cook RNR was ordered to take troops from the Mole, as *Medway Queen*'s First Officer, Sub Lieutenant John Graves RNR, remembered: 'Off the entrance the flotilla came under very heavy fire from shore batteries, and some of the ships hauled out of the line as the sea spouted columns of water around them. The scene was awe inspiring. Rows of great oil tanks were blazing furiously and the glare was reflected on the clouds.

'Heavy shells plunged into the harbour which was littered with wrecks. It was enough to daunt the stoutest navigator but still the ships came and went, feeling their way past uncharted obstructions and avoiding each other.'

The ships tied up against the Mole and, as it was low tide, men had to climb down ladders to reach the decks of the paddle steamer, several feet below. 'It was while we were tied to the Mole that we were most vulnerable,' said the *Medway Queen*'s signaler, Eric Woodroffe. 'There was much more enemy activity then.

I remember the bombs coming down, other ships being hit including a cruiser, and getting the soldiers on board as fast as we could.'

One of those rescued by *Medway Queen* was Alf George, of Ashford, Kent, who served with the Royal Artillery:

> There were stretchers and bodies all along the Mole as we made our way along. We were given a tin of bully beef and a big packet of hard biscuits and told to share it among five of us. We'd been without food for three days. I looked over and there was this little paddle steamer about six feet below me. A sailor helped me down and I went to the after cabin and sat on a bench seat where I dropped off to sleep. Then I was woken up by an airburst of shell fire. I looked out of the window and there were all these flashes. The floor was completely covered with stretchers and injured men. I slept again and was awoken by a shuddering and a rattling, then everything went quiet. We thought we would be taken back across to France to continue fighting, but instead we were taken to Ramsgate Pier and unloaded. There were people at the end of the pier all cheering us.

Second Lieutenant David Smith's detachment of Engineers had been relieved of its duties and was placed under the command of II Corps, which was making its way to the coast:

> The force moved away to the village of Vincquin and a most depressing journey it was. On all sides were parks of vehicles which were being systematically destroyed. On arrival at Vincquim all papers were destroyed and after saving what personal kit could be conveniently carried, the detachment destroyed the vehicles. After the vehicles had been destroyed the personnel of the detachment were carried on the 12th Royal Lancers' vehicles to Ghyvelde where the regiment R.V.'d. Here all the remaining armoured cars were destroyed. All the guns were salvaged and during the evening all available Bren Guns were mounted and two enemy machines were shot down. As darkness fell away to the west could be seen the glow of fires which marked Dunkirk.[25]

LOSSES

Day 4 of Operation *Dynamo* was one of heavy losses amongst the Royal Navy ships and the civilian vessels. HMS *Wakeful*, as we have read, was the first to go down on the 29th, and many more would follow. In total, seventeen Royal Navy ships were sunk and eleven others were damaged and put out of action, mostly by the intense bombing. At 15.50 hours HMS *Jaguar* was subjected to an attack over the course of fifteen minutes in which she was targeted by fourteen salvos of bombs, with the German planes releasing four bombs in each salvo. The destroyer never stood a chance. 'There were many near misses, and towards the close of the attack a bomb exploded close on the port side abreast the break of the forecastle,' wrote Lieutenant Commander J.F.W. Hine:

> This did considerable damage to ship and personnel, and engines and steering were put out of action. Steering was carried out from tiller flat, and … headway was soon lost and ship stopped close to a wreck whose upperworks were visible… Messengers had to be sent to engine room to ascertain damage, owing to break-down of telephone, and the report seemed serious, holes above and below the water line, leaking oil fuel tanks, and pierced steam, oil and water pipes indicating that ship was likely to be out of action for some time.
>
> Water was flowing into number one and two boiler rooms, and low power room, an increasing list to port developed, and it was feared that ship would sink slowly until those holes above the water line were also submerged, and thus increase the likelihood of foundering, unless steam could be raised. An additional handicap was the extra load of seventy tons of troops, who hampered all movement above and below decks. Under these circumstances, it was decided to jettison torpedoes and depth charges.[26]

The disarmed torpedoes were fired but the stop valves on four of them failed to function and they ran onto the beach at Braye, though there are no indications that they did any damage. *Jaguar* continued to drift towards one of the many wrecks and was only fifty yards away when another destroyer came to her rescue. '*Jaguar* was sighted, stopped and disabled as a result of the attack,' recalled Commander Jack Grant Bickford of HMS *Express*:

She had a large number of Troops on board and was very close to a wreck. *Express* went alongside – towed her clear – and took off some of her troops and approximately 45 wounded. Later *Jaguar* was towed astern while bombing attacks were continued in the vicinity. At about 1830 the tow parted and in view of the number of men and the condition of the wounded I ordered *Jaguar* to anchor, transferred the remaining troops, and proceeded to Dover leaving a trawler to escort *Jaguar* who was later able to proceed at slow speed.[27]

Jaguar reached Dover at 23.50 hours, even though she was subjected to two further attacks on the passage home.

The sloop *Bideford* anchored off Bray beach at 17.30 hours and twenty minutes later the first boat-loads of troops (mostly French) came alongside. The event was recorded by her skipper, Lieutenant Commander J.H. Lewes:

The boats were dangerously overcrowded and several swamped on the way off from the shore. On arrival alongside, the men would all jump on board and let their boats drift off on the tide. Paddles were lost overboard, rendering the boats useless. *Bideford*'s M/B was lowered and ordered to collect and tow inshore any empty boats. The whaler was lowered and 2 officers and a signalman were sent in to endeavor to take charge on the beach ... this was next to impossible. The men rushed the boats and capsized them in shallow water, and then left the boats without making any attempt to right them and use them again. There were only 2 motor landing craft in the vicinity. One had one engine out of action; the other [*A.L.C. 16*] was blown up subsequently when laying alongside the ship.[28]

At around 19.00 hours *Bideford* was the target of Stukas. She was then machine-gunned at low level and a few minutes later was bombed again. One bomb landed just thirty yards away and another hit the stern, detonating one of the sloop's depth charges. About forty feet of *Bideford*'s stern was blown away and a further forty feet was reduced to tangled mass of metal. The main mast was blown down, wrecking the searchlight and the machine-gun platform.

The bridge superstructure was damaged as were other parts of the sloop. Two officers and thirteen men of the crew were killed and a further nineteen wounded, with the troops on board also having two officers and ten men killed and two officers wounded.

The M/S *Halcyon* witnessed what appeared to be the deliberate bombing of the Hospital Carrier *Isle of Guernsey*. She was bombed by ten German aircraft off Dunkirk whilst attempting to pick up a downed airman. Although damaged by near misses, *Isle of Guernsey* entered the harbour after dark and embarked 490 wounded over the course of many hours. The airman was picked up by *Halcyon*.

It is interesting to note that this intentional bombing of ships bearing the Red Cross was similarly noted by ambulance drivers who believed that they were being specifically targeted. Attacks upon ambulances became so prevalent that the committee in charge of the American volunteer ambulances took a quite remarkable step:

> All our drivers agree that the Red Cross only attracts the attention of German pilots. In the past ten days, Nazi airmen have been bombing or machine-gunning our ambulances, sometimes from only fifty feet. The Red Cross no longer protects our men, and we are removing it in their interests.[29]

After dropping off the landing craft, as mentioned earlier, *Clan Macalister* was bombed and sank in shallow water, her upper structures remaining above water. She continued to serve, even though abandoned, as the German bombers thought that she was still afloat and continued to waste their bombs on her. The trawler *Calvi* was also hit by bombs and sank.

Others amongst those lost was the steam packet SS *Fenella* which came under aerial attack as she was loading troops from the East Mole. She had more than 600 men on board when she was hit by three bombs in quick succession, the first bomb hitting her directly on the promenade deck, the second bomb hitting the Mole, blowing lumps of concrete through the ship's side below the waterline, and the third exploded between the pier and the ship's side, wrecking the engine room. *Fenella* was clearly unable to move, and likely to sink, so the troops were disembarked back onto the Mole.

Luckily, the paddle steamer *Crested Eagle* was nearby and the troops were re-embarked.

The destroyer HMS *Grenade* also went to *Fenella*'s assistance, on board which was Bob Bloom, who was part of the warship's medical team:

> We went in and we lay alongside and then they brought a seaman in from the *Fenella*. He had shrapnel in his shoulder. They took him on the seaman's mess deck and I went down with the doctor. I said, 'Right, we'll fix him up in a minute,' because we'd been summoned aft to the search light platform, which we used to call the 'bandstand'. I was taking the stretcher as it came down from the bandstand. Then the German aircraft started to machine gun us. And the Doc' called out to me, 'Drop!' So I dropped down and let go of the stretcher. The bullets went fore and aft — the wounded fella didn't get another one; he was lucky.
>
> I went to the sick bay. I was climbing down the ladder on my return when – whoof! – I went up in the air! My tin hat must have stayed up there, because I've got a hole, a dent in my skull where the nut inside the hat penetrated my skull. As I came down I fell straight into a flash because the oil went up. The oil tanks were under the stoker's mess deck and a bomb broke through and set light to the oil, which flashed up in front of me. It was like being whipped. I prayed to god to take me home quickly, and with that somebody lifted me up, turned me round and pushed me. I could see daylight. I could also see steam and I made for the daylight - before I knew it, I was on the upper deck by the engine room.[30]

Grenade had been struck by two bombs from Stukas that had attacked the destroyer as it lay alongside the East Mole. Fourteen sailors were killed instantly and another four were mortally wounded. The warship was badly damaged and fire took hold. The ship was cast off from her berth, in case she sank there, and then drifted into the harbour channel. Bob Bloom was still on the deck of the burning destroyer:

> I took one look round me and saw my hands - the skin was hanging off my hands like plastic gloves. I tried to pull it back on again, and

then I just went bump, bump over the wires surrounding the ship and into the water. When I came up the oil was on fire and had caught my legs, around my ankles. I swam. I was fully clothed, but I swam towards three tugs. I couldn't get to them but I saw there was a ladder alongside, made of rough wood - I remember because I pulled the wood out of my hands after I reached the top ... I realised that I was on the 'Crested Eagle'.

The trawler *John Cattling* towed *Grenade* over to the west side of the outer harbour where her magazines exploded later that evening.

Crested Eagle, meanwhile, had set off back for England with the men it had rescued. This included Sergeant W. Clarke of the RAMC who had in his care a number of injured men, including No.534973 Private C.T. Newell:

We were about half a mile out when we were hit by incendiaries and fire rapidly gained control of one end of the ship. A cry then came from the upper deck, 'Get the wounded on top'. Pte. Newell, in company with several other disabled men, was then dragged up through the hatchway but the press and throng of the crowd was so great that I was unable to keep with him, nor did I see how the wounded were eventually disposed of. It was some considerable time afterwards (I think about 15 minutes) before, through the smoke and falling woodwork, I myself managed to gain the upper deck. The boat was, by this time, well ablaze and I had to jump into the water and swim about 200 yards before finally being picked up by the minesweeper *Oldbury*. I never saw Pte. Newell after he left me on the lower deck.[31]

Second Lieutenant F.E. McMaster of the Royal Signals had a fortunate escape from the sinking paddle steamer:

I was at the left and the bottom of the staircase when I heard the A.A. machine-guns firing and suddenly the explosion of the first bomb. Instinctively I bent myself as much as possible, protecting my eyes with my hands. Then I heard a terrific noise, saw a big flash, fell down on the back, and fainted. I recovered after a few seconds and was expecting the sinking of the boat. My hands and my face were terribly burnt. The staircase near me was destroyed and all around me some soldiers were killed or wounded trying to extinguish the flames off their burning clothes.

Then I saw a window on [the] port side and managed to drop myself through it and fell down on a small triangular deck between the side and the left wheel of the paddler. There I recovered with the fresh air and saw that the *Crested Eagle* had been set on fire but the engine was still running. A short time later she was beached near the French shore.[32]

Crested Eagle was hit by four bombs and, as Lieutenant McMaster observed, she was set on fire but her engines kept on running out of control. The destroyer HMS *Verity* signaled for the paddle steamer to stop so that she could transfer her passengers, but *Crested Eagle* could not stop, and, blazing from fore to stern, she ran aground to the west of Bray beach. The 200-or-so survivors in the water were machine-gunned by the *Luftwaffe*, some being picked up by the minesweepers *Lydd* and *Hebe*.

In this latest German attack, the Southern Railway Steam Ship *Normania* was also hit off Dunkirk. She was towed clear of the Dunkirk channel by the gunboat *Mosquito*, her crew and the troops on board being taken off by the minesweeper *Ross*. *Normannia* sank at 02.45 hours on the morning of the 30th.

HMS *Pangbourne* was on her second trip to Dunkirk, an account of which comes from an unnamed sub lieutenant:

We are back near where we went aground last night [off Bray], and the sea is a mass of boats and debris. A destroyer on fire is being towed out on one side, and gaping holes in her side show where the bombs went home. Men are struggling in the water all around us, and we are stopping to pick them up.

'What is that on the port quarter? – It looks like a tiny cloud. I strain my eyes through the glasses. It's Jerry again. I give the orders mechanically, and the gun swings on to the bearing. They come relentlessly on like great black vultures. No use opening fire yet; they are not yet within range. These are a different kind, with queer wings and fixed undercarriages. I rack my brain to think what they are. Suddenly the penny drops. They are Stuka dive-bombers.

'They wheel round in a circle and peel off one by one. Each has selected his prey, and here comes ours. In a screaming vertical power dive he is tearing down towards us at four hundred knots. The noise is terrifying. I am shouting ranges at the top of my voice. Surely to God nothing can stop him crashing on our decks! – he'll never pull out of this. He starts to spit fire at us, and the tracer shells from his cannon blind me as I watch for the bombs to fall.

'Our machine-guns are chattering back at him, and the red tracer bullets seem to be passing through his wings. My head will burst with noise soon. ... The scream of the bombs is masked by the roar of the diving plane as it sweeps the masts. The world goes mad. The ship leaps in the air and cold salt water souses me as I shrink into the deck. The spanging of bullets and flying shrapnel is added to the explosion of the bombs. The breath is knocked out of my body and then for a brief moment there follows a stillness broken only by the retiring plane.

'I stagger to my feet and gaze at a picture of utter horror. Blood and flesh is everywhere; mutilated bodies that ten seconds ago were men I knew personally, are flung in grotesque heaps all about me. The gun is pointing drunkenly at the sky, knocked completely from its bearings. Three of my seven men are standing with me stunned by the desolation around them. I climb with difficulty to where the gun layer is lying, his neck and stomach torn open and his hand blown away. We have no doctor – none could help him anyway. He is still breathing and moaning faintly. I slip a morphia tablet under his tongue and move across to the breech worker. No need for morphia here; he is dead. The loading number is lying with his eyes open and looking at me. I kneel beside him before I find what is wrong. A shrapnel splinter has fractured his jaw on the side away from me. He will be all right. I give him a tablet and cushion his head on a life jacket.[33]

At the same time as *Pangbourne* came under attack so too did the paddle steamer *Gracie Fields*, which was also on her second trip to Dunkirk. She had taken on board four British officers and some 800 other ranks from La Panne, before setting off back for the UK at around 18.00 hours. She did not get far. Whilst still in sight of land she was hit amidships. One bomb penetrated the engine room, though it did not hole the ship. Her steering was also jammed at

15 degrees starboard. As with *Crested Eagle*, her skipper, Captain N.R. Larkin was unable to stop *Gracie Fields*' engines and she started going round in circles at six knots. Fortunately, the skoot *Twente* was on its way back from La Panne with 275 French troops on board. The Dutch skipper was able to secure his ship alongside *Gracie Fields* – an act of considerable skill – and received as many of the wounded and others as he could. Another skoot, *Jutland*, then secured itself on the other side of the paddle steamer and took off some more of the men. Finally, the rest of the soldiers were rescued by the minesweeper *Pangbourne*. It was at approximately 18.30 hours that the last man was taken off *Gracie Fields*. The rescue of the men from *Gracie Fields* had taken just thirty minutes. What is equally astonishing is that *Pangbourne* had been holed on both sides above and below the waterline when off Bray beach having had thirteen men killed and eleven others wounded.

After taking eighty men off *Gracie Fields*, *Pangbourne* took her in tow, but the paddle steamer did not reach England, sinking in mid-Channel.

The Southern Railways steamer SS *Canterbury* had embarked 1,960 troops from the East Mole in the midst of the German air attacks. In a brief lull in the bombing, she set off from Dunkirk but was severely damaged by a near miss as she was leaving the harbour. Amongst those that had been taken off the East Mole was Albert George Heath of the Royal Artillery, whose leg had been badly wounded by a German shell on 21 May, his leg being shattered below the knee. He had also received a gunshot wound at the back of his shoulder. Gangrene set in and his leg had to be amputated. He was moved to Dunkirk in stages, and eventually reached the port. 'Whilst in the ambulance on the quayside a bomb exploded nearby,' the courageous gunner recalled. 'Shrapnel ripped into the ambulance severing my right arm, the ambulance then caught fire! French sailors pulled me from the burning ambulance, but I suffered burns to my head and face.'

Albert was embarked on *Canterbury* but when the ship was tossed by the exploding bomb he was pitched into the sea. He was pulled out of the harbour by the crew of the former ferry. *Canterbury* made her way slowly back to Dover and Albert was treated for his many wounds. Over the course of the following five years, Albert underwent thirty-one major operations on both his arm and leg. He overcame his disabilities to work until he retired at the age of sixty-five. He died in 1985 at the age of seventy-five. In many ways, the story of this brave man epitomized the 'Dunkirk Spirit.'[34]

HMS *Sabre* had set off from Dover at 16.00 hours and arrived at Dunkirk in the evening. *Sabre* pulled alongside the East Mole but found that due to the air raids the Mole had been cleared of troops. A request had been made for a party of Royal Navy officers to help organise the evacuation on the beaches, as it had been reported that the troops were completely disorganised, were discarding their rifles, lying down on the beaches and refusing to get into the small boats.[35] Consequently, Captain J.M. Howson with two commanders, two lieutenant commanders and two lieutenants had travelled across the Channel on *Sabre*. The officers were dropped off on the East Mole.

Whilst Howson's party was disembarking, a few troops were seen running down the Mole and so Commander Brian Dean waited to take these on board. The *Luftwaffe* continued to bomb the port and the East Mole but, inexplicably, did not appear to target *Sabre*. Regardless, the destroyer expended 'prodigious' quantities of ammunition at the raiders and one bomber was seen to crash and one appeared to be damaged; both were Ju 87s.

After the first raid *Sabre* left the Mole and saw some men struggling in the water. Having no boats left it was necessary to place the ship alongside each man and hoist him in with a bowline. The survivors included the Second Engineer of the *Crested Eagle* and a stoker from *Grenade*, both badly burned. *Sabre* also took on some Frenchmen from a raft. Throughout this time, *Sabre* was repeatedly attacked by dive bombers but suffered no damage.

Sabre then made its way to lie off Bray to land a portable wireless set, loudspeakers, etc., that would be used by Howson and his officers. Some time was spent in searching for a boat (*Sabre* having none), and a small motor launch was eventually headed off and pressed into service. The equipment for Howson's team was dropped off along with the telegraphists in charge of them. The air attacks persisted during this time, forcing *Sabre* to zig-zag around at high speed and the destroyer was severely shaken by near misses, with every man on deck being blackened with oil-fuel splashes. At 20.10 hours, by which time *Sabre* was out of all ammunition, she was ordered to withdraw, returning in the company of *Verity* and *Saladin*, the latter only able move at fifteen knots.[36]

All together on Day 4 of Operation *Dynamo* twenty-four vessels were sunk and another twelve severely damaged and put out of action, but it was a day of remarkable achievement. In total, 13,752 men were taken off the beaches and 33,558 from the harbour and the East Mole. This made a total of 47,310 men landed in England on 29 May. It may be recalled that the Admiralty had originally estimated the most that they were likely to be able to save would be 45,000. This figure had been exceeded on one day alone. The total recovered from France now amounted to 72,783. It was also seen that General Adam, the perimeter being well-established, had done his job and he was evacuated on the evening of the 29th.

As a result, Churchill decided that efforts should be made to help take off as many French troops as was possible, whilst still continuing to evacuate the BEF. He, therefore, sent the following message to Prime Minister Reynaud for onward transmission to *Général* Weygand:

We have evacuated nearly 50,000 from Dunkirk and beaches, and hope another 30,000 tonight. Front may be beaten in at any time, or piers, beaches, and shipping rendered unusable by air attack, and also by artillery fire from the south-west. No-one can tell how long present flow will last, or how much we can save for [the] future. We wish French troops to share in [the] evacuation to fullest possible extent, and Admiralty have been instructed to aid French Marine as requested. We do not know how many will be forced to capitulate, but we must share this loss together.[37]

Amongst the last ships to reach France on the 29th was the skoot *Patria*, which arrived off Bray from Ramsgate at 23.00 hours. Her skipper decided that the quickest way to embark troops off the beach was, like the *Oriole*, to run her aground and hope that her engines could pull her off as the tide rose: 'The troops, holding hands, waded out and clambered on board by nets, ladders and ropes' ends. The sight of two solid phalanxes of men, delineated by phosphorescence in the water and steadily advancing to the ship will be memorable ... over 1,000 men were embarked in just over two hours.'[38]

This exemplified the manner in which the sailors were going beyond the call of duty to rescue the soldiers of the BEF. The feared-for disaster was beginning to look increasingly like a success.

Ramsay, consequently, felt able to reduce the number of destroyers involved in *Dynamo*. In the course of the two previous days, eleven destroyers had been either sunk or disabled, leaving Dover Command with only seven modern destroyers to defend the Channel. In an agreement with the Admiralty, Ramsay withdrew these destroyers, leaving fifteen to continue with the evacuation. Even with this reduced capacity, Ramsay calculated that he could still maintain a rate of one destroyer per hour reaching Dunkirk, which meant these ships alone would be able to lift 17,000 men every twenty-four hours.

With these considerations in mind, Ramsay spelt out his arrangements for the night of 29/30 May in a signal to Tennant:

> Evacuation of British troops to continue at maximum speed during the night. If adequate supply of personnel vessels cannot be maintained to Dunkirk east pier [Mole], destroyers will be sent there as well. All other craft except hospital carriers to embark from beach which is extended from one mile east of Dunkirk to one mile east of La Panne. Whole length is divided into 3 equal parts referred to as La Panne, Bray, Malo, from east to west with a mile gap between each part. La Panne and Bray have troop concentration points each end and in the middle; Malo at each end. These points should be tended by inshore craft.

Tennant was told to pass this information verbally on to those vessels not equipped with radios. However, Captain Tennant would not have to bear that responsibility alone, as shortly before midnight Rear Admiral William Wake-Walker arrived in the destroyer *Esk*. From that night onwards, Wake-Walker would be the Senior Naval Officer afloat, directing the ships from a motor boat or a warship, while Tennant directed operations on the shore, and Captain Howson organised the troops on the beaches. Howson split his party into two groups with one group under Commander H.J.O. Otway-Ruthven at Bray and the other group at La Panne led by Commander H.G. Gorton. What difference these officers would make to evacuation from the beaches remained to be seen.

Chapter 7

Operation *Dynamo*: Day 5, Thursday 30 May

Operations during the night had been disappointing, as Tennant complained in his first situation report of the 30th: 'Enemy activity was reduced during the night, only two bombing attacks being made. It was intended to recommence embarkation from Eastern Arm under cover of darkness but apparently due to some misunderstanding the only ships that arrived were four trawlers and a yacht. Consequently, a great opportunity was missed. Probably 15,000 troops could have been embarked had the ships been forthcoming.'[1]

As dawn broke that morning, the recently arrived Rear Admiral Wake-Walker was able to see the magnitude of the task that confronted him. Along the beaches, long dark lines of men stretched to the water's edge and larger groups of men were gathered on the sands. He could also see the effects of the German bombing – *Bideford* aground with her stern blown off and the burnt-out remains of *Crested Eagle*.

In his report, Wake-Walker described the beaches as ships began to arrive: 'Long stretch of sand dunes rising fairly steeply in places from a gently shelving beach which dries for 200 yards or more at low water. Offshore the water deepens very gradually and a destroyer cannot get nearer than half a mile.'[2] After remarking on the dark line of men formed along the shore, Wake-Walker wrote that: 'Lying off were destroyers, sloops, drifters etc., and men making their way off in whalers, motor boats and pontoon craft. A slight swell made landing difficult, and many boats broached to and were stranded on a falling tide.'

To help coordinate the evacuation, Captain J.M. Howson was appointed Naval-Officer-in-Charge of beaches. As the first light of day broke over Dunkirk, Howson had his first glimpse of the scene off Bray, 'in the lightening dawn, a number of destroyers, sloops and skoots were seen to be lying off, and embarkation was proceeding in such boats as were available. Several boats were aground, others holed, and some had no oars ... By about 06.00 all destroyers, sloops, etc., had cleared for England and there were no further ships available.' This demonstrated the urgent need for more ships, and reinforced Tennant's statement that a great opportunity had been lost during the night.

As Wake-Walker had seen, an increasingly fresh breeze from the north-east was causing a line of breakers that extended to about fifty yards off shore. This, together with the small number of available boats, meant that embarkation was frustratingly slow. The shortage of boats was because the destroyers' whalers were crewed by their gun teams and these men were obviously wanted by the warships on their return trips. So, once each destroyer was full, the whalers and their crews were taken back on board. 'To anyone with an appreciation of the practical difficulties of embarking in small boats with a long pull to seaward, the sight of that beach black with troops was dismaying,' confessed Wake-Walker. 'The numbers increased steadily as more men filed down the sand dunes and at the back of our minds all the time was the question and fear of how long the defence line could hold and the weather remain fair.'[3] The rear admiral confessed that, as he saw it, the picture was a confused one, 'and so far as operations off beaches were concerned organization was not possible. The most that could be done was to exercise some control and direction.'[4]

HMS *Vivacious* had arrived off Bray at about 07.00 hours and by 17.00 hours had only received 175 British troops. 'It was particularly distressing to see an increasing number of troops assembling on the beach,' complained Commander Dechaineux, 'which in the circumstances prevailing gave me a feeling of impotence.' This frustration was relayed to Ramsay by Wake-Walker at 11.07 hours: 'Beaches crowded ... Until more boats [are available] strongly of opinion ... essential to concentrate on evacuating from Dunkirk itself.'

One of the Beach Officers at Bray was Lieutenant J.G. Wells, who soon worked out the most efficient way of embarking the troops:

> The system that produced the best results was to organize them into a long queue at each of the three embarkation points at Bray beach. The queues were three deep and were spaced out in groups of ten, this number being most suitable for the types of boat available. The following group could be used for shoving off a loaded boat, which took a good deal of moving at half-tide owing to a bar running parallel to the sea.

The Army pontoon boats proved most suitable owing to their draught, double ended construction and general handiness. Fortunately, the weather was favourable for the operations, the sea remaining calm all day and a gentle Northerly breeze assisting in the recovery of drifting craft. An overcast sky and the presence of our fighter patrols seems to have deterred the enemy aircraft from bombing.[5]

Tennant continued to bombard Dover with requests for more ships, and at 09.50, he wrote that if the overcasts sky that was keeping the *Luftwaffe* grounded was to continue, he wanted a ship to arrive every thirty minutes. He later complained that: 'The whole morning was misty and ideal for embarkation but few ships arrived and a great opportunity was again lost. Hospital ships also did not arrive until afternoon and there were over one thousand wounded waiting for transportation.'

There was soon to be another wreck on the Dunkirk shore to accompany *Crested Eagle*. This was one of the ships of the Red Funnel Line that took holidaymakers on excursions along the Bristol Channel. The steel paddle steamer *Devonia* had seen service in the First World War as a minesweeper and in October 1939, she was again called upon by the Admiralty. After being appropriately re-equipped at Milford Haven, which included the addition of a single 12-pounder gun on the forecastle and Lewis guns on each paddle sponson, she sailed up to the Firth of Forth to help guard the East Coast. When Operation *Dynamo* began, *Devonia* was summoned to help, she moved down to Harwich before coaling up for the passage along the swept channel to France.

Devonia arrived off La Panne on 30 May. Amongst the crew was Signalman Leslie Rashleigh:

There was a lot of air activity, mainly bombing, and the Germans were also in Nieuport, in sight of the beaches, which they shelled spasmodically. We manned the 12-pounder and popped off a few shells and also the Lewis guns, which helped morale if nothing else. After passing a Clan Line freighter which had been hit and abandoned while at anchor, we launched our boat to make a couple of runs to inshore, off-loading on to the *Hilda*, a small, one hold, high poop Dutch coaster manned by a Royal Navy lieutenant with three ratings. Before long the bombing and shelling came too close for comfort and then we reeled from a stick of bombs immediately astern. Because of the severity of the damage we were instructed to beach as far in as possible in the hope that the ship would act as a jetty for the troops – although at the time we were still too far out for the soldiers to wade … After we beached I took the ship's confidential books and papers to the stokehold to be burnt and only the second engineer remained to assist, and then opened the seacocks. We left *Devonia* – and her unfinished day trip to France – in style and rowed across to the *Hilda*.[6]

Devonia was never recovered and her stark remains can still be seen, and visited, on the beach at La Panne.

As Wake-Walker had remarked, lying off the beaches were a small number of destroyers and other vessels to which men were making their way in tiny craft, but the swell continued to make beach work difficult and many boats lay stranded by the tide. The troops, orderly and under control, continued to file down from the dunes, but the need, still, was for boats and more boats. Part of the problem was that, quite often, once the troops had climbed on board the ships, they just left the boats to float away on the tide as there were few naval ratings to act as boat-keepers to return the boats to the shore.

LIFEBOATS TO THE RESCUE

It is surprising, in view of the problems being experienced off the beaches, that it was not until 13.15 hours on 30 May, that the War Ministry made contact with an obvious source of suitable vessels – the Lifeboat Institute. A phone call was made to the R.N.L.I. which was asked to send as many of its boats as possible to Dover at once. That was all that was said and the instruction was not queried, though the reason for the call was easily guessed.[7]

As soon as the Institute received the call, it telephoned the eighteen stations around the south and east coasts within practicable sailing of Dover, from Gorleston in Norfolk, which is 110 miles north-east of Dover, to Shoreham Harbour in Sussex, eighty miles to the west.

The lifeboat coxswains were ordered to make their way to Dover immediately for special duty with the Admiralty. They were told to take a full crew, full fuel-tanks and towing ropes. The first boats arrived at Dover that evening and another three reached the port early the next day. Within twenty-nine hours of the summons all bar three of the lifeboats had reached Dover.

The lifeboats were going to war.

When the first of the lifeboat-men to arrive at Dover were told that they would be taking men off the beaches of Dunkirk, three of the crews, which manned heavy boats with deep keels that would have to be winched off the beaches, refused to go. Their boats were therefore taken over by the Royal Navy. The other lifeboat crews to arrive were given their course for Dunkirk and ordered into Dover for re-fuelling before their departure. They had not refused to go across the Channel but the Navy, worried about the morale of lifeboat-men after the refusal of the first three crews, decided to seize the boats and man them with their own officers and men. The brave, volunteer, lifeboat-men were very upset at this slight upon their honour, especially as some had anticipated being called into war service and had turned up at Dover with borrowed steel helmets.

However, two of the lifeboats were already at sea heading not for Dover but straight for Dunkirk and manned not by the Royal Navy but by the lifeboat crews themselves.

Earlier that morning, the naval officers-in-charge at Ramsgate and Margate had asked their lifeboats if they would sail for Dunkirk. Both crews agreed and, at 14.20 hours, the *Prudential* left Ramsgate and a little more than three hours later the *Lord Southborough* departed from Margate.

The eight-man crew of the *Prudential*, under the command of Coxswain Howard Primrose Knight, was issued with gas masks and steel helmets and cans of fresh water for the soldiers they would saving from the beaches of Dunkirk. Coxswain Knight was also given four coils of grass warp rope. This particular type of rope is made from cocoa-nut fibre. It is not as strong as manila but it is much lighter and floats in the water. The advantage of this is that, when towing, there is far less chance of the rope becoming entangled in the boats' propellers. It is interesting to note that one of the things that delayed the transport of some of the Little Ships was a shortage of hawsers in and around the south coast ports and appeals were made to other ports further north to send what suitable towing ropes they could.

Prudential took in tow eight boats manned by eighteen men from the Royal Navy. Most of these boats were wherries, i.e. simple, light rowing-boats. It would be the task of the Ramsgate lifeboat to tow the wherries between the beaches and the ships standing out to sea. By contrast, the *Lord Southborough* herself was towed across the Channel by a large Dutch barge commanded by a naval officer. Coxswain Edward Drake Parker's ten-man crew was supplied with steel helmets and food and cigarettes. Their journey to Dunkirk was featured in an article in the *Daily Mirror*:

> Standing on the beach at Dunkirk helping to embark BEF men amid bombs and machine-gun bullets, a young British sailor, Jim Parker, of Margate, turned as someone slapped him on the shoulder and said: 'Well, fancy meeting you here, Jim!' When Jim turned round it was his elder brother, Ted, aged twenty-eight.
>
> Unknown to each other, the brothers had been working like heroes with only a few yards between them, getting the tired troops aboard their ships. Neither brother had any idea the other was at Dunkirk and it was this amazing meeting which saved Jim's life. For after chatting for a few minutes, Ted asked his brother to go along with him to a small motor-boat off the jetty for a drink of water and some food.
>
> 'While I was aboard the motor-boat the part of the jetty [presumably the East Mole] was smashed by German dive bombers,' Jim told the *Daily Mirror*.

The brothers decided to try and get back to England on the motor boat. As they headed away from Dunkirk, they were passed by a lifeboat, the coxswain of which was none other than their father Edward in the *Lord Southborough*![8]

E. Jordan was *Lord Southborough*'s Mechanic:

> We went inshore, with the engine running dead slow and with a small anchor astern. We got in as close as possible and saw masses of troops assembled at the water's edge; we got about 80 aboard at first and they were French, we put off and got them aboard a nearby craft and returned to the shore. A British officer swam to us and came on board telling the Coxswain that he had a large number of his men further along the shore and guided us to the spot.

He instructed his men how to make their way to us, telling them it was their last chance. They soon began swarming through the water to us, up to their armpits, and practically everyone had his rifle slung across his shoulder. Some had removed their boots and trousers. They were assisted aboard, among them were several badly injured and their mates were holding them high on improvised litters. We then put off again and got them aboard another craft.[9]

The beaches themselves, after four days of bombardment, presented a sorry spectacle, as Sergeant A. Bruce of the 7th Field Company, Royal Engineers saw:

As we trudged on, we passed horses, their stomachs ripped apart and entrails scattered all over the place. Men were lying there in grotesque attitude of death, eyes and mouths wide open; it was hard to believe that they had ever been human beings … here they lay where they had died, like dogs that had been run over in the street.[10]

Just what it was like that day for the troops waiting on the East Mole or the beaches was also described by Ernest Long:

I could see the masts of sunken ships all over the harbour. Some had been blasted onto the beach, and there, and there was evidence of aircraft dogfights with parts of shot-down planes of both sides littering the sands. There were hastily prepared slit trenches dug by those who had preceded us and in quite a lot of these trenches were dead bodies of those who had been killed by enemy action. It was a terrible gruesome sight. The harbour master and his assistants were trying desperately hard to organise the embarking troops into any boat or ship that had managed to reach the side of the Mole. When my turn came I remember having to balance across a gangplank that had been put across a part of the Mole that had received a direct hit. That hit had left a wide gap between the two sections.[11]

For some, the gaps in the Mole proved fatal. 'We got on the long jetty and were told to march along,' recalled Private Victor Burton of the 1st Battalion of the East

Lancs later in the day. 'There were shell holes in it, and every now and then – it was dark now – there were people falling through the holes. You could hear a splash, and you couldn't help them because you couldn't see what was happening.'[12]

Despite such difficulties, embarkation continued from the Mole, the ships having to manoeuvre round the growing number of wrecks. Nevertheless, Tennant felt that he had organised affairs as well as he could and he handed over responsibility for monitoring the embarkations to Commander G.O. Maund while he met with the other senior military and naval officers at Gort's HQ at La Panne.[13]

It was on La Panne that many of the retreating troops were converging, including Sid Seal of the 4th Battalion, Sussex Regiment:

> It was the 30th of May when we got there and we could already see Dunkirk in flames. We could see crowds of troops at Bray-Dunes, there was plenty of panic there, thousands of men were on the beach. But where we were wasn't so busy. We were just fortunate. On the night of the 31st we found a rowing boat. It had probably come off one of the ships that had been bombed. The Germans were shelling and bombing De Panne, so it was get into the boat or stay in the town and get blown to pieces. So seven or eight of us – just one of them was a chap from my battalion – got in and rowed out into the Channel, just hoping we were going in the right direction. Fortunately, we were. A fishing boat picked us up and took us back to Ramsgate.[14]

Signaller Wilf Saunders with the 48th Division reached the evacuation areas on the 30th:

> For miles, we could see the pall of smoke over Dunkirk from that flaming oil … All the French and many of the English were just straggling along, a proper rabble … We went the last miles through densely packed horses left by the French … We went to the shores and walked about two miles up and down soft sand – agonies of agonies after our march – looking for our unit. Huge masses of men, and apparently, the only way of getting onto a boat was to wade … Chief trouble was too many men trying to get on a boat.[15]

Allied troops on one of the soft, sandy beaches which stretch for sixteen miles eastwards from Dunkirk to Nieuport, beaches at places such as Malo-les-Bains, Bray-Dunes and La Panne, forming into long winding queues ready to take their turn to board small boats which took them to larger vessels during Operation *Dynamo*. (Historic Military Press)

British troops entering Dunkirk pass the smouldering wreckage of a lorry, a small part of the debris of war that came to increasingly litter the streets of the port. (Historic Military Press)

A busy scene in the English Channel as ships of all shapes and sizes, military and civilian, make their way back to the South Coast laden with their valuable cargoes of evacuated Allied troops. (Historic Military Press)

Allied troops wade out into the water near the imposing Maritime Hospital at Zuydcoote, near Bray-Dunes, to the east of Dunkirk. (Historic Military Press)

The author sailing past the Steam Tug, and Dunkirk 'Little Ship' veteran, *Challenge* whilst it was berthed in the harbour at Shoreham-by-Sea. (Author)

Loaded with evacuated soldiers, *Emperor of India* sets out from Dunkirk to return to the South Coast ports during Operation *Dynamo*. (Historic Military Press)

The Dunkirk gateway at Bergues, as with other parts of the town's old fortifications, still bear the scars of the fighting in 1940. (Author)

The re-built 'Massacre Barn' at Wormhoudt. This exceptionally atmospheric site is open to the public and is well furnished with information panels describing the terrible events of 28 May 1940. (Author)

Safely home. The original caption to this image, dated 31 May 1940, states that it shows some of the men landed that day at one of the Kent ports having arrived in London, 'still smiling', by train. (Historic Military Press)

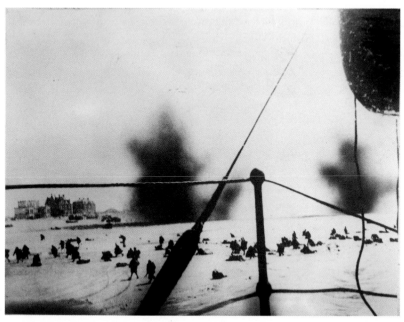

A remarkable shot of the beach at La Panne during a German air raid. It was taken from the decks of HMS *Oriole* by Sub-Lieutenant John Crosby; he had turned and captured the very moment that a pair of German bombs fell on the sands and exploded. (Historic Military Press)

Taken by a German soldier in the immediate aftermath of Operation *Dynamo*, this picture shows abandoned British and French vehicles on the quayside in the harbour at Dunkirk, with, in the background, the East Mole or jetty that proved so important during the evacuation. The East Mole was not a stout stone wall with berthing places along its length, as might be imagined around a harbour. It was a narrow plank-way barely wide enough for three men to walk abreast. On either side was a protective railing made of strong timbers with, at intervals, taller posts which could be used by ships to secure themselves against the Mole in emergencies. (Historic Military Press)

The East Mole at Dunkirk, as it was in 1940, no longer exists, though this is the spot from where it reached out into the harbour. (Author)

The wreck of the paddle steamer *Devonia* on the beach at La Panne, where it was deliberately beached after being damaged in an air raid on 30 May 1940. *Devonia* had made several journeys to and from the beaches before it was abandoned. (Historic Military Press)

The wreck of *Crested Eagle* can still be visited at low tide on the beach at Bray-Dunes. (Author)

German personnel inspecting the remains of one of the improvised piers constructed from assorted military and civilian vehicles on the beaches to the east of Dunkirk. (Historic Military Press)

Abandoned vehicles and equipment litter the seafront at Dunkirk in the immediate aftermath of Operation *Dynamo*. The abandoned Thames sailing barge in the centre background is believed to be *Ethel Everard*, which had been towed across the Channel by the tug *Sun XII* in company with another barge, *Tollesbury*. The building in the distance with the round tower is the Malo Terminus Casino. (Historic Military Press)

Wilf Saunders managed to find an abandoned boat, but he was followed by other soldiers and, once again, the boat was swamped when too many tried to climb onboard. Saunders then waded out to a lifeboat manned by a single Royal Marine but, once more, too many men tried to get in and it filled with water and sank.

> Staggered to the shore exhausted and collapsed on the stones. Heavy, wet clothes and full kit, less rifle dropped when the first boat turned over, had reduced me to such a state that I didn't care if I did die. Continued wading into a heavy sea had also sapped my strength, and at the end of that three weeks ... I decided it was impossible to get a boat and for a third successive day gave myself up as finished.

The perimeter was, by 30 May, beginning to take on a solid form, running for twenty-five miles from the right of Nieuport to the town of Bergues, which was the only position held forward of the Bergues-Furnes canal and formed the limit of the British line, and then westwards along the French-held sector to Mardyck. I Corps held the western half of the British sector, from Dunkirk to the French frontier, with the 1st Division pushed forward alongside the 42nd and the unattached 46th Division; whilst II Corps occupied the eastern part from the frontier to the sea at Nieuport. The weakest point of the perimeter was in the area of Dunkirk itself where III Corps' severely-mauled 44th and 48th divisions were in no state to mount a determined defence.

Over at Nieuport during the night, Brigadier Clifton's men had managed to tow a disabled tank onto the bridge over the canal, which had helped to block the enemy's persistent efforts to cross the water. But at around 02.00 hours on the 30th, a Royal Engineer officer, who he had not previously met, had approached him, saying that he was holding a sector of the line near Nieuport, but that most of his men were old, being mostly enlisted pioneers who could barely handle a rifle. They had, so far, escaped most of the action, 'but were very shaken and very apprehensive of a tank attack.' The officer was 'certain' that they would give way if they came under heavy fire. Clifton had no spare men and could not help the Engineer, and he responded in the only way he could, telling the worried officer that 'it was imperative he should maintain his position'.[16] Clifton, though, admitted that he was perturbed by the Engineer's defeatist attitude, which did not bode well for the coming day – and soon, as Clifton described it, 'things began to boil up'.

It was at Nieuport that the Germans established a battery of guns with the capacity to reach the ships anchored off shore. This, it was believed, consisted of two, later four, 4-inch guns. Throughout the afternoon this battery was only firing occasionally and somewhat ineffectually, however, at 18.00 hours, the German guns targeted the destroyers off La Panne: '*Vivacious* was hit on the *fo'c's*le by what is believed to be a 4-inch graze fuze shell, causing three deaths and twelve casualties to the troops on the upper mess deck,' reported Commander Dechaineux. 'Two near misses caused about forty small shrapnel holes on the waterline abreast the engine room and the after torpedo tubes. These near misses punctured two fuel tanks rendering them unfit for use. The central store was flooded partially, the lubricating pipe to the stern was punctured and the De-Gaussing circuits were cut in eight places.'[17] *Vivacious* moved about two miles to the west, out of range of the German guns, and continued to embark troops.

During the morning sappers and troops of the 1st Division built a long pier of lorries stretching into the sea at Bray and decked it with planks. This would help speed up the embarkation as at low tide even many of the Little Ships, could not get close to the beaches. Around fifteen three-ton lorries were placed end to end on Bray-Dunes' hard sand during low tide. Bullets fired at their tyres punctured them and this, together with sand thrown into the backs of lorries and the fact that the lorries were lashed together after the covers were stripped of their superstructure, ensured that they did not move when the tide came in. Decking panels from bridging trucks laid across the backs of lorries, along with planks 'liberated' from a local timber yard, served as the walkway along which soldiers could make their way out to the launches and boats that came to collect them.[18]

'The hard part,' remembered one member of the naval beach parties, 'was the organisation of the assembly of the pier between bouts of shelling, low-level bombing and machine gunning from enemy aircraft. Once it was done, though, this procedure was a most welcome break for us. It made filling the boats so much easier. There was no more brute force required to push out the boats and get wet through in the process.' Though the pier was too unstable for larger vessels to risk going alongside, or for small boats to use when the sea was a little choppy, it did increase the rate of embarkation and a similar one was built at La Panne, as were others later in the operation. The pier also gave the troops who had waited patiently for many hours added hope that they would soon be rescued and morale amongst the tried and anxious soldiers lifted immeasurably.

PLANNING THE FINAL DAYS

During the morning of the 30th, Gort and Wake-Walker met with Tennant Abrial, Fagalde and *Général* de la Laurencie (commander of the French 3rd Corps) at Bastion 32 to discuss the final phase of the evacuation. Gort had already agreed with Laurencie that 5,000 of his picked men who had fought alongside the BEF and had proven to be excellent troops, should be found space on British ships, but Abrial told the British commander that he had received orders from *Général* Weygand that priority should be given to members of the French Cavalry Corps instead. Gort also invited Fagalde and Laurencie to go with him when he departed from Dunkirk, but both these proud French generals declined, preferring to remain to the end with their men.[19]

It was arranged that the 3rd, 4th and 5th divisions of II Corps would withdraw from the perimeter to the beaches and the Mole, whilst 50th Division was to fall back to the French defences on the Belgian frontier, and then be under command of I Corps. These moves were to take place on the morning of the 31st, by which time it was hoped that most other units would have been evacuated.

It was accepted that the last reasonable date at which the BEF might be expected to hold its part of the perimeter was daybreak on 1 June, with the army being reduced by that time to a rearguard of just 4,000 men. Wake-Walker knew that by then he would have a large number of suitable boats at his disposal – ocean-going tugs and lifeboats – to bring off these last men in one lift. It was therefore agreed that Wake-Walker would ensure that he retained the necessary craft for this last lift which was to begin at 01.30 hours on 1 June and be completed by 03.00 hours.[20] Hopefully, by the time it was light enough for the Germans to see the beach clearly, the BEF would have gone.

Heavy cloud and poor visibility made air operations very difficult during the 30th and it brought some respite from the German attacks. Fighter

Command, on the other hand, patrolled at three- or four-squadron strength at frequent intervals throughout the day and the only enemy bombers they met were driven off. Gort paid tribute to the help given by British aircraft: 'Am extremely grateful for the valuable work of [the] RAF. Presence and action of fighters is of first importance in preventing embarkation being interrupted and is having most heartening effect on troops.'[21]

Bomber Command also played its part, with Blenheims attacking the German forces south of Dunkirk during the day and Wellingtons bombing the German columns heading for Dunkirk. Major L.F. Ellis, the official British historian of the fighting in France and Flanders, described one of the successful examples of the RAF's operation which took place late in the evening: 'There had been fighting all day at Nieuport and while attack and counter-attack had led to no great change, the enemy was moving up additional troops and the threat of a real break-through was serious. In the early evening six Albacores of the Fleet Air Arm and eighteen Blenheims bombed the enemy in Nieuport and troops behind the town massing for a further attack. The enemy's concentration there was broken up and no further attack was made before the 4th Division retired to the beaches. There were other successful sweeps by bombers of Bomber Command which attacked enemy columns moving towards the bridgehead from east and south and both Bomber Command and the Advanced Air Striking Force continued all night to attack enemy supply lines and communications.'[22]

The rate of embarkation was still increasing, helped by the arrival of private, what Ramsay called 'freelance', boats. As well as helping to take men directly off the beaches, they also recovered many of the small boats that had been abandoned and drifted out to sea. These small boats, of all kinds, were arriving in convoy after convoy. These included five little vessels, *Bee, Bat, Chamois, Hound* and *M.F.H.*, from Pickfords the removal firm which had been built to carry items between the mainland and the Isle of Wight. Three of these were manned by their own civilian crews. *Chamois* came under air attack and was twice forced to pull back. When she made a third attempt, she got to within two miles of Dunkirk but went to the help of two ships that had been bombed and were on fire. This 25-metre-long steel barge with its two–man crew, of E. Brown and L. Church, rescued 130 men from the burning ships, all of whom were French or Belgium.

Duncan Nicol, a former navy stoker, was assigned to the *Elizabeth Green*, a small pleasure craft with a rowing boat attached. He helped row the little boat backwards and forwards, taking as many men as it could carry to an anchored warship:

> We continued ferrying from the beach to the sloop, but on leaving the beach each time there was appeals to come back and on one occasion, when I said we have enough, we can't take any more, a little man, wearing glasses, a little soldier, he put his four fingers to hold the side of the whaler, and he said, 'will you please take me because I don't think I can stand any more. I shall be dead before you get back.' There was a sergeant in the whaler and he crashed his rifle down on this man's fingers and said, 'You heard what the man said and we can't take any more', and he completely severed the four fingers which fell into the bottom of the boat. The little man just fell back into the water and presumably died.[23]

The exact number of Little Ships that took part in the evacuation has never been officially confirmed. They included private sailing yachts and steam pinnaces, fishing boats, seaplane tenders, picket boats, and motor-boats. Six tugs from Tilbury were on their way to Dunkirk towing between them sixty-nine other small craft, all manned by eager crews, naval and civilian, willing to risk their lives and their boats to help the stranded soldiers.

One of those small boats that had made its way across the Channel to arrive off La Panne was Albert Harris' 35-foot cabin cruiser *Berkshire Lass*. Mr Harris had left Ramsgate on the morning of the 30th, in convoy with other such boats. He had taken two dinghies in tow. It was late evening when *Berkshire Lass* moved close inshore towards the soldiers standing waist-deep in the water: 'They piled aboard *Berkshire Lass* heavy boots playing havoc with the precious paint-work. Hobnails gashing the afterdeck and the white canvas roof of the cabin. They piled into the three boats, so many of them that Harris feared they would overturn the little craft, but an officer, who did not himself go aboard, saw to it that this did not happen. Then Harris put about and made for a drifter which lay out to sea.' Harris, like so many others, continued throughout the evening and into the night. Also, like so many others, *Berkshire Lass* was later lost, and Harris was wounded.[24]

The flow of troops through the perimeter had also improved throughout the day, meaning that there were fewer men crowding onto the beaches, making for less inviting targets for the *Luftwaffe* on the few occasions they appeared on the 30th. The German aircraft also had to deal with the RAF, which inspired Commander Dechaineux, to write: 'At 15.00 a very thrilling dog-fight between nine spitfires and a larger number of Messerschmitts and various types of German bombers was witnessed. Two spitfires were shot down and two enemy bombers. A fifth unaccounted plane was also shot down.'

It is also interesting to note the comments of one of the Royal Navy officers regarding the German aerial attacks. Commander Hector Richardson was the Senior Naval Officer at Bray Beach:

When being bombed in daylight and at night it is apparently the Army training for the men to lie over on their faces in a huddled heap and to await the completion of the air raid. I consider that if one lies over on one's face during an air raid, one gets the impression that the bombs when falling with very horrid shrieking noises are each and all coming to land right in the small of one's back. There is little doubt that the Army were considerably cowed by the bombing and I do feel that this form of inactivity during a raid is psychologically bad. I would have thought it better that the men be trained to stand up and take cover and loose off their rifles and anyhow look at the bomber, especially by day.[25]

The intense bombing of shipping the previous day had resulted in the order being given that on the 30th only one destroyer at a time should berth against the East Mole. But the reduced effort by the *Luftwaffe* on the 30th because of the poor weather encouraged Commander Maund at 17.00 hours to try to improve the rate of embarkation still further by instructing ships waiting off shore to use the Mole if they could find berthing space.

The German Air Force was far from idle, though, and it delivered a number of attacks, with many of the aircraft targeting not the ships loading troops but the already wrecked vessels. 'We got a great deal of amusement and satisfaction from this, for loading was proceeding apace with no casualties,' as Maund later reported:

I decided that the rate of embarkation must in some way be speeded up as the capacity of the ships now alongside was more than adequate for the rate of the flow of troops. This laid our vessels open to attack from the air … I therefore went down to the Eastern Arm [Mole] and rigged up a loud speaker [which had been sent over on the 30th] and addressed the troops in the following terms: 'Remember your pals, boys. The quicker you get on board, the more of them will be saved'.

This worked like a miracle. The thousands of troops, tired, depressed, and without food or water for days, broke into a double and kept it up for the whole length of the Eastern Arm for more than two hours.[26]

Maund's encouragement certainly paid dividends as around 15,000 men were taken off the East Mole between 18.00 to 21.00 hours. During that time, apart from other vessels using the East Mole, eight destroyers rescued 8,528 men and the packets *Prague*, *Royal Sovereign*, *St Helier* and *Tynewald*, recovered 5,694 troops. The hospital carrier *Dinard*, which berthed at the far end of the Mole also took a number of wounded on board.

THE FRENCH EVACUATION

French ships also began to arrive on the 30th. Some fifteen vessels reached Dunkirk harbour, including the destroyers *Foudroyant* and *Branlebas* and the torpedo boats *Bourrasque*, *Bouclier* and *Siroco*, two minesweepers, four trawlers, a tug and three fishing vessels.[27]

Bourrasque's participation in Operation *Dynamo*, however, did not last long. Amongst those onboard *Bourrasque* was a young French sailor, Quartermaster Louis Spitaels, who had been ordered with other sailors from the Ronarc'h barracks in Dunkirk to move to the harbour. The sailors marched from the barracks at 10.30 hours, reaching the harbour thirty minutes later. 'Everywhere, visions of horror;' Spitals recalled. 'Ambulances in flames, burning ruins, burnt corpses. The ground was covered with all kinds of debris … While we wait for the ship to arrive, we pick up a few wounded and put them behind a heap of coal. We also bury the corpses in the bomb holes that litter the ground.'

At 15.30 hours the first two French ships, *Branlebas* and *Bourrasque*, reached the Quai Felix Faure, and Spitals climbed aboard the *Bourrasque*. Taking on around 800 men (and one woman), *Bourrasque* set off for Dover along Route Y at its full speed of twenty-eight knots. 'But we're not safe,' exclaimed Spitals: 'Three aircraft spotted us and attack us without respite. Their machine-guns and those of the destroyer crackle. The bullets sweep the bridge, and the bombs whistle and burst around us.' Then, as *Bourrasque* was passing Nieuport, she came under fire from a German battery. The French boat moved as far over as she could to the edge of the swept channel, but when the torpedo boat was about five miles north of Nieuport, she was shook by a violent explosion. 'Is it a mine, a bomb, a torpedo? I do not know,' continued Spitals, 'The deck which is strewn with corpses, the officers intervene to maintain order. The boat was badly hit. Already it sinks slowly … Panic-stricken soldiers throw themselves into the water with their packs still on their backs. Orders are flying from all sides, given in vain.'

The first explosion was followed by a second even more violent one and Spitals was thrown into the sea: 'I find myself swimming in the middle of sailors, suitcases, wood debris of all kinds, losing blood through my ears and through my nose. I witness excruciating scenes that remain engraved in my memory.'

The ship came to a halt, badly damaged. Understandably, there was a degree of panic amongst the passengers, who believed the ship was sinking. Even though the captain had not declared that the warship should be abandoned, the ship's boats were lowered but so many crowded into them that they sank. Others jumped into the water. Yet *Bourrasque* was indeed sinking, having either struck a mine or been hit by artillery, sources disagree on this point, and broke in two. *Branlebas*, with 300 troops on board, was astern of *Bourrasque* and picked up 100 survivors. The Admiralty drifter *Yorkshire Lass*, and the armed trawler HMT *Ut Prosim* also helped. Amongst those saved by the trawler was Louis Spitals, who survived by clinging onto a canteen chair. Remarkably, at 05.30 hours on the 31st, fourteen hours later, the Pickfords' boat *Bat* picked up another fifteen survivors from the partially submerged wreck. They were found completely naked and covered in oil.[28]

The few French vessels that reached Dunkirk was not nearly enough shipping for the French troops gathered there and this formed the subject of a telephone conversation between Gort and Ironside. Gort complained that his orders and those of the French generals differed. Gort said that he had been told that the British were 'to stand together and share the evacuation facilities'. To this Ironside agreed. Unfortunately, Gort believed that this was incompatible with his prime consideration, which was for the safety of the BEF, and with large numbers of French troops pouring into the Dunkirk area, if he tried to evacuate the French and British troops in equal proportions, 'he would be prejudicing the successful evacuation of the BEF.'

Ironside gave an entirely unsatisfactory reply, saying that, indeed, saving the BEF was Gort's first objective but that he must 'do his best' to take away 'a fair proportion' of the French. This was far too vague an instruction, so Gort asked the C.I.G.S. for a written instruction from the Prime Minister to settle the matter officially which he could also show to *Général* Blanchard.[29]

Lieutenant J.A. Simpson was in command of minesweeper trawlers *Lord Grey* and *Clythness* engaged in sweeping for magnetic mines. Being based at Dover, he had seen a lot of what had taken place over the last few days, and had heard 'tragic stories, humorous stories [and] stories of great courage'. As the work the two trawlers were engaged upon was highly secret (even the Germans did not know how to sweep their own magnetic mines) they did not expect to be sent to Dunkirk unless the Germans seeded the approaches with fresh mines. However, on the 30th, Simpson was given one hour's notice to sail for Dunkirk, as indeed the enemy had dropped some mines into the waters off the evacuation beaches. 'We sailed out at 15.30 on a dull, cloudy day and the sea was as calm as a lake,' he later wrote:

Dunkirk was visible about 30 miles distant as it was burning furiously. On the way across we had met numerous British & some French Destroyer going 'full bat' for home, their decks a mass of khaki & all their guns at maximum elevation – ominous! We seemed to be the only people going our way and I suspected the worst – that we were too late. My orders were to enter the harbour and make fast to the most convenient stone quay, and report to Captain Tennant.

As no-one on board the ship had been to Dunkirk before, we approached very gingerly to the accompaniment of the most outrageous din and guided by a furious blaze. Hell itself could not put up a better show, I'm sure.[30]

Simpson saw that there were various destroyers and some six Yarmouth drifters off the harbour entrance which, owing to all the wrecks, were a bit 'chary' of entering. But then a Dutch skoot shot boldly past, which gave Simpson the confidence to enter Dunkirk. As Simpson moved slowly into the harbour, the skoot rushed back past *Lord Grey* and *Clythness* going the other way, 'as if he had definitely decided that it was no place for him!' Simpson persisted and *Lord Grey* tied up to the East Mole, with *Clythness* lying astern. 'We now had time to survey the situation by the eerie light of numerous oil fires and the flaming wreck of a British destroyer,' related Simpson:

> Bombing was continuous as was the whine of whistling bombs. There was no sign of anyone on the quay, which was – I now saw – completely severed just shoreward of us … This of course meant that we should have to move further into the inferno before I could land and endeavour to report to Captain Tennant. I may say I had the gravest doubts about that officer's safety, for it looked impossible to exist anywhere near the town.

Along with the skipper of *Clythness*, Tony Heckstall-Smith, Simpson stepped out onto the East Mole to try and find Captain Tennant:

> Armed to the teeth we now both clambered ashore and found the quay piled high with equipment of every description. Rifles, Bren guns, petrol, bicycles, ammunition, kitbags, coats, belts, gas masks, in fact every conceivable variety of gear. Aircraft were flying low over us and we felt no inclination to delay and examine some of the stuff.

The two men picked their way through the debris on the quay and came upon the steamer HMS *King Orry*. They hailed the skipper, who told them that the Mole was broken in a second place even closer to the town. Simpson considered that it would be too hazardous to try manoeuvring so close to shore and he decided to wait until daylight.

King Orry had sailed for Dunkirk on the 29th, and as she approached the harbour she was the target of an attack by German dive-bombers. Though straggled by six bombs, none caused any serious damage. It was a different matter, however, after the steam-packet turned-Armed Boarding Vessel moved towards the East Mole, as bombs rained down on all sides. The ship was violently shaken and the steering gear was put out of action. All instruments, woodwork, etc. were shattered. 'We were now attacked again but no direct hits were made,' reported Commander J. Elliott, 'bombs falling so close, however, as to give the impression of direct hits, especially as various debris flew up at every explosion'. With Elliott unable to steer the ship, he crashed against the Mole, but without causing any further real damage. Conscious that his ship would be unable to move until the steering gear had been repaired, Elliott sent his crew off *King Orry* to find shelter in Dunkirk.

On examining his ship, Elliott found that *King Orry* had been holed below the waterline in two or three places and that a fire had broken out on the starboard side. This Elliott was able to extinguish. Further damage was found and it was evident that, with the best will in the world, the steamer would not be capable of leaving the harbour before daylight.

Elliott found Tennant and discussed *King Orry*'s plight. Tennant told Elliott that if *King Orry* remained where it was when morning came, the steamer was certain to be destroyed by the *Luftwaffe*. Elliott had little choice but to try and manoeuvre his ship out of the harbour using his engines to steer, and at 03.00 hours, the crew of *King Orry* cast off.

Lord Grey's Lieutenant Simpson takes up the story again at this point:

> Things now were a little quieter and in preparation for an arduous day I decided to take a short rest. Hardly had I sat down and put my feet on the wardroom table, hopefully closing my eyes, when I was awakened – or rather disturbed – by the announcement that people could be heard calling for help, apparently just off the harbour mouth. Both ships [*Lord Grey* and *Clythness*] launched their boats in the direction from which the shouts came, and as they got louder, we could faintly discern part of the funnel & foremast of *King Orry*.

Water had poured into the stokehold of *King Orry* and, as she cleared the harbour, the steamer took on a severe list. It was immediately obvious that the ship was sinking and Elliott had no hesitation in ordering the crew to abandon ship.

Lord Grey's and *Clythness*'s boats rescued fourteen crew from *King Orry*, including Elliott, who was the last to leave his sinking ship. He stepped aboard *Lord Grey* with a cheery, 'Good evening, thanks!' The destroyer *Vivacious* picked up the rest of *King Orry*'s crew.

The destroyer *Anthony* anchored off Bray at 07.41 hours and landed a Royal Marine staff officer. She then embarked 620 troops which were brought off by small craft of every kind. But *Anthony* could not yet return to the UK as she had another task to perform – to land maps at Dunkirk, presumably to be taken to the naval HQ at Bastion 32. *Anthony* was not able to set off for Dover until after 11.00 hours.

After dropping off the troops at the Admiralty Pier, the destroyer was back in Dunkirk by 19.15 hours. An hour and ten minutes later *Anthony* sailed from the East Mole with another load of troops, but at 21.55 a lone enemy aircraft appeared at just 500 feet above her stern. 'He appeared to be correcting to starboard and revved up his engines,' wrote *Anthony*'s captain:

> Put wheel hard a port and eased on ship answering because of topweight. Observed 5 cylindrical bombs drop in a salvo of 4 and followed by 1 single. They fell on the starboard bow or on what would have been the original course, and were delay action. The fifth felt similar to the salvo of 4 but deeper and closer. Aircraft also machine gunned ship but no casualties ... When the lights went out and the ship considerably shaken, it was quite understandable that the Army Officers and soldiers in messdecks and enclosed spaces below attempted to gain the upper deck as quickly as possible. A 'panic' was entirely prevented by the various ratings present in the spaces who forcibly stopped and explained that the shakes were our own depth charges.[31]

The destroyer's Gyro and its magnetic compass were put out of action, as were its wireless receivers. Damage to elements of its turbines was also sustained, but its hull was still intact. *Anthony* was able to make its way back to Dover but only at ten knots going backwards, stern first.

HMS *Sabre* had reached Dover at 05.15 on the morning of the 30th, and just over three hours later, after borrowing a whaler from the depot ship HMS

Sandhurst, she was heading back to Dunkirk. By 11.45 hours she had secured alongside the East Mole and had filled up with troops. On shoving off it was found that the ship was aground, but by moving troops forward she lifted off and headed for England. In the struggle to get free *Sabre* had suffered some damage to her propellers and the asdic dome.

Nevertheless, she reached Dover at just 15.30 and was back at sea again just forty-five minutes later. Visibility was poor in the Channel and *Sabre* took the chance of crossing via Route Z. A drifting mine was sighted and was sunk by machine-gun fire.

The fog gradually dispersed and *Sabre* was spotted by a German reconnaissance aircraft, and as she was opposite Calais came under fire from shore batteries. 'Speed was increased to "Full"', wrote Commander Dean, 'and the wheel put over at each gun flash, keeping them between 20 and 70 degrees abaft the beam':

> The range was quickly found, however, and several hits sustained on the bridge and upperworks. Course was therefore altered to the northward, smoke was made, and the ship continued to zig-zag as much as possible without showing herself clear of the smoke. Just before turning away however, a shell passed through the Petty Officer's messdeck. It did not explode, but it passed through the Master Gyro compass, and a splinter from it penetrated the deck and so admitted water to No.2 Oil Fuel tank. With this tank out of action there was insufficient oil fuel remaining for the round trip to be completed. The D.G.[32] cable had been pierced in four places and the magnetic compass was therefore practically useless. The ship was therefore steered by the sun (fortunately visible) until traffic on Route 'X' was discerned. Thereafter it was possible to go from buoy to buoy. *Sandhurst*'s whaler was severely riddled with shell splinters but the damage to the ship (except for the gyro compass and oil fuel tank) was only superficial and not a man was touched.

Sabre reached Dover at 20.30, and repairs to the destroyer were put in hand immediately. She would be ready again for service in little more than twenty-four hours.

It was also on a destroyer that Lieutenant General Alan Brooke returned to England on the 30th. He had been instructed to hand over II Corps to Major General Bernard Montgomery (commander of the 3rd Division) and report to the War Office, where he was to be instructed to take command of a secondary force that would operate with the French Army after the evacuation from Dunkirk.

In his diary, he described his journey back to the coast: 'Congestion on roads indescribable. French army became a rabble and complete loss of discipline. [French] troops dejected and surly and refusing to clear road, panicking every time a Boche plane came over.'[33]

He was taken from the beach in an open boat at 19.15 hours, but the warship did not leave until after midnight:

> The five long hours at anchor with repeated visits from German bombers, the crash of bombs on the sea, the continuous firing of A.A. [anti-aircraft] guns, and the horrible sight of a destroyer being blown up by a bomb which we had witnessed the previous afternoon continually before our eyes [HMS *Grenade*].
>
> I am not very partial to being bombed whilst on land, but I have no wish ever to be bombed again whilst at sea. I have the greatest admiration for all sailors who so frequently were subjected to this form of torture during the war.[34]

The paddle steamer *Glen Gower* undertook its maiden trip to Dunkirk in the early evening of the 30th, her skipper, Acting Commander M.A.O. Biddulph, saw the evacuation areas for the first time:

> At 20.58 we turned to run along the coast past Dunkirk. Gunfire could be heard and a large fire was blazing in Dunkirk itself sending up columns of thick smoke which hung about like a pall over the beleaguered city ... At 21.21 there was heavy H.A. fire heard ahead and the tracers from Bofors guns could be seen streaking into the sky. Bombs could be seen exploding on the beaches and in the water close to. The noise of aeroplane engines could be heard but at this we could not see the planes themselves. We passed a number of sunken vessels of various types and a burned-out paddle minesweeper on the shore.[35]

It was completely dark when *Glen Gower* anchored off the beach in between its sister ship *Glen Avon* and another requisitioned paddle-steamer HMS *Snaefell*, some eight miles to the east of Dunkirk, on an ebb tide. Commander Biddulph sent its boats to the beach, but the boats reported back that they were having difficulty re-floating when full because of the rapidly falling tide. *Glen Gower*'s coxswain explained that the tired and dispirited troops were disinclined to help get the boats off the beach. Biddulph saw only one course of action open to him – to run his ship onto the beach in the hope that *Glen Gower* would lift off at the next high tide:

> Weighed anchor at 02.05 and ran the ship into the beach taking the ground at 02.20. The kedge anchor was laid out to prevent the stern swinging in. The idea of the beaching was that ladders and hawsers, hanging alongside, would be used by the troops to climb aboard with, after wading out to the bows. This idea proved to be impracticable, the ship being still some way from the water's edge, and the embarkation was continued by means of the ship's boats ... In the meantime, the ship became hard and fast broadside to the beach due to the fact that the kedge anchor dragged.

By 04.25 hours, *Glen Gower* had embarked 530 troops, but then a message was received from Wake-Walker for all paddle minesweepers to proceed alongside the East Mole. *Glen Gower* was pulled clear by *Snaefell*.

Glen Gower tied up against the East Mole shortly after 06.00 hours. Before she was able to take on any of the troops on the Mole, a whistling sound was heard and then an explosion, followed by ten more:

> I saw from the bridge a mass of black fragments leap up on the fo'c'sle ... The other explosions occurred very close to the ship, following rapidly upon one and other ... When the explosion ceased a hole was found in the fo'c'sle and I was informed that a shell had burst inside the ship on the stokers mess deck, killing five soldiers and wounding seven ... I proceeded later to the mess deck, which was a shambles of blood and brains.

Despite the casualties, there was no serious structural damage to the paddle steamer and the engines and steering remained unaffected. So the crew of *Glen Gower* stuck to their task, and waited for more troops to arrive. It proved to be an agonisingly long wait, as the troops that reached the Mole were directed to embark on the destroyers. It was only when the last destroyer was full, that *Glen Gower* could take more troops on board, allowing Biddulph to sail for England at 08.10 hours.

THE OTHER LIFEBOATS ARRIVE

The lifeboat *Prudential* reached Dunkirk at 20.00 hours. A light westerly wind was blowing and a dense black cloud of smoke from the burning oil-tanks swirled around and above the shore and the sea. Howard Knight moved the *Prudential* two miles along the coast to Malo-les-Baines to lie alongside a Dutch coaster until it was dark.

With the fall of night, Coxswain Knight sent three of his wherries to the shore each with one of his lifeboat-men on board. They rowed carefully towards the land shouting into the dark until they heard an answering call. Locating the desperate soldiers, the boats filled up with men. Knight then sent three more boats with twelve of the naval men. The sailors were to man the oars of the six boats and push the boats off the beach. The three boats set off but never returned.

So Knight sent a seventh boat with three sailors and, along with the other three boats, ferried increasing numbers of troops back to the *Prudential*. It was a slow and difficult operation. Each boat was rowed in stern first. The sailors would grab the rocking boat and hold it steady in the rolling surf until the troops waded out. There was no rush or panic. The soldiers only moved forward, waist-high in the water, when their officers gave the word. Just one man at a time could climb over the stern and a full boat amounted to a mere eight men.

The *Prudential* could hold 160 men fully-laden and eventually she reached capacity and Knight had to transfer the troops to a ship that lay further out in the deeper water. Back to her post went the Ramsgate lifeboat and by daybreak she had taken some 800 men off the Dunkirk beaches.

On one of its trips to the shore during the night a voice called out to the *Prudential*, 'I cannot see who you are. Are you a naval party?' 'No, sir', replied one of the lifeboat-men, 'we are the men of the crew of the Ramsgate lifeboat.' The voice called back, 'Thank you, and thank God for such men as you have this night proved yourselves to be.'[36]

Towards the late afternoon and into the early part of the night the Germans intensified their efforts to cross the canal at Nieuport. One of the most exposed parts of the line, and one that came under the severest pressure, was held by HQ troops. These men were mainly fitters, storemen and transport drivers. These were young, inexperienced soldiers, who had received only the barest minimum training on the weapons they carried since joining the army in France. Yet, according to Brigadier Clifton, they showed remarkable 'tactical sense, fire discipline, initiative and tenacity', even though they had never expected to find themselves in the firing line.

Clifton's mixed force held on until after nightfall, when it was relieved by the 10th and 12th infantry brigades. Due to continuing fire from the enemy, and the difficulty of communication in the darkness, the relief was not completed until the following morning.

The onset of night also saw a renewed attempt by the Germans to cross the canal just north of Furnes. Earlier, the Germans had launched their most determined effort of the day against this section of the perimeter, which was held by the 7th Guards Brigade and the 8th Brigade. The attack was beaten off, but the 4th Battalion, Royal Berkshire Regiment was so severely depleted in numbers that a company of the 1st Coldstream Guards was sent to take over that part of the line. Harry Dennis of the 1st Battalion, East Surrey Regiment, had been ordered to take a message to the Berkshires:

> I eventually found them. They looked as though they had been put through a mincer. I approached a young officer. 'I'm looking for the Commanding Officer of the Berkshires,' I said. 'That's me,' he replied. He was a Lieutenant, not a Colonel or Major or Captain. It appeared they were down to 87 men in the battalion.[37]

Furnes itself was held by 1st and 2nd battalions, Grenadier Guards. Signalman George Jones was with the 1st Battalion: 'We saw and felt the town of Furnes tumble about us. The Germans expended untold quantities of ammunition upon the area, and us! Driven into the depths of cellars, rows of red bricked houses became an inferno of exploding rooftops.'[38]

At around 22.00 hours the attack was renewed and the enemy succeeded in breaking across the canal. But the Guards counter-attacked, drove them back across the water and restored the front.[39]

Over to the west of the perimeter, the men holding Burgues also came under an intense bombardment during the night. Private Hector Morgan was with 'D' Company of the 1st Battalion the Loyal Regiment near the town's Ypres Gate:

> We were jumping from door to door. The German gunners were dropping shell after shell and as soon as they had dropped one, off we'd go into another doorway. It so happened that I was flattening myself in one of the doorways when he [the enemy] dropped one about fifty yards from me. All of a sudden I felt this terrible bash on my back and I said to one of my mates, that's my lot. I've had it.[40]

As it happened Private Morgan had been struck by a cobblestone that had been blasted up by the exploding shell and was not seriously wounded. There were, nonetheless, heavy casualties from the shelling mounted and it was only a matter of time before the town would have to be abandoned, or its defenders overrun.

By the end of Day 5 of Operation *Dynamo*, 53,823 men had been rescued, of which 29,512 had been taken off the beaches and 24,311 from the harbour and the East Mole. The total recovered for these five days was 126,606. According to Gort's estimation, there remained just 80,000 British troops within the perimeter. His job was all but done. This was made clear to him in a message from the Secretary of State:

> Continue to defend the present perimeter to the utmost in order to cover maximum evacuation now proceeding well. Report every three hours through La Panne. If we can still communicate we shall send you an order to return to England with such officers as you may choose at the moment when we deem your command so reduced that it can be handed over to a Corps Commander. If communications are broken

you are to hand over and return as specified when your effective fighting force does not exceed the equivalent of three divisions. This is in accordance with correct military procedure and no personal discretion is left to you in the matter. On political grounds, it would be a needless triumph to the enemy to capture you when only a small force remained under your orders. The Corps Commander chose by you should be ordered to carry on the defence in conjunction with the French and evacuated whether from Dunkirk or the beaches, but when in his judgement no further proportionate damage can be inflicted on the enemy he is authorised in consultation with the senior French Commander to capitulate formally to avoid useless slaughter.

Gort had been sent to defend the great nation of France and had found himself defending just a few square miles by the sea. Though he had been forced to withdraw, there was no ignominy in the retreat to Dunkirk. The BEF had not been defeated, and now he could hand over command in the knowledge that the bulk of the army was already safely back in the UK, and would be able to fight again another day.[41]

Chapter 8

Operation *Dynamo*: Day 6, Friday 31 May

It had been thought that the evacuation would only last for forty-eight hours before it was terminated by enemy action but after five days the perimeter still held, despite repeated attempts by the Germans to cross the Furnes-Bergues canal in rubber boats throughout the 30th. The Germans, therefore, concentrated their efforts on the town of Furnes, held by 1st and 2nd battalions, Grenadier Guards, during the night of 30/31 May. It seemed evident that this part of the perimeter could not hold much longer and if the enemy could break through at this point they could swoop down on La Panne, and the tired and almost defenceless troops on the beaches would be slaughtered.

One Guardsman, whose name was withheld, spoke of the German attacks:

> They came over absolutely regardless of our bullets, all of them great big fellows. They were armed with Tommy guns and sometimes would stand a few yards in front of us, spraying us with bullets – but not for long.
>
> The shock troops were good. The infantry who came after them were different altogether. Some of them were mere children. Among those we captured were some only 17 years old.
>
> The shock troops came over with nothing but a Tommy gun and spare ammunition hanging on their belt – no gas mask, no pack, no gas cloak. They also wear armour-plated waistcoats. We examined some and found that this was so.[1]

The whole of the German operations against Dunkirk were finally put under a single command – that of General George von Kuechler's Eighteenth Army of Army Group B – the change taking place at 02.00 hours on the 31st. This was to release Rundstedt's panzer divisions for the drive south towards the Somme, where it was believed that a large French army was still intact. The Battle of France was still not won and, as had already been seen, it was the panzer divisions that were the most effective element of the German forces, and already Rundstedt had lost nearly half of his armoured strength. To waste any more of his tanks in the broken, ditch-strewn fields around Dunkirk against an enemy that no longer posed a threat and was evacuating would have been a poor use of such a resource. So, the Eighteenth Army, which had been engaged in Holland and against the Belgian Army, was now made responsible for the destruction or capture of the Allied troops in the bridgehead. The forces that came under General von Kuechler's command were the IX, X, XIV and XXVI Corps, which included the S.S. Adolf Hitler Regiment.[2]

As a result of these changes, heavy shelling of the beaches by the German artillery during the night had ceased by 03.00 hours, allowing large numbers of troops to be evacuated and by full dawn the beaches were very nearly clear of troops. The Senior Naval Officer at Bray, Commander Hector Richardson, had been told not to allow either himself or any of his party be taken prisoner and, as no further large-scale embarkation seemed possible, he calculated that the time had arrived for him to make his getaway: 'We decided to take over a whaler that we had salved and to go to the nearest destroyer to report to the Senior Naval Officer (Wake-Walker). We waited for high water and at about 07.30 put to sea. There was a very heavy surf running and we had only an uneven set of oars, rope crutches and only an oar to steer by. We approached two destroyers but they both got underway. Two other destroyers passed us at about 7 cables but paid no attention to us.

'After about an hour as if from nowhere appeared the Margate lifeboat. We asked the Coxswain to take us to the nearest destroyer but all were underway at this time. He was returning to Margate and so we came back with him. The men in my party were completely exhausted and were asleep within five minutes of being onboard the lifeboat.'

The Naval Officer-in-Charge, Beaches, Captain John Howson, was still on the beach at Bray, however, and his report illustrates conditions at this time:

At 0400 there was a very considerable number of destroyers, paddlers, trawlers, skoots, etc., off Bray, and embarkation was proceeding satisfactorily, but a lop [choppy sea conditions] had already started. There were about 10 motor yachts which had arrived from England. These craft drew 6-7 feet and were unable to get close in to any of the beaches. During the forenoon, considerable towing of empty craft towards the beach was carried out, and only about two boats were allowed to get adrift and ultimately ground. With the falling tide, however, a number of boats were seen to ground and remain ashore until the tide rose in the afternoon … Other power boats broke down. Nevertheless, the embarkation, much hindered by the lop, proceeded satisfactorily. As further destroyers and sloops arrived, they were directed to lower their motor boats and whalers as this had not already been done; these boats were quite invaluable. About noon, the lop began to subside and with the rising tide conditions for embarkation very greatly improved, more boats were sent in and more boats floated off and matters were proceeding very well.[3]

The respite from the shelling did not last long and it was still early morning when German artillery near Nieuport opened-up and began shelling the shore at La Panne with great accuracy. A number of the small boats were sunk and the embarkation was disrupted as the ships moved westwards out of range of the enemy guns.

The Eighteenth Army launched a major assault upon the perimeter held by II Corps. The 4th Battalion, East Yorkshire Regiment and the 4th and 5th battalions, the Green Howards of 150th Brigade, found themselves in an almost indefensible position, as the Officer Commanding 'C' Company 5th Green Howards, Captain Tony Steele, was all too painfully aware:

My Company had a frontage of 800 yards, which was far too big to hold successfully. More important still, the German side of the canal in front of us was completely wooded, whereas on the Dunkirk side the terrain was completely flat and open. We dug in in sections and there was absolutely no way to camouflage the trenches; the enemy just climbed trees on the other side, spotted every last one of our positions on ground that was as flat as your hand, then brought up their heavy mortars and systematically plastered us.[4]

The 1/6th Battalion, East Surrey Regiment of the 10th Brigade also came under heavy pressure, the Germans crossing the canal at first light and storming the brickworks it held as a strongpoint. The East Surrey's 1st Battalion from the 11th Brigade was sent to help. The perimeter held, but only just. At one stage the two battalion commanders had to man a Bren gun together, with one lieutenant colonel feeding the gun while the other fired it.[5]

There was an even closer call when a massive assault upon the 8th Brigade saw the Germans break through the perimeter near Furnes. The 2nd Battalion Grenadier Guards was sent to plug the gap. Second Lieutenant Jones found two battalions of the brigade in a state of panic, abandoning their positions. The fate of the BEF hung in the balance. The men had been spooked and nothing, it seemed, could stop them running away – until they faced the bayonets of the Grenadiers. Jones managed to restore order, even being forced to shoot some of the panicked troops. The line held and by the middle of the afternoon the enemy pulled back.[6]

The Germans, though, were far from finished. The Durham Light Infantry, its 6th, 8th and 9th battalions, forming II Corps' 151st Brigade, held the small village of Les Moeres ten kilometres north-east of Bergues. Again, the Germans stormed across the canal, and again the line held. The Germans then did what they should have done before their attack and bombarded the DLI's positions. The German shells hammered into the main building in the village, the château, which the DLI had to abandon.

Furnes itself, held by the 1st Battalion Grenadier Guards, also came under attack, as did the positions along the canal to the east of the town where the 2nd Battalion Coldstream Guards were posted. These battalions of I Corps held their ground until nightfall when the decision to thin the line came into effect and the Grenadiers were told to make their way to the beach. From 1 June onwards the perimeter would be occupied by far fewer troops and it would require heroic action to hold it. This would result in the first Army Victoria Cross of the war, the story of which will soon be told.

MORE LITTLE SHIPS

Tennant spent the night of 30/31 at G.H.Q. A number of meetings took place there, in which Tennant was at lengths to explain to the Army commanders that if the rest of the BEF was to be saved it could only be accomplished by using the East Mole to its maximum. Even given good sea conditions, embarkation from the beaches would be a slow and lengthy process. He explained that a destroyer 'going full out with her boats to the beaches' could only embark 600 men in about twelve hours, whereas this could be done in twenty minutes at the Mole. This information was received with some misgivings:

> Some of the G.H.Q. staff expressed disappointment that more could not be done to push on with the embarkation off the beaches in a surf. I was satisfied that when the weather permitted everything possible was being done by the officers I had placed there, but I continually stressed that troops should be moved to Dunkirk and maximum numbers should also be available.
>
> Political pressure was now being brought to bear on the C. in C. that the evacuation must be on a fifty-fifty basis with the French. My only stipulation was that at all costs we should be allowed free use of the Eastern arm while the French used the port, outer harbour and beaches.[7]

The Little Ships, while only playing a supporting role, would still be required to lift men from the beaches. Tennant's estimate was based on a destroyer using only its own boats and clearly if more boats were available, embarkation would be much quicker.

Consequently, Tennant continued to urge the Admiralty for more vessels. These are the signals he sent during the morning:

> 0320. Request more ships to load Dunkirk.
>
> 0445. Every available ship will be required at Dunkirk during the next two hours to evacuate rest of army.
>
> 0605. Embarkation proceeding satisfactorily in spite of bombardment. I would again stress the need for more ships and constant fighter protection.

The slow state of embarkation from the beaches was exemplified in the experiences of HMS *Impulsive*. The destroyer sailed from Dover at 04.00 hours, arriving off the beaches to the east of Dunkirk three hours later having travelled along Route X. Lieutenant Commander William Scott Thomas reported that there were thousands of soldiers on the beach but very few boats to take them off. *Impulsive* had, by this time, just one whaler. The only power boat in the area was a large War Department motor boat with an Army officer, a Colonel Hutchings, in charge. Hutchings towed *Impulsive*'s whaler and a cutter backwards and forwards from the beach and loaded 450 men onto the destroyer, but it took over five hours. Though Tennant may have exaggerated a little in his calculations, he was clearly right in his conviction that it was only with more ships and boats that the rest of the BEF could be saved.

As it happened, as *Impulsive* was waiting for more soldiers to be brought out to it that it grounded aft on a wreck, damaging both its propellers and shafts. Thomas abandoned *Impulsive*'s embarkation efforts and it made its way back across the Channel on one engine.

The morning had seen the loss of the French destroyer *Siroco* after being attacked by German E-boats. She was on her way to Dover with 770 troops from Dunkirk when the noise of aircraft was heard overhead and the skipper slowed to seven knots to reduce her phosphorescent wake. Waiting silently in the dark was *Oberleutnant zur See* Christansen's *S-23* and *S-26*. At 01.45 hours *Siroco* was hit by two torpedoes. A column of flame was seen to shoot 200 feet into the air. Moments later she rolled over and sank. Only 252 men survived.[8]

Nevertheless, vessels of all descriptions arrived throughout the 31st. A semi-official record of the services of many of the Little Ships was compiled after Operation *Dynamo* by one of the Naval officers who travelled with the first flotilla, Temporary Lieutenant A. Dann, in which he portrays the assembly of these vessels with eloquence:

> From all around the compass they came. From up the river, along the coast, from the yachting harbours, the pleasure beaches, Naval ports and fishing towns – anything that would float, move under its own power, or collect a dozen or so men from the beaches where they waited. Each boat with its own tiny crew was thrown more or less upon its own resources; and upon the fortunes of war and the initiative of each boat's captain depends the story each may subsequently tell.[9]

These included cockle boats from the Thames Estuary that had never ventured beyond those waters and only one of the crews had travelled further than Ramsgate. Six of these came from Leigh-on-Sea – *Renown, Reliant, Endeavour, Leticia, Resolute* and *Defender*. When they arrived off the beaches of Bray and

La Panne, it was found that the swell was too great for the small boats to try and take men off the beaches. Instead, they operated a form of ferry service, taking troops off the East Mole to the larger ships waiting in deeper water. On board *Leticia* was 'Jimmy' Dench:

> During the penultimate ferrying trip from the small fishing boats to the larger ships out at sea: a shell burst between the last boat and us. We turned back to go out, but the signaller that we had on board, and who had only been 'out' for about six weeks and never been under fire, said, 'We've got to go in again' (to rescue more soldiers). So we went in.

The eighty-foot former First World War submarine-chaser *Tigris 1*, which had been converted by Tough Brothers at Teddington to a passenger boat and normally took tourists from Richmond to Hampton Court during the summer months, had been under Admiralty orders since early on the 27th. By Friday the crew was thoroughly worn out. This following passage from one of the crew members gives some indication just how exhausting and difficult rescuing the troops could be:

> Ships sunk everywhere, fuel oil as thick as could be, wreckage all over the place ... it took the heart out of us ...
>
> We start to load up with French troops. What a sight they look! Dirty, unshaven, tired – and hungry too, I expect. Some were crying at the start of coming aboard. I wonder how long they have been on the beach? Nearly a week by the look of them. They came aboard each side of the boat. I was leaning over the side, over the safety chain that went around the boat. I leaned down over the chain to pull one man up. He was a big chap. He took my right hand in his left hand and with his right hand he grabbed hold of the stanchion which is attached to the flange and screwed to the deck with screw four inches long. I had my left foot on the fore side of the flange. It gave me more purchase for helping him aboard. My toe had got under the flange somehow when this Frenchman started to pull himself up. The flange came down on my foot. That with his weight and a screw in the flange! Did I shout! The screw had gone through the top-cap of my shoe between my big toe and the one next to it.[10]

One of the most remarkable little boats to cross to France on the 31st was the 45-foot ex-naval steam pinnace *Minotaur* – it was remarkable in that it was crewed, in part, by sea scouts! The Mortlake Group Scout Master, believed to be Mr Tom Towndrow, took the scout's boat across to France:

> Destroyer after destroyer raced past, almost cutting the water from beneath us, and threatening to overturn us with their wash. We approached the beach with great caution at Dunkirk, because of the wrecks. We found things fairly quiet, and got on with our allocated job of towing small open ships' boats, laden with soldiers, to troop transports anchored in deep water, or of loading our ship from the open boats and proceeding out to the transports.
>
> Conditions did not remain quiet for long. We were working about a quarter of a mile away from six destroyers. Suddenly all their anti-aircraft guns opened fire. At the same time we heard the roar of 25 Nazi planes overhead. Their objective was the crowded beach and the destroyers. Salvo after salvo of bombs was dropped. Adding to the deafening din were air raid sirens sounding continuously on the shore. One 'plane made persistent circles round us. Another Nazi 'plane was brought down in flames, far too close for our liking![11]

James Christmas was also on *Minotaur*: 'We were ordered to only save able-bodied men, as their fighting ability may be required at any time on their arrival. This was one order we quickly forgot, as there were many men standing in the queues with water up to their chins that were wounded. It would take a much braver man than myself to say, "Sorry mate, but can't take you aboard", men who had been walking targets as they headed towards the beaches under constant enemy action, totally exhausted, but with one object in mind – survival.'[12]

Minotaur continued to operate off the beach until she was low on fuel, and then she sailed back to England. *Minotaur* did not return to Dunkirk, but the sea scouts did, returning as crew on another boat for the final evacuation.

Sub Lieutenant A. Carew Hunt took charge of the little Dutch eel boat *Johanna* which had a diesel engine and was capable of about six knots. The crew consisted of a Leading Hand and four ratings and three Dutchmen, who owned the boat and could not speak English. They set off from Ramsgate on the night of 29 May in convoy with two other boats. Soon, though, Sub Lieutenant

Hunt found himself and his crew alone and with no charts. He cast around and saw a ship anchored off Goodwin Sands, to which he secured his little boat, remaining there throughout the night.

The next morning, Hunt returned to Ramsgate where he succeeded in joining up with the Dutch skoot *Jutland*, which towed *Johanna* across to France that evening, the two vessels anchoring around two miles east of Dunkirk at 23.30 hours on the night of the 30th, sending in the boat's whaler and cutter:

> By this time the beach was swarming with French soldiers [but] I could not get my boats within 100 yards of the shore because of the shallowness of the water. I summoned my limited store of French to my aid and with cries of 'En Avant mes heros' and '*Courage mes enfants*' I tried to tempt them into the water. My efforts were unavailing and so I had to go and fetch them myself. My first leap into the water took me into the only deep patch for miles and I went in up to my neck. Struggling out of the hole I waded ashore. Seeing me only up to my waist the French came on in a rush and I was compelled to draw my revolver and brandish it threateningly. This quietened them down a bit but when they got to the boats only a few were strong enough to get in so my crew and I had to lift them on board.
>
> We did six trips and brought off about 200 in all, each time I had to go into the water and get them. At 02.30 the captain of the Schoot reckoned it was time to go. I only had ten Frenchmen on board the *Johanna* as it was a bit choppy and all had to go below. They all suffered from sea sickness on the way back.[13]

After reaching Ramsgate, Sub Lieutenant Hunt was re-assigned to another vessel and we will read of his further exploits in due course.

The increasingly heavy seas experienced on the 31st also caused problems for Lieutenant R.H. Irving, who commanded a crew of five on the motor boat *Triton* which arrived off La Panne on 30 May. Irving placed *Triton* just beyond the surf, from where he towed boatloads of troops out to destroyers and trawlers. He continued in this work until 02.00 hours on the 31st when he went just a little too close to the beach and the motor-boat grounded. He threw out the anchor as far astern as he could and tried to pull the boat off. As the tide was coming in, he was able to pull the boat clear at 04.00 hours and then carried on as before. At about 08.00 a strong north wind developed causing a heavy swell which made going alongside the larger ships a difficult operation as the boat was rolling and pitching at every turn. Irving continued ferrying from the beach until 13.30:

I was heading close inshore at this time, no boats in sight, and heavy shelling was taking place, suddenly the shelling became terrific, and my Cox. called out 'For God's sake get off, Sir, look, all the Destroyers have left'. It was as he said, but a small Merchant ship remained. I closed her and saw she too was heaving up, so I proceeded after the destroyers towards Dunkerque. I was the last Naval Officer to leave La Panne, and the last Naval Boat. The troops had all disappeared from the beach. I proceeded along the beach close inshore, until I came to the most Easterly position from Dunkerque in which our ships lay. I got a very heavy boat load of troops in tow.

At this time a terrific aerial battle was on, shells from shore batteries were falling around and bombs dropping all over the place in close proximity. As I was towing this boat I saw a bomb hit the pleasure steamer *Prince of Wales*. I closed her and took aboard two badly wounded Officers and two ratings. I offered to go aboard as she was sinking slowly, but was told only two dead remained on board.

Just before this, ordinary seaman Purbrick fell overboard from exhaustion and I picked him up somehow. My Cox. was sleeping on his feet on and off and the two others lay down and stood up as strength permitted. The C.O. of the *Prince of Wales*, although covered in blood, offered to try and steer the boat.

I then saw a man swimming naked in the water. Stopped and got him. Next a heavily loaded boat of soldiers turned right over close inshore, and left the men struggling in the water. I got down to them and rescued the lot personally hauling them aboard with my crews' feeble assistance. While doing this, I got a rope round my Starboard screw and fouled the rudder. I now had a full load of soldiers on board (six wounded) a full boat load towing and soldiers clinging to the stern.

With what I thought was the last of my strength, I got my launch alongside a lifeboat and from there hauled her hand over hand, by means of a grass rope, up to the sloop *Mosquito*.[14]

Over the course of eight hours, as the evacuation was reaching its conclusion, these small boats helped rescue hundreds of troops as the Germans closed in upon the Dunkirk perimeter. When there was no more that they could do, many returned to England, including the Essex cockle-boats – but then tragedy struck. *Leticia*'s Jimmy Dench described the incident: 'we saw another boat coming up behind us. It was the *Renown*, and, yelling that they had engine trouble, they made fast to our stern … We towed them 3.5 fathoms of rope being the distance between us. That was 1.15 am [1 June] … Tired out, the engineer, seaman and signaller went to turn in, when, at about 1.50 am, a terrible explosion took place, and hail of wood splinters came down on our deck. In the pitch dark, you could see nothing, and we could do nothing … except pull the tow rope which was just as we passed it to the *Renown* about three quarters of an hour before.'

Renown had hit a mine and little fishing boat and all three fishermen from Leigh-on-Sea that were onboard were blown to pieces, along with a young seaman from the Merchant Navy who had volunteered to join the crew.[15] Ramsay wrote of these that, 'They were all volunteers who were rushed over to Dunkirk in one day, probably none of them had been under gunfire before and certainly not under Naval discipline … In spite of this … all orders were carried out with great diligence even under actual shell fire and aircraft attack.'[16]

A reporter for the *Daily Mirror*, Ewart Brookes, volunteered to help crew a private motor-yacht, the name of which, due to wartime censorship, could not be named. All we know is that the owner of the yacht was a grey-haired London doctor and that he had two sons with the BEF:

> We were the Harry Tate navy – open motor-boats, slick varnished motor-cruisers, hard-bitten fishing boats, Thames barges and the 'shilling trip round the lightship' pleasure boat of the peacetime beach. It looked like a holiday cruise as we set course …
>
> When the [French] coastline was only a grey smudge, above us was heard a deep drone. Bellowing German machines flew low over the bigger ships off the coast, ships we were to unload from our trailing string of small boats.
>
> 'Close in, put your small boats ashore, fill them up and take them off to the large craft.' These were the simple orders …

The dark waters splashed whitely. The solders waded out to us, dead beat, heavy-eyed, bomb-stunned, and clambered aboard with the help of our crew. On the beach were thousands, many wounded. Hour after hour we helped them aboard, until our arms ached, pulling them over the side, giving them a drink of water, giving them coats, life-belts, anything on which to rest their heads.[17]

Captain Lemon Webb was sailing up the River Thames on his barge *Tollesbury*. He was passing Erith when a naval launch came alongside and instructed him to proceed to Cory's jetty for orders. There, Webb and his young lad of nineteen, were given a choice to leave the ship or to volunteer to help evacuate the BEF from Dunkirk. Neither of them hesitated and by 14.00 hours *Tollesbury*, with the larger *Ethel Everard*, was on its way across the Channel, towed by the tug *Sun XI*. Webb wrote of his experiences when he reached the beaches, around midnight, in a letter two his two children:

The tug shot us off but we had not enough way to reach the beach so we got out the oars and rowed her on. We had to stop at times breaking water as planes came over and the water was like fire.

A French battery was close and they took up firing protection. The French soldiers were shouting 'barge, barge,' frantic to get aboard, they waded in up to their armpits to meet us.

I dropped leaboards to hold her, it was calm, we put the ladders over, but the cabin one broke, then we lowered the boat for them, and they got in and my cook was pulling them up over the rails; it was a job to get their knees up on the gunwale with all their gear on.[18]

Tollesbury was stuck on the beach for hours. The crew set the sails and tried to push her off the beach with the boom, but she was simply too overloaded and the wind was against her. Eventually, she got into deeper water and the barge's naval gunner managed to signal with flags to a British destroyer, 'and was fast coming alongside to get men off,' continued Webb, 'when scores of jerries came over and our ships both sides let go all their guns at them, the planes nearly touched us; they raced off full speed circling round us. Firing also [came from the] shore batteries. They made dives at us dropping bombs just clear. We had about four hours of that altogether as they kept coming at us, until we were nearly half way back to England.'

Henry John Osborne was hoping to gain a commission with the RNVR and was, on 30 May, actually attending a lecture for a qualification in 'practical piloting' that would help his application, when the lecture was interrupted and the attendees asked to report to the Port of London Authority Building near the Tower of London at 18.30 that evening. They were told to man lifeboats that had been taken from sea-going ships. These were then formed in lines of four or five boats and towed over to Dunkirk by tug. Henry takes up his story after they had reached the beaches:

> The troops were very well disciplined, just waiting in long columns, hoping to be taken off. They were all dead beat, having had a terrible time fighting their way to the beaches. We were able to get right to the sandy beach and took on board about 30 British soldiers. They were travelling 'light' having discarded most of their equipment. We rowed away from the shore and took our 'passengers' to the nearest craft lying off shore that we could find, a tug, a drifter, a trawler, anything that could risk coming in so close.
>
> We returned to the beach; probably a different section because as soon as we approached a crowd of French soldiers, with all their equipment, rushed out into the water and climbed on board before we had a chance to turn the boat around and headed out to sea. As the tide was falling we became stuck on the sand. With great difficulty, we persuaded the Frenchman to get out of the boat and we were then able to turn it round and prevent it broaching (getting broadside onto the sea). At one time, I was almost up to my neck in the water holding the bow of the boat pointed out to seawards — still in my 'interview' suit! We transferred that load eventually to one of the waiting craft and made one or two more trips before deciding dawn was approaching and it was our turn to make the return journey and get on the way before daylight.
>
> Through all this time we were so occupied with what we were doing that we were hardly aware of all the other activity going on all around us. It is always like this 'in action'. There were aircraft overhead, friend and foe, all the time; continual bombardment of the town, harbour and of the beaches by the Germans. Ships were being sunk and survivors rescued. All around the town and harbour of Dunkirk fires were blazing, a heavy pall of smoke hanging over it all. From much further off shore the British ships were bombarding the German positions.

We eventually left the beaches just before dawn on Saturday, 1st June.[19]

As seems to be the case, quite the opposite from the ordered, controlled embarkation was experienced by others, and Colonel Whifeld was scathing in his criticism in his report to Lieutenant Brownrigg, the Adjutant General:

> It is with regret that I must bring to your notice the behaviour of many officers, both junior and senior, who passed through Dunkirk during the evacuation. During the heavy and incessant air raids both by day and by night it was more than essential that the officers should stay with the men and attempt to calm them and lead them, if possible, to a place of safety. In many instances, however, the officers departed for the boats leaving their men behind to be rescued later by members of my staff. Officers whom I detained for jobs which might delay their departure for a day or so disappeared and I have no doubt embarked for England without permission.[20]

Whitfeld also complained about the military police, who were obviously essential in maintaining discipline: 'These men awaited the arrival of darkness, left their positions and embarked for England without permission.'

Somewhat surprisingly, considering their humanitarian role, some members of the Royal Army Service Corps also looked first at their own survival: 'On more than one occasion,' Whitfeld continued, 'these men drove their ambulances down to the docks, and slipped away in the dark onto the boats, leaving the wounded or empty ambulances on the quayside. It is due to this disgraceful conduct on the part of certain R.A.S.C. drivers, that the evacuation of the wounded at one time almost failed to function.'

Similar ill-discipline with troops that had been left to fend for themselves was noted by Coxswain Parker of the *Lord Southborough*:

> The wind had by this time veered to the N.W. and was making a nasty surf on the shore. We continued to make further trips to the destroyer, how many times, I do not know. By this time things were getting bad. Troops were rushing out to us from all directions and were being

drowned close to us and we could not get them, and the last time we went into the shore, it seemed to me we were doing more harm [than good] by drawing the men off the shore, as with their heavy clothing, the surf was knocking them over and they were unable to get up. The whaler from the destroyer which went into the shore with us on our last trip was swamped, so was the motor pinnace that was working with the whaler; and so it was all along the sands as far as I could see. Both sides of us there was not a boat left afloat.[21]

The swell, caused by a stiffening on-shore breeze, was indeed making things very difficult. Many of the towing-boats had capsized and had lost their crews, and the motor-boats were being tossed around so much in the surf that they could not reach the beach. The problems facing the skippers of the ships is exemplified by that encountered by Temporary Lieutenant A.L.U. Braithwaite, the captain of the paddle mine-sweeper *Westward-Ho*:

I arrived at Dawn and in the first place attempted to put the ship ashore close enough to embark troops by wading. This proved futile as the water on this coast is so shallow that the ship was aground over a mile from the beach. I then sent the boats in but there was a ground swell which was breaking too heavily on the beach for the boats to get off without immense difficulty.

The boats were repeatedly swamped and matters were not made easier by the reluctance of the troops to wade out. Some of my crew managed to assist a Motor Boat which made several trips towing the lifeboats but the engine seized up & this too drifted ashore and capsized.

Both my lifeboats were by this time hopelessly waterlogged and damaged but a Naval Cutter which was adrift was picked up and made two trips. On the second of these such difficulty was experienced in getting the heavily loaded boat clear of the beach that I was seriously afraid I should lose the crew, and when the cutter finally arrived along-side I decided that the risk was too great, and that I would shift the ship nearer to Dunkirk in the hope of finding better conditions. It had been necessary the whole time to manoeuvre the ship as the tide was falling and the boats were being swept down the coast as they pulled off, a grass rope streamed to assist them being useless as it was carried away by the tide.[22]

It was evident that what was urgently needed was a second lorry pier, and the men were set to work at La Panne which, it was hoped, would be beyond the range of the German artillery at Nieuport.

Nowhere though, was beyond the range of the *Luftwaffe*, and once the early morning haze had burnt off, the Luftwaffe mounted three raids during the day, at 14.15, 17.00 and 19.00 hours. Fighter Command did what it could, flying eight patrols with 289 Spitfires, Hurricanes and Defiants in large multi-squadron sorties. It proved to be a bad day for the RAF, losing nineteen aircraft whilst only able to claim ten enemy machines.[23]

The skipper of HMS *Express* witnessed some of those successes of Fighter Command:

On arrival off Dunkirk roads all ships present engaged enemy aircraft intermittently who were carrying out bombing attacks, and the prospect of going alongside the Eastern side of Dunkirk Pier was investigated. At about 1700 dive bombing attacks on Destroyers off Bray was particularly heavy. Two attacks were carried out on *Express*, one salvo was a near miss ahead, and the other straddled, five depth charge type bombs falling close all round the ship. Aircraft were heavily engaged and no damage was sustained except for small breakages. At 1830 *Express* again entered Dunkirk and embarked about 700 troops sailing at 1900.

Shortly after a large number of enemy bombers and fighters attacked ships approaching Dunkirk including a large number of small craft. Several aircraft were seen to be destroyed as a result of our aircraft attacking.[24]

The Fleet Air Arm provided the second fighter patrol of the day, watched by Pilot Officer D.H. Clarke who had reported for duty at RAF Detling earlier on the 31st:

The thirty-seven Skuas and Rocs were a splendid sight as they took off in mass formation …They came back just before lunchtime, so I stayed to watch them land. There were not many – I counted six; where were the others? One belly-flopped and I went across to see what had happened, the blood-wagon passing me on the way. That aircraft was a complete write off. Bullets and cannon shells had ripped the fuselage from end to end – the after cockpit was sprayed liberally with blood, the inside of the glass-house reddened throughout by the forward draught. The front cockpit, if anything was worse. Two bullet holes through the back of the pilot's seat showed where he had been hit, and his parachute, still in position, was saturated with blood. The instrument panel was shattered wreckage, and on the floor was a boot – and the remains of a foot

I was nearly sick with the horror of it. How that pilot flew home will never be known, for I found out that he was dead when they dragged him out. Of those thirty-seven Skuas and Rocs, nine came back; of the nine only four were serviceable.[25]

It was on 31 May that Pilot Officer Al Deere of 54 Squadron reached Dunkirk after crash-landing onto the beach to the north of Nieuport. After a series of adventures and help from the Belgians, plus a lift from three British troops, he finally arrived at Dunkirk. There he saw that discipline had largely been maintained, as the troops understood that their best chance of getting away was by being orderly and efficient. But, having just arrived, he was at the back of the queue. Not being part of any infantry unit, Deere looked around for someone who could provide some guidance, and saw the navy-blue uniform of a RN lieutenant who directed him to the beach commander, who was shepherding small boats around near the shore. Deere asked if he could be given a place on one of the boats. The sooner he could get back to the squadron, the sooner he could be back up in the air fighting the *Luftwaffe*.

Deere was advised to wait for the next HM destroyer as that would carry him back to England far quicker, and in more comfort. After a prolonged, and nerve-wracking wait, a destroyer came into view and was soon tying up alongside the Mole:

We set off at once for the causeway leading to the mole, weaving our way through the long lines of troops who still maintained some semblance of order despite the constant attention of Hun aircraft. Just as we reached the causeway a formation of three Junkers bombers appeared overhead, hotly pursued by a single Spitfire. There was a mad scramble for cover, available only to those near the sand dunes or those who could shelter behind the rock causeway. Mostly the troops just dived into the water, re-emerging at neck level to fire their rifles in desperation and defiance in the general direction of the attacking bombers. From the comparative safety of the causeway I watched the Spitfire as it closed to attack only to see white smoke begin to pour from its engine as the pilot, obviously badly hit, turned away and glided inland. Silently, I wished him luck.[26]

The troops had little choice but to continue to try and reach the ships, air attacks or not. 'Ammunition was going up like fireworks,' recalled one soldier:

I waded out to my armpits and scrambled aboard a boat. Two others jumped onto the boat and completely swamped her. We spent about two hours trying to re-float her, but the seas were too strong. I decided to look for a change of clothes and searched the beach, where I soon picked up some short pants and socks. On returning, I found my party gone.[27]

Such incidents demonstrated the need for proper organisation on the beaches and to help with this a contingent of twelve Royal Navy and sixty ratings was sent on the 30th, beginning work in the early hours of the 31st. They were split into parties of one officer, one petty officer, one leading seaman, two able seamen, and one signaller. One of those officers, J.G. Wells from the shore-based training establishment HMS *Excellent*, saw that the troops were, 'eager to get off the beach at any cost. Some had been waiting for forty-eight hours and all had witnessed the bombing that day by German aircraft.'

With insufficient naval ratings to man the boats, they were simply abandoned by the soldiers, and the sailors often had to swim out to recover the empty boats. Nevertheless, Lieutenant Wells was complimentary about the conduct of the troops: 'Their behaviour under shell fire ... was a fine example to the sailors, who soon picked up the idea of lying flat on the stomach and singing "Roll out the barrel"'.

The destroyer *Venemous* had left Dover at 09.40 hours and was off Bray at 15.30. Lieutenant Commander John Edwin Home McBeath submitted the following report for that day's operations:

> Finding no small craft available, I lowered my motor boat and whaler to embark troops. The motor boat broke down and was towed back to the ship. HM Motor Boat *Balquhain* (a Sub-Lieutenant was in command) used the whaler and ferried some 200 troops from the shore to the ship. During this period, repeated high level bombing attacks were carried out on the beach and ships lying off. Barrage fire was opened as opportunity presented.

The *Daily Mirror*'s Ewart Brookes in a small private yacht, continued to lift men from the beaches in what seemed to be reasonable order:

> From the golden sands more British soldiers staggered, with an NCO in charge. 'Fifty to a boat', he said. And not a man moved in the water until the NCO said so.
>
> I saw British soldiers, bombed and shelled, with cracked lips, covered in mud, on the sand playing football with a half of French bread, a grotesque, staggering dribble, while bombs marked out touch-lines of this bizarre ground.
>
> The bombardment went on incessantly – crushing artillery well in shore, bombs to seaward, and on the beach still the khaki procession, seemingly endless, came on. Up to their knees, up to their waists, even up to their necks, they waded … I saw men die, shattered and bloody. I saw men die ashore before we could get to them … The darkness came again as we went across the Channel, and the last we saw was a line of fire red with the incessant overture of artillery and bomb fire that we left behind us.[28]

The water supply situation had seriously deteriorated for all units still in the beachhead. The compiler of the War Diary of the Royal Artillery's 7th Field Regiment was, however, still able to find some humour in his regiment's dilemma in the entry for 31 May:

Regtl H.Q. Water trailer had been abandoned on the journey from Oostvleteren, and by the start of the day the water situation had become precarious. The Officers Mess had a fairly large supply of whiskey and gin left, and this was used for washing up. This procedure was started by the M.O.; a strange thing for a true Scotsman!

At 17.00 *Venomous* was ordered by Wake-Walker to sail over to the East Mole where there were troops waiting to be embarked. When she reached Dunkirk, however, there was no space along the Mole and *Venomous* had to wait. This made her a perfect target for the *Luftwaffe*, but *Venomous* put up a terrific barrage and none of the bombs that were dropped hit the destroyer, and it was thought that it was her gunfire which resulted in one aircraft crashing onto the beach to the west of Dunkirk.

It wasn't until 19.00 that a berth became available on the East Mole – just as sixty German aircraft roared into the attack from the south-east: 'Fire was opened with all guns, wrote Commander McBeath. 'The gun recoil parted all my wires and as no berthing party was available on the jetty, I proceeded out of harbour so as to retain mobility of the ship during the air attack. All H.A. ammunition was now expended.'

With no more ammunition, and, in fact, no more troops on the Mole, there was little point in the warship remaining exposed, so Wake-Walker ordered *Venomous* back to Dover, where it was just as important to have a speedy turn round of ships as it was at Dunkirk. G.D. Lowe was the master of the Thames tug *Simla* which was one of four tugs employed in Dover harbour to help with the berthing of the arriving ships:

The main berths for the landing of troops, is at Admiralty Pier, the western end of the harbour. It has eight berths for ships like the cross-Channel boats.

During the busy time, there were as many as sixteen to eighteen ships using the Pier at one time, landing the troops and going to make room for other vessels, to attend to them. They practically all required the assistance of tugs, one or two, whatever the position they were in. Some had to be held off while the inside ship got away, or shifted here and there to allow room for others to berth, for which the tugs

Simla, *Gondia*, *Roman* and *Lady Brassey* were ordered to attend to
them, but also, these tugs had other work to attend to, such as ships
for the Submarine Camber Dock, which is at the eastern end of the
harbour, where they go for repairs. Then there is the Granville Dock,
the Wellington Dock, and the Eastern Arm.

In the main harbour, there are forty-odd buoys for ships to berth.
The oil tanker *War Sepoy* is at one of these, and the ships berth alongside of her with the assistance of the tugs ... The tugs are also required
to convey ammunition and stores off the destroyers and other Naval
vessels in the harbour.[29]

Lowe estimated that from 20 May until the completion of *Dynamo*, *Simla*
assisted more than 140 ships at Dover.

Once disembarked, the men had to be processed as quickly as was practicable.
They were asked which unit they belonged to, and which part of the country
they were from. After a cup of tea and a bun or piece of cake from the ladies
of the Red Cross, they were moved onto one of the 186 ten-carriage troop
trains that had been requisitioned by the Railway Executive Committee from
the various railway companies and whisked out of the port to be taken to large
military camps at Aldershot, Blandford, Dorchester, Oxford, Tetbury and
Tidworth to be reunited with their respective parent units.[30]

One of the more unusual boats to reach the evacuation beaches was the
Massey Shaw which was the River Thames fire float. Whilst there was some
suggestion that she might be able to put out some of the fires raging in Dunkirk
harbour, it was *Massey Shaw*'s shallow draft of less than four feet, that was of
the greatest appeal to the Admiralty. She set off on 30 May with a volunteer
crew of thirteen under Sub-Officer A. J. May. The fire float was never expected
to leave the calm waters of the Thames and was not built to withstand the
waters of the English Channel.

Having picked up a naval lieutenant, and a chart, at Ramsgate, *Massey Shaw*
arrived off Bray-Dunes on the late afternoon of the 31st. According to thirty-
year-old Auxiliary Fireman Francis George Codd, the crew had no idea that
they were being sent to France to rescue British soldiers:

From about a mile away ... we could see it was a flat beach, and then
we saw the silhouette of houses against this sky, the setting sun. We

couldn't see what was on the beach. We gradually saw reflections on the calm water, and I thought I could see a wrecked small craft, and then a bigger craft. Gradually we could see dark shapes against the sand; and then we saw that there were hundreds, thousands of people on this sand, and stretching up to the line of houses which stood, presumably, on the road that ran along the coast.

It was an extraordinary sight. Nothing seemed to be happening. They didn't seem to be moving in any organised way; not marching. They were standing or sitting, but mainly we noticed that they were columns of men waiting to be picked up.[31]

She moved close into the shore, sending a light skiff that had been picked up at Ramsgate, to one of the many queues that Francis Codd had seen formed along the beach. The moment the boat was close enough the troops at the head of the column rushed onto the boat, which promptly sank. The crew then saw a stranded RAF speedboat which they salvaged and sent to the beach, only for the scene to be repeated and the speedboat went down under a mass of desperate soldiers. It was not until 23.00 hours that another boat was found, by which time the crew of *Massey Shaw* had worked out a solution to the problem. A line was run from the fire float to an abandoned lorry on the beach and the new boat was pulled along this rope like, as one historian described it, a 'sea-going trolley car'.[32] The boat could only carry six men at a time. 'Whoever was in charge of the column of men,' Francis Codd explained, 'lined up near the shore end of the line [and] detailed six men into the rowing boat to pull along the line till they reached *Massey Shaw*, [they would then] climb on board and send their rowing boat back for another half-dozen.' Forwards and backwards the little boat travelled until she was full, having taken on board forty men of a company of Royal Engineers. *Massey Shaw* made her way back to Ramsgate during the night, surviving an attack from a German bomber that had spotted its phosphorescent wake.

The evacuation, though, was now going much better than expected and Churchill issued the instructions, as agreed earlier with Weygand, that the French troops should be given an equal opportunity of being evacuated in British ships and boats. This was relayed to Alexander, by Secretary of State Eden, at 20.15 hours: 'You should withdraw your force as rapidly as possible on a 50-50 basis with the French Army, aiming at completion by night of 1-2 June. You should inform the French of this definite instruction.'

In fact, numbers of French and Belgium ships arrived during the 31st. The French destroyer *Léopard*, two French trawlers, three French motor fishing vessels and ten Belgium trawlers as well as French cargo ships all reached Dunkirk. One of the French trawlers, *Pierre*, was carrying munitions which exploded when hit by a German shell.

Some of these French vessels rescued British as well as French troops, as Ken Potter of the 98th Field Regiment, Royal Artillery, remembered:

> Dunkirk beach looked as crowded as any holiday beach on a summer bank holiday. The moving ones were still alive.
>
> Constantly dived bombed by Stukas six or seven at a time we had nothing to throw back at them. From time to time, but not as frequently as we would have liked, a single Hurricane, sometimes two, would scream in out of the sun and knock hell out of them. They stayed as long as they could before making for home, presumably for more fuel. Those Hurricanes did more for morale at that time than anything else.
>
> In the meantime, everyone waited for the opportunity to get off the beach … Many of the small rescue craft had been sunk by the dive bombers and offshore one could see all kinds of craft trying to get closer through the wreckage. Some were standing off while troops waded out to them. All the time dive bombers were strafing everything and everyone.
>
> There were a number of Beach Masters who struggled to control the flow of men into likely avenues of escape. Together with another group I was directed back to the dock area to a bombed jetty with several corpses on it. Luckily for us a small French 'packet boat' was able to get alongside and take us off. Normally it would have carried 20 or 30 passengers.[33]

It was the German artillery, rather than the German aircraft, that caused Tennant the most problems throughout the 31st, with the German gunners maintaining a heavy and continuous bombardment of the beach and the inshore boats at La Panne. At 10.44 hours, Tennant signalled that: 'We have been continually, heavily bombarded and they [the Germans] are gradually finding the range of our loading berth.'[34] Tennant decided that he could not risk ships waiting idly for long periods of time for men to be transported to them. He therefore limited the number of ships going inshore so that they could be quickly filled by the boats. Of these boats, sixteen were either sunk or disabled by shells or 'misadventure', such as grounding, swamping, machine failure or striking wreckage.

The shelling seriously affected the rate of embarkation at La Panne which slowed to a trickle of about 150 an hour. The Germany artillery was so effective because of two observation kite balloons that had been deployed above Nieuport. Tennant called for Fighter Command to shoot these down, but when the RAF appeared the balloons were hauled down only to be released back into the sky as soon as the fighters had flown away. One attempt at bringing down the balloons was made by six Hurricanes, only for them to be engaged by around thirty Bf 109s.

Coastal Command was also in action over Nieuport, with ten Albacores and nine Skuas sent to bomb German pontoon bridges over the Nieuport Canal, with direct hits being claimed. On returning home the Skuas were engaged by twelve Bf 109s of I/JG20, and two Skuas of 801 Squadron (L2917 and L3005) were shot down. Another Skua crash-landed back at Detling. The battle was not all one-sided, as the Skuas claimed one Bf 109 shot down and another damaged.[35]

DIFFICULTIES IN THE DARK

The hope was that as soon as night fell the German guns, denied their aerial observation, would be less accurate and the remaining 7,000 troops at La Panne would be lifted before the German guns recommenced their barrage at dawn. These hopes were communicated to Dover by Tennant:

As it is vital to carry on the evacuation of troops throughout every available moment day and night it is intended to place two white lights at eastern and western pier head as a guide to ships in the hours of darkness. It is requested that all HM ships and other vessels who are likely to enter port to-night be warned accordingly … Slow British progress in the port due to shelling, bombing, and wounded and

French troops using quay. Weather fine and clear, sea moderate, good prospects for night embarkation from beaches.[36]

The dark, though, brought confusion, with large numbers of men crowding around the beach and scores of little boats skidding around the shallows. Lieutenant Commander J.W. McClelland was the SNO at La Panne, and with the approach of night, he gave orders for the destruction of all equipment and confidential gear that was not in actual use. At 20.30, two ships arrived and the boats on the beach, which had already been filled, put off. As, however, no additional boats had arrived, the rate of evacuation was only about 300 an hour and, as darkness set in this fell to about 150 an hour. With as many as 7,000 men gathering on the beach, and with the expectation that at first light the German artillery would start up again, an embarkation rate of at least 1,000 an hour was needed.

Accordingly, McClelland sent urgent messages to Ramsay and Wake-Walker for more vessels to be directed to La Panne. No more boats arrived – but the *Luftwaffe* did, patrolling almost continually and bombing any lights that were shown at sea. This made communication with the ships extremely difficult.

By 22.00 hours, the situation had become serious, as only about 600 troops had been embarked and the few boats available had dwindled to just three. This, McClelland believed, was mainly owing to mismanagement in the darkness by the inexperienced soldiers, who were having to try and handle the boats unsupervised. By 23.00 hours a frustrated McClelland reported that the situation had become critical: 'Troops, for whom there were no boats, commenced to pile up on the beach and the withdrawal [westwards], which would leave La Panne in No Man's Land by 04.00 the following morning, was in full swing. To make matters more awkward, the enemy battery near Nieuport opened a slow fire on the beach, which caused casualties with almost every shell and must have been very nerve racking to the waiting men.'

McClelland walked up and down the beaches and could not find any boats of any description. He went to the senior Army officer at La Panne, Major General D.G. Johnston, who commanded the 4th Division, to discuss the prevailing state of affairs. The meeting was recorded in the Division's War Diary: 'By 01.00 hrs [on 1 June], not more than three to four hundred men of the Division out of eight thousand to be embarked had been put on transports.

A conference was called at Divisional HQ, which had now opened in a house by the side of the beach where it was decided that it was useless to continue the embarkation from La Panne.' Together the decision was reached that they should march the 6-7,000 or so men still at La Panne westwards to Bray-Dunes. McClelland, consequently, informed Dover that the headquarters at La Panne was being abandoned, and he closed down the telephone link that had operated throughout the evacuation. As if to confirm that the correct decision had been made to leave La Panne, more German artillery batteries came into action and the rate of fire upon the British troops increased.

The men marched off westwards, with McClelland gathering up bunches of stragglers and sending them off towards Bray-Dunes and the East Mole. Embarkation at La Panne was officially terminated at 02.00 hours.

According to Captain R. Pimm, who assumed the role of Beach Master at Bray, by midnight the beaches were empty: 'Just before midnight I went along certain beaches to look for stragglers. A Staff Officer informed me that no more troops would embark from these beaches [La Panne] but that they would march to Dunkirk, as it was anticipated these beaches would be shelled and would probably be in German hands the following day.'[37]

Wake-Walker was still at sea off La Panne, 'wondering how things were going. Everything was black, ships and boats and shore showed no lights.' The messages he was receiving were contradictory, with ships' masters claiming that their boats could find no men on the beach, whilst from the shore, the news was that there were thousands of men on the beach and no boats to be seen. 'The ships and the boats were there,' declared a baffled Wake-Walker, who may have been unaware of the decision to close down operations from La Panne, 'and the troops ashore, and one could do no more ... I do not know to this day,' he conceded, 'what really took place there.'[38]

Even on the East Mole, embarkation was at times patchy, as can be seen in the account of an unnamed soldier who was one of those who waited through the night to be embarked:

We reached the East Jetty at 11 p.m. On one place, there had been a direct hit on the Mole. The gap had been patched with boards. A final halt was made 200 yards from the end, which was altogether about a mile long. Most of the men laid down on the jetty and went to sleep in spite of the cold. A German bomber flew over us at one o'clock, dropping bombs. The battalion just behind us was heavily shelled and machine-gunned and suffered severe casualties.[39]

The situation towards the end of the day was communicated to the War Office, after discussions between Brigadier Sir Oliver Leese, the Deputy Chief of Staff of the BEF, and Lord Gort. The latter said that pressure had increased along the whole front during the day, in particular noting that there had been a great deal of mortar fire directed at the men holding the perimeter. Gort made it clear that the rearguard would not be able to hold for long under such pressure, even though the front would be reduced as the final hours of the evacuation drew near. He estimated that after the night's evacuations there would be just the rearguard left, numbering around 12,000 British troops. There would, in addition, be a number of men of the French Cavalry Corps and *Général* de Laurencie's Corps at Dunkirk expecting to be rescued. This would depend on the rearguard holding on until 2 June, and no one knew if this was possible.[40]

THE BALANCE SHEET

As night fell on the 31st the order was given for the remnants of II Corps to withdraw from the perimeter and make their way to Bray-Dunes. Some of the men joined the long, patient queues lined up in front of the improvised piers to wait for the small boats to pick them up. Most, though, continued for a further ten miles to the Mole.

Also moving onto the beach that night was the headquarters of the 1st Division's 3 Brigade. Earlier in the day the men of the 1st Division had learnt that they were to form the rearguard – the last to leave. To prepare for their last stand on the beach, it was suggested that Brigadier T.N.F Wilson should take his headquarters down to Bray-Dunes to prepare for the final evacuation in two days' time. The brigade's journey to Bray-Dunes was recorded in the Brigade War Diary for that night:

The scenery provided a ... picture of the abomination of desolation. Ruined and burnt out houses ... salt water spreading everywhere, vehicles abandoned, many of them charred relics of twisted metal on the roadside and overturned in the ditches. Light tanks and guns poking up … Horses dead or dying for want of water. Here and there civilian or French Army corpses in the open. An unforgettable spectacle.[41]

Corporal W.L. McWilliam was with 145th Field Ambulance RAMC (48th Division) at La Panne and had helped evacuate the last of the casualties that were in a fit state to be moved at 18.00 hours. Leaving a small team to look after those men who were left in the hospital, the rest of the medics were relieved of their posts:

We marched off down the beach in single file, past the debris of war: lorries of every description, stores, arms, ammunition, the wreckage of aircraft – and the bodies of our comrades. Behind us, shells screeched into La Panne, and we saw one explode on the rear of the building we had just left. In front of us Dunkirk was ablaze, and we could see shells dropping into the sea close to the ships. Halfway along the beach were machine-gunned from the air and took refuge in a concrete shelter. Packed inside like sardines we heard a bomb drop and a puff of sand blew in through a small window. When the noise had subsided we resumed our trek towards the ships.[42]

The corps commander Gort chose (or was persuaded to choose by Major General Montgomery) to command the rearguard and oversee the final evacuation was Major General Harold Alexander who had commanded the 1st Division, but who was told to take over the rump of I Corps and the final defence of Dunkirk. That evening Lord Gort was collected from the beach at La Panne by the Inner Patrol Yacht, *Lahloo*. Her skipper was Lieutenant J.V. Ould, R.N.V.R.:

1700. Lay off La Panne as ordered and, while waiting for Lord Gort, took several boat loads of soldiers who had rowed out from shore and put them aboard destroyers.

1830. Boat brought out Lord Gort and his Aide de Camp to me. He came aboard and I took him over and put him aboard HMS *Hebe*. It appeared to me that the enemy knew of his departure as they shelled the beach and bombed it as he left and a very large enemy formation flew over and bombed as I put him aboard the *Hebe*.[43]

With Gort's departure, Harold Alexander assumed command of the remnants of the BEF. Gort's decisiveness had helped save the BEF from complete annihilation, but his last act in France showed none of that strength of mind. This was revealed by Tennant:

> I returned Dunkirk with General Alexander and discovered that totally different instructions had been given to General Alexander by Lord Gort and by Lord Gort in writing to Admiral Abrial and *Général* Fagalde.
>
> Lord Gort had told the French authorities that General Alexander would assist in holding the 'Perimeter' for the French to embark and that he was to place himself and his divisions under General Fagalde's orders. General Alexander, however, was told by Lord Gort in my hearing that he was to do nothing to imperil his army and was ultimately responsible for their safety and evacuation.
>
> I suggested to General Alexander that he should at once return to La Panne before the telephone was cut off to telephone to the Secretary of State for War, and to get the matter cleared up. This he did. The Secretary of State instructed General Alexander to act on his own discretion and to proceed with the evacuation.[44]

The day ended with 22,942 men being lifted from the beaches, 45,072 from the harbour and the Mole, making 68,014. As we have seen, there are many stories of periods of time when there were no ships available, yet this was the most successful day of the evacuation, with the greatest number of troops being rescued.

Each day, Berlin issued a communiqué, which was usually reproduced in British newspapers. The communiqué relating to 31 May, after stating that the remaining French forces in north-east France had been encircled, and large numbers of French troops had been taken prisoner in the region around Lille, turned its attention to the British:

> The attack against the rest of the BEF on both sides of Dunkirk, which is meeting with stubborn resistance in very difficult terrain, is making good progress.

Despite the bad weather our air force made further successful attacks yesterday on troops embarking at Dunkirk, and intervened in the protection of our army in ground operations.

Five transport vessels were sunk and three cruisers or destroyers, as well as 10 merchant ships, of a total tonnage of 70,000, were badly damaged by bombs.[45]

The truth was that only one HM ship, the minesweeper *Devonia*, was sunk, with the destroyers *Vivacious* and *Hebe* being damaged and *Wolsey*, *Impulsive*, *Scimitar*, *Icarus* and *Malcolm* being involved in accidents. It had been a remarkable day, and if the last few thousand troops could be evacuated over the course of the next twenty-four hours or so, the impossible would have happened. The BEF would have been saved.

Chapter 9

Operation *Dynamo*: Day 7, Saturday 1 June

A
t around, 04.00 hours on 1 June, J.V. Ould with *Lahloo*, which had assisted with the departure of Lord Gort the previous evening, was ordered to collect up the numerous boats that had been abandoned and were drifting around:

> While doing this we were bombed and continually shot at by enemy fighter aircraft. It occurred to me as poetic justice that I who had been on night bombing duty at Dunkirk in the last war should now be well bombed myself in this war … Collected several boats as ordered and also picked up several boat loads of soldiers from shore again, putting them aboard a sloop. While putting the last of these aboard a bomb fell right alongside and a splinter broke the fore skylight and hit one of my crew on his steel helmet. This ship seemed to bear a charmed life and though we had several bombs alongside I can only think that they were so close as to be ineffective.[1]

Lahloo was ordered back to Ramsgate, her crew having had no sleep for five consecutive nights. The boat's charmed existence continued, as she was bombed and strafed on the way back yet suffered no further damage.

Back in the UK, watching the returning troops from the previous night's operation arrive, was a BBC reporter:

> At dawn this morning, I stood on the quays of a south coast port and watched the hundreds of men to whom the sight of their relatives must have meant all and more than England herself.
>
> I saw several ships coming in, and every one of them was crammed full of tired, battle-stained and bloodstained British soldiers. Soon after dawn, I watched two warships steam in, one listing heavily to port under the enormous load of men she carried on her deck.

In a few minutes, her tired commander had her alongside, and a gangway was thrown from her decks to the quay. Transport officers counted the men as they came ashore.

No question of units, no question of regiments, no question even of nationality, for there were French and Belgian soldiers who had fought side by side with the British in the battle of Flanders. All were tired. Some were completely exhausted.[2]

Across the Channel, the cold light of dawn revealed not a horizon filled with ships, but an almost empty sea, most of the vessels heading for England. Even the small boats had moved westwards away from the reach of the German artillery at Nieuport. The ships would return later and the first day of June would see tens of thousands of troops evacuated, but until then the men had to endure a day of terror and frustration, under enemy attack from the sky unable to retaliate. All they could do was dig in, keep their heads down and hope.

La Panne was as deserted at the sea opposite, but at Bray there was still some loading taking place and it was to there that the troops were trudging along the sand. Corporal George Leger was with the 8th Battalion, Durham Light Infantry, which, with the 6th and 9th battalions formed the 151st Brigade, reached the coast on 1 June:

> When we got to Dunkirk on Saturday, there was just a feeling of dejection, and we were that tired and filthy dirty. We were picked up in lorries on the outskirts and taken the last few miles, to drive through the people who were guarding the perimeter, you couldn't just walk through. They were fighting a rearguard action, keeping the perimeter open for us. When we got through, we got out of our lorries and started walking through Dunkirk. It was one horrific sight. Machines, lorries, guns, armaments, strewn both sides of the road ... I walked halfway along the beach and there were rows and rows of troops, five or six deep, right up to the water's edge, and there was an officer standing at the head of each one.[3]

The destroyer *Codrington* had arrived off La Panne at 03.45 hours to find only a few minesweepers embarking equally few men from the beaches. *Codrington*'s Captain, G.F. Stevens-Guille, had expected to see masses of men and ships. He had not been told that the evacuation had been moved westwards:

The general situation ashore was unknown to me and I did not know what area was being evacuated, nor in fact, whether Dunkirk itself was still being held. It was while under the impression that a general evacuation with the possible exception of a very small rearguard was taking place that my enquiry to Rear Admiral Dover Straits as to the direction of the withdrawal ... was made. When ordered by Rear Admiral Dover to proceed to Dunkirk after daylight and on arrival there I realised that the evacuation of the previous night was of the eastward positions only.[4]

At last aware of what was happening, Stevens-Guille sailed for Dunkirk and tied up alongside the East Mole at 05.25 hours. There *Codrington* embarked around 900 men, including Major General Bernard Montgomery, who had been placed in temporary command of II Corps. Stevens-Guille noted in his after-action report that, 'While in Dunkirk harbour low cloud persisted and several low bombing attacks took place. It was most noticeable that accurate and heavy close range A.A. fire had a great deterrent effect and also caused poor aim. The experience of this occasion convinces me that the strengthening of A.A. armament of destroyers and other small vessels, even with close range weapons only, is of great utility.' The effectiveness of the *Luftwaffe*, which it appeared was often able to operate in empty skies, is a subject that has long been in question. For it would seem, that even when the RAF was not on patrol over Dunkirk, the German Air Force had no easy task attacking the Allied ships.

Out in the Channel, the low cloud reported by Stevens-Guille manifested itself in a dense fog with visibility down to fifty yards. In these difficult conditions, the destroyer HMS *Malcolm* struck a French trawler, which was heading in the opposite direction. The correct procedure is for ships to pass each other port side to port side, but instead of turning to starboard the trawler swung towards port and the destroyer's bows rammed into the side of the French boat, holing it above the waterline.

When *Malcolm* reached Dunkirk, she berthed against the East Mole and amongst the 1,000 men that were embarked was Tom Whelan with 107 Battalion, 32nd Field Regiment, Royal Artillery:

We reached the beach at Bray-Dunes, to find a chaotic situation. On the shoreline, there were floating bodies everywhere – mostly sailors, both British and French, washed up from destroyers sunk by Stukas, just a short time earlier … What a time to arrive … We joined a queue further along, near the East Mole. We sat on the sand, making sure we didn't lose our places, and taking pot shots at the Stukas as they came in to bomb the Mole – we wondered if it would still be there when our turn came …

We eventually got onto the Mole, where moored alongside was HMS *Malcolm*. We had to negotiate a narrow plank to get into the ship, and I soon found myself in the bowels of the ship drinking a cup of navy cocoa. After this I went to sleep and didn't wake up until we arrived at Dover.[5]

HMS *Sabre* had left Dover at 21.20 hours on the 31st and reached Dunkirk again at 01.15 on the morning of the 1st, making for Marlo-les-Bains. No troops were found there, so *Sabre* started searching further east. As she made her way towards Bray the crew heard an 'S.O.S.' being sounded on a siren. *Sabre* steamed towards it and found a drifter stranded on a submerged wreck. The destroyer went alongside and took off the crew and troops.

Just before dawn, *Sabre* reached Bray where other destroyers were at work. *Sabre* sent in her two boats and started taking off the soldiers that were found there in large numbers. She was also directed by Wake-Walker, who was aboard HMS *Keith*, to take off troops from a tug that was needed to pull the minesweeper *Speedwell* off the beach where she had grounded. During this time a single aircraft (apparently, a Bf 109) approached and made what was considered to be 'rather half-hearted' machine-gun attacks, the Messerschmitt being driven off by intense fire from *Sabre*. There was also an unsuccessful attack on the destroyer by a Stuka, but Commander Brian Dean reported that Fighter Command was seen in strength over the beaches and that his ship's freedom from serious interference by the *Luftwaffe* was due to the presence of the British aircraft. *Sabre* took on board 451 troops and headed back to Dover, which was reached at 10.00 hours.[6] *Sabre* was able to make another round trip on the 1st, reaching Dunkirk at 23.15, and pushing off from the East Mole before midnight.

Charles Herbert Lightoller, who was the Second Officer on the *Titanic* when she sank in 1912, being rescued by SS *Carpathia*, owned the fifty-two-foot motor-yacht, *Sundowner*. Following the instructions he received from the

Admiralty, he had taken *Sundowner* to Southend on 31 May. From there he was ordered to Ramsgate, and at 10.00 hours on 1 June, *Sundowner*, along with five other vessels, set off for France. With Lightoller was his eldest son Roger, and a sea scout called Gerald Ashcroft.

After narrowly avoiding a mine in mid-Channel, *Sundowner* encountered enemy aircraft for the first time, when two German fighters appeared overhead. Luckily HMS *Worcester* happened to be steaming by and drove off the attackers with its anti-aircraft guns.

At 14.25 hours, Lightoller sighted the 25-foot motor-cruiser *Westerly* broken down and badly on fire. This little boat, smaller than the Admiralty minimum requirement for *Dynamo* of thirty feet, had a crew of two and had picked up three naval ratings from Dunkirk. Lightoller went alongside the burning boat and took off all five – who then had to return to Dunkirk on board *Sundowner*, 'facing the hell they had just left'.

Steaming through the wreckage off Dunkirk, *Sundowner* headed for the beach:

> For some time past we had been subject to sporadic bombing and machine-gun fire, but as *Sundowner* is exceptionally and extremely quick on her helm, by waiting until the last moment and then putting the helm hard over – my son at the wheel – we easily avoided every attack – though sometimes nearly lifted out of the water.

It had been Lightoller's intention to go straight to the beaches, from where his second son, Second Lieutenant Trevor Lightoller had been evacuated just four hours earlier. But he was told by the crew of *Westerly* that there were no longer any troops on the beaches to be picked up, so Lightoller headed for the East Mole:

> By now dive bombers seemed to be forever dropping out of the cloud of enemy aircraft overhead. Within half a mile of the pier heads a two-funnelled transport had overhauled us on a converging course and was just passing us to port when two salvos were dropped in quick succession right along her port side. For a few moments, she was completely hidden in smoke and I certainly thought they had got her,

but she reappeared out of the smoke gaily streaming on and heading for the piers which she entered ahead of us.

When Lightoller reached the East Mole he saw that, being such a small vessel, it would be almost impossible for him to safely take off men from the structure high above. So he went alongside HMS *Worcester* and hailed the destroyer, telling its crew that he could take 100 men, even though the most he had ever had onboard had been twenty-one. When he had taken on seventy-five men, the boat was completely filled below and above decks and from stem to stern. At that point, Lightoller called a halt and set off back to England.

The Thames barge *Shannon* left Southend at 12.00 hours on 31 May with three other boats towed by *Sun III*, arriving at Ramsgate at 17.15 that evening. The little convoy left for France on the morning of the 1st, spotting a lifeboat en route. Arthur William Joscelyne was on board *Shannon*:

We saw a ship's boat full of soldiers, and they were resting on their oars. In front of it there was a smaller dingy, with about a dozen dark-skinned fellows in, who hardly spoke any English at all. They were part of a Spanish labour corps, and they had attached themselves to this ship's boat full of soldiers and they were doing all the work, rowing like mad, while these soldiers were sitting back and letting them pull it.[7]

Sun III and its gaggle of boats reached the waters around Dunkirk at 12.30 on the 1st and was directed to two further boats overloaded with troops. 'The soldiers were not used to boats, and they all rushed to get on board,' continued Arthur Joscelyne:

We could have capsized at any moment. An officer stood up in the bows and got his revolver out. He said, 'I'll shoot the first man who makes a move before I give you permission to board. You will do it in an orderly manner.' He stood there with his revolver, while we got about fifty of them on board. They were in such a state that they just lay down anywhere. A couple of them threw their rifles overboard and said, 'We shan't want these anymore.'

The tug boat took these troops on board, and with 148 passengers filling its decks, Master F. W. Russell decided to return to England. Though damaged, *Shannon* reached Ramsgate on 2 June.

Able Seaman Samuel Palmer had taken charge of the 30-foot, 7-ton motor-yacht, *Naiad Errant*, which started from Sheerness early on Friday the 31st as one of a convoy of seven motor boats. By around 12.50 hours *Naiad Errant* was approximately three miles from the French port when Palmer saw a German plane burst into flames and tumble out of the sky, and with it a dark object, which he assumed was the pilot:

> As he landed in the water I made my way over to him and fished him out with my boat hook, but as he was dead and a German at that, I pushed him off and got on my way.
>
> A few minutes later, I saw a French destroyer doing about twenty-five to thirty knots, making her way into Dunkirk. I took my eyes off her for a minute or two and then glanced back, but there was nothing there. She must have had a direct hit from a bomb and sunk within a few minutes.[8]

The French destroyer was *Foudroyant*, which was attacked at 12.55 hours by a mass of Heinkels and Stukas, and was hit by three 250kg bombs, the third of which penetrated her hull. She broke in two and although orders were given to abandon ship, she rolled over so quickly there was no time to launch any boats or floats. According to French accounts *Foudroyant* went down in less than a minute. Only twenty of her 138 crew were saved, most of those being rescued by *Naiad Errant*. When he was able, Palmer transferred the French sailors to the tug *Notre Dame de Lourdes*.

On arrival off the beaches, French soldiers swarmed over his boat preventing him going astern so that he drifted ashore where the boat was stranded. He left *Naiad Errant* and swam off with his crew to a minesweeper, whose name he did not know. Shortly afterwards the minesweeper also went aground, but, as the tide rose, both the minesweeper and *Naiad Errant* floated off. Palmer asked permission to swim back to his boat, but this being refused, he shouted to some soldiers on the beach to bring her alongside. This they managed to do and Palmer jumped on board, cast off from the minesweeper, and set course for home.

Palmer was the only naval rating in a small boat without a chart, with one sergeant and eight other soldiers from the Middlesex Regiment. Shortly after trying to head out to sea, the yacht's engines broke down. Knowing little about engines, Palmer broke up the door of the yacht's cabin into long pieces, handed them to the soldiers and told them to start paddling! Luckily one of the engines started up and at about 22.00 hours he left the vicinity of Dunkirk and headed west-northwest for England. As none of the soldiers had any boating experience, Palmer had to remain at the wheel all through the night. He reached Ramsgate at 11.00 hours on 1 June.[9]

The captain of the auxiliary minesweeper, the former Caledonian Steam Packet Company paddle steamer *Duchess of Fife*, had a remarkable tale to tell of his experiences on 1 June:

> The pier was stiff with French troops. They took my lines and then refused to come aboard. One of my men got one by the leg and hauled him down the brow, but none others would follow.
>
> Accordingly, I climbed the brow and harangued them in a strange language, which I doubt had little effect. But, as is my custom, I happened to be wearing a beret, and at sight of the familiar headgear some 25 of them followed me down the brow. Again, there was a hold up and going on the bridge I hailed to inquire if were was a British Officer within hearing. At the third hail a man forced himself to the rail … [I asked him if] there any British troops on the quay? He replied that there were no British troops on the quay, that these 'yellow bellies' would not board, and that I might as well let go my ropes and clear.
>
> It seemed I could do nothing but land a party and drive them aboard, when I was hailed from up the quay to bring my ship 200 yards further ahead. Accordingly fleeted along and found Col. Winterton at the head of a detachment of disciplined British troops in threes who marched on board.[10]

Further indication of the difficulties the British experienced with some of the French soldiers was highlighted by Major Miles Reid, who was a liaison officer to the First French Army:

> Although the French and Belgians had been allocated a beach further south for their assembly and embarkation … every conceivable type of

car sought access to the beach. A cordon of Welsh Guards with fixed bayonets blocked the entrance, but still the motors came worming their way round the cordon. Their occupants, mainly French and Belgian officers, were deaf to entreaties or orders to drive to their own beach. When it was seen that force might have to be used, the cars were deliberately put out of action by their drivers. I gave the occupants of one motor instructions to turn round, and the result was the ripping of all the wires from under the dashboard. Every step was taken to interfere with the task of organising the beaches to make full use of the available space and craft ... Finally, in desperation, we had to call on two Welsh Guardsmen to remove forcibly a French Air Force Colonel, who, obviously the senior, obdurately refused to help us in any way whatsoever.[11]

There were also reported problems with fifth-columnists. Unlikely though such tales were, they found their way into the British newspapers. One such story from a British officer was reported in the *Liverpool Daily Post* of 1 June:

On one of the beaches a man in the uniform of a British officer and speaking good English, came up to him and said: 'I have just got orders that you are to take all your men two miles further along.

The officer was just about to do so when he met a naval officer and said: 'Surely, it is rather stupid of you to try and take us off down there because the Channel is so much further out.' The naval officer replied that there was no intention of doing so. An hour afterwards the point two miles further on was bombed to pieces.

THE LUFTWAFFE ARRIVE

It was at 04.15 hours that the *Luftwaffe* appeared in the skies above Dunkirk in force. Forty Stukas attacked the shipping at sea. Fighter Command's 11 Group squadrons were soon in the air, flying a total of 267 sorties in eight missions throughout the day. But the RAF could not be present all the time, and the *Luftwaffe* had long periods in which it could operate freely against the beaches and the boats.

In the first raid the main target was the large destroyer *Keith*, where Wake-Walker was directing operations. The warship's manoeuvrability was severely restricted in the shallow waters but she managed to avoid being hit. However, what was believed to have been a delayed-action bomb exploded immediately astern of the destroyer, which caused the ship's wheel to jam. Temporary steering was rigged up, but by the time the next attack came, at around 08.00 hours, her anti-aircraft guns were out of ammunition and all that the skipper, Captain E.L. Berthon, could do was turn the ship in tight circles as fast as the destroyer was able.

Three Stukas headed directly for *Keith* and Wake-Walker watched as the enemy's bombs plunged straight towards the destroyer:

> I looked up as they dived at us, saw the bombs released and watched them as they fell. Everyone on the bridge was lying or crouching down but there was not much room and I could only find room to crouch a bit. It was an odd sensation waiting for the explosions and knowing that you could do nothing. When they came, it was obvious that the ship had been hit. She shook badly and there was a rush of smoke and steam from somewhere aft.[12]

Wake-Walker made his way aft to examine the damage. He found the Chief Engineer hurriedly trying to turn off steam valves. The Rear Admiral asked the Engineer what damage has been caused, and he replied that the Senior Engineer was lying dead on the floor plates:

> A man [then] passed me carrying a wounded man on his shoulders from right aft on his way to the sick bay; his face was cut and covered in blood. Smoke and steam were coming out of the after funnel and the ship was listing to port, but could see no signs of damage and learnt later that the bomb had gone down the funnel and burst below.

Able Seaman Reginald Heron was on the warship's switchboard:

> There was a hell of a crash and everything shook like hell. We knew we'd been hit because we were more or less expecting it ... A bomb

from a Stuka went down the funnel, and blew out the whole of the underpart of the ship. We grabbed the codebooks, and put them in a specially-weighted bag and threw it over the side. Then someone shouted, 'Abandon ship! Throw everything floatable overboard'. So I threw a dan-buoy overboard … I jumped in behind it and started swimming with one arm. I swam over to a tug a few hundred yards away and grabbed hold of a rubber tyre on the side.[13]

Able Seaman Heron was one of the lucky ones. A hole had been blown in the side of the destroyer at the forward end of the starboard engine room below the waterline and the bulkhead between there and the boiler room was ruptured, allowing the sea to pour in, drowning those inside. A fire then started in the boiler room. *Keith* was hit two more times on the port side and she took on a severe list. Seeing that he was unable to carry out his duties on the immobile destroyer, Wake-Walker transferred to *MTB 102*.

After disarming the depth charges and jettisoning them along with its torpedoes, *Keith* was abandoned. Vessels nearby rushed to help as more bombs were aimed at the destroyer, dropping amongst the men struggling in the water. Slowly the men were picked up by tugs, the minesweeper *Salamanca*, a skoot and the motor-barge *Sherfield*. But an unidentified grey yacht was hit and sunk as it was collecting survivors – an anonymous victim, crewed by courageous volunteers, their names lost to posterity.

In a further raid at around 09.40 hours, *Keith* was attacked by approximately fifty enemy aircraft and the destroyer sunk amidst a salvo of bombs. The last survivors, struggling to stay alive in the destroyer's oil slick, were not picked up until around 11.00 hours. Three officers and thirty-three men were lost.[14]

The loss of HMS *Keith* was witnessed by Bren Gunner First Class, James Bradley:

Eventually I did get to the coast. When I came to the sand dunes, I could see that Dunkirk was a blazing mass of burning oil and a battle was going on.

I moved along the sand hills to Le Panne, a little to the right of Dunkirk, and there were hundreds and hundreds of soldiers on the sand. Ships were coming in, trying to pick up the soldiers. I thought, they'll never get these people off here, but we just had to be disciplined.

I saw the most magnificent bit of British discipline there. They went down in the water, stood in rows of four, and the tide came in and then the tide went out, and then it came back again. I remember three tides, and I stayed there a night. There was the odd guy who left for obvious purposes – to nip back over the sand dunes. Then he'd come back and a hand would go up and someone would say, 'Over here, over here!' It was terribly British - I think I became a man there.

Unfortunately, the dive bombers were knocking out the ships and terrible things were happening. I saw them hit a destroyer, packed with men on board, and it went on its side. Hundreds of men went into the sea, thrashing about there. Many of them couldn't swim, I'm sure.[15]

One of those vessels that went to the assistance of *Keith* was the HM Tug *St Abbs*. She had arrived some six miles off Dunkirk with two Thames barges in tow at 00.30 hours (a third barge had broken away on the crossing), waiting then until daylight before closing in on the shore. Lieutenant Brooker slipped the two barges at 06.30 and then moved towards the beaches. When *Keith* was hit, *St Abbs* went alongside and took off many of the survivors from the destroyer as well as picking up some from the sea. Then disaster struck. At 09.30 hours, *St Abbs* ran into four delayed-action bombs that had been dropped into the water ahead of the tug. The bottom and stern of *St Abbs* were blown off and she went down in less than a minute. Approximately 135 officers, ratings and troops were on board, but only thirty were seen swimming in the water after the tug disappeared beneath the waves, amongst whom was *Keith*'s Captain Berthon.[16]

The minesweeper HMS *Skipjack*, which had been receiving troops off Malo beach had been fighting off air attacks since 05.30 hours, which had reduced her ammunition to only about twelve rounds per gun. At 08.45 no less than ten Ju 88s singled her out, with two bombs striking her. A minute later, *Skipjack* was hit by three more bombs. W. T. Emslie, serving aboard another minesweeper, HMS *Dundalk*, saw what happened:

She was lying at anchor still taking on troops, when she took the full delivery from a dive-bomber and went up in a terrific explosion. When the smoke cleared, she had vanished; there was simply nothing there any more.[17]

Bill Stone was the chief stoker on *Skipjack*'s sister ship *Salamanca*:

> Our final trip was on 1st June by which stage there was the wreckage
> of sunken ships all around and burning oil tanks by the dockside.
> Lines of troops were all marching towards the sea. We were anchored
> off the beach with one of our sister ships, the *Skipjack*, only about
> fifty yards away. At about 8 am the German dive bombers came over
> and attacked *Skipjack*. One of the attacking planes was shot down
> but *Skipjack* was badly hit and capsized. She must have had about 200
> men on board. I had to say 'God, help us'. I believe to this day that
> He did.[18]

At the time she sank, *Skipjack* was loaded with troops, nearly all of whom were
below deck and had no chance of escape when the minesweeper turned turtle
and floated bottom-up for a few minutes before sinking. A total of nineteen
crew and 275 soldiers were lost.

Another destroyer, HMS *Ivanhoe*, was also attacked as she was leaving the
beaches with 1,000 soldiers on board. In the early hours of 1 June, she had gone
to La Panne to find the beach deserted. She moved westwards where a large
body of British troops had gathered. As the men were being embarked, *Ivanhoe*
was strafed repeatedly and subjected to high-level, but fortunately inaccurate,
bombing.

After loading the troops *Ivanhoe* moved off, but as she was passing Dunkirk
she was straddled by two bombs whilst a third hit the port whaler's after davit
and exploded a few feet above the upper deck near the base of the foremost
funnel.[19]

No.2 Boiler room was pierced by bomb splinters, damaging the boiler and
causing a fire which began to spread. Many of the deck fittings were destroyed
and the ship's secondary armament was put out of action. She avoided further
attention from the *Luftwaffe* by igniting a smoke-float in the bows which
convinced the German pilots that the ship was severely crippled. Casualties were
heavy, with twenty-six killed and thirty wounded. Most of the soldiers were taken
off by HMS *Havant* which had berthed alongside the East Mole at 07.30 hours.

The Mole had become badly damaged by the incessant German shelling
and aerial attacks. Gaps in the decking were covered with trestles, planks of

wood, ladders and anything that could be found. The job of loading the troops was made even more difficult by the number of ships sunk alongside. There was, though, only a trickle of men in the early morning and after half-an-hour *Havant* had taken on board only about fifty men. Then, at around 08.00 hours, the *Luftwaffe* arrived overhead and *Ivanhoe* was seen to be hit and on fire.

Havant cast-off from the Mole and went to *Ivanhoe*'s assistance. She went alongside and took off approximately 500 men, some of whom were wounded. Lieutenant Commander A.F. Burnell-Nugent, then decided to make for Dover. 'On the way down the channel parallel to the beach to the west of Dunkirk we were subjected to intense dive bombing and high and low-level bombing and also bombardment from shore,' reported Burnell-Nugent. 'These were avoided by zig-zagging as much as the width of the channel permitted. *Havant* had just turned to the North Westward at the end of the channel when, at 09.06, we were hit by two bombs in the Engine Room which passed through the starboard side. Almost immediately afterwards a large bomb fell in the water about 50 yards ahead. This had a delay action and exploded right underneath the ship as she passed over it, momentarily giving the impression of lifting the whole ship.'[20]

The bombs that hit the engine room killed the Engine Officer and all the Engine Rome Artificers were either dead or wounded, the after ready use ammunition lockers had blown up, and there were many casualties amongst the soldiers on the upper deck. The ship was continuing to steam at moderate speed, out of control and gradually circling to starboard.

The destroyer was in serious trouble, approaching the sandbanks opposite Dunkirk. Somehow *Havant* had to be stopped. This could only be done by letting steam out of the boilers, and Chief Stoker Gallor bravely stepped forward and let out the steam, even though there was a fire in one of the boiler rooms. *Havant* was eventually brought to a halt using the starboard anchor as a brake.

Signals for assistance were then made to HMS *Saltash* and a large private yacht. These came alongside, one on each quarter, and all the soldiers were transferred under almost continuous bombing. *Havant* was then taken in tow by *Saltash* but after another bomb had dropped between the two destroyers it became clear that *Havant* was not going to make it back to England and the captain decided to abandon ship. The magazines were flooded, she rolled over and sank at 10.15, after a few rounds had been fired into her by *Saltash* to make sure that she went down.

HMS *Grive* also responded to *Ivanhoe*'s distress call, but seeing that she was already being helped, made her way to the East Mole where troops were waiting. Captain Lambert placed *Grive* alongside the inside of the Mole and took 700 troops onboard under heavy air attack. She left the harbour as a 'tremendous' air battle raged overhead. *Grive* arrived at Dover and discharged her human cargo. At 22.00 hours Lambert set off again for Dunkirk, even though she had only three rounds of ammunition left for each of her guns. At around 23.30, the sound of an aircraft was heard. 'We could not see anything,' Sub Lieutenant J.K.B. Miles later wrote, 'a few minutes later there was a tremendous explosion and *Grive* was literally blown to pieces and sank in a few seconds ... Together with three others of the ship's company I was picked up by a boat from a drifter.' A further fifteen of *Grive*'s crew were picked up by other ships.[21]

It was a difficult day not just for the Royal Navy but also for the RAF. Already having lost dozens of aircraft in the Battle of France, Keith Park's 11 Group was stretched to the limit trying to find enough men and machines to give the BEF the air protection it so badly needed. This meant pressing into action aircraft that were not really a match for the Messerschmitt fighters. These included four Blenheim IVF aircraft of 254 Squadron which had been flown down from RAF Sumburgh in the Shetland Islands to RAF Detling in Kent to operate with the Blenheims of 248 Squadron. Their task was to undertake sea patrols to cover the evacuation. The Blenhiems conducted their first patrol between North Foreland and Calais-Dunkirk on 29 May which was repeated the following day. Their third patrol began at 04.50 hours on 1 June in which two aircraft from both squadrons were to operate together. First one then the other 248 Squadron planes returned to Detling with mechanical faults. The two other two aircraft carried on with the patrol and, at 07.50 hours, they began their last circuit. Ten minutes later, as they were approaching Dunkirk, they were pounced on by eleven Bf 109s. The Observer on board Blenheim L9481 was Pilot Officer G. W. Spiers:

> I was sitting in the seat on the right-hand side of the pilot. Looking out to my right I could see the sand beaches with numerous clusters of troops queueing to embark on small craft. As I looked up I saw

recognisable ME 109 German aircraft diving in line astern towards our rear starboard quarter. I managed to count eleven 109s and as I looked downwards I saw our other Blenheim who had, been flying in line astern of us, pass beneath to starboard with both engines on fire.

As soon as I had seen the enemy, I had yelled to [Flying Officer J. W.] Baird 'fighters' and in the meantime, he turned to port and headed for North Foreland giving the engines full power. We were slowly picking up speed in a shallow dive but a cold feeling in the small of my back, made me realise we were 'sitting ducks' for fighters.

In temper and fear I shouted to Baird to manoeuvre the aircraft about, at the same time I made demonstrations by waving my hand in front of him. Whether or not he understood I never found out, as the cockpit suddenly filled with acrid smoke and flying fragments as the dashboard and instruments disintegrated in front of me, under a series of violent crashes and flashes. Suddenly it stopped. The smoke started to clear and I looked back through the armour plate to see what had happened to [LAC R.] Roskrow the Gunner. The fuselage down to the turret was a mass of bullet holes which which were accentuated by the sun beams that shone through the smoke. All I could see of Roskrow was a bloody green flying suit slumped over the gun controls.

Turning to Baird I immediately realised he had been hit although he still held the controls. His head was slumped forward on his chest and blood ran down his right cheek from a wound in the temple that showed through the side of his helmet. Another wound in his neck had covered him with blood and it had gushed all over my left shoulder. He looked very peaceful with his eyes shut; I was sure he was dead. It was miraculous that I had survived that burst of gunfire into the cockpit. The two-foot square Perspex panel had many holes in it. The bullets had passed me and gone into Baird and the cockpit panel.

Spiers was alone in a damaged aircraft and, naturally, his first instinct was to bale out, but he found he could not lift the Navigator's seat which was on top of the bale-out hatch. The Blenheim was also staring to roll. Spiers had no choice but to try and fly the plane himself. He lifted Baird's hands from the controls and, leaning over the dead pilot, he eased back the throttles:

Yellow flames from the port engine were beating against the front and side windows and standing at the side of Baird I was about to level the aircraft to prevent the vicious sideslip, that was causing the flames to play on the cockpit, when suddenly the windscreen shattered. I felt a hot searing wind on my face, I felt my cheeks, nose, throat and mouth shrivelling under the heat but have no recollection of any pain. As soon as the aircraft righted, the cockpit cleared of fire and smoke and a noticeable peace descended as the cut back engines purred and the wind gently whined through the shattered glass.

He saw a trawler some miles away and decided to try and ditch the Blenheim as near to it as he could. He slowly pulled the throttles back and, as the aircraft lost speed, it lost height. Gradually the Blenheim dropped towards the sea, until the waves seemed to rush up at him. Then there was a sudden jolt:

I can still visualise the water bounding in through the nose like a dam which had burst; I remember turning my back to the barrage and gently cushioning on it. The silent cockpit was now full of blood coloured sea and I struggled to reach the normal entry sliding hatch above the pilot's head. My feet kept slipping on the floor and I could make no progress despite the numerous attempts.

The Blenheim sank downwards but, with his lungs bursting and his pulse pounding in his ears, Spiers felt the floor of the aircraft fall away and he was able to swim up to the surface. Spiers was rescued by the trawler men, and lived to become a squadron leader and a Member of the British Empire.[22]

Recovering pilots who had been shot down was not merely a humanitarian deed. Over the previous six days since the start of Operation *Dynamo*, Fighter Command had lost more than ninety aircraft, but of even greater concern for Air Chief Marshal Dowding was the loss of experienced pilots, for trained flyers could not be replaced as quickly as machines. Nothing was more important for the protection of the men and the ships at Dunkirk than getting downed pilots back to England and back in the air.

One such airman was Sergeant Jack Potter, who was up before dawn on 1 June and was soon heading across the Channel in his 19 Squadron Spitfire Mk.1 coded K9836. The squadron found itself over the French coast at around 05.40 hours and immediately ran into a group of enemy aircraft from

Zerstörergeschwader 1. 'On 1 June 1940, I was on patrol with Red Section,' Potter later recounted:

Shortly after reaching the patrol line we found twelve Me 110s over Dunkirk. We moved into attack. Whereupon they turned very quickly back over the town as if trying to escape. However, we soon engaged them and they broke up and most of them appeared to turn steeply to the left. This appeared to be the only means of escape they knew and they became quite easy to shoot at.

I fired at several without apparent effect and then engaged one which had just begun a steep diving turn to the left. I had a full plan view of the top of the aircraft and opened fire at about 400 yards. I held my fire for almost eight seconds and could see my bullets going into the front half of the fuselage. At about 150 yards my ammunition ran out and I had to avoid the shell fire of another enemy aircraft which was firing at me from my port side.[23]

Potter tried to escape from the melee so that he could return home to re-arm:

As I reached the outskirts of the fight a metallic 'bang' from my port side made me look at my port mainplane and saw a hole about eight inches long and about two inches wide just above the position of the oil cooler … At about ten miles out from the coat the engine became very rough and glycol smoke started to appear. Finally, the engine seized up at about 4,000 feet and fifteen miles out from land.

Looking around at the sea I saw a small boat and decided to stay with the aeroplane as the sea was very calm and I thought my chances of being picked up were greater if I landed alongside the boat than if I took to my parachute.

I circled the boat at about fifty feet and then, being very close to the sea, straightened out to land … On first touching the water the machine skimmed off again, and after one more such landing it dug its nose into the sea. I was flung forward and my forehead and nose met the reflector sight … I stood up in the cockpit and found the aircraft still afloat but it sank almost immediately … As the aircraft sank I tried to get out but the parachute caught on the sliding hood and I was taken down with the aircraft. However, I was soon released and pushed off with my feet only to be struck by the tailplane as it went past.

Potter swam upwards and broke the surface to discover that he was just fifty yards from the boat. This was a French fishing vessel, the *Jolie Mascotte*. Potter was hauled on board by the crew of four, none of whom could speak English. As it happened, Potter's appearance was a fortuitous event for the French fishermen, as they were lost! Potter, of course, knew exactly where he was and, with the aid of a chart, was able to show the Frenchmen the bearing for Dunkirk.

As *Jolie Mascotte* approached Dunkirk the men spotted a British destroyer and a naval motor-boat was sent across to the fishing boat. A Royal Navy lieutenant climbed aboard and told Potter that his ship, HMS *Basilisk*, had already been bombed and that the engines and wireless were both out of action. The destroyer, which had a displacement of more than 1,800 tons, was loaded with soldiers and the lieutenant asked if the little boat could tow the warship out to sea away from the enemy bombers.[24]

A line was duly attached and *Jolie Mascotte* began to pull the 323-foot warship round when a mass of enemy aircraft filled the sky, 'There were about thirty Dornier 17s and Heinkel 111s', Potter noted:

> Above them were about twenty Me 109s. I informed the lieutenant that the ship was about to be bombed and we decided to cast off. At about three-quarters of a mile from the destroyer we watched the bombing operations.
>
> The enemy aircraft did not appear to adopt any particular formation, but at about 3,000 feet turned singly over the target and jettisoned all their bombs. The bombs left the aircraft in a string of about ten. There appeared to be very little attempt at precision bombing, but rather as if they let all their bombs go hoping that one would hit.
>
> As they bombed, others opened fire with machine-guns on the destroyer. During the course of the whole action they did not score a single hit – despite the fact that the target was stationary and had only two pom-poms with no anti-aircraft shells.

Jolie Mascotte returned, re-attached the line and began towing again. Yet shortly afterwards, the fishing boat had to cast the line off again as about twenty Ju 87s dived down from a height of around 400 feet to deliver their deadly cargoes – this time with the precision that was lacking in the earlier attacks. The ship was hit by possibly four of the bombs, one of which detonated inside No. 3 boiler room, killing all of her boiler and engine room personnel, as well as fracturing her steam lines and knocking out all her machinery.

When the Stukas flew off, *Jolie Mascotte* returned to the destroyer once more only to find that the ship was sinking and the order to 'abandon ship' had been given. *Basilisk* had heeled to starboard when first hit but had then momentarily righted itself. But she then sank in about three minutes, settling on the sea bed on an even keel in some four fathoms of water.

The little fishing boat picked up six officers and seventy-one ratings from the stricken warship, but there were still many others stranded onboard. Some were able to take to the ship's motor-boat and the whaler (which actually made its own way across to Dover) and, luckily, another destroyer, HMS *Whitehall*, appeared and some of the remainder of the crew were saved.

It was not just the ships at sea off the beaches that came under attack from the *Luftwaffe*. At 10.09 hours, SS *Prague*, which had earlier suffered damage from the German artillery, had loaded 3,000 French troops from the East Mole and set off for England when she was attacked by Ju 87s. Her skipper was Captain Cliff Baxter:

> Suddenly an aircraft appeared out of the clouds almost directly overhead, and swinging round, dived the *Prague*.
>
> Releasing three bombs together while still at a considerable height, the aircraft escaped without coming into effective machine gun range, and the bombs fell very close to the stern of the ship which was swinging hard round to starboard. The force of the explosion was terrific, and the ship seemed to be lifted almost out of the water.
>
> Although not actually hit, it was evident that the ship was very badly damaged aft. The stern settled down considerably and the starboard engine had to be stopped immediately as the shaft was bumping round in the stern very badly. The watertight doors were closed at the time in accordance with wartime procedure, but the force of the explosion had evidently made them considerably distorted, as the ship filled up to the after engine room bulkhead and the water rose to the level of the main deck.

It was clear that she was taking in vast amounts of water and was in danger of sinking. The troops, therefore, were transferred to other ships, most of these being taken on board the paddle minesweeper *Queen of Thanet*. *Prague* was taken in tow by the tug *Lady Brassey*, which attempted to take her back to Folkestone; but as she was in danger of sinking, she was beached at Deal. Over the course of four days, *Prague* had taken from Dunkirk more than 6,000 soldiers.

The ship losses continued to mount. The paddle minesweeper *Brighton Queen* arrived at Dunkirk at 10.35 hours, having been under constant attack for the previous hour. She collected 700 French colonial troops and set off back to Margate thirty minutes later. Just as she started on Route X, *Brighton Queen* was attacked by a formation of Ju 87s, and a 500-pound bomb exploded close to her starboard quarter, blowing a hole in her side. Water poured into the paddle steamer and she began to sink quickly. The minesweeper *Saltash* sped to *Brighton Queen*'s assistance and was able to save around 400 men, but the rest of the French troops were lost.

Close behind *Brighton Queen* was the SS *Scotia* which had also picked up French troops, in her case some 2,000 men. She too came under attack from the Stukas and at least four bombs hit her and she began to sink by the bows. The destroyer *Esk*, with guns blazing, came to *Scotia*'s rescue, driving off her attackers. *Esk* took on board approximately 1,000 men and HMS *Worcester* collected a few more, but twenty-eight of *Scotia*'s crew were lost, as were 200 or 300 of the French soldiers.

French ships also suffered when, at approximately 16.00 hours, a convoy of French minesweeper-trawlers, which was returning to Dunkirk after landing troops in England, was attacked by dive bombers. In the space of just five minutes, three of them, *Denis Papin*, *Venus* and *Moussaillon*, were sunk.

On what the Admiralty called 'this black day', thirty-one vessels were sunk, including three Royal Navy destroyers, and eleven were damaged. Yet these bleak figures hide the true story of the day, which was that almost as many men had been landed in England as had been on 31 May. From the beaches 17,348 men had been saved and 47,081 from the East Mole, giving a total of 64,429. These figures were further broken down by the Admiralty to show that motor-boats and small craft had rescued 2,334 men, hopper barges had collected 1,470, private yachts 1,831, skoots 3,170, special service vessels 1,250, drifters 2,968 and trawlers had saved 1,876. French ships lifted 3,967, Belgian trawlers 402 and a Dutch yacht took 114.

One reason for such success was that the rate of embarkation was considerably increased during the day due to improved organisation. The destroyer *Vivacious*, for example, spent only fifteen minutes at the East Mole to collect 475 men, and *Shikari* needed only twenty minutes to take on board 623 troops.

With most of the ships having departed from Dunkirk after the morning rush, there was little that Wake-Walker could do until the coming night's evacuation, and he returned to Dover to confer with Ramsay. For his part, Tennant sent the following report to Dover on the situation, stating that, 'Things are getting very hot for ships, over hundred bombers on ships near here since 05.30, many casualties. Have directed that no ships sail during daylight. Evacuation for transports therefore ceases at 03.30.' He remained optimistic, nevertheless, finishing his message by declaring, 'If perimeter holds, will complete evacuation tomorrow, Sunday night, including most French.'[25]

Amongst those who had already reached England on 1 June was Lionel Tucker, who was serving with the RAOC as a motor engineer and attached to the 1st Battalion Oxford and Buckinghamshire Light Infantry:

> After spending a day trying to get aboard a boat of any kind without success an officer with a pistol in his hand ordered a large number of us to leave the beach and make our way to the 'Mole' which we found already packed with hundreds of troops.
>
> The trek to the end of the 'Mole' was disastrous, Jerry came over and made a direct hit causing many casualties, also a long delay in proceeding any further along.
>
> Eventually the gap was bridged and we were able to proceed, at that point I decided to remove all my webbing and equipment into the sea in case I had to swim for it. Eventually our savour was in sight, a fairly large ship which I learnt later was the 'Maid of Orleans'. By this time I had lost any idea of time and was thoroughly exhausted, got on board, flopped down on deck amongst the others and fell fast asleep, I remember nothing about the journey until I had a friendly kick from someone saying On your feet mate we are in Dover, I really couldn't believe what I was hearing was true. This was 09.45hrs on the 1st of June 1940.[26]

Just what it was like along the evacuation areas that first day of June was described by Squadron Leader C. G. Lott of Fighter Command's 43 Squadron:

> Big boats, little boats, boats with brass funnels, boats with strings of smaller boats strung out behind them like a duck with her ducklings. In a never-ending stream they crept over the water in both directions. The slowness of their movement was anguishing. Their vulnerability to air attack was so obvious as to make the spectacle truly heroic, and I could have both cheered and wept as I watched.[27]

Also still at Dover was Wake-Walker who, after a short sleep, went to the Dynamo Room to speak to Ramsay and the Dover staff. There he watched Captain M. M. Denny, who was in charge of the finer details of the operation. With him in the Dynamo Room were around twenty officers, both naval and military, Board of Trade and Sea Transport officials, who were supplying, controlling and fuelling the many warships and civilian vessels. Sometimes, after making one trip to Dunkirk, a merchant crew might refuse to go back again, but within a few hours, the officers and officials under Denny had found another crew, and the ship would be on its way once again.[28]

THE DUNKIRK VC

It was only because of the stubborn resistance of the soldiers holding the perimeter that so many men had been saved. General Küchler had aimed to bring the defence of Dunkirk to an end on 1 June with a major assault upon the southern part of the perimeter line, while diversionary attacks were carried out to the east and the west. The main assault would be undertaken by *Generalleutnant* Hansen's X AX corps, which would strike at Bergues where the British and French forces joined hands. Once Bergues was taken the flanks on both sides could be rolled up, while other forces drove through to Dunkirk.

The German assault began with a bombardment of Bergues and the adjacent canal line. Twenty-eight-years old Captain Harold Marcus Ervine-Andrews commanded a company of the 1st Battalion, East Lancashire Regiment and had been ordered to take over approximately 1,000 yards of the defences along the line of the canal to the east of Bergues. Ervine-Andrews later told of his experiences: 'I went up there on the evening of the 31st May to relieve one of my companies, D Company of my regiment. We knew we were in for a big attack the next day because all that day D Company had been having it pretty hard and at dawn on the 1st June the enemy attacked.'[29]

The Dunkirk perimeter was hardly distinguishable as a defensive line, being nothing more than an irregular chain of strong points. This meant that the intense artillery barrage put down by the Germans for some two or three hours had comparatively little effect and the East Lancs were able to hold back the enemy throughout the morning. One of Ervine-Andrews' forward posts, however, was running desperately short of ammunition. This was because during the retreat to Dunkirk, the men had been instructed to dispose of surplus ammunition and the supply dumps on the lines of communications had been destroyed to prevent their contents falling into the hands of the enemy. The men of the East Lancs, in particular, had been ready to embark when they were 'whipped up' and ordered back to the perimeter, and they had to search amongst dead bodies to try and find ammunition for their rifles.

Under mounting pressure, the East Lancs held on, but the shortage of ammunition became increasingly grave. The Germans had also succeeded in crossing the canal on both flanks and one of his sections was cut off, as Ervine-Andrews related: 'One of my sections was in a very, very, very, very, bad way. They had had a tremendous onslaught onto them, they were running very short of ammunition and they sent back and asked for urgent help and I looked round and I had no reserves whatsoever so I looked at the few soldiers who were with me in the company headquarters and said "look I am going up who's coming with me?" I said "give me that rifle" and I picked up a rifle and some ammunition and every single man there came forward with me. We went up, took over the position and the Germans had been lulled into a false sense of security and we were able then to hold up the attack on the position, and we held then for quite a long time until we ran out of ammunition.'

What Ervine-Andrews didn't say, was that the strong point he and his few men held was in a small barn across from the canal. The terrain, according to Ervine-Andrews was 'pretty good it was low lying, low land, intersected by dykes with very, very, few farm buildings here and there and a few folds in the ground but a very open area which gave me personally a very good field of fire'. Ervine-Andrews used that good field of fire to great effect by mounting the roof of the barn from where he could pick off the enemy with his rifle. It is believed that he personally accounted for seventeen Germans with his rifle before taking over a Bren gun in the barn and killing many more.

Though a company commander, Ervine-Andrews took it upon himself to fire most of the depleted stock of ammunition. He explained his reason for doing this in a later interview: 'We had the dominant position in that they were out in the open I was in a barn, they didn't know where I was and it's all very, very, quick you are firing ammunition and if you fire accurately and you hit men they are discouraged; it's when you fire a lot of ammunition and you don't do any damage the other chaps are very brave and push on, but when they are suffering severe casualties they are inclined to stop or as in this case they move round to the flanks because there is no point in going up and getting a bloody nose if you can avoid it by going round to a weaker position on either flank. Which is what the Germans did.'

Private Frank Curry was with Ervine-Andrews:

> We could see hundreds of Germans appearing in front of us. Captain Andrews shouted, 'Don't fire until they get right down to the canal.' …
> They'd fire their mortars, and try to come across in little rubber boats. We repulsed them, simple as that. We were behind the hedges with Bren guns and plenty of ammo, and we just riddled them like stupid. They were like suicide squads. Andrews was on top of a barn and could see them coming, and he'd send a runner down to us who'd say, 'Somebody coming on the left-hand hedges.'; or 'Enemy troops on the far right.'
> But then I could see the Germans stacking up on the hill, hundreds of them, and I thought, 'We can't keep this up. If 100 come at us and we shot half of them, some of them are still going to get across.'[30]

The odds were indeed too great for Ervine-Andrews' little band, which eventually could do no more, and succumbed to the inevitable; the burning barn having been all but blown to pieces and the men finally out of ammunition. Ervine-Andrews had held the position along the perimeter for more than ten hours – effectively holding up the Germans for a full day. He sent his wounded back in a carrier and then, with his remaining eight men he tried to lead his men back to the beach.

By this time his party was cut off from the rest of the BEF and all but surrounded. Taking advantage of any cover, they also had to swim or wade up to their chins in water along the canal for more than a mile to escape. Yet, thanks to Ervine-Andrews' determination, they made it through the enemy lines to the blood-soaked beaches and finally escaped back to England three days later.

It is with little wonder that Harold Ervine-Andrews was recommended for the Victoria Cross. According to the words in his citation in *The London Gazette*, 'Throughout this action, Captain Ervine-Andrews displayed courage, tenacity, and devotion to duty, worthy of the highest traditions of the British Army, and his magnificent example imbued his own troops with the dauntless fighting spirit which he himself displayed.'[31]

Ervine-Andrews' heroics may have been exceptional, but acts of courage were repeated along the perimeter as German pressure increased. The 1st Battalion, Loyal Regiment, was another of those that had started to move down to the evacuation area only to be recalled and thrown back into the firing line on the 29th, the men having to hold the perimeter for the next three days. With the Loyals, was a far from happy Lieutenant Richard Doll:

> During the previous night fifty of the battalion had been allowed to go down to the beach and embark, so we were expecting to get off at any minute. However, we were to be disappointed, for we were suddenly ordered forward to Bergues where we were told the Germans had broken through. The Adjutant borrowed four lorries from an artillery regiment and sent off D Company to hold the canal in front of Dunkirk while the rest set off the seven miles on foot.[32]

As it transpired, the Germans had not broken through, but Major General Curtis was grateful for the reinforcement of his composite garrison, which included stragglers from the Lincolnshire Regiment, the Welsh Guards, the Royal West Kents and a 'reliable' French battalion.

The bombardment of Bergues continued until the town was in ruins and the defenders exhausted. So, on the afternoon of the 1st, orders were issued to evacuate Bergues. Richard Doll, who was the 1st Loyals medical officer, was determined to save as many of the wounded in the now almost deserted town as he practically could, filling a 30cwt lorry with all those who were still able to fire a rifle:

> A difficulty soon arose, for the town was so shattered that we were unable to recognize our way about. We made one false attempt to get out, being halted by a blown-up bridge, when to our delight, we found a soldier who was apparently still on duty; he turned out to be a Royal Engineer who was dealing with the last bridge, and he directed us to it. Once again, we lost our way, and following a dispatch rider, we came out near the crest of the hill well in sight of the enemy. We turned at full speed and tore back over heaps of bricks and rubble into the town; two shells must have landed very near to us, for twice the car was shaken as loud explosions seemed to crash above us.[33]

Doll escaped to Malo-les-Bains, finding room on the SS *Maid of Kent*.

The defenders along the perimeter were forced to give ground in other areas, particularly to the east where the Coldstream Guards and the 2nd Battalion the Warwickshire Regiment were overwhelmed, but, by nightfall, the line had been stabilized. With only three-and-a-half divisions left on the ground, the perimeter had been reduced, with the eastern beaches being given up, so that the eastern flank, which was held by the 50th Division, ran along the Belgian border. The southern line of the perimeter, from Ghyvelde along the Furnes-Bergues Canal, was defended by the 1st Division and the 126th Brigade of the 42nd Division, whilst the 46th Division held the west flank which interfaced with *Général* Fagalde's men. No less than four German divisions were pitted against just six battalions holding the Bergues-Furnes Canal line, with a further two divisions pressed against the eastern perimeter held by only two battalions.[34]

The French had more than played their part, with *Général* Louis Janssen's 12th Division holding off a systematic attack by Kuechler's forces along the Belgium border – the months spent building defences throughout the previous winter proved not to have been wasted after all. The few tanks left with Kuechler had also been stopped by the French; *Général* Beaufrère's artillery firing over open sights each time a panzer rumbled into view.[35]

The RAF had also experienced success, shooting down six enemy aircraft. The Air Ministry made an announcement designed, no doubt, to lift morale at home and to counter complaints from the troops about the lack of protection from the *Luftwaffe*. The figures quoted, as with so many 'claims' from pilots on both sides, are considerably inflated:

> On Saturday. June 1, 78 enemy bombers and fighters were destroyed or severely damaged over the beaches between dawn and 7 p.m. Squadrons of Hurricanes and Spitfires flew above the French fens all day, guarding the convoys that were bringing home the B.E.F. rearguard. Huge formations of German bombers, escorted by fighters, came out and attempted to sink the ships. They did not lack targets, for the sea was thick with craft of all kinds. But when they attempted to bomb, our fighters attacked and drove them off. Most of the bombs fell into the sea [that, at least was true]. Many Junkers, Heinkels, Dorniers and Messerschmitts soon crashed into the sea after their bombs; 32 fighters were certainly destroyed.[36]

Much would depend on Fighter Command and the French over the course of the next twenty-four hours as the British rearguard took up its final positions and the last men prepared to escape. This was discussed by the First Sea Lord and the Chief of the Imperial Staff that evening. They had been asked to provide air cover for four hours on the 2nd, but Admiral of the Fleet Dudley Pound, the First Sea Lord, pointed out that it would take a destroyer ninety minutes to cross the Channel and therefore three hours for a round trip. If cover was provided only for four hours, it would leave just one hour for all the ships to find a berth and load up troops. This was clearly impossible, so it was agreed that evacuation could continue until 07.00 hours, with Fighter Command keeping its planes in the air until 08.30.[37]

There were still thousands of men in and around Dunkirk. If the Germans broke through the perimeter there would still be a bloodbath on the beaches regardless of the operations of the Royal Navy or the RAF.

Chapter 10

Operation *Dynamo*: Day 8, Sunday 2 June

A fter the heavy losses to shipping on 1 June from the attacks of the German Air Force, and the fact that the only route that was not previously dominated by enemy artillery, Route X, was now coming under fire from German artillery, Wake-Walker's decision to end all evacuations during daylight hours was entirely correct. But with part of I Corps, two French divisions and the 4,000 men of the rearguard still to be lifted, it was recognised that an enormous effort would be required during the night of 1-2 June. It was hoped in London that the evacuation would continue until all the troops had been rescued, but because so many men had been drowned by enemy action on the 1st, it was accepted that a point would be reached where it was more dangerous for the troops to attempt evacuation than to try and save themselves or surrender. The decision when to terminate Operation *Dynamo* was left with the men on the spot, this being communicated by General Ironside on the evening of the 1st:

> We do not order any fixed moment for evacuation. You are to hold on as long as possible in order that the maximum number of French and British may be evacuated. Impossible from here to judge local situation. In close co-operation with Admiral Abrial you must act in this matter on your own judgement.[1]

By using both sides of the East Mole and the beach, it was estimated that between 21.00 and 03.30 hours (this being the last time ships could depart Dunkirk and get safely past the German guns before daylight) 17,000 men could be evacuated. To enable this, the troops were to concentrate by the East Mole and one-and-a-half miles to the east. All minesweepers, as well as skoots and small craft, were to operate off the beaches, as well as about 100 small French vessels such as beach fishing boats, whilst seven personnel ships and eight destroyers were use the East Mole. The French troops were mostly posted to the west of Dunkirk, and drifters and MTBs were to go into the inner harbour to lift these soldiers from the West Mole, whilst small private boats used the Quay Félix Faure. The destroyers were to operate in pairs and the Admiralty ordered that these ships should continue to operate from the East Mole until 07.00 hours. Predictably, not all the vessels reaching Dunkirk were aware of these instructions and some embarkation continued during the daylight hours.

The owner of a Thames launch *Curlew* set off for Dunkirk on 1 June, arriving in French waters during the night of 1-2 June. With him was his friend and two young naval seamen lent as deckhands. He later wrote of his experiences:

As we made our way up the channel leading to the port we could see the flashes from the artillery holding the coast and a vast pall of smoke hung over the town itself. One of our destroyers, apparently damaged, was tied up to the mole and firing furiously, but our orders were not to stop at the harbour but to push on past it to a beach about two miles to the east. The whole place was littered with wrecks, and the only vessels under way were Cairngorm and ourselves. Cairngorm sounded her way carefully towards the beach, and we were able to follow in her wake at full speed. So we drew up to her and both of us went alongside a pair of Thames barges, the Glenway and the Lark, which were aground and apparently deserted. But they made good landing-stages for us, though we could not tie up because of the danger of grounding on the ebbing tide. Had we touched bottom we probably could not have got off again.

We were at the beach from 4.40 until 6.25 and this was the most uncomfortable hour and three-quarters that I have ever spent, because until we had got our troops aboard it was a question of putting our engines astern and ahead, astern and ahead, so as to hold the boat just clear of the sand. Meanwhile, we were bombed at intervals, and so were the troops waiting on the beach.

It had been our plan, had there been any destroyers or other large vessels nearby, to put our troops aboard them and go ashore for more, but the only other vessel was the destroyer that was firing shells from her berth at the mole ... So we had no option but to make off for Ramsgate with our load of troops.[2]

Another small craft that reached Dunkirk during the night was *Elvin*, a six-berth, thirty-six-foot 'gentleman's' motor-yacht, which went to France under Lieutenant Commander Archie Buchanan:

> We lay off the entrance until first light. We could hear gunfire to the eastward and saw a great pall of smoke over the town and flashes in the inner harbour. As soon as we could see we went alongside the eastern pier where a column of soldiers was drawn up. An officer called out '*Combien de soldats?*', and as I could not remember the French for twenty-five I replied '*Trente*', but before we could take on the thirty that had been detailed by the officer the sub rushed up from below and said that we were full.[3]

After speaking to a Royal Navy sub lieutenant in a small open motor-boat, Buchanan decided to try and take the soldiers out to a destroyer, but when he sailed out of the harbour he found that all the destroyers had gone:

> So we chased after some French minesweepers to westward hoping to put our soldiers on board, but they were unable to take them so decided to set course for Ramsgate. We had no idea where the swept channel was, but as we drew only three feet six inches and it was not low water we didn't think that there was much danger from mines.

Archie Buchanan also recalled one of the lighter moments that day: 'Fighters flew over us on four occasions, I pointed a rifle at the first one, but the soldiers in the cockpit shook their heads with rather amused smiles – the fighters were all RAF planes.'[4]

Elvin survived the return trip and has also survived the ravages of time and still sails today as a proud member of the Association of Dunkirk Little Ships.

The Hunt-class minesweeper *Lydd* reached Dunkirk just before midnight on 1 June. Her skipper was Lieutenant Commander Rodolph Cecil Drummond Haig:

> The beach and roads were being shelled, and there did not appear to be much boat traffic. I sent the motor boat inshore and it brought

off the Brigadier of the Brigade then embarking, who asked that a
message from the acting C–in–C might be sent to V.A. Dover [Ramsay]
asking that the embarkation should be diverted to the beach, as French
soldiers were causing congestion on the piers. It was also stated that
the rearguard would arrive about 0230. I informed V.A. Dover and
all the forces at Dunkirk of this by W/T. The difficulty at the beach
appeared to be lack of boats. With *Lydd*'s boats about two hundred
were embarked by 0245, 2nd June.

The ASW trawler HMS *Portsdown* also dropped anchor off the beaches late
on 1 June. 'Then,' wrote her skipper, Sub Lieutenant Richard H. Church, 'the
fun commenced':

> The first salvo landed 10 feet for'd of the stern, the next to port but in
> line. By this time all ships in the harbour were illuminated by the inferno
> of the oil dump. Anchor hove up and proceeded to move to 2 cables
> ahead, next salvo landed 50 feet astern. My 1st Lieutenant returned
> shortly after this to report that no troops were in evidence ashore. We
> proceeded towards the breakwater [Mole] inside the shipping, my
> draft being only seven feet, but were compelled to pull out owing to
> shells landing uncomfortably near, where we again dropped anchor. By
> this time the bombardment was continuous. We saw a number of large
> boats pulling or being towed ashore and hailed them. On their return
> journey none, however, came to our ship. I was informed that each ship
> had to do it's own ferrying. We possessed two 15 foot dinghies!

So Church moved inshore, dropping the anchor again and sending off his
two tiny boats which, between then, made seven trips. On the last trip, fifteen
'sodden' soldiers taken on board one of the boats proved too much and she sank
'like a stone' under the weight.

It was at that point that Church encountered a man in a large motor-boat
who answered the Sub Lieutenant's call in the dark for help. 'I want a thousand
men,' said Church. 'He gave me about 500 and plugged away in that inferno
and din, like a true Englishman. It is with regret that his name is unknown.'
He was just one of the many forgotten heroes of those nine days at Dunkirk.

Church, nevertheless, still had room for more men but by 04.00 hours the harbour seemed deserted and just a few men were visible on the beach, which the Anti-Submarine Warfare trawler could not reach. With dawn breaking, Church had decided to make for England but, a mile west of the East Mole, a French vessel was seen hard aground with approximately 1,000 soldiers on board. *Portsdown* went alongside and in half-an-hour had taken everyone off the stranded French ship. 'Never have I seen a man's face look so pleased or express such gratitude,' remembered Church of the French captain. 'He exclaimed in broken English words to the effect of what a "sitter" he would have been for a Nazi dive bomber!'

Church set off for Dover, but he had not finished saving people, for on the way back home, he picked up twenty-five British troops from a motor boat. Finally, he came across a motor-driven naval pontoon, which was steering out of control and collected the naval party of twelve.[5]

Also amongst those who got back to England on 2 June was Albert Powell, a driver with the Royal Signals attached to III Corps Medium Artillery Headquarters. His unit had been heavily bombed on 24 May at Poperinghe, the commanding office being killed. During the retreat to Dunkirk the unit had become dispersed and by the time Albert reached the beaches on 1 June there were only three other men with him:

We huddled together in the sand-dunes for protection from constant bombing and machine-gunning. To complete this nightmare scene, there was smoke coming from the oil tanks on fire at Dunkirk. At dawn the next day we were marshalled in groups of fifty by an officer or senior N.C.O., and marched down to the water's edge, where discipline was maintained by a naval beachmaster. Each group was called in turn – woe betide anyone who stepped out of line and tried to go out of turn! I saw one group run out of line and the person in charge was promptly shot by the beachmaster.

Owing to the shallow draft of the beach, the first job was getting on to a rowing boat which took us a little way out, and where we were transferred to a launch which then took us to the larger vessels laying further off. On the way out to the bigger ships, out launch was bombed, and although we didn't suffer a direct hit, one bomb hit the water close enough to us to swamp the boat and I found myself in the water ... I surfaced and looked around and saw there was a ship closer to me than the shore, so I struck out for her. She was a converted minesweeper called the *Medway Queen*. I was hauled out of the water totally exhausted – so were my mates.[6]

One Frenchman, Paul Dervilers, was fortunate in being picked up by *Medway Queen* as she made her way into Dunkirk:

I was on the beach walking up the coast towards Belgium when I saw some Englishmen getting into a dinghy and I joined ten of them who tried to get aboard. But the dinghy became waterlogged. We all began bailing hopelessly with our helmets. Fortunately, half-way to an off-lying ship, we picked up an abandoned little skiff in good shape and we got into it. It was 23.00 when we climbed up the ladder of the *Medway Queen*.[7]

Medway Queen left Dunkirk at 02.45 hours with 426 soldiers on board, and on the way back to England picked up ten Spanish labour force men, and the crews of two motor boats whose engines had broken down. The first ship to sail from Malo-les-Baines on 2 June was the paddle-steamer *Emperor of India*, which set off back to the UK at 02.38 hours with 213 troops.

Another group that was picked up in mid-Channel was that under Major Mark Henniker, who was in command of 253rd Field Company, Royal Engineers. Being frustrated at not being able to find a ship, Henniker decided that he would take matters into his own hands. He found two beached rowing boats and, stocking them up with food and water, hauled them off the sand and into the water:

After we had been rowing for about two hours we were out of sight of land. We then saw what I took to be a Royal Naval pinnace pointing towards us. The sea was like glass and, as we got closer, it seemed to be stationary or moving very slowly, for she had no bow wave ... We rowed towards her and found she was deserted, so we tied up astern and boarded her, there was a half eaten meal on a table and food and water in plenty aboard. A lieutenant commander's jacket was hanging on the back of the stateroom door with his name on the tailor's tab in the back.[8]

The vessel was a small armed yacht which showed signs of it having been damaged by the *Luftwaffe*. The engineers managed to get the yacht moving again, but, at 05.45 hours, HMS *Locust* overtook them heading for England. Lieutenant Ackroyd Norman Palliser Costobadie took Henniker and his twenty-eight men onboard the gunboat, which reached Dover safely at 10.05 hours.

The Troop Transport Ship, *Manxman*, under the command of its Master, P.B. Cowley, reached France just a few minutes after 05.00 hours:

Arrived at Dunkirk Mole. To our surprise, no Naval vessels of any description were present. Approximately 200 troops amongst whom was Brigadier Massey of the R.A. were on the Mole. These men moored us, and then embarked. As the visibility was poor I twice sounded the ship's siren to attract the attention of any more troops at the head of the Mole. A few soldiers carrying one wounded man came, which party were taken on board. A German bomber appeared and launched one aerial torpedo which fell 200 feet on the East side of the Mole. This bomber was chased away by three of our aircraft. As there was no person left on the Mole to let go ropes, we cut them and backed out and proceeded down the East channel in case any small boats might be coming off with troops. None came and I deemed it prudent to get out.[9]

As the destroyers (and a few other vessels unaware of the order to restrict evacuations to night time) would still be passing the German batteries in daylight, the RAF was asked to help, and twenty-four sorties by Blenheims were directed to the area near Pointe de Gravelines. They operated from first light until 07.45, when the last of the destroyers should have passed the crucial spot.

After the heavy attacks by the *Luftwaffe* on the 1st, Fighter Command put five full squadrons into the air over Dunkirk. The Spitfires and Hurricanes claimed eighteen enemy bombers and ten fighters, for the loss of just seven of their own machines. Further air protection was provided by Coastal Command between 08.30 and 11.00 hours with aircraft from 206, 235, 801 and 806 squadrons.

One of those Fighter Command pilots who flew on the early morning patrols was Flight Lieutenant Frankie Howell, in a Spitfire of 609 Squadron:

Dover, Ramsgate and Folkestone and all piers around Kent were crowded to overflowing, disembarking the troops and setting off again on the suicide journey. Naturally there were some pretty terrible sights as well, ships on their sides burning furiously, ships sinking and beached, and I even saw a salvo of bombs land smack in the middle of one large boat – it burst into flames, slowly turned over and sank in about 2 minutes.[10]

Howell found himself alone, having lost the other aircraft in his section:

I whistled around at 0 feet for a bit about 15 miles from Dunkirk. I thought I saw a boat, just a speck on the water, so I went to have a look. There were 8 or 10 Tommies and sailors rowing for dear life in a ship's lifeboat for England about 70 miles away! The way they were rowing they would miss England altogether, so I flew three times in the direction. They all stood up and waved and cheered poor devils. I only hope they were picked up alright, as I reported their position as soon as I landed.

Flying Officer Barrie Heath was also in the air over Dunkirk:

Dunkirk was seen from miles away by a the column of black smoke going up to over 30,000 feet. We did two tours at 24,000 feet along the beach and then we saw a large formation of Ju 87s below us. At that moment we turned and [Flight] Sergeant Sadler missed the turn, so I went out to bring him back and one of my colleagues told me later that as I broke away an Me 110 took my place which was lucky for me. We shot down a number of Ju 87s, but of course the whole squadron had split up. I got mine and my hand was shaking so much that I went on firing into the sea as I was pulling out of my dive.[11]

The efforts of the RAF formed the subject of an article that appeared in a number of American newspapers on 2 June. One such, carried the headline 'PARIS SENDS U.S. ENVOY FROM FLANDERS "HELL"', with the envoy being Count René de Chambrun, who was reported to be travelling to Washington to advise President Roosevelt on events in France. The Count had been the liaison officer between the 1st French Army and the BEF. He wrote of his Dunkirk experience:

> As we left the French coast, three squadrons of Heinkels, twenty-seven in all, converged from three directions … six British fighters [of 264 Squadron] appeared in the sky at the precise moment that the Germans jettisoned their mines, they dived on them. They fought under our eyes the finest air battle I have ever seen. In a few minutes, almost all the Heinkels had been hit and fell in the sea, leaving behind them long trails of smoke. Only when I reached Dover did I learn the news: the first 'Bolton [Boulton Paul] Defiants' with their revolving turrets had been sent that very morning over the Channel by the R.A.F. This extraordinary sight, which has come to my mind often since, convinced me with absolute certainty, that any German attempt at a landing on British soil would be doomed to fail.[12]

The determined display by the RAF cost it dear in both men and machines, as this eye-witness account of aircraft returning from Dunkirk to RAF Hawkinge describes:

> Pilots flew in with petrol gauges reading empty, hydraulics shot away, ammunition expended, engines smoking, tail sections crumpled, and trailing fabric like bunting.b Some of the hasty landings would have made the hair of any instructor stand on end. Aircraft clipped the perimeter trees and hedges, ploughed through the fences, and dug deep grooves in the turf. Machines stood up on their propellers, some

cartwheeled, some skidded across the field on their canopies [i.e. upside-down]. Even a pirouette was not uncommon.[13]

This had been 611 Squadron's first day of combat, and they were able to claim three Ju 87s and three Bf 109s destroyed plus one Bf 109 as a probable and another damaged. The squadron's achievements that morning were celebrated upon its return to RAF Digby with a champagne breakfast.

The skipper of the motor-yacht *Marsayru* also had cause to comment on the actions of Fighter Command that day:

> We were of course under constant fire of various kinds, but I have the honour to report that the ship was not hit by anything. On one day – Sunday 2nd June I think – we were singled out for attention (we were alone, nearest ship being about 2½ miles away) by 4 brave Messerschmitts who dived and machine-gunned us with much vigour but exceedingly poor aim for about half an hour. We had a Bren and 2 rifles but did not use them as the German pilots seemed disinclined to come nearer than 2,000 feet and I had given orders to hold our fire to 1,000 feet range. A pity. After half an hour of this three Hurricanes hove in sight and we saw no more of the Messerschmitts after that.[14]

Helped by the support given by the RAF, the Allies also took to the offensive on the ground, with the bridgehead the Germans had established on the north bank of the Bergues-Furnes canal being driven back over the water by the 21e Centre d'instruction divisionnaire supported by six Somua 35 tanks.

After the evacuations of the morning just how many troops remained in and around Dunkirk was not known with any degree of precision. It was thought there might only be 2,000, plus the 4,000 British rearguard, but the number of French troops remaining was increasing by the hour and was now in the region of 50,000 to 60,000.

At 10.30 hours, an urgent request was sent to Ramsay from Dunkirk for Hospital Carriers: 'Wounded situation acute and Hospital Ships should enter during day. Geneva Convention will be honourably observed it is felt and that the enemy will refrain from attacking.'[15]

As this appeared to be the only way of evacuating the wounded, observing that the whole facilities of the port during the night evacuation hours would be required for fighting troops, it was decided to send two Hospital Ships during the daylight, hoping that, indeed, the Germans would not attack them.

The first to head for Dunkirk was *Worthing*, which sailed at 13.00, followed by *Paris* four hours later. At 14.40 *Worthing*, which was about two-thirds of the way across the Channel, was attacked by twelve Ju 87s. There were no casualties but she had suffered some superficial damage and returned to England.

Then at 19.15 *Paris* reported that she had also been attacked at roughly the same point as *Worthing*. She had been bombed and badly damaged with her engines rendered useless. A little while later she was attacked again by three aircraft and damaged still further. At 19.47 hours, she sent out an SOS, and tugs *Sun XV*, *Sun IV* and *Lady Brassey* were sent to her assistance. Another tug, *Foremost 87*, also rushed to her aid. *Foremost 87* had left Dover at 16.00 hours with the lifeboats *Cecil and Julian Philphott* and *Thomas Kirk Wright* in tow. As the tug approached the pre-determined point where the lifeboats were to be released, *Paris* was spotted in difficulties. *Foremost 87*'s skipper was Captain James Edwin Fryer:

I at once altered course and steamed towards *Paris*. On approaching her I noticed several explosions and machine gunning. I also saw several lifeboats with survivors from *Paris* who had taken to their boats owing to *Paris* being bombed and machine gunned causing *Paris* to slowly fill with water. I at once gave orders for every possible assistance to get survivors taken from these lifeboats which were half-full of water. Managed to get 95 survivors in all from lifeboats – some seriously injured. Also took on board 13 Spaniards who were in lifeboat. Interviewed these but could not get any satisfaction as to how they came to be adrift in a boat, so handed them over to the Army authorities on reaching Dover.[16]

Paris was abandoned by her medical team and all her crew except the captain and some of his officers. This meant that the last attempt to evacuate the wounded by Hospital Carrier from Dunkirk failed. *Paris* subsequently sank shortly after midnight on 3 June, ten miles off the French coast, after being attacked a third time. Ramsay informed the Admiralty of these appalling attacks by the *Luftwaffe*, making it plain, that the circumstances admitted 'of no mistake of their identity.'

The loss of *Paris* was also reported by Commander Dean in HMS *Sabre*. The destroyer had left Dunkirk at 18.45 in company with her sister ship *Shikari*. As the two destroyers were passing near the Ruytingen bank buoy, *Paris* was seen to be sinking and to have boats away. Dean saw that the hospital ship was receiving assistance and, after sending a signal back to Dover continued to Dunkirk.

Shortly afterwards, *Sabre* herself came under fire, but she made smoke and suffered no damage, tying up alongside the East Mole at 21.10, and immediately embarking troops. These soldiers earned Commander Dean's praise: 'These were all part of the rearguard of the B.E.F. and included men of the Green Howards. Only 15 came on board in stretchers, but a further 50-odd were carried by their comrades and the seamen: most of these collapsed on arrival and over 50 had to be hoisted out on stretchers at Dover. Their courage was magnificent and I never heard a complaint and hardly ever a groan.'[17]

As *Sabre* left the East Mole flashing signals were observed from the wreck of *Mosquito*. Dean went to investigate, placing *Sabre*'s bows gently against the abandoned destroyer. Three men were taken off. They turned out to be Royal Artillery officers who had evaded capture by paddling off in a small boat. The boat had evidently been made fast to *Mosquito* with what Brian Dean mockingly called a 'Soldier's hitch' knot which had come undone. The boat drifted away leaving them stranded. They were fortunate in finding a signal lantern and so were able to attract *Sabre*'s attention. The rest of *Sabre*'s trip was uneventful as she arrived at Dover at 01.20 hours on the 3rd.

With no hospital ships coming to their rescue, the men of the Royal Army Medical Corps were placed in the situation of knowing that if they wanted to escape to England they would have to leave their wounded and, in all too many cases the dying, to the mercy of the enemy. This, these courageous doctors, nurses, assistants, orderlies and drivers simply could not do. They would stay with their patients. They knew that in doing so they would inevitably be taken prisoner. What lay ahead for them was, at best, the humiliation of defeat and years behind barbed wire; or at worst, if the Germans didn't play by the rules, a bullet in the head or a bayonet in the chest. The fact that the Hospital Carriers had been bombed indicated all too clearly that there was a distinct chance that the men would be treated badly.

The 11th Casualty Clearing Station had set up its operating rooms at La Panne, which was soon to be overrun, and the stark reality was that space on the other ships, Churchill had told Gort, had to be reserved for men who were able to carry a gun, 'the country's imperative need', the Prime Minister had earlier said, 'is for men with whom to reconstitute fresh divisions without loss of time'.[18] The severely wounded, who could be of no immediate use to the Army, would have to be left behind. Rather than let all the medical staff be captured, the colonel in charge decided that it was only necessary for one doctor and ten orderlies to remain for every 100 patients. The question of who remained was settled by drawing lots.

THE LAST ESCAPE

An impressive collection of vessels was assembled for the night evacuation. These were eleven transports, one 'autocarrier', two stores carriers, one paddle-steamer, eleven fleet minesweepers, two yachts, nine drifters, four tugs, one gunboat, fifteen motor-boats, with a further four motor-boats for 'traffic control'. The total capacity of these, in one lift, it was calculated, amounted to 34,000 men, but because of the limitations of the port facilities and the available hours of darkness, it was thought that only 18,000 could be evacuated. Large numbers of French ships would also be available, including destroyers, drifters and trawlers. They would be using the western side of the port and the adjacent beaches. It was estimated that 20,000 French could be embarked.[19]

Earlier in the day, Ramsay had sent an inspirational signal to all the HM destroyers and minesweepers: 'The final evacuation is staged for tonight, and the Nation looks to the Navy to see this through. I want every ship to report as soon as possible whether she is fit to meet the call which has been made on our courage and endurance.'[20]

The fifteen destroyers that declared they were fit and ready for service were given specific time slots in which they had to arrive at Dunkirk, with *Shikari* and *Sabre* to berth against the eastern side of the East Mole at 21.00 hours, with the other destroyers to arrive every thirty minutes. As the rearguard might have to withdraw in a hurry if pursued by the enemy, the warships were issued with special brows and ladders at Dover, and the destroyers were told to have boxes ready to form steps to help the troops embark as quickly as possible.

After seeing the last of the ships leave Dunkirk on the morning of 2 June, Wake-Walker had gone back to Dover again. There he saw the harbour, 'full of destroyers, sloops and minesweepers, many with the signs of their strenuous time upon them – bent bows, holes and the evidence of bumps and collisions. Some were out of action altogether and all were enjoying the first few hours at rest in harbour that many of them had had for days.'[21]

Feeling somewhat refreshed after a brief rest at Dover, Wake-Walker returned to Dunkirk and disembarked at the shore end of the East Mole to discuss the coming night's arrangements with Tennant: 'From there I went to the "Bastion" which was the headquarters of the Army and the local French Naval and Military Command. From the root of the pier [Mole] it was a ten-minute walk along a road which ran behind the old ramparts of the town facing seaward on the left hand. On the right were buildings and sheds, mostly roofless or damaged, that hid shipbuilding slips or shipyards. Mounted on the embrasures was a French field gun which was firing back over the town. The road was fairly clear but littered with lorries and cars the whole way, leaving little room to dodge others which careered along the road at intervals. Men straggled along the road and one Frenchman asked for directions, but there were very few troops to be seen as they were kept away on the beach behind the shelter of the wall except when ships were coming alongside.'

Commander James Campbell Clouston, pier master on the East Mole, also headed back to Dunkirk after returning from a meeting at Dover, sailing on the fast motor-boat *Seaplane Tender 243*, which was accompanied by her sister boat *S.T. 276*. It was intended that these two nimble boats would act as 'runners' for Wake-Walker during the night's operations. At approximately 18.55 hours, when around six miles off Gravelines, four enemy aircraft attacked the two boats, with *S.T. 243* being fatally damaged by a bomb that hit the water nearby. Clouston ordered *S.T. 276* to get away before it too was sunk, and it carried on to Dunkirk.

Only one other officer as well as Clouston survived the attack on *S.T. 243*, and these two abandoned the sinking vessel in a bid to reach another boat they had spotted a couple of miles away. But Clouston soon realised that he was too exhausted after his long nights on the Mole to reach the boat, and he turned back to the sinking launch. He did not make it. The other officer did swim to the boat, which turned out to be an abandoned ship's cutter. He drifted around in this for some time until he was picked up by a French trawler. It later transpired that one of *S.T. 243*'s rating had also been rescued.[22]

Motor Anti-Submarine boat *MASB 6* was sent to look for the drifter *Girl Gladys*, which had been reported broken down seven miles east of Dunkirk. After picking up eighteen soldiers from an open boat, *MASB 6* continued along the French coast looking for *Girl Gladys*, as her skipper recalled:

> At approximately 1720 when out of sight of land we were attacked by either six or eight dive-bombers, 20 to 30 bombs were dropped and fell at distances varying from 10 to 50 yards of the ship. The bombers appeared to attack in pairs out of the sun and having released their bombs continued their dive firing machine-guns.
>
> Course was altered frequently in an endeavour to miss the bombs. Some appeared to explode after entering the water, some on striking the surface and a certain number appeared not to explode at all. One exploded under the bow right ahead and the ship passed through the splash. A certain amount of discomfort was experienced by myself and members of the crew who were exposed to the splash in the eyes for the next twelve hours or so.
>
> Able-Seaman Power was wounded in the leg when manning the port turret also one of the soldiers in the fore peak. As I now had wounded on board I considered it advisable to return to Dover forthwith … The bombing to which the ship had been subjected had caused leaks to the hull and the petrol tank and the ship was not used again for that night's operation.[23]

At 15.38, Tennant submitted a situation report to Ramsay in which he stated that in general the French were holding the perimeter and he declared, 'Present situation hopeful.' If the French could hold the line until nightfall when the evacuation would recommence in earnest, the last of the BEF could well get away without too much resistance from the enemy.

In fact, the Germans had resumed their assault upon the perimeter just half-an-hour or so earlier when 61 Infanterie Division, supported by tanks from 9 Panzer Division had attacked along the road to Spycker, while over to the east 56 Infanterie Division had tried to break through the positions held by the French 12th Division. In both instances the defenders had shown the kind of determination that saw them hold back the Germans for four years in the First World War. In the fighting, the 12th Division lost its fine commander, General Janssen. Though the perimeter held in most sectors, a major assault upon Bergues, preceded by a heavy bombardment by Ju 87s, saw the town taken by Küchler's 18th Infanterie Division. The Germans, however, were halted on the banks of the Canal des Moëres.

Wake-Walker and the senior officers held back all the ships and boats that had approached Dunkirk until nightfall when they would be released for the mass descent upon the harbour and the beach. In preparation for the evening rush, minesweepers, destroyers, anti-submarine trawlers and drifters worked to ensure that the swept channel remained clear of any danger – yet this placed some of those vessels within range of the enemy. At 16.15 the anti-submarine trawler *Blackburn Rovers* was struck by a torpedo, probably fired from a small coastal submarine. Two other anti-submarine trawlers were also hit; *Spurs* was bombed and severely damaged, and *Westella* was sunk by a torpedo – possibly from the same submarine that attacked *Blackburn Rovers*. These losses notwithstanding. the channel was rendered safe as evening approached.

At 17.00 hours, the movement of the great armada towards Dunkirk began. As well as the destroyers, this collection of vessels consisted of thirteen personnel ships, two large store carriers, five paddle minesweepers, nine fleet minesweepers, one special service vessel, nine drifters, six skoots, two armed yachts and one gunboat. There was also a large number of tugs, lifeboats, etc. formed either in organised tows or operating independently. The exact composition of the French contingent was unknown, though it was thought to consist of six small destroyers, four despatch boats and about 120 fishing craft.

One of those that went in that evening was Sub Lieutenant (Acting) G.A. Cadell who took over command of HM Motor Boat *Lady Cable* earlier on 2 June from a Mr Goodall, who had operated the boat for the owner and who had already undertaken one trip to Dunkirk. After taking on water, provisions and fuel, she was taken in tow by *Sun VI*, along with two life-boats and one other craft, setting off for Dunkirk at approximately 15.30. Sub Lieutenant Goodall submitted the following report:

After uneventful trip arrived off Dunkirk harbour at about 2230 and received orders to proceed in harbour and go a long way up the Mole to embark soldiers – fill up and return to tug, then go in for further loads. At times had difficulty in persuading French troops to embark in *Lady Cable*, the reason apparently being reluctance to break their units or to act without definite orders from their officer who was probably still in the town of Dunkirk. However, we took four boat loads off – each load containing between 40 and 50 soldiers. Three loads I took to tugs – and one to HMS *Wishart* when tug was not in usual position.

Spoke to tug after forth trip and was informed that it would soon be light and that she couldn't wait much longer. In reply to a question if any British Officers were still left on the Mole, I replied that on earlier trips I had seen one who had asked me not to leave him behind. This Officer was engaged in helping the embarkation of the troops. I had not seen him on my last trip but told tug I would make another trip to see if he was there. Informed tug would be as quick as possible and if tug could not wait, would return to England under own power. Tug said she could only wait a short while.

On going in for fifth time engines began to go badly and stopped altogether before reaching point of embarkation. Engines got going again and we went alongside and collected about 24 more French soldiers. There was no sign of British Officer and Price reported to me that French on the Mole told him he had gone. I sent Price up on to the Mole to make enquiries. Owing to the improbability of tug waiting for us, I only took 24 soldiers as a greater number would have made trip back to England under own power too hazardous.[24]

Some indication of the conditions around the harbour and the Mole, with scores of ships dashing around the waters, can be gleaned from the report of Sub Lieutenant M.J.R Yeatman, who took charge of the Lowestoft lifeboat *Michael Stephens* with just three other crew. The lifeboat, which was towed across the Channel by the tug *Sun XI*, reached Dunkirk at around 22.00 hours.

As *Michael Stephens* entered the harbour she was rammed by a motor-boat, but without causing serious damage. Yeatman tied up against the East Mole and, with difficulty, persuaded twelve French soldiers to get on board. He pushed off from the Mole to find *Sun XI*, but the tug had moved on. He did find a trawler, nevertheless, and was able to transfer the Frenchmen. Yeatman returned to the harbour – being rammed by another MTB on the way in – to see a sloop trying to berth against the Mole but being repeatedly pushed away by the 'swish' of the tide. Using the powerful engines of the lifeboat, Yeatman was able to push the sloop against the Mole and hold her there while her crew made her secure.

Yeatman then tied his own vessel against the Mole: 'Climbed onto the Mole, which was being shelled, and by means of some forceful language and a rifle butt, induced the French troops who were lying on the Mole to start down on to the sloop. Once a few had started they all began to go down.' Yeatman took fifty-two of the French soldiers on board *Michael Stephens* and returned to Dover under the lifeboat's own power – and being rammed yet again, this time by a fishing boat. *Michael Stephens* reached England at 07.10. In his report, Yeatman commented on the accuracy of the German artillery, writing that he found 'considerably greater risk from the movements of Allied craft than from Nazi shelling'![25]

Despite the obvious difficulties and dangers, the evening evacuation went very smoothly with the shipping being well-controlled. There was, though, one unfortunate incident, involving the French cross-Channel ferry, *Rouen*. As the tide began to ebb, *Rouen*, which had collected a number of men from the harbour, became stranded on the mud. The tug *Foremost* went to help pull the French ferry clear but herself grounded and only just managed to reverse engines and get back into deeper water. A smaller tug, *Sun X*, then went in, but found that even 200 yards from *Rouen* there was only ten feet of water beneath her keel, and it was evident that *Rouen* could not be moved until the next tide.

Rear Admiral Taylor, who it may be recalled was the Maintenance Officer for *Dynamo* at Sheerness, whose work was done, decided to sail to Dunkirk to see if he could help with the evacuation from Malo-les-Bains, where the little boats he had prepared were due to operate. He crossed the Channel in the motor cruiser *White Wing*, on board which was David Devine.[26]

Having an Admiral on board, we were not actually working the beaches but were in control of small boat operations. We moved about as necessary and, after we had spent some time putting boats in touch with their towing ships, the 5.9 battery off Nieuport way began to drop shells on us. It seemed pure spite. The nearest salvo was about twenty yards astern, which was close enough. We stayed there until everybody else had been sent back and then went pottering about looking for stragglers.

At 21.45 it was learned that the former LNER train ferry converted to a landing ship, *Royal Daffodil*, had been bombed and strafed near the North Goodwin Light Vessel on the outward passage, from where she returned to England. Her skipper was Captain A.P.J. Paterson:

> On our sixth trip we were attacked by a group of dive bombers that had just sunk the hospital ship *Paris*, and we received a direct hit from a delayed-action bomb. This penetrated two decks and came out at the waterline on the starboard side and burst in the sea astern. By shifting all moveable gear to the port side and filling the swung-out lifeboat on that side with water, we listed the vessel and were able to raise the hole clear of the water. We then patched it with tarpaulins and bedding.
>
> Meantime, the shock of the explosion had flooded the engine room and we were being rapidly carried by the spring tide towards a mined area. However, the Chief Engineer managed to get the engines to move in time and we arrived safely back in Ramsgate.[27]

When *Royal Daffodil* reached Ramsgate, a 16-year-old apprentice with the General Steam Navigation Company based at Deptford, Tom Mogg, was asked to count all the bullet holes in the ship, 'and there were thousands of them,' Tom recalled:

> When I walked into the ship, it was a bright sunny day outside, and it gave the impression that I was walking into a colander – there were so many shafts of light beaming in through the holes. We circled every bullet hole we found, measured it, and made a note of it. If the hole was more than two inches across it had to be fixed by a shipwright, less than two inches and it could be done by a carpenter. The Royal Daffodil had also been dive-bombed on its final crossing and the bomb had passed through three decks into the engine room, missing the fuel tank by inches, and exited the hull before it exploded. It had been a

very lucky escape for those onboard. The captain had to instruct all the soldiers to move to the port side to try to raise the hole in the starboard side out of the water.[28]

The Halcyon-class minesweeper *Leda* set off from Dover at 16.45 hours and was off the entrance to Dunkirk Harbour by 23.00. She went in and berthed against the East Mole as German artillery shelled the harbour entrance. Not a single soldier was seen along the Mole, and, after fifty minutes, Lieutenant Commander Harold Unwin was ordered to slip his berth and go back to the UK. He returned empty.

Yeoman/Signaller Victor Chanter, with the naval beach party, was still helping to organise the embarkation:

Soon, with the evacuation of the gun crews along the beach, it would be time for the demolition of everything of use to the enemy ... devastation strewn over miles of sand.

As the number of those awaiting evacuation dwindled, our chance of being left behind increased. Consequently, our officer began letting our group off one at a time along with the army. Night time on what was to be our last day found us searching for suitable floating material for our own departure.

During the hours of darkness later that evening, while the officer and I were helping some of the remaining soldiers into a boat from what was left of our pier, he asked who I was and suggested that I should leave with the next lot.

With just three others, Vic wandered along the beach and eventually they found two dinghies:

We waded out until we were able to pull ourselves into the floats. The officer and I were in one ... and his orders were that both dinghies should stay as close as possible to each other we paddled into the dark.

How far out we went with the receding tide I've no idea, but out of the blackness a voice hailed us, and we came alongside. Scrambling nets were already down the ship's sides, and a voice rasped, 'Up you go.'[29]

With the French stoutly holding the perimeter and darkness concealing movement, the rearguard slipped away from the positions in front of the enemy and made its way towards Malo-les-Bains and the harbour, and by 23.00 most of the British troops had been embarked. The last unit to be lifted from Dunkirk was the 1st Battalion King's Shropshire Light Infantry, which departed on the Channel ferry *St Helier*, which slipped the East Mole at 23.00 hours. It was that moment when Captain Tennant despatched a short message to Dover. Though it was the briefest signal sent since *Dynamo* began, it was the most welcome message of all. It simply read: 'B.E.F. evacuated. Returning now.'[30]

Chapter 11

Operation *Dynamo*: Day 9, Monday 3 June

On 2 June, 26,265 men reached England, of which 6,695 had been lifted from the beaches and 19,561 from the harbour and the East Mole. A similar number would be rescued on 3 June, mostly from the night evacuation of 2/3 June.

Amongst those vessels that joined in the evacuation on the night of 2/3 June was the Kingfisher-class Patrol Sloop *Guillemot*, commanded by Lieutenant Commander Henry Maxwell Darrell-Brown. The ship was off Dunkirk at 23.00 hours, and reached the West Mole at 23.55:

It was high water and owing to the shape of the Mole the ship could not lie close enough for the brow to reach. This difficulty was solved by heaving the bow in and utilising the flare of the bow. The ship secured past HMS *Speedwell* which was lying at the outboard end of the Mole.

There were about six hundred French troops ashore, and after thirty-one minutes of embarkation the ship was full, and cast off from the Mole, leaving about two hundred troops behind. Boats were seen approaching the Mole and it was thought that the remaining troops would be collected by them. *Guillemot* cast off at 02.25. There was considerable congestion at the entrance and collision was with difficulty avoided. Aircraft flares were seen on the return journey but no attacks were made on the ship. Thick fog came down at daylight, and the ship anchored near the Foreland Buoy at 04.28 for one hour, arriving at Margate at 07.00 and disembarked 387 Officers and men.

Commander C. Hammond, was placed in charge of five Dutch skoots – *Pascholl*, *Bornrif*, *Lena*, *Reiger* and *Hornsrug* – and instructed to sail into Dunkirk harbour and use the West Mole and the inner new disembarkation pier. After leaving behind *Reiger*, which ran aground, Hammond, sailing in *Pascholl*, took the remaining ships into the harbour, but found that the water by the inner pier was too shallow. He backed out towards the West Mole, which he could see silhouetted against the burning town:

> Meanwhile, two of my boats went passed me and tried to go alongside the west side of the West Pier [Mole]. They got their bows up to the pier but had a job getting their stern to, and *Lena*, which was the outside ship of the two, grounded just off the pier. I got alongside the east side and *Hornsrug* came alongside me.
>
> The pier was full of French troops and I was very glad to find Commander [H.R.] Troup who said he had appointed himself pier-master. He and I were unable to get a tug to pluck *Lena* off and finally had to take the men off and leave her.

Meanwhile, the other skoots were taking the French troops off the West Mole, urged on by Troup who was becoming hoarse from shouting. 'At about 00.30,' continued Hammond, 'we had a good load, though we could have taken more. There was a lull in the arrival of troops and there were ships waiting to get alongside, so I decided, after consulting Troup, to go with what I had.[1]

The skipper of the paddle-steamer *Marmion* was Temporary Lieutenant H.C. Gaffney, who wrote a staccato report of his ship's actions on the morning of the 3rd:

> Vessel under gunfire – aircraft active. Entered harbour 0100. Vessel alongside mole – considerable swell – no troops for some time – much shelling. Embarked 204 troops and told to clear off as no more troops arriving. Port paddle fouled by floating rope. Cleared harbour at 0233 – proceeded to Dover.

The last of the vessels left Dunkirk as day was breaking, leaving behind tens of thousands of French troops, as well as numerous British wounded, whose only hope of salvation was in being rescued by the Royal Navy and the Little Ships that might return in the coming night. But many of the crews had been working almost without respite since 26/27 May, and this was not just ordinary labour. They had to operate under bombardment from the sky and the land, with the decks of their ships crowded with soldiers, allowing little or no space for the crews, either volunteer civilian or naval, to rest or relax. It was even remarked upon by one Royal Navy officer that as the days wore on it was the crews who were looking more dishevelled and exhausted than the soldiers they were embarking.[2]

The crews had been pushed to the very limit but with what had been estimated to be as many as 30,000 men still to be saved, Ramsay knew every effort had to be made to try and rescue as many of them as he could in the hours that were left, not least because the actions of *Général* Fagadle, and the men who had come under his command, had enabled the BEF to be saved. Ramsay understood the importance of saving as many of the valiant French troops as possible, but he told the Admiralty that asking his men to make yet another trip into the horror of Dunkirk, might prove beyond them:

> After nine days of operations of a nature unprecedented in naval warfare, which followed on two weeks of intense strain, commanding officers, officers and ships' companies are at the end of their tether.
>
> I therefore view a continuation of the demands made by evacuation with the utmost concern as likely to strain to breaking point the endurance of officers and men.
>
> I should fail in my duty did I not represent this to Their Lordships the existence of this state of affairs in the ships under my command, and I consider it would be unfortunate after the magnificent manner in which officers and men of the surviving ships which have faced heavy loss and responded to every call made upon them, that they should be subjected to a test which I feel may be beyond the limit of human endurance.[3]

Ramsay accepted that one more attempt would have to be made, but he told the Lords of the Admiralty that if the evacuation continued beyond the night of 3-4 June, fresh crews would have to be found, as he would not ask his men to go again. This was accepted by the Admiralty and was relayed to the French Admiralty, which agreed that the operation on the coming night would be the last.

Ramsay now had to communicate this to his tired and nerve-shattered sailors, sending what would prove to be his last signal of Operation *Dynamo*, to all the destroyers, minesweepers and auxiliary vessels:

> I hoped and believed that last night would see us through but the French who were covering the retirement of the British rearguard

had to repel a strong German attack and so were unable to send their troops to the pier in time to be embarked.[4]

We cannot leave our Allies in the lurch and I must call on all the officers and men detailed for further evacuation tonight to let the world see that we never let down our ally.

The approach will be made later and the retirement earlier. The night protection of our fighters which stopped all bombing of the harbour last night will be repeated.

THE FINAL NIGHT

With no daylight movement of shipping close to the French coast, it meant that the RAF could concentrate its efforts in a far narrower time-frame. Protection was therefore arranged by Coastal Command between Dover and Dunkirk from 19.30 until nightfall on the 3rd, and then on 4 June four squadrons from Fighter Command were to patrol from 04.30 until 06.15 hours, by which time it was expected that the last ships would be in home waters.

The actual final lift was to take place between 22.30 on the 3rd to 02.30 on the 4th. The destroyers, personnel ships, corvettes, skoots and paddle steamers would operate from the East Mole. The ships were to use the full length of the Mole, being sent in and despatched as quickly as possible. There would be no time to hang around. The drifters and small craft were to go directly into Dunkirk harbour, and any other British craft were to use the West Mole (called the New Avant Port). French vessels, of an unknown number, were to pick up any soldiers they found at Malo-les-Bains beach, the Quai Félix Faure and the West Mole.

At Ramsay's disposal were nine passenger ferries, nine destroyers, four paddle minesweepers, seven fleet minesweepers, nine drifters and two corvettes. The Dragonfly-class River Gunboat *Locust* would also accompany the flotilla and would wait off Dunkirk where it would receive men ferried out to her from smaller vessels.

The French were to send craft to Dover during the day where they would be organised into flotillas for the crossing to Dunkirk for the night-time evacuation. In addition to this, four French torpedo boats were available.

This was enough shipping to embark the 30,000 French troops that the British Naval Liaison Officer at French Naval Headquarters had told Ramsay were at Dunkirk. Such a number was estimated to be around 5,000 more than could be taken from Dunkirk harbour, the rest would have to be lifted from Malo beach. In reality, there was around double that number of French soldiers in and around Dunkirk. Many would be left behind.

Even though there was a full night of evacuations ahead, the original timetable for the blocking of Dunkirk's Inner Harbour, to render the port unusable by the enemy (Operation *C.K.*), was to be maintained. Admiral Abrial had asked if the blockade ships could arrive at Dunkirk at 03.00 hours on 4 June but when he was made aware of just how many French soldiers remained to be evacuated, he asked that the blockade be postponed. Ramsay, nevertheless, believed that the evacuation would be unaffected by blocking the Inner Harbour, and so the blockade ships were ordered to sail as previously planned.

The three blockships, *Westcove*, *Edward Nissen* and the MV *Holland*, arrived at Dunkirk in the company of *Vivacious* and two naval motor boats (Motor Anti-Submarine boat *07* and Motor Torpedo Boat *107*) which the destroyer had towed across the Channel. At 02.45 the blockships entered the harbour, just as a long line of destroyers was making its way out to sea laden with rescued troops. Concealed behind the destroyers was a large and fast transport ship which, appearing out of the semi-darkness, bore down on *Holland*. Even before she was hit, the skipper of *Holland*, knowing exactly what was going to happen, called out 'Abandon Ship!' The transport crashed into *Holland* just before the boiler room bulkhead. The ship went down by the bows almost immediately. Luckily, she was only in eight feet of water and all the crew were saved, though two were severely injured in the collision.

The other two blockships continued into the Inner Harbour. At the allotted point, *Westcove* swung hard to starboard with the intention of smashing into the Inner West Jetty, but her bows got stuck in the mud while still fifty feet from the jetty. Likewise, *Edward Nissen* put her wheel about to charge into the East Jetty. Though the operation had not gone to plan, both crews fired their scuttling charges, but when the charges exploded on *Westcove* she shifted off the mud and came to rest on her keel in mid channel. The result of the blockade attempt was that there was still a gap of some fifty feet through which ships could pass at highwater. This was one of *Dynamo*'s few failures.

The crews of the blockships were taken off by MASB *07* and MTB*107* and transferred to *Vivacious* which had by this time moved three miles to the west, just as shore batteries opened a well-directed fire at the destroyer.

LAST CHANCES

The fifty or so ships and boats gathered beyond Dunkirk as night fell, and at 22.00 hours they were released and the rush began 'The congestion [in the harbour] was chaotic,' wrote Lieutenant J.N. Wise in the skoot *Pascholl*, 'ships going astern into others coming ahead. French destroyers shrieking on their sirens, small craft nipping here and there, rendering the exit most dangerous.'[5] Wake-Walker had returned to Dunkirk to help with the final evacuation in *MTB 102*, and he also found the harbour 'swarming with French fishing craft and vessels of all sorts. They were yelling and crowding alongside the East Pier which was already thick with French troops. At one time it looked as if they would get in the way of the transports and destroyers which were on their way, but I managed to get them to go on up the inner harbour and out of the way in time.'[6]

HM Transport *Princess Maud* reached Dunkirk just before midnight. Forming part of the volunteer crew was Bill Birtles:

> Dunkirk was being shelled and bombed. The smoke was that thick, oily smoke blowing inland. We managed to dock at the mole with difficulty and by 2 am on the 4th June we were overloaded with 2,200 British and French Army and Naval personnel. How we got out, God only knows. Harry [surname unrecorded] played a great part in marshalling them. One of the destroyers pulled us off by the stern and at 2.30 am we were clear, leaving stern first, out into the Channel and headed for Folkestone. We had to wait for high tide to get in. The troops were very restless, so near, yet so far. Harry took the loudhailer from the bridge and used it as only service men understood. He told them that they must be patient. We would be going on the tide within the hour.[7]

The experiences of Lieutenant Commander George Anthony Mayhew Vaughan Harrison of the Patrol Sloop *Kingfisher*, were in marked contrast to those of most of the British skippers: 'Went alongside West Pier, Dunkirk Harbour and embarked 210 French troops, who were very well organised for embarkation, and appeared much fresher than any of our own. They also still possessed practically all their equipment.'[8]

Sub Lieutenant Carew Hunt, who we last heard of on the 31st in the Dutch eel boat *Johanna*, had volunteered to be a Lewis gunner on the War Department speed-boat *Marlborough*. The crew of *Marlborough* exemplifies the nature of the Dunkirk evacuation and the spirit in which ordinary people came forward to help rescue the soldiers, for it was composed of six Royal Navy personnel, two solicitors from the Treasury, and two sergeants of the RAF. *Marlborough* carried off forty French soldiers on 2 June, returning them to Ramsgate. Learning that one last effort was to be made on the night of the 3rd, Hunt was eager to go back to Dunkirk again. But the two Treasury men were due back at their desks, being a Monday, their places being taken by two Army officers, one who had been invalided out of the forces and the other a retired colonel. *Marlborough* left Ramsgate at 19.30 hours, picking up Rear Admiral Taylor half-way across the Channel from the motor-boat *Mermaiden*. 'When we got to Dunkirk,' continued Sub Lieutenant Hunt:

> We went inside the harbour and quite a long way up the canal and secured. The Admiral went ashore accompanied by two of our crew armed to the teeth. The rest of us occupied our time looting and trying to start up derelict cars. Sub. Lt. Poole found a very nice motor cycle and rode it round the docks.
>
> We went off once to bring boats to the point of embarkation and then secured again. Shortly afterwards machine gunning started quite near and a shell landed in a warehouse about 150 yards away. Fortunately, our job was done so we were able to leave. On our way down the canal we came on a blockage of shipping, and going too near the shore went aground on some rubble knocked into the water by a shell. We had the bad luck to lose both our screws and our rudder.[9]

The crew of the stranded boat called out to three French tugs that were nearby, but they refused to come to *Marlborough*'s aid. Fortunately, a Royal Navy Anti-Submarine trawler pulled *Marlborough* out to the main harbour where it was taken in tow by the motor-yacht *Gulza* and taken back to Dover.

HMS *Sabre* left Dover at 20.20 hours on 3 June for its final trip and entered Dunkirk harbour at 22.50 hours where she lay off while the numerous transports berthed. *Sabre* then berthed on the Mole between two transports where there would not have been room for a larger destroyer. This move did in fact allow a larger destroyer – HMS *Whitshed*, which had arrived earlier but had not yet berthed – to place her bows against *Sabre*. Troops were then passed across *Sabre* until there was room for *Whitshed* to berth against the Mole

By this time *Sabre* was full up, having embarked nearly 600 French troops and Admiral Abrial's Flag Lieutenant. Commander Dean shoved off at 00.25, getting out with some difficulty owing to the mass of ships trying to berth or to get away. A number of imminent collisions were narrowly averted and *Sabre* eventually got clear and headed westward.

Heavy fog was encountered on the way back across the Channel and *Sabre* along with a minesweeper and one of the transport ships, went slowly along until the North Goodwin Light Vessel was spotted. The three ships then passed carefully from buoy to buoy through the fog until Dover was reached at 05.00 hours. 'The French troops were in excellent spirits,' wrote Brian Dean, 'and keenly appreciated being addressed in their own language, however imperfectly. Jokes about the comparative comfort of *Sabre* and [the luxury liner] *Normandie* were well received.'

With so many vessels rushing in and out of the harbour it was probably inevitable that there would be accidents, and *Kingfisher* was rammed by the French trawler *Edmond René*. The trawler ripped a hole in *Kingfisher*'s bows, almost down to her waterline. In the collision, the two boats swung alongside each other and, as the trawler was undamaged, the French troops were transferred from *Kingfisher*. The sloop was able to limp slowly back to England.

The dense fog in the Channel added to the confusion, and on her passage back to England, the minesweeper *Leda* struck the Belgian skoot *Marechal Foch*, which sank. *Leda* sustained damage to her bows, but the forward bulkhead held.

One ship that did not make it back to England was the French Navy's Fleet Auxiliary, *Emile Deschamps*. She had been spotted by the Clyde passenger turbine steamer, *King George V* which had been requisitioned by the Admiralty for use as a troop transport, as she passed North Foreland with 817 men on board. It was at about 03.00 hours when a heavy explosion was heard astern of *King George V. Emile Deschamps* had struck a magnetic mine as she headed for the North Goodwin Light Vessel. She sank within a minute. There were a few other vessels in the vicinity that were able to save some of the survivors. *King George V* managed to save sixty-seven from the sea. Among the survivors landed later at Margate were seven French women and a boy.[10]

E.A. Leppard was the owner of a former 52-foot naval harbour launch *Letitia*, which was normally berthed in Chichester Canal. He had set off from Chichester at 06.00 hours on 2 June, reaching Hythe on the morning of 3 June where a Royal Navy sub lieutenant and three sailors went on board and took over. The boat's masts were taken down and a machine-gun was fitted to the deck. Mr Leppard stayed on board as the launch, along with three other yachts, was towed across the Channel by the tug *Sun XV* and he later wrote of his experiences:

> Arrived off Dunkirk at 11.30 p.m. and cast of from tug. Proceeded into Dunkirk past the Mole, and up the Canal for about two miles. Moored alongside the quay and proceeded to take troops on board. Could find no Englishmen so took on board forty Frenchmen. Left the quay and proceeded outside the Mole to HMS *Walrus*[11], who took troops on board. Swell from other craft made ship dash into the side of the warship, tearing rails down and breaking ropes. Had orders to load on board about 400lbs of T.N.T., in two barrels. Five naval ratings came on board and proceeded to wreck of HMS *Mosquito*. Went alongside and put on ratings and T.N.T. Waiting there for ratings to fix charge to blow up the wreck. When all was ready naval ratings jumped on board and we got away from the wreck in quick time.[12]

Mr Leppard also wrote that artillery shells were exploding all the time *Letitia* was in Dunkirk and off the Mole, the shrapnel falling all around. With the town of Dunkirk in flames and the explosions overhead there was enough light to see the masts and funnels of the ships that had sunk outside the harbour.

The demolition party Mr Leppard refers to was from the gunboat *Locust*, its skipper, Lieutenant Ackroyd Norman Palliser Costobadie, provided a little more detail:

Demolition party consisting of Lieutenant Holdsworth and 6 men left by Motor boat for wreck of *Mosquito*. On arrival, it was found that the wreck was submerged to the level of the battery deck, and despite repeated efforts of Lieut. Holdsworth who attempted to enter the Captain's Quarters, the forward charge had to be placed in the wheelhouse. The after charge was placed in the after magazine. The demolition party were working under great difficulties due to the movement of the wreck in the swell and to the darkness, and great initiative was displayed by Lieut. Holdsworth in placing the charges which were heavy and difficult to handle, and were somewhat dangerous.

The demolition party returned on board at 02.05 having fired the charges. The explosion blew off the fore part and after part of the wreck and should have prevented anything of value falling into enemy hands.[13]

Mick Wenban, a licensed waterman, volunteered to join the Thames tug *Challenge*, which had made repeated trips to Dunkirk and on 3 June was back in Dover harbour when the destroyer HMS *Worcester* collided with the passenger ferry SS *Maid of Orleans*. The collision was the result of *Worcester*'s manoeuvrability being severely restricted due to damage to her two screws and her rudder.

At 20.00 hours, *Challenge*, along with the other tugs *Crested Cock*, *Sun VII* and *Sun XIII*, took them in tow, hauling HMS *Worcester* to the Prince of Wales Pier. Then at approximately 21.30 hours, *Challenge* was ordered to steam back to Dunkirk and 'pick up or rescue anything'. At 23.00 hours, she was off North Goodwin in a line with *Ocean Cock*, *Crested Cock*, *Fairplay I*, *Sun VII*, *Sun XI* and *Sun XII*, all heading towards Dunkirk with the same orders. 'We were under command of a naval officer this time, although the vessel was still under the red ensign,' said Mick Wenban describing that final trip across the Channel. 'When we got there, there was a lot of noise going on from German guns. There were many big fires.'

The great risk the ships faced at Dunkirk was in becoming stranded on the sands. To avoid this, the ships would drop anchor in deep water and then go astern on it, so that the vessel was facing out to sea, ready for a quick getaway.

Challenge was anchored in just such a fashion whilst Captain Parker scanned the shore with his binoculars. Mick Wenban junior recalled what he was told by his father: 'He [Charlie Parker] was looking on the quay and he was saying there are all these soldiers there. So Dad jumped up on the stern of the tug and he was shouting to them on the beach "come on lads we'll take you back" and they all start saying "*Achtung*" and they start firing at them and someone said, "Jesus Christ they're bloody Germans!"'

If the Germans were in Dunkirk harbour it meant that there were no more Allied troops left to save. 'It was obvious that our little tug could do no more, although we were told to try and bring back anything we could see,' Mick Wenban senior related. 'Our officer eventually ordered the tug back to Dover.' *Challenge* was one of the last vessels to leave Dunkirk.

HMS *Vanquisher* experienced problems loading at the East Mole, as Lieutenant Commander C.B. Alers-Hankey described:

> Owing to strong offset from the pier and delay in securing the stern wires, considerable difficulty was experienced in berthing the ship alongside the pier at Dunkirk. This delayed the embarkation of troops by about five minutes but I was able to remain alongside ten minutes after the time I had been told to leave by the Pier Master. The French soldiers were very slow embarking and were much hampered by their equipment.

Similar difficulties were experienced by the destroyer *Malcolm* which tied up against the East Mole at 02.10 hours and embarked approximately 800 French troops, much less than Captain T. Halsey would have wished: 'This disappointing number,' he complained, 'was due to difficulty of stowing French troops with the enormous packs they carried. The ship seemed fuller than it had ever been.'

While *Malcolm* was embarking troops, *Locust* had completed the embarkation of troops from small boats and signalled that she had room for about another 100 or so and although her job had been to stay further out, she berthed alongside the East Mole ahead of *Malcolm* at about 02.25 hours and filled up.

At about this same time, Wake-Walker called out to Captain Halsey in *Malcolm* from *MTB 102* by loudspeaker, that the last two ships were to use their discretion about remaining later than 02.30 hours. Halsey told Commander Jack Bickford in HMS *Express* that he should leave not later than 03.00. But he stayed for a further eighteen minutes to pick up the Naval Beach Party and as many French troops as he dare, before heading out across the Channel as fast as the destroyer could go.

An unnamed French officer was interviewed when he landed in the UK:

> We were heavily shelled as we were embarking. At one time the German long-range batteries were dropping shells in the sea just beyond the quay, and then they shortened their range and commenced shelling immediately behind us. We were caught between two fires, but nearly all the men managed to get safely away. But fires are still raging in many parts of the town, which is now nothing more than a shambles.[14]

Captain Aubrey Lamplough-Lamplugh's company of the RASC had reached Bray-Dunes, it may be recalled, on 28 May, but few of them had been able to find a ship. 'All during those days on the beaches – altogether we spent seven days on them – we were subject to machine-gun fire, air bombing and artillery fire from the approaching German artillery,' Lamplough-Lamplugh later told a journalist. 'Throughout this time, we had no proper food at all and all we ate was a few biscuits which had had been scrounged by somebody from I don't know where.' He continued with his somewhat confused narrative:

> On the 29th I was picked up unconscious on the beach and taken to a French hospital in Dunkirk. I lost my memory for a time, and was later recalled to the facts by the sight of my officer's identity card. I remembered then who I was. Asked where I was making for, I answered 'Bruges', to be told that far from being able to get there the Germans were but already eight miles from the hospital! I then said that I wanted to get to England. They replied that practically all the English troops had gone. I looked out of the hospital window and saw a lot of tin-hats. 'I'm going with them,' I told the nurses. I was told this was not possible in my state. So I later slipped out of the hospital without permission and headed for the beach … We walked right back to the beach, and were in time to see a paddle-boat manned by Navy men preparing to leave. We semaphored an S.O.S. to the paddle-boat: 'Seven days on beach; starving; please take us off'.

Although the engines had already been started, they swung round to respond to our message. Some eighty of us were got onboard.[15]

It was also on Monday 3 June 1940, that the *Medway Queen* set out on her final voyage of the evacuation. 'Whilst we were in Ramsgate getting ready to go over for that last time,' Albert Mason later wrote, 'Lieutenant Cook called the men together and told everyone to write a postcard to their families and then all hands went ashore to the pub on the jetty where the Captain bought us all a drink.'

Another man on *Medway Queen* who wrote about that last night of the evacuation, was Sub Lieutenant Graves. 'We berthed alongside the Mole for the last time at midnight. Machine-gun fire could be clearly heard. This time we took on about 400 French soldiers, all the BEF had by this time left.

'A destroyer astern of *Medway Queen* was hit and flung forward onto our starboard paddlebox, extensively damaging the sponson. The Captain nursed us away from the berth with difficulty and the *Medway Queen* made off very slowly down the harbour, with the familiar Mole still lit by blazing oil tanks falling astern.'

In what was a remarkable achievement, the little paddle steamer made a total of seven trips to Dunkirk and back. In the course of these journeys the *Medway Queen* and its crew rescued 7,000 soldiers – more than any other vessel smaller than a destroyer. Captain A.T. Cook and Sub Lieutenant J.D. Graves each received the DSC, two of her petty officers, A.E. Crossley and H.J. McAllister, as well as Seaman K.R. Olly, were awarded the DSM and two other members of the crew were Mentioned in Despatches.

As the battered little paddle boat limped into Dover, her crew utterly exhausted, the ships in the harbour sounded their sirens and Vice Admiral Ramsey sent the signal, 'Well done *Medway Queen*'!

There was no such rejoicing, however, for the French rearguard. *Général* Barthélémy hoped to be able to slip away undetected by the Germans soon after nightfall to reach the harbour before midnight. His hopes were dashed, as the French historian Jacques Mordal cuttingly commented, his words being translated by David Devine:

As he approached Malo with the rearguard, he saw a vast crowd of troops materialize suddenly as the news of the last departure spread.

Out of the cellars and the holes, streams of unarmed men appeared, emerging everywhere, converging on the Mole, until they became an immense river of men frozen solid at the approaches. These hidden heroes, these warriors who for days had not left their shelters, had no intention of giving up their chances of escape to those who had been fighting for them.[16]

Nevertheless, before he departed, Barthélémy conducted a moving ceremony on Dunkirk's central pier, watched by Commander Troup:

About 1,000 men stood to attention four deep about half-way along the pier, the General and his staff about thirty feet away; and after having faced the troops, whose faces were indiscernible in the dawn light, the flames behind them showing up their steel helmets, the officers clicked their heels, saluted, and turned about and came down to the boat [the Admiralty motor boat *Haig*] with me and we left at 03.20.[17]

The last acts of the Dunkirk evacuation were related by Commander Richardson, whose ship, the destroyer *Shikari*, acted as the guide for the blockade ships with Captain Dangerfield, who led the blockading operation, on board. Richardson takes up the story after leaving the blockading ships:

Shikari, in waiting, proceeded alongside and embarked 400 French troops who had been left after the last ship evacuating had sailed. Among these troops was *Général* Barthelemy, commanding the Flanders Garrison, who stated that 12,000 still remained in Dunkirk. This was reported. By this time, it was light and firing at the jetty had commenced, one shell hitting the jetty, causing many casualties. 03.40. Ordered to withdraw by Captain Dangerfield.[18]

These were the last of Barthélémy's men to be rescued, the rest of the rearguard fell into enemy hands. 'No episode in the epic of Dunkirk,' wrote Mordal, 'caused more heartbreak.'

At 08.00 hours, German troops reached Bastion 32, the French naval headquarters in Dunkirk, where *Général* Beaufrère formally surrendered, bringing the fighting to a conclusion. An hour and a half later the Germans were at the foot of the East Mole, which was still packed with helpless French soldiers. The official end of operations against Allied forces at Dunkirk was marked shortly afterwards with the raising of the swastika over the East Mole at 10.20 hours.

Yet, astonishingly, there was still another rescue from Dunkirk to relate. Sixty-eight French soldiers reached Margate on 5 June, it was reported in the *Evening Telegraph and Post* of that day:

> These were the only troops to arrive. There was not a sailor among them, but rather than be taken prisoners of war, they decided to make a dash for it ... Forty-eight were in a motor-boat. The remainder were in a ship's lifeboat which they had salvaged. They had been towed by their comrades.
>
> The motor-boat made for the direction of the English coast but when it was near the coast the petrol supply ran out. Without food or water the men were drifting helplessly when a blanket they had hoisted as a signal was observed by Mr Howard Knight, coxswain of a lifeboat [the Margate boat, *Lord Southborough*] which had been standing by another ship, and was about to return to port as her services were not required. The lifeboat immediately made towards the two small craft, and after having taken aboard the men on the ship's boat, they set it adrift.

The French troops said that they had been bombed and machine-gunned as they made their escape, and they were proud to claim, that the officers on board had taken their turn on the oars. There would be no more escapes from Dunkirk by sea, and most of those left behind became prisoners of the Third Reich. But the great bulk of the BEF had got away, to the bewilderment of *Luftwaffe* pilot, Bernt Engelman, who flew over the now empty beaches of La Panne, Malo and Bray:

> On the beaches and in the sand dunes north of Dunkirk, thousands of light and heavy weapons lay on the sands, along with munitions crates, field kitchens, scattered cans of rations and innumerable wrecks of British army trucks.

'Damn!' I exclaimed to Erwin. 'The entire British Army went under here!' Erwin shook his head vigorously. 'On the contrary! A miracle took place here! If the German tanks and Stukas and navy had managed to surround the British here, shooting most of them, and taking the rest prisoner, then England wouldn't have any trained soldiers left. Instead, the British seem to have rescued them all – and a lot of Frenchmen too. Adolf can say goodbye to his *blitzkrieg* against England.[19]

That was the true significance of Operation *Dynamo*.

Chapter 12

The Dunkirk Spirit

Hitler was ecstatic at the news that his troops had taken Dunkirk: 'Dunkirk has fallen! 40,000 French and English troops are all that remains of the formerly great armies. Immeasurable quantities of material have been captured. The greatest battle in the history of the world has come to an end.'

The truth was that Hitler had failed to prevent the BEF from escaping. It would prove a catastrophic error. On 4 June 26,175 men were landed back in the UK to make a grand total of 338,226 that had been rescued from France since the 27 May. Winston Churchill told the House of Commons that Operation *Dynamo* was 'a miracle of deliverance'. It was achieved, he said:

> by valour, by perseverance, by perfect discipline, by faultless service, by resource, by skill, by unconquerable fidelity, is manifest to us all. The enemy was hurled back by the retreating British and French troops. He was so roughly handled that he did not harry their departure seriously. The Royal Air Force engaged the main strength of the German Air Force, and inflicted upon them losses of at least four to one; and the Navy, using nearly 1,000 ships of all kinds, carried over 335,000 men, French and British, out of the jaws of death … Could there have been an objective of greater military importance and significance for the whole purpose of the war than this?[1]

It certainly felt that a victory had been snatched from the jaws of defeat, though, as Major General Julian Thompson wrote, the only miraculous element of Operation *Dynamo* was that the weather stayed benign for nine days and nights, and the success of the evacuation owed more to the efforts of the Royal Navy than any mystical intervention.[2]

Remarkably, what should have been seen as a humiliating disaster had been turned into a national triumph. That was certainly how the *New York Times* saw it:

In that harbour, in such a hell as never blazed on earth before, at the end of a lost battle, the rags and blemishes that had hidden the soul of democracy fell away. There, beaten but unconquered, in shining splendour, she faced the enemy, this shining thing in the souls of free men which Hitler cannot command. It is the great tradition of democracy. It is the future. It is victory.[3]

Even the French, for whom the magnitude of disaster that had befallen their country had yet to be fully understood, appeared to have much to celebrate, publishing the following communiqué on 4 June:

The embarkation of Allied troops from Dunkirk was completed today in conformity with the pre-arranged plan. Until the last moment, first in the suburbs, and then in the town itself, from house to house the rearguard put up a heroic resistance. The enemy, constantly reinforced, ceaselessly continued his assaults and was ceaselessly counter-attacked.

The last embarkation took place under the fire of German machine-guns. This implacable defence and the success of these difficult and vast operations under the orders of Admiral Abrial and *Général* Falgade have had a definite influence on the development of the struggle. Our soldiers returning from the north, whose energy remains intact, are ready for fresh battles.[4]

Churchill wisely sought to dampen down the widespread jubilation with which *Dynamo* was reported by the press and received by the public: 'We must be very careful not to assign to this deliverance the attributes of a victory,' he told the House. 'Wars are not won by evacuations.'

Nevertheless, the manner in which the country had responded to the plight of the BEF was magnificent, not just the service men of the BEF, RAF and Royal Navy, but also the volunteer crews of the civilian ships and, the ones that had caught the national imagination more than any other, the little private yachts and boats that could be seen in normal times tied up against wooden jetties in south coast harbours or bobbing at local moorings. Their owners risked everything – their lives and their beloved boats – to try and save a few soldiers; mere strangers in arms. After the BEF had been let down by its allies, with the Belgians having surrendered and the French all-but given up, these, the ordinary folk of southern England, young and old, had sailed to rescue the beleaguered troops. 'These small craft lifted more than 100,000 men,' wrote the Poet Laureate, John Masefield, 'no boat ceased work as long as troops were in sight on shore ... As the boats were sunk, the crews went elsewhere, into other boats and carried on.'[5]

On 5 June, J.B. Priestley delivered a broadcast on the BBC:

> Here at Dunkirk is another English epic, and to my mind what was most characteristically English about it, so typical of us, so absurd and yet so grand and gallant, I hardly know whether to laugh or to cry when you read about them, was the part played in the difficult and dangerous embarkation, not by the warships, magnificent though they were, but by the little pleasure steamers ... and our great-grandchildren, when they learn how we began this war by snatching glory out of defeat.

This created a powerful image, one that brought the nation together as never before or since, and the so-called 'Dunkirk spirit' carried the British people through five further years of war. The term Dunkirk spirit has become embedded in the British psyche and is part of the English lexicon, being defined by the Oxford Dictionary as 'stoicism and determination in a difficult or dangerous situation, especially as displayed by a group of people'. This is the received understanding of how the British united during those momentous few days in May and June 1940 that has been passed down through the decades since that time. But just how accurate a picture is that?

Firstly, the little private boats so often portrayed as the saviours of the BEF only took part in the last few days of the operation, and most of the Little Ships were crewed, and certainly skippered, by Royal Navy personnel. It was the Royal Navy, and especially its destroyers, that carried the bulk of the BEF and the 110,000 French troops to safety.

Lieutenant Bruce Junior, who served on HMS *Wolfhound*, was particularly aggrieved with the false impression that it was the Little Ships that had saved the BEF:

The evacuation of the beaches was a magnificent piece of organisation but it has gone down in history that the whole of the British Expeditionary Force came off on Dunkirk beaches, which is nonsense. Thirty to forty thousand men were evacuated from the beaches by the Little Ships, which was a magnificent effort. It was, however, a drop in the ocean compared to the evacuation by the Royal and Merchant Navy from the jetty [Mole], of some 220,000.[6]

Nevertheless, it was these vessels that caught the imagination, not just of the UK but of the wider world. This image was reinforced by the British Council which produced a war-time film entitled *The Little Ships of England*. Its commentary played as follows:

Our men gathered on the bullet-swept sands, while the Little Ships: fishing boats, yachts, motor boats, barges, canoes, anything that floated, steamed to the rescue. That strange fleet came somehow back to port. But all along the coast of England were moorings that lay empty and unclaimed. Just as the fishermen had answered the call to Dunkirk, so the age-old craft of ship building rose to the nation's call and on Britain's hillsides and in her woods the sound of axes echoed.

Whilst there were countless instances of heroism and self-sacrifice displayed by both service and civilian personnel, there were also cases insubordination, bordering on mutiny, with entire crews refusing to sail to France. One such example, as has been touched on earlier, was the case of the Hythe lifeboat, whose coxswain persuaded not only his own crew to refuse to take their boat over to Dunkirk, but also the crews of two other lifeboats, those of Walmer and Dungeness. The consequence was that the Admiralty had to find Royal Navy personnel to crew the three lifeboats at a time when they were desperately short of experienced sailors. The Coxswain told a reporter at the time that he refused to go to Dunkirk because he had been asked to drive his boat onto the sand: 'I knew we could never get away again, because at Hythe it takes 50 men and a steam winch to get us off one bar of sand when we launch.'[7] The coxswain. H. Griggs, was dismissed from the Lifeboat Service.

There were other incidences of crews refusing to sail, though admittedly only after performing heroic work for days before their nerves finally cracked. The following account was provided by Lieutenant Commander, R.H. Buthy, Officer in Charge, No.3 Party, Royal Marines:

At 05.00 on Sunday 2nd June, 1940, it was reported that three ships – S.S. *Malines*, S.S. *Ben-my-Chree*, S.S. *Tynewald* – were giving trouble. An armed party under Petty Officer Hollingsworth was sent over to take guard duties on these ships. The Petty Officer had instructions that no-one was to leave these ships under any circumstances. Shortly after the arrival of this party the ships were sent out to anchorage. Nothing untoward occurred before 1400 when a relief party under Leading Stoker Booth took over duties.

At 1850 S.S. *Ben-my-Chree* came alongside the jetty. Three sentries ... were placed on the gangway, the remainder being posted at intervals along the ship. As the ship was being berthed the crew were demonstrating and shouting that they were going to leave the ship, and on the brow being run out they attempted to do so with their kits.

Leading Stoker Booth ordered his men to come on guard and advance up the brow. The crew thereupon returned on board at once, where they remained until the relief crew arrived.

S.S. *Tynewald*, came alongside at 19.10. The crew did not attempt to leave the ship, but contented themselves with shouting abuse at the sentries. Relief crews for these two ships arrived at 19.50, and the old crews were then allowed to leave. Complete lists of their names and addresses were taken and given to the S.T.O. Folkestone. These ships subsequently sailed as ordered.

S.S. *Malines*, had left the harbour with no instructions at about 16.00, and was subsequently found to have proceeded to Southampton.[8]

These were not the only instances of crews or captains refusing to sail. But, except for Coxswain Griggs, whose actions could not be disguised, such episodes did not feature large in the newspapers. In times of national peril, it was the duty of the British press to paint an entirely positive picture. Which is why the image of the valiant fighting retreat, the heroic Little Ships and the 'miraculous' salvation of the BEF, was created and nourished. So, on 31 May, the *News Chronicle* declared, 'Thousands of BEF Men Successfully

Withdrawn from Trap', the *Daily Express* ran with the headline, 'Tens of Thousands Safely Home Already', the *Daily Mirror* announced, 'Navy Fight for BEF – Thousands Home', and later *The Times* told the nation that, 'What is supremely important is that the men now being brought back to England are not fugitives from a lost battle but unbroken units ... their discipline forged to a steely edge by experience of war'. In particular, the story of the Little Ships, as Major General Thompson wrote, 'was milked as hard as it could be.'[9]

This continues to be the case to the present day with the 2017 film *Dunkirk*, and a TV documentary narrated by Tony Robinson, *Witness to War*, which focuses almost entirely on the Little Ships, mentions the Mole only once and the destroyers not at all. There is also a book written recently (2014) by a best-selling author which states that: 'Dunkirk is woven into the tapestry of national identity. This is the story of the people, the events, and the little ships, that make the tapestry so moving and vivid.'[10] In all fairness to these little boats, it should be stated that around 700 took part in the evacuation and more than 100 never made it home, constituting almost half of the 220 vessels lost during Operation *Dynamo*.

But, amidst the relief and the rejoicing over the evacuation, and the undoubted heroism of so many individuals, the fact was that 68,000 men of Britain's only field army had been killed, wounded, taken prisoner or listed as missing, many of the latter lost in the seas off Dunkirk. The RAF lost 1,526 killed in action, died of wounds or injury, lost at sea, wounded or taken prisoner. Losses were not confined to serving men, as 125 civilians were killed or wounded in the bid to save the soldiers.[11]

The BEF also abandoned almost all its equipment. The numbers are staggering. There were 2,472 guns, 20,000 motorcycles, and almost 65,000 other vehicles abandoned, including virtually every one of the 445 tanks sent to France. In addition, 416,000 tons of stores, more than 75,000 tons of ammunition and 162,000 tons of fuel were destroyed or left behind. The RAF also lost 145 aircraft, including forty-two invaluable Spitfires. Total RAF losses for the Battle of France were 959, a number only marginally less than the Battle of Britain which was to follow.[12] It was, at the time, the heaviest defeat that Britain had ever suffered.[13]

Yet, it was essential that the true nature of Britain's weakness at this time was not revealed to Hitler. It had to be seen that the British Army was still intact and capable of resisting an invasion, backed by the British public. Unlike the Belgian and French civilians who had fled before the approaching enemy, the ordinary British people had left their homes, not to run away, but to get into their little boats to face the Germans. It sent a powerful message to the enemy, reinforced by Churchill's refusal to discuss peace terms, despite Hitler's repeated appeals after the fall of France for the British Prime Minister to see 'reason'. When Winston ignored Hitler's peace offer, the Führer saw that he could never conquer Britain and, in July 1940, little more than a month after the last troops had been whisked away from Dunkirk by the Royal Navy, the German leader turned his attention away from the UK and began planning the invasion of the Soviet Union.

The truth, though, was that Britain's finest military leaders had been out-thought and out-manoeuvred by their German equivalents, and as a result, heavily defeated. The retreat to Dunkirk was a disjointed affair, with an almost complete breakdown in communications, as so many of those involved recalled, such as Gunner Doug Dawes:

> One day was just like the previous day and the next — chaos. We had very little to eat ... I don't remember any other rations being available, the whole supply system had broken down. It did not appear that we were going to stop and make a stand. We heard that the B.E.F. was being evacuated by sea. We didn't believe it. We came to a cross road in the Armentieres area — a terrible traffic jam. French troops were crossing at right angles — vehicles and marching men.[14]

George Gordon, with a Royal Army Medical Corps Field Ambulance, paints a similar picture:

> From then onwards it was a continual retreat ... Our Field Ambulance had problems evacuating casualties along roads clogged with refugees escaping the Germans, and there was strafing by the Messerschmitts. ... This was the chaos prevailing at the time ...I cannot remember ever having received an order to make for Dunkirk, and was never in that port. At times we were out of contact with our officers and did not know what was happening, except that we were continuing to retreat.[15]

To Sergeant Norman Smith, also of the RAMC, the retreat was 'all confusion and occasional panic'. Signaller Albert Henry Powell recalled that his unit was informed that it was 'every man for himself', and Sapper, later Major C. R. Wampach of the Royal Engineers complained that, 'The greatest problem was communication. Most of us did not know where we were going or what we were supposed to do.'[16] Much of the cause of this breakdown in communication was the result of Lord Gort's decision to move his headquarters near Lille whilst leaving his operational and intelligence staffs at Arras.[17]

This is not, of course, how it could be presented to the general public. It is interesting to read Tennant's comments of 29 May, 'The French staff at Dunkirk feel strongly that they are defending Dunkirk for us to evacuate, which is largely true', compared with the Pathé news: 'The greatest tribute must go to the men of the rear guard. Their job was to fight on until the evacuation was almost complete. They have suffered terribly; they have left behind thousands of dead. They fought their last battle from the water's edge, before they dived in and swam out to the ships.' Whilst there is no denying that the troops that had held the perimeter did so heroically and magnificently, the reality is that it was the French who had helped to hold off the Germans and had facilitated the evacuation of the last British soldiers.

When John Masefield asked for access to official reports and documents concerning the Battle of Flanders and Operation *Dynamo* in the summer of 1940 for a proposed book, there was panic in Whitehall. It was feared that the truth, Mr T. Cash at the War Office confessed, would be 'disastrous, the general impression left, so far as the Army was concerned, being one of general chaos redeemed by occasional gleams of individual bravery, but otherwise putting both the Army and its leadership in a very poor light'.

This is certainly how some if not most of the soldiers themselves saw it. But this, of course, could never be publicly admitted, much to the annoyance of many, including Lieutenant Anthony Rhodes of the RAMC:

> We listened to the nine o'clock news, to see how our retreat was viewed
> by the Government, or rather, to see how the Government thought
> it ought to be viewed. The announcer said we had made a 'strategic
> withdrawal according to plan'. It appeared, according to him, that we
> had always intended to abandon Brussels, it was all part of a devilish
> scheme. 'The bloody liars' said the doctor.

Yet such was the perceived integrity of the British press and the BBC, that even servicemen believed the withdrawal was well-organised and planned. That was certainly what Squadron Leader Al Deere was led to understand, after he had crash-landed his Spitfire to the north of Dunkirk:

> The tide was out, and I got down on the beach, but I knocked myself out on the edge of the windscreen. When I came to, I got out and was looked after by a girl who stitched me up with an ordinary needle and put a plaster on me. Then I headed for Dunkirk, where I knew the BEF was intending to evacuate. We had been reading in the newspapers that the British Army was retreating 'according to plan'. Somewhere en route to Dunkirk, I went into a small café where I saw two Tommies. I asked, 'Am I heading for the army at Dunkirk?' They looked at me and said something to the effect of, 'What British Army?' There's no retreat, chum. There's bloody chaos'. Dunkirk was a complete shambles: burning buildings, abandoned vehicles and falling masonry.'[18]

Some, though, were not so easily convinced by the stirring rhetoric of the media, such as Ordinary Seaman Stanley Victor Allen serving on HMS *Windsor*, who viewed the retreat and evacuation as a disaster and feared for the future:

> We saw all the all the soldiers coming back without their equipment and we began to think this was the end of our way of life. We didn't know how long we'd be able to hold Jerry off in England. We knew we had the navy, and that we would fight, but we didn't know what the soldiers would be able to do if Jerry landed, because they had nothing.[19]

Away from the public glare, at a meeting in France with Weygand and Reynaud on 31 May, Churchill had expressed similar views as Ordinary Seaman Allen, conceding that the enforced evacuation, with the loss of equipment it entailed, placed Britain in a highly perilous situation: 'Our Army will have lost everything but its rifles, everything the men do not actually carry. We shall have lost 1,000 guns, which is extremely serious; there are not more than 500 guns in England today. We have lost thousands of lorries.

'The loss of guns is most grave and presents a terrible danger in case of an attempted invasion. Should a small German force, well equipped with artillery, land in England, it could not be opposed by a force of equivalent strength.'[20]

General Ironside wrote in his diary six days later: 'The withdrawal of an army with the destruction of all its equipment. Something quite unknown in history ... What an extraordinary thing to have to do, to give up all your equipment ... A disaster.[21]

Even more alarming was the collapse in morale of the BEF, as was later revealed to one newspaper editor by the Director of Statistics:

> The Dunkirk episode was far worse than was ever realised in Fleet Street. The men on getting back to England were so demoralised that they threw their rifles and equipment out of railway-carriage windows. Some sent for their wives with civilian clothes, changed into these, and walked home.[22]

In a secret session of the House of Commons, several Members of Parliament told how large numbers of officers had 'run away and deserted their troops so as to get on the earliest boat'.[23] Similar scenes were witnessed by the men waiting to be rescued. The following story was given by Barry Ainsworth, of the Royal Artillery, who had been seconded to a field ambulance unit:

> Near the mole I came to the tail end of a queue of troops. There was a lot of tension amongst the men, if anyone attempted to strike a match they were shot at. Royal Marines were patrolling the queue to stop men sneaking ahead and causing a panic ... Some Officers had the trick of moving along the queue asking the men if they were all right, but were really making their way to the front of the line.[24]

Sid Crocket was happy to have escaped, but, 'we thought we had let England down, we've retreated, we've lost the war for them. God knows what people are going to think of us now because we have come back and we were very upset; we all thought we would be disgraced because we'd give in.[25]

Der Adler, though a Nazi propaganda magazine, wrote with some truth, when, on 5 June, it declared: 'For us Germans the word "Dunkirchen" will stand for all time for a victory in the greatest battle of annihilation in history. But, for the British and the French who were there, it will remind them for the rest of their lives of a defeat that was heavier than any army had ever suffered before.'

It was certainly a rude awakening for the British leaders, demonstrating that the British Army could not contend with the Germans and their 'lightning war', *blitzkrieg*. Particularly embarrassing was Britain's deficiency in tanks, considering that it was this country that had first developed tanks more than twenty years previously. In May 1940, while the Germans could boast of not just tank brigades and divisions, but entire armoured corps, the BEF had only twenty-four tanks fitted with guns other than machine-guns. 'It must be said to our shame,' General Montgomery admitted, 'that we sent our Army into the most modern of wars with weapons and equipment that were quite inadequate … In September 1939, the British army was totally unfit to fight a first-class war on the continent of Europe.'

It would be another two years before the British Army would inflict a heavy defeat upon the Germans on land, as the war began to turn in favour of the Allies.

The loss of millions of poundsworth of supplies, ammunition and equipment, especially the expensive items such as destroyers, artillery and tanks, had other, and in the long-term more serious, consequences for the UK than homeland defence. All these items had to be quickly replaced and, coming off the back of the Depression of the 1930s, this was beyond the UK's means. The immediate consequence of the 'miracle' of Dunkirk was that the UK Government was placed in serious financial trouble. Indeed, Britain was still in debt to the USA from the First World War and would have to go cap-in-hand to the US once again.[26] This was agreed at a Cabinet meeting on 22 August. That day, Clive Ponting believes, marked the end of Britain as a world power.[27]

The first move was to replace the destroyers that had been lost in Operation *Dynamo*. On 2 September, President Roosevelt agreed to the transfer of fifty obsolescent destroyers (only nine of which were fit for immediate service) in return for granting the US long-lease military bases in British territories in the Caribbean and the North Atlantic. This hugely one-sided deal amounted, in Churchill's words to 'a blank cheque on the whole of our trans-Atlantic possessions.'[28]

By the end of 1940, Britain was effectively bankrupt, almost all her gold having gone to the US. The first shipment to the US took place on 5 June, the day after the last of the troops landed in England from Dunkirk, as a precaution against invasion. On that day it was announced in the UK press that 'the greatest mass movement of gold in history is now under way' with Britain's gold reserves being deposited in the US Federal Reserve Bank.[29] It would be the last that Britain ever saw of that bullion – and worse was to come. Six months later the Americans sent a warship to Cape Town to take £42 million in British gold held in South Africa.

Before the end of 1940, Britain could no longer afford to buy any more goods from the US, but with the US economy gearing up for the production of war materiél, Roosevelt needed to keep Britain spending and, as he put it, 'milking the British financial cow.'[30] So, the President devised a brilliant scheme, Lend–Lease, which enabled Britain to continue to buy items from the UK, which would be paid for later, after the war. The Lend–Lease Act was no act of generosity as Churchill tried to paint it, but a hard-headed business deal.

In return for the goods the US would provide the UK, a heavy price was to be extracted. Britain had to allow the US access to the markets of the Empire, to which it had previously been denied. Furthermore, Britain was not permitted to export any of the same type of products that it was receiving from the US and, indeed, Britain agreed to reduce *all* exports to 'the minimum necessary to supply or obtain materials essential to the war effort.' meant that the US had virtually no competition in markets around the world, and by the end of the war British exports were just one-third of their pre-war level whilst America's quadrupled.[31] As one historian put it, 'During the 18 months between Dunkirk and Pearl Harbour, Britain mortgaged its future as a world power.'[32]

'WHERE ARE OUR AEROPLANES?'

Another of the myths surrounding the Dunkirk evacuation was that the RAF failed to give the troops on the beaches the protection they expected from the attacks of the *Luftwaffe*. The Ministry of Information compiled reports from around the UK during this crucial period and, on 3 June noted: 'The return of our soldiers from Flanders ... has brought to the forefront certain critical discussions. In particular the BEF are found to be stating on all sides that the RAF was not in evidence during the retreat. These first-hand stories are throwing some doubt on the truthfulness of the broadcast news reports of RAF exploits.' In this national survey was a report from Bristol, 'BEF men's stories of sky black with Nazi planes and few British ones'. Cardiff reported, 'Returning troops question "Where are our aeroplanes"', and in Edinburgh, 'BEF speaking freely of lack of planes', whilst the report from Reading began with 'Growing stories of RAF v BEF controversy'.[33]

The pilots, such as Pilot Officer H.A.C. Bird-Wilson of 17 Squadron, who had been heavily engaged throughout the evacuation, were angered to learn what was being said of them:

> The squadron having completed some twelve patrol missions over Dunkirk, and achieved some success and a few casualties, it was a great surprise and somewhat annoying to hear from the returning BEF Army, 'Where the hell was the RAF?' and 'Why weren't they there to protect them from the bombs on the beachhead?' The RAF could understand the bad feelings, particularly when the pilots had witnessed the appalling congestion on the beaches at Dunkirk. Continuous aerial combats were taking place all around and many miles from the beaches, thus greatly reducing the number of attacks on the endless queues of troops waiting to get on board ships.[34]

This was elaborated further in the Whitehall history of *Dynamo*, which detailed the efforts of the five Fleet Air Arm squadrons that operated under Coastal Command, with their Albacore, Swordfish and Skua aircraft. 'They carried out attacks on tanks, transport, batteries, gun emplacements, enemy positions in the Calais and Dunkirk areas, and E-boats. In spite of their inadequacy for the purpose the Skuas were also detailed for fighter escort for ships.'[35]

It is true that the men stranded for days on end may not have witnessed many British aircraft over the beaches, but that is because the RAF was in action further inland, where its efforts were focused on hampering the build-up of German forces around Dunkirk.

In his review of air operations, the official historian, Major L.F. Ellis, lists the objectives of the RAF during the Battle of Flanders and the evacuation. Firstly, he enumerates those of Bomber Command:

1. to reduce the enemy's total resources of oil;
2. to disorganise his lines of communication, especially railways on which he must rely for long-distance supply of his armies;
3. to compel him to hold back from the battle fighters for home defence;
4. to divert his bombers from France by inducing retaliation on England.

Just how much the bombing raids undertaken by the RAF hampered the Germans in their advance towards Dunkirk has never been quantified, but the fact that the French and British troops were able to hold the Dunkirk perimeter for nine days – a seemingly remarkable achievement – must, at least in part, be attributable to the efforts of Bomber Command and the AASF.

With regards to Fighter Command, Ellis lists its objectives as:

1. to protect our own troops and our Allies from enemy air attack;
2. to defend their own airfields and other bases and key positions from enemy bombers;
3. to protect our own aircraft in their bombing attacks and reconnaissance;
4. to protect troops and shipping during evacuation.

It will be seen from the above that only two of Fighter Command's objectives related directly to protecting the troops and the ships. There were greater strategic goals than simply affording immediate support for the troops.

What must also be borne in mind is that when over France, Keith Park's men of 11 Group were operating beyond the range of the Chain Home radar system. Meeting the enemy was, therefore, largely a matter of chance, or as one pilot put it, 'it was a game of blind man's buff and we were the ones with the blindfold'.[36] They also had very limited time over France. It took around fifty minutes to take off, reach altitude and fly to Dunkirk. A Spitfire, for example, flying conservatively at high altitude, could stay in the air for almost three hours. At low altitude and high speed, this could be reduced by almost half. The British fighters, therefore, had precious little time over Belgium and France if they were engaged in combat before they were compelled to return.[37]

It was also the case that the troops on the ground may not have seen the RAF in action even when the British aircraft were fighting in the sky directly above them, as can be gleaned from the account of 92 Squadron's Pilot Officer A.C. Bartley in a letter to his father in June:

This is the true story as I saw it over Dunkirk and Calais. Fighter Command were at first disinclined to send the Spitfires out of England at all. We are primarily home defence. Anyhow, we went and at first, just as single squadrons (12 aircraft). You have had my accounts of how we used to run into fifty and sixty German machines every time we went over there, and fought them until our ammunition ran out. While this battle was going on up at 10,000 feet, the dive bombers which did the chief damage, were playing havoc down below us. The fact was that they had layers of bombers and fighters, with which twelve Spitfires had to cope.[38]

'Looking back at it,' wrote Pilot Officer Hugh Dundas of 616 Squadron, who admitted at the time he found the accusations of the soldiers distressing and bewildering, 'the explanation seems quite simple. Firstly, the enemy had far more planes available to use over Dunkirk than we had. Secondly, those planes could be based closer to the scene of action than ours. And thirdly, the nightmarish, smoke-laded conditions ... worked to the advantage of the Germans. They were able to nip in and out round the curtains of smoke and smog and cloud, at varying altitudes and from varying directions, on bombing and strafing missions which might only last a few seconds but were none-the-less devastating to the defenceless men who formed their targets ... In such circumstances it is not at all surprising that, again and again, our troops and transport vessels were bombed and strafed by German planes which we never saw, even though we were somewhere in the area, and that the victims of those attacks felt themselves to have been terribly let down by the RAF.'[39]

The troops on the beaches and the ships would only have been conscious of the bombers diving down to attack them, being mostly oblivious of the life or death struggle thousands of feet higher up in the sky.

William Tennant, whilst persistently requesting more help from the RAF, did acknowledge on more than one occasion that the *Luftwaffe* were often prevented from attacking the port and the beaches by Fighter Command. In his report on Operation *Dynamo* Tennant gave his assessment of both the RAF and the *Luftwaffe*. It is surprising to note that the impression one gets from the recollections of many of the soldiers of the beaches being under almost incessant attack is not supported by Tennant's account and that he believed the

German Air Force, which had the BEF at its mercy, could have achieved far more than it did:

On our arrival, they [the enemy aircraft] were chiefly occupied in wrecking Dunkirk and the port. It was quite out of the question to use the harbour at all, and my first reaction was that evacuation would have to be done from the beaches. It soon became obvious, however, that they were not including the pier in their attentions.

At times they were held off by a fine morning mist which some-times persisted until afternoon. At times, when the wind was favourable, a heavy pall of smoke from burning oil tanks, to the westward, largely obscured the pier. During the morning, they made attempts to machine-gun the beaches, but were held off by anti-aircraft fire. The beaches were also bombed but only for a brief period. Had they persisted, they would have inflicted terrible losses on us, for there were seldom less than 10,000 troops on the beaches. They later attacked the pier, with dive bombers, sunk three ships and damaged the pier. Had they persisted in these suc-cessful attacks on the pier and ships alongside, the evacuation could never have been achieved. They soon, however, turned their attention to ships lying off the beaches, and on one day (31st), no less than 100 bombing attacks were made on ships within two miles of the pier. Happily, at least twenty-four bombs were dropped on one large wreck and many bombs on other wrecks. By this time also, Bofors guns were being collected and this seemed to make them more shy of attacking the pier. The heavy attacks on ships at sea compelled me to stop all sailings and arrivals during daylight.

On the last day, they appeared once more to return to the bombing of Dunkirk and its port and bastion.

Enemy fighters were occasionally in evidence escorting their bomb-ers. At times our own fighters gave us a great measure of relief, but the sky is a big place and it was often difficult to know if our aircraft were present or not. When our aircraft did arrive the French, and less fre-quently the British, opened fire on them.[40]

An unnamed 'independent' American journalist wholeheartedly agreed, declaring that:

The withdrawal was accomplished primarily because of British local superiority in the air. This may sound astonishing to those who over estimated the strength of the German air force, and I do not underestimate its quantitative importance. But it remains true that British fighters like Spitfires, Hurricanes and Defiants are masters of any German chasers, and actually achieved mastery in the air over the Channel.[41]

Nevertheless, some airmen were publicly jeered at by the returning soldiers, which led to the Ministry of Information to announce that, 'Evidence of the strength and spread of this feeling is very marked and its repercussions, unless checked by some statement, or explanation of the facts, are likely to be most unfortunate in both military and civilian circles.'[42] Relationship between the two services was so strained that there was even a story of a pilot from 213 Squadron, who had crash-landed on one of the beaches being prevented from embarking on a ship by an embittered Army officer.[43]

Churchill therefore had to act in defence of the RAF, particularly as it would be Fighter Command that Britain would look to primarily over the coming months to hold back the Germans whilst the Army was in such a weakened state. After conceding that, 'many of our soldiers coming back have not seen the Air Force at work; they saw only the bombers which escaped its protective attack,' he said:

This was a great trial of strength between the British and German Air Forces. Can you conceive a greater objective for the Germans in the air than to make evacuation from these beaches impossible, and to sink all these ships which were displayed, almost to the extent of thousands? Could there have been an objective of greater military importance and significance for the whole purpose of the war than this? They tried hard, and they were beaten back; they were frustrated in their task. We got the Army away; and they have paid fourfold for any losses which they have inflicted. Very large formations of German aeroplanes – and we know that they are a very brave race–have turned on several occasions from the attack of one-quarter of their number of the Royal Air Force, and have dispersed in different directions. Twelve aeroplanes have been hunted by two. One aeroplane was driven into the water and cast away by the mere charge of a British aeroplane, which had no more ammunition. All of our types – the Hurricane, the Spitfire and the new Defiant- and all our pilots have been vindicated as superior to what they have at present to face.

Thus, the scene was set for the next great conflict between the two nations. The Battle of France would soon be over, and the Battle of Britain set to begin.

But the British Army had been returned to England to defend its shores and after the heroics of Dunkirk, as it had been portrayed in the media, few doubted that it would fight on the beaches, the landing grounds, in the fields the hills and the streets. The people of Britain swallowed whole the fable that the valiant BEF had been rescued from the beaches of Dunkirk by the great armada of little fishing smacks and private yachts, and therefore nothing could defeat them. It was not true, but that didn't matter. It was what was believed that counted.

Thus, the rescue of the BEF from France, and only the rescue of the BEF from France, enabled Churchill to declare to the nation and the world with absolute conviction, that Britain would 'never surrender'. After the miracle of Dunkirk, who could doubt him?

Appendix I

The British Expeditionary Force (As Organised On 10th May 1940)[1]

Commander-in-Chief
General The Viscount Gort

Chief of the General Staff	Lieutenant-General H. R. Pownall
Adjutant-General	Lieutenant-General Sir W. D. S. Brownrigg
Quarter-Master-General	Lieutenant-General W. G. Lindsell

G.H.Q. Troops

Royal Armoured Corps

    1st Light Armoured Reconnaissance Brigade—Brigadier C. W. Norman

    1st Fife and Forfar Yeomanry 1st East Riding Yeomanry

2nd Light Armoured Reconnaissance Brigade—Brigadier A. J. Clifton

    5th Royal Innisikilling Dragoon Guards

    15th/19th King's Royal Hussars

1st Army Tank Brigade—Brigadier D. H. Pratt

    4th and 7th Battalions Royal Tank Regiment

Not brigaded

    4th/7th Royal Dragoon Guards; 12th Royal Lancers; 13th/18th Royal Hussars; 1st Lothians and Border Yeomanry

Royal Artillery

    1st and 2nd Regiments Royal Horse Artillery; 32nd, 98th, 115th, 139th Army Field Regiments; 1st, 2nd, 4th, 58th, 61st, 63rd, 65th, 69th Medium Regiments; 1st, 51st, 52nd Heavy Regiments; 1st, 2nd, 3rd Super Heavy Regiments.

1st Anti-Aircraft Brigade—Brigadier E. D. Milligan

    1st, 6th, 85th Anti-Aircraft Regiments

2nd Anti-Aircraft Brigade—Brigadier E. W. Chadwick

    60th Anti-Aircraft Regiment, 51st, 58th Light Anti-Aircraft Regiments

4th Anti-Aircraft Brigade—Brigadier J. N. Slater

      4th Anti-Aircraft Regiment1st Light Anti-Aircraft Battery

5th Searchlight Brigade—Brigadier E. Rait-Kerr

      1st, 2nd, 3rd Searchlight Regiments

Royal Engineers

      100th, 101st, 216th Army Field Companies; 228th, 242nd Field Companies; 223rd Field Park, 19th Arm Field Survey, and 58th, 61st, 62nd Chemical Warfare Companies. In addition, there were thirty-eight General Construction companies; two Road Construction, one Excavator, four Tunnelling companies and one Workshop and Park company; one Field Survey depot; and two Water-Boring section

Infantry

      1st Battalion, Welsh Guards

—Machine Gun

      7th Battalion Cheshire Regiment; 1st/8th Battalion Middlesex Regiment; 4th Battalion Gordon Highlanders; 6th Battalion Argyll and Sutherland Highlanders

—Pioneer

      6th, 7th, 8th and 9th Battalions King's Own Royal Regiment; 7th Battalion Royal Norfolk Regiment; 6th Battalion Royal Scots Fusiliers; 1st/6th Battalion South Staffordshire Regiment

—Garrison

      9th Battalion West Yorkshire Regiment

I CORPS

Lieutenant-General M. G. H. Barker

Corps Troops

Royal Artillery

      27th, 140th Army Field Regiments; 3rd, 5th Medium Regiments; 52nd Light Anti-Aircraft Regiment; 2nd Light Anti-Aircraft Battery and 1st Survey Regiment

Royal Engineers

      102nd, 107th, 221st Army Field Companies; 105th Corps Field Park and 13th Corps Field Survey Companies

Infantry—Machine Gun
>2nd and 4th Battalions Cheshire Regiment; 2nd Battalion Manchester Regiment

1ST DIVISION
Major-General The Hon. H. R. L. G. Alexander

1st Guards Brigade—Brigadier M. B. Beckwith-Smith
>3rd Battalion Grenadier Guards
>2nd Battalion Coldstream Guards

2nd Battalion Hampshire Regiment

2nd Brigade—Brigadier C. E. Hudson
>1st Battalion The Loyal Regiment
>2nd Battalion North Staffordshire Regiment
>6th Battalion Gordon Highlanders

3rd Brigade—Brigadier T. N. F. Wilson
>1st Battalion Duke of Wellington's Regiment
>2nd Battalion Sherwood Foresters
>1st Battalion King's Shropshire Light Infantry

Divisional Troops

Royal Artillery
>2nd, 19th, 67th Field Regiments; 21st Anti-Tank Regiment

Royal Engineers
>23rd, 238th, 248th Field Companies; 6th Field Park Company

2ND DIVISION
Major-General H. C. Loyd

4th Brigade—Brigadier E. G. Warren
>1st Battalion Royal Scots
>2nd Battalion Royal Norfolk Regiment
>1st/8th Battalion Lancashire Fusiliers

5th Brigade—Brigadier G. I. Gartlan
>2nd Battalion Dorsetshire Regiment
>1st Battatlion Queen's Own Cameron Highlanders
>7th Battalion Worcestershire Regiment

6th Brigade—Brigadier N. M. S. Irwin (to 20th May)
>1st Battalion Royal Welch Fusiliers
>1st Battalion Royal Berkshire Regiment
>2nd Battalion Durham Light Infantry

Divisional Troops

Royal Artillery
>10th, 16th, 99th Field Regiments; 13th Anti-Tank Regiment

Royal Engineers
>5th, 209th, 506th Field Companies; 21st Field Park Company

48TH (SOUTH MIDLAND) DIVISION
Major-General A. F. A. N. Thorne

143rd Brigade—Brigadier J. Muirhead
>1st Battalion Oxfordshire and Buckinghamshire
>Light Infantry
>1st/7th and 8th Battalions Royal Warwickshire Regiment

144th Brigade—Brigadier J. M. Hamilton
>2nd Battalion Royal Warwickshire Regiment
>5th Battalion Gloucestershire Regiment
>8th Battalion Worcestershire Regiment

145th Brigade—Brigadier A. C. Hughes (to 15th May)
>Brigadier The Hon. N. F. Somerset (from 15th May)
>2nd Battalion Gloucestershire Regiment
>4th Battalion Oxfordshire and Buckinghamshire

Light Infantry
>1st Buckinghamshire Battalion, Oxfordshire and Buckinghamshire
>Light Infantry

Divisional Troops

Royal Artillery
>18th, 24th, 68th Field Regiments; 53rd Anti-Tank Regiment

Royal Engineers
>9th, 224th, 226th Field Companies; 227th Field
>Park Company

II CORPS
Lieutenant-General A. F. Brooke
Corps Troops

Royal Artillery
>60th, 88th Army Field Regiments; 53rd, 59th
>Medium Regiments; 53rd Light Anti-Aircraft Regiment and
>2nd Survey Regiment

Royal Engineers
>222nd, 234th, 240th Army Field Companies;
>108th Corps Field Park and 14th Corps
>Field Survey Companies

Infantry—Machine Guns
>2nd Battalion Royal Northumberland Fusiliers; 2nd and 1st/7th
>Battalions Middlesex Regiment

3RD DIVISION
Major-General B. L. Montgomery

7th Guards Brigade—Brigadier J. A. C. Whitaker
>1st and 2nd Battalions Grenadier Guards
>1st Battalion Coldstream Guards

8th Brigade—Brigadier C. G. Woolner
>1st Battalion Suffolk Regiment
>2nd Battalion East Yorkshire Regiment
>4th Battalion Royal Berkshire Regiment

9th Brigade—Brigadier W. Robb
>2nd Battalion Lincolnshire Regiment
>1st Battalion King's Own Scottish Borderers
>2nd Battalion Royal Ulster Rifles

Divisional Troops

Royal Artillery
>7th, 3rd, 76th Field Regiments; 20th Anti-Tank Regiment

Royal Engineers
>17th, 246th, 253rd Field Companies; 15th Field Park Company

4TH DIVISION
Major-General D. G. Johnson

10th Brigade—Brigadier E. H. Barker

   2nd Battalion Bedfordshire and Hertfordshire Regiment

   2nd Battalion Duke of Cornwall's Light Infantry

   1st/6th Battalion East Surrey Regiment

11th Brigade—Brigadier K. A. N. Anderson

   2nd Battalion Lancashire Fusiliers

   1st Battalion East Surrey Regiment

   5th Battalion Northamptonshire

12th Brigade—Brigadier J. L. I. Hawkesworth

   2nd Battalion Royal Fusiliers

   1st Battalion South Lancashire Regiment

   6th Battalion Black Watch

Divisional Troops

Royal Artillery

   22nd, 30th, 77th Field Regiments; 14th Anti-Tank Regiment

Royal Engineers

   7th, 59th, 225th Field Companies; 18th Field Park Company

5TH DIVISION (in G.H.Q. reserve on 10th May)
Major-General H. E. Franklyn

13th Brigade—Brigadier M. C. Dempsey

   2nd Battalion Cameronians

   2nd Battalion Royal Inniskilling Fusiliers

   2nd Battalion Wiltshire Regiment

17th Brigade—Brigadier M. G. N. Stopford

   2nd Battalion Royal Scots Fusiliers

   2nd Battalion Northamptonshire Regiment

   6th Battalion Seaforth Highlanders

Divisional Troops

Royal Artillery

   9th, 91st, 92nd Field Regiments; 52nd Anti-Tank Regiment

Royal Engineers

   38th, 245th, 252nd Field Companies; 254th Field Park Company

50TH (NORTHUMBRIAN) DIVISION
Major-General G. le Q. Martel

150th Brigade—Brigadier C. W. Haydon
    4th Battalion East Yorkshire Regiment
    4th and 5th Battalions Green Howards

151st Brigade—Brigadier J. A. Churchill
    6th, 8th and 9th Battalions Durham Light Infantry

25th Brigade—Brigadier W. H. C. Ramsden
    2nd Battalion Essex Regiment
    1st Battalion Royal Irish Fusiliers
    1st/7th Battalion Queen's Royal Regiment

Divisional Troops

Royal Artillery
    72nd. 74th Field Regiments; 65th Anti-Tank Regiment

Royal Engineers
    232nd, 505th Field Companies; 235th Field Park Company

Infantry
    4th Battalion Royal Northumberland Fusiliers (motor-cycle)

III CORPS
Lieutenant-General Sir R. F. Adam, Bt.

Corps Troops

Royal Artillery
    5th Regiment Royal Horse Artillery; 97th Army Field Regiment; 51st, 56th Medium Regiments; 54th Light Anti-Aircraft Regiment and 3rd Survey Regiment

Royal Engineers
    213th, 214th, 217th Army Field Companies; 293rd Corps Field Park and 514th Corps Field Survey Companies

Infantry—Machine Gun
    7th Battalion Royal Northumberland Fusiliers;
    1st/9th Battalion Manchester Regiment;
    1st Battalion Princess Louise's Kensington Regiment,
    Middlesex Regiment

42ND (EAST LANCASHIRE) DIVISION
Major-General W. G. Holmes

125th Brigade—Brigadier G. W. Sutton
    1st Battalion Border Regiment
    1st/5th and 1st/6th Battalions Lancashire Fusiliers
126th Brigade—Brigadier E. G. Miles
    1st Battalion East Lancashire Regiment
    5th Battalion King's Own Royal Regiment
    5th Battalion Border Regiment
127th Brigade—Brigadier J. G. Smyth
    1st Battalion Highland Light Infantry
    4th Battalion East Lancashire Regiment
    5th Battalion Manchester Regiment

Divisional Troops

Royal Artillery
52nd, 53rd Field Regiments; 56th Anti-Tank Regiment
Royal Engineers
200th, 201st, 250th Field Companies; 208th Field Park Company

44TH (HOME COUNTIES) DIVISION
Major-General E. A. Osborne

131st Brigade—Brigadier J. E. Utterson-Kelson
    2nd Battalion The Buffs
    1st/5th and 1st/6th Battalions Queen's Royal Regiment
132nd Brigade—Brigadier J. S. Steele
    1st, 4th and 5th Battalions Queen's Own Royal West
    Kent Regiment
133rd Brigade—Brigadier N. I. Whitty
    2nd. 4th and 5th Battalions Royal Sussex Regiment

Divisional Troops

Royal Artillery
    57th, 58th, 65th Field Regiments; 57th Anti-Tank Regiment
Royal Engineers
    11th, 208th, 210th Field Companies; 211th Field Park Company

SAAR FORCE
51ST (HIGHLAND) DIVISION
Major-General V. M. Fortune

152nd Brigade—Brigadier H. M. V. Stewart

  2nd and 4th Battalions Seaforth Highlanders

  4th Battalion Queen's Own Cameron Highlanders

153rd Brigade—Brigadier G. T. Burney

  4th Battalion Black Watch

  1st and 5th Battalions Gordon Highlanders

154th Brigade—Brigadier A. C. L. Stanley-Clarke

  1st Battalion Black Watch

  7th and 8th Battalions Argyll and Sutherland Highlanders

Divisional Troops

Royal Artillery

  17th, 23rd, 75th Field Regiments; 51st Anti-Tank Regiment

Royal Engineers

  26th, 236th, 237th Field Companies; 239th

  Field Park Company

When the 51st Division moved to the Saar in April 1940, the following troops were attached to the division:

Royal Armoured Corps

  1st Lothians and Border Yeomanry

Royal Artillery

  1st Regiment, Royal Horse Artillery (less one battery)

  97th Field Regiment (one battery)

  51st Medium Regiment

Royal Engineers 213th Army Field Company

Infantry—Machine Gun

  7th Battalion Royal Northumberland Fusiliers

  1st Battalion Princess Louise's Kensington Regiment, Middlesex Regiment

—Pioneer

  7th Battalion Royal Norfolk Regiment

  6th Battalion Royal Scots Fusiliers

FORMATIONS UNDERGOING TRAINING AND PERFORMING
LABOUR DUTIES
12TH (EASTERN) DIVISION
Major-General R. L. Petre

35th Brigade—Lieutenant-Colonel A. F. F. Young (acting 10th–12th May)

    Brigadier V. L. de Cordova (from 13th May)

    2nd/5th, 2nd/6th and 2nd/7th Battalions Queen's Royal Regiment

36th Brigade—Brigadier G. R. P. Roupell

    5th Battalion The Buffs

    6th and 7th Battalions Queen's Own Royal West Kent Regiment

37th Brigade—Brigadier R. J. P. Wyatt

    2nd./6th Battalion East Surrey Regiment

    6th and 7th Battalion Royal Sussex Regiment

Divisional Troops

Royal Engineers

    262nd, 263rd, 264th Field Companies;

    265th Field Park Company

23RD (NORTHUMBRIAN) DIVISION
Major-General A. E. Herbert

69th Brigade—Brigadier The Viscount Downe

    5th Battalion East Yorkshire Regiment

    6th and 7th Battalions Green Howards

70th Brigade—Brigadier P. Kirkup

    10th and 11th Battalions Durham Light Infantry

    1st Battalion Tyneside Scottish, Black Watch

Divisional Troops

Royal Engineers

    233rd, 507th Field Companies; 508th Field Park Company

Infantry

    8th Battalion Royal Northumberland Fusiliers (motor-cycle);

    9th Battalion Royal Northumberland Fusiliers (machine gun)

46TH (NORTH MIDLAND AND WEST RIDING) DIVISION
Major-General H. O. Curtis
137th Brigade—Brigadier J. B. Gawthorpe
    2nd/5th Battalion West Yorkshire Regiment
    2nd/6th and 2nd/7th Battalions Duke of Wellington's Regiment
138th Brigade—Brigadier E. J. Ginling
    6th Battalion Lincolnshire Regiment
    2nd/4th Battalion King's Own Yorkshire Light Infantry
    6th Battalion York and Lancaster Regiment
139th Brigade—Brigadier H. A. F. Crewdson (to 22nd May)
    Brigadier R. C. Chichester-Constable (from 22nd May)
    2nd/5th Battalion Leicestershire Regiment
    2/5th and 9th Battalions Sherwood Foresters

Divisional Troops

Royal Engineers
    270th, 271st, 272nd Field Companies; 273rd Field Park Company

LINES OF COMMUNICATION TROOPS
Royal Artillery
    3rd Anti-Aircraft Brigade—Brigadier W. R. Shilstone
    2nd, 8th, 79th Anti-Aircraft Regiments4th Light Anti-Aircraft Battery
Royal Engineers
    104th, 106th, 110th, 212th, 218th Army Troops Companies
In addition, there were four Road Construction companies, twelve Artisan Works companies, three General Construction companies, one Map depot, two Engineer Stores (Base) Depots, Engineer Base Workshop, one section Foresty company, and lines of communication depot.
Infantry
    4th Battalion The Buffs, 14th Battalion Royal Fusiliers,
    12th Battalion Royal Warwickshire Regiment,
    4th Battalion Border Regiment,
    1st/5th Battalion Sherwood Foresters
    In addition, there were two infantry and two general base depots.

With the Advanced Air Striking Force

Royal Artillery

   12th Anti-Aircraft Brigade—Brigadier W. T. O. Crewdson
   53rd, 73rd Anti-Aircraft Regiments

Units Of The BEF Arriving In France After 10 May 1940[1]

1ST ARMOURED DIVISION
Major-General R. Evans

2nd Amoured Brigade—Brigadier R. L. McCreery
- The Queen's Bays
- 9th Queen's Royal Lancers
- 10th Royal Hussars

3rd Armoured Brigade—Brigadier J. H. Crocker
- 2nd and 5th Battalions Royal Tank Regiment
- (The 3rd Battalion was detached and sent to Calais—see below)

1st Support Group—Brigadier F. E. Morgan
- 101st Light Anti-Aircraft and Anti-Tank Regiment
- (The infantry battalions were detached and sent to Calais—see below)

Divisional Troops

Royal Engineers
- 1st Field and 1st Field Park Squadrons

52ND (LOWLAND) DIVISION
Major-General J. S. Drew

155th Brigade—Brigadier T. Grainger-Stewart
- 7th/9th Battalion Royal Scots
- 4th and 5th Battalions King's Own Scottish Borders

156th Brigade—Brigadier J. S. N. Fitzgerald
- 4th/5th Battalion Royal Scots Fusiliers
- 6th and 7th Battalions Cameronians

157th Brigade—Brigadier Sir J. E. Laurie, Bt.
- 5th and 6th Battalions Highland Light Infantry
- 1st Battalion Glasgow Highlanders, Highland Light Infantry

Divisional Troops

Royal Artillery

70th, 71st, 78th Field Regiments; 54th Anti-Tank Regiment

Royal Engineers

202nd, 241st, 554th Field Companies and 243rd Field Park Company

DEFENCE OF BOULOGNE

20th Guards Brigade—Brigadier W. A. F. L. Fox-Pitt

2nd Battalion Irish Guards

2nd Battalion Welsh Guards

Royal Artillery

275th Anti-Tank Battery, less one troop; 69th Anti-Tank Regiment

DEFENCE OF CALAIS

30th Brigade—Brigadier C. N. Nicholson

2nd Battalion King's Royal Rifle Corps 1st Battalion The Rifle Brigade

3rd Battalion Royal Tank Regiment

(all the above from 1st Armoured Division)

1st Battalion Queen Victoria's Rifles, King's Royal Rifle Corps (motor-cycle)

Royal Artillery

229th Anti-Tank Battery, less one troop; 58th Anti-Tank Regiment

Appendix III

The Royal Air Force During The Battle Of Flanders And In France[1]

BRITISH AIR FORCES IN FRANCE

Air Officer Commanding in Chief
Air Marshal A. S. Barratt
Senior Air Staff Officer
Air Vice-Marshal D. C. S. Evill
Headquarters—North: Group Captain S. C. Strafford
East: Squadron Leader R. Cleland

AIR COMPONENT

Air Vice Marshal C. H. B. Blount
No. 14 Group—Group Captain P. F. Fullard
No. 60 (Fighter) Wing—Wing Commander J. A. Boret
    Nos. 85 and 87 Squadrons
No. 61 (Fighter) Wing—Wing Commander R. Y. Eccles
    Nos. 607 and 615 Squadrons
No. 70 (Bomber Reconnaissance) Wing—Wing Commander W. A. Opie
    Nos. 18 and 57 Squadrons
No. 52 (Bomber) Wing—Wing Commander A. F. Hutton
    Nos. 53 and 59 Squadrons
No. 50 (Army Cooperation) Wing—Group Captain A. R. Churchman
    Nos. 4, 13 and 16 Squadrons
No. 51 (Army Cooperation) Wing—Wing Commander A. H. Flower
    Nos. 2 and 26 Squadrons
No. 81 (Communication) Squadron

ADVANCED AIR STRIKING FORCE

Air Vice-Marshal P. H. L. Playfair

No. 71 (Bomber) Wing—Air Commander R. M. Field
    Nos. 105, 114, 139 and 150 Squadrons

No. 75 (Bomber) Wing—Group Captain A. H. Wann
    Nos. 88, 103 and 218 Squadrons

No. 76 (Bomber) Wing—Group Captain H. S. Kerby
    Nos. 12, 142 and 226 Squadrons

No. 67 (Fighter) Wing—Wing Commander C. Walter
    Nos. 1 and 73 Squadrons

No. 212 (Photographic Reconnaissance) Squadron

(II) HOME COMMANDS

Groups principally concerned in Air Fighting in France and Belgium

FIGHTER COMMAND

Air Chief Marshal Sir Hugh Dowding

No. 11 Group—Air Vice-Marshal K. R. Park
    Nos. 3, 25, 32, 54, 56, 64, 65, 74, 79, 92, 111, 145, 151, 253, 501, 600,
    601, 604, 609 and 610 Squadrons

The following squadrons were also temporarily under operational command
of No. 11 Group:
    (from No. 12 Group)—Nos. 17, 19, 66, 213, 222, 229, 264, 266, 504,
    and 611 Squadrons
    (from No. 13 Group)—Nos. 41, 43, 72, 242, 245, 605, and 616
    Squadrons

BOMBER COMMAND

Air Marshal C. F. A. Portal

No. 2 Group—Air Vice-Marshal J. M. Robb
    Nos. 15, 12, 40, 52, 82, 107, 110 Squadrons

No. 3 Group—Air Vice-Marshal J. E. A. Baldwin
    Nos. 9, 31, 37, 38, 75, 99, 115 and 149 Squadrons
No. 4 Group—Air Vice-Marshal A. Coningham
    Nos. 10, 51, 58, 71, 77 and 102 Squadrons
No. 5 Group—Air Vice-Marshal A. T. Harris
    Nos. 44, 49, 50, 61, 83 and 144 Squadrons

COASTAL COMMAND

Air Chief Marshal Sir Frederick Bowhill
No .16 Group—Air Vice-Marshal J. H. S. Tyssen
    Nos. 22, 48, 206, 220, 235, 236 and 500 Squadrons
With the following temporarily under operational control:
    (from No. 17 Group)—No. 248 Squadron
    (from No. 18 Group)—No. 254 Squadron
The following squadrons of the Fleet Air Arm were also temporarily under operation control of No. 16 Group:
    Nos. 801, 812, 815, 816, 818, 819, 825, and 826 Squadrons

Material Losses Of The British Army In France And Belgium, May To June 1940[1]

	Shipped to France (September 1939–May 1940)	Consumed and expended in action or destroyed or left behind	Brought back to England
Guns	2,794	2,472	322
Vehicles	68,618	63,879	4,739
Motor Cycles	21,081	20,548 533	
Ammunitions (tons) 109,000	76,697	32,303	
Supplies/Stores (tons)	449,000	415,940	33,060
Petrol (tons)	166,000	164,929	1,071
Only thirteen light tanks and nine cruiser tanks were brought back to England from a total of 445.			

Daily List Of Disembarkation In UK Ports, Classified By Types Of Ships[1]

| | DATE | | | | | | | | | | |
| | MAY | | | | | | JUNE | | | | TOTALS |
	26	27	28	29	30	31	1	2	3	4	
Destroyers	–	–	11,327	15,972	18,554	25,722	14,440	5,649	6,432	5,303	103,399
Personnel Ships	2,287	3,168	2,161	17,525	2,981	12,477	11,314	4,977	7,477	10,013	74,380
Mine-sweepers	–	–	420	4,307	7,671	4,714	594	1,842	2,552	1,940	31,040
Paddle Minesweepers	–	–	1,336	1,454	1,477	2,682	9,148	2,075	1,777	1,079	21,028
Trawlers	–	–	100	3,894	7,405	3,976	2,760	900	50	1,200	20,287
Skoots	–	–	–	90	1,116	1,797	647	1,975	418	418	6,461
Drifters	24	–	3,138	3,158	2,931	2,938	1,797	2,632	2,526	2,023	20,167
Hospital Carriers	–	–	–	818	780	907	130	–	–	–	2,635
Miscellaneous	1,936	2,550	45	3,133	5,293	4,596	10,803	2,649	3,018	2,637	36,660
French Destroyers	–	–	–	460	2,620	2,026	615	–	750	1,116	7,623
Other Vessels	–	–	–	520	2,399	2,306	2,271	905	4,641	1,960	15,002
Totals	4,247	5,718	18,526	50,331	53,227	64,141	61,557	23,604	29,641	27,689	338,682

Appendix VI

No. 11 Group Fighter Patrols – Dunkirk Area
26 May To 4 June 1940

Date	Patrols	Total flying hours daily	Enemy aircraft assessed as destroyed
26th May.	22	480	20
27th May.	23	536	38
28th May.	II	576	23
29th May.	9	674	65
30th May.	9	704	–
3Ist May.	8	490	38
Ist June.	8	558	43
2nd June.	4	231	35
3rd June.	4	339	–
4th June.	3	234	–
Details from Ramsay's despatch of 18 June 1940.			

Appendix VII

A Brief Example of Some of the Boats Commandeered by Tough's at the time of 'Dunkirk' Together with Brief Details of the Various Crews put aboard[1]

Gay Crusader:	B. Kearns (Skipper)	L.R. Messenger (Engineer)	C. Newens (1st Lt.)
	55, The Vale	104, Dowanhill Road	98, Brackenbury Rd
	N.W. 11	Catford, S.E.6	Hammersmith
Aloha:	R.W.A. Winter (1st Lt.)		A.B Dann (2nd Lt.)
	24, Rosefont Road		35, Holmes Road
	Richmond		Twickenham
	R.R Thornton (3rd Lt.)		G.R Talbot
	16, Ailsa Road		7, Vernon Road
	Isleworth		East Sheen, S.W.14
Nanette II:	H.C. Boyle		C. Forester
	Shadbrook Road		1, Strawberry Vale
	W.11		Twickenham
Also Friday Engineer and hand			
Cairn Gorm:	W. Bray (3rd Lt.)		P. Kratz
	43, Eddly Cresent		37, Claremont Road
	S.W.5		Surbiton
Transferred from *Schesdeen*		H. Brooks (Skipper) & P. Nichols (Engineer)	

Vessels to be Returned to Owners

Sambre   21st June 1940

Anthony   F. Winter, 'Braedoone', Woodlands Road, Surbiton

Major   21st June 1940. B.R. Bunn, St Bernard Road, St Albans

Boats to Claygate Surrey, Essex, London, Burnham in Bucks, Cambridge

Skylark II   27th June 1940, Myalls Ltd., 46, Pleasant Road, Southend

Our Lizzie   H. Bevan Penketh, Ingatestone, Essex.

Notes

Chapter 1: The British Expeditionary Force In France

1. J.E. & H.W. Kaufmann, *Fortress France. The Maginot Line and the French Defences in World War II* (Connecticut, 2005), p.15.
2. Vivian Rowe, *The Great Wall of France: The Triumph of the Maginot Line* (Putnam, London, 1959), p.16.
3. A. Danchev and D. Todman, *War Diaries 1939-1940, Field Marshal Lord Alanbrooke* (Phoenix Press, London, 2002), p.25.
4. Account by Captain Jones, 1st Battalion King's Shropshire Light Infantry, courtesy of The Shropshire Regimental Museum.
5. ibid.
6. *War Magazine*, 9 February 1940, p.481.
7. L.F. Ellis, *The War in France and Flanders, 1939-1940* (HMSO, London, 1953), pp.20, 249 & 366.
8. Saul David, *Churchill's Sacrifice of the Highland Division, France 1940* (Brassey, London, 1994), pp.12-45.
9. Quoted in Mike Rossiter, *I Fought at Dunkirk* (Bantam Press, London, 2012), p.70.

Chapter 2: 'The Greatest Battle Of History'

1. Alex Danchev and Daniel Todman, *War Diaries 1939-1945 Field Marshal Lord Alanbrooke* (Weidenfeld & Nicolson, London, 2001), p.59.
2. Winston S. Churchill, *The Second World War*, vol. II (Cassell, London, 1949), p.38.
3. Danchev and Todman, p.64.
4. Grehan, J. & Mace, M., *The BEF in France, 1939-1940, Manning the Front Through to the Dunkirk Evacuation* (Pen & Sword, Barnsley, 2014), p.45.
5. Ian Hay, *The Battle of Flanders 1940*, (HMSO, London, 1941), pp.36-7.
6. Churchill, vol. II, p. 52.
7. R. Macleod and Dennis Kelly (eds.), *The Ironside Diaries, 1937-1940* (Constable, London, 1962), p.321; Private Papers of Lieutenant Colonel J.S. Watson, IWM Document no.16543.
8. Marcus Cunliffe, *History of the Royal Warwickshire Regiment, 1919-1955*

(William Clowes and Sons, London,1956), p.36.

9. Quoted in Hugh Sebag-Montefiore, *Dunkirk, Fight to the Last Man* (Penguin, London, 2007), pp.157-8.

10. Quoted in Richard Holmes, *War Walks 2, From the Battle of Hastings to the Blitz* (BBC Books, London, 1997), p.171.

11. Charles Gardner, *A.A.S.F.* (Hutchinson, London, 1940), p.171.

12. Quoted in John Hammerton, *The Second World War Illustrated*, Vol. II, p.636.

13. Charles Gardner, pp.192-3.

14. Quoted, unsourced, in Geoffrey Stewart, *Dunkirk and the Fall of France* (Pen & Sword, Barnsley, 200), p.54.

15. Leith Hay, p.41.

16. S. Prichard, *Life in the Welsh Guards 1936-46* (privately published, Wales, March 2007), p.7.

17. J. Armengaud, *Le Drame de Dunkerque* (Plon, Paris, 1948), p.105.

18. Ellis, p.157.

19. J. Cooksey, *Boulogne 20 Guards Brigade's Fighting Defence – May 1940* (Pen & Sword Books, Barnsley 2002), p.126.

20. Prichard, p.14.

21. The French troops in the Citadel were not informed that the Guards Brigade was going to be evacuated and they, with some justification, felt that they had been callously abandoned by the British. All the French in Boulogne were either killed or captured and Churchill wrote that he 'regretted' evacuating the Guards and leaving the French on their own. He was wrong, of course, because Windsor-Lewis held the port for just as long as the French held the Citadel, Churchill, p.68.

22. Churchill, pp.70-1.

23. ibid, p.70. Churchill was so annoyed about this that he was still complaining about this the next day and he sent a letter to the Chief of the Imperial General Staff demanding to know who had sent the instruction to evacuate Calais.

24. Douglas C. Dildy, *Dunkirk 1940, Operation Dynamo* (Osprey, Oxford, 2010), p.19.

25. ibid, p.73.

Chapter 3: Operation *Dynamo*: Day 1, Sunday 26 May

1. TNA WO 197/134.

2. Roy S. Humphreys, *Hellfire Corner - Reminiscences of Wartime in South East England* (Sutton, Stroud, 1994), p.31.

3. Walter Lord, *The Miracle of Dunkirk* (Allen Lane, London, 1982), p.20.
4. TNA WO 197/119.
5. Lieutenant Colonel David Smith, *Retreat to Dunkirk* (unpublished memoir, HMP collection), pp.7-8.
6. Paul Addison and Jeremy A. Crang, *Listening to Britain, Home Intelligence Reports on Britain's Finest Hour – May to September 1940* (Bodley Head, London, 2010), pp.11-13.
7. Ian Hay, p.50.
8. Grehan & Mace, p,70.
9. Danchev and Todman, pp.67 & 70.
10. Ellis, p.171.
11. Walter Lord, p.25.
12. *Général* Billotte was fatally injured in a motor accident on 21 May.
13. Hay p.31.
14. Robert Jackson, *Dunkirk: The British Evacuation, 1940* (Cassel, London, 2002), pp.101-2.
15. Danchev and Todman, p.69.
16. Ellis, p.178.
17. Grehan and Mace, P.65.
18. Levine, p.172.
19. Mike Rossiter, *I fought at Dunkirk, Seven Veterans Remember the German Invasion of France* (Bantam, London, 2012), p.214.
20. Len Deighton, *Blitzkrieg, From the Rise of Hitler to the Fall of Dunkirk* (Jonathon Cape, London, 1979), p.294.
21. David Divine, *The Nine Days of Dunkirk* (Ballantine Books, New York, 1959), pp.82-3.
22. TNA ADM 199/792
23. TNA ADM 234/360.
24. TNA ADM 199/792.
25. W. J. R. Gardner, *The Evacuation from Dunkirk, 'Operation Dynamo 26 May-4June 1940* (Frank Cass, London, 2000), p.16.
26. David J. Knowles, *Escape from Catastrophe, 1940 Dunkirk* (self-published, Rochester, 2000), pp.77-8.
27. TNA ADM 234/360, Battle Summary No.41.
28. Divine, p.85.

Chapter 4: Operation *Dynamo*: Day 2, Monday 27 May

1. IWM Sound Archive, catalogue no.10695.
2. Daily Mail, 28 March 2014.

3. Quoted, unsourced, in Gregory Blaxland, *Destination Dunkirk, The Story of Gort's Army* (William Kimber, London, 1973), p.258
4. Hammerton, p.644.
5. Gardner, pp.18-9
6. TNA CAB 106/243.
7. ibid.
8. Anthony Rhodes, *Sword of Bone, The Phoney War and Dunkirk 1940* (Severn House, London, 1975), pp.188-9.
9. Dildy, p.30.
10. Graham Wallace, *RAF Biggin Hill* (Pace Reprographics, Denham,1975), p.123.
11. TNA WO 106/1607.
12. TNA ADM 199/786.
13. Quoted in Knowles, p.44.
14. Quoted in Knowles, pp.44-5.
15. Rhodes, p.198.
16. Divine, p.95.
17. TNA ADM 234/360.
18. Jackson, p.123.
19. Dildy, p.36. The *Luftwaffe* flew only marginally more sorties than Fighter Command = 225 bomber and seventy-five dive-bomber, totalling 300, just thirteen more than the British fighters.
20. TNA ADM 358/110
21. TNA ADM 199/786. Commander Dechaineux took over from Vivacious's captain Lieutenant Commander F.R. Parish R.N. who, due to overstrain was granted sick leave.
22. Denys Thorp's story can be found at http://website.lineone.net/~tom_lee/monas%20isle%20hms.htm.
23. Quoted in Divine, pp.93-4.
24. TNA WO 197/119.
25. Rhodes, p.207.
26. TNA WO 197/119.
27. Quoted in Patrick Wilson, *Dunkirk, From Despair to Deliverance* (Pen & Sword, Barnsley, 1999), p.45.
28. Dildy, p.32.
29. BBC People's War, ID:A2663660.
30. Danchev and Todman, p.71.
31. Tennant's report can be found in TNA ADM 199/789.
32. Gardner, p.25.

Chapter 5: Operation *Dynamo*: Day 3, Tuesday 28 May

1. Quoted in Basil Liddell Hart, *History of the Second World War* (Putmam, New York, 1970), p.41.

2. IWM Sound Archive Catalogue no. 10433.
3. *Jerry Murland, Retreat and Rearguard – Dunkirk 1940: The Evacuation of the BEF to the Channel Ports* (Pen & Sword, Barnsley, 2016), p.217.
4. TNA WO 197/119.
5. BBC People's War, Article ID: A2663660.
6. *North Devon Journal*, 20 June, 1940.
7. Rhodes, p.203.
8. Dr John Rickard, *Operation Dynamo, the evacuation from Dunkirk, 27 May–4 June 1940*, http://www.historyofwar.org/articles/operation_dynamo.html
9. TNA ADM 199/786.
10. Quoted on the Queen Alexandra's Royal Army Nursing Corps website, www.qaranc.co.uk.
11. Pennant No. L. 20 was allocated to HMS Garth.
12. TNA ADM 199/786.
13. ibid.
14. For example, Russel Plummer, p.34.
15. Quoted on the Medway Queen website: www.medwayqueen.co.uk.
16. Lord, p.117.
17. ADM 199/789.
18. ibid.
19. Tom Vigors, *Life's too Short to Cry: The Compelling Memoir of a Battle of Britain Ace* (Grub Street, London, 2006), pp.154-6.
20. BBC People's War, ID A3542339.
21. This is from Gunbuster, *Return via Dunkirk* (Hodder & Stoughton, London, 1940), p.249, which, because of wartime restrictions, did not give the true Royal Artillery regiment in question.
22. TNA ADM 199/787.
23. Gardner, W.J.R., p.26.
24. TNA ADM 199/786.
25. TNA ADM 199/786.
26. Peter Hadley, *Third Class to Dunkirk* (Hollis and Carter, 1944), quoted in Nicholas Harman, *Dunkirk, The Necessary Myth* (Hodder and Stoughton, Sevenoaks, 1980), p.161.
27. Lieutenant A. Dann's report, TNA ADM 199/788.
28. TNA ADM 234/360.
29. *Voices of Dunkirk*, BBC history.
30. TNA ADM 199/787.
31. IWM Sound Archive Catalogue no. 6973.
32. BBC People's War, Article ID: A2528138.

Chapter 6: Operation *Dynamo*: Day 4, Wednesday 29 May

1. BBC People's War, Article ID: A2528138.
2. BBC History Archive, 'Voices of Dunkirk'.
3. IWM Sound Archive, Catalogue no. 16722.
4. Hilary Heptinstall, Forces War Records Blog.
5. TNA WO 197/119.
6. TNA ADM 199/789.
7. BBC People's War, Article ID A4612484.
8. TNA ADM 199/786.
9. Basil Bartlett, *My First War: An Army Officer's Journal for May 1940 Through Belgium to Dunkirk* (Chatto and Windus, 1941).
10. BBC People's War, Article ID: A2298495.
11. BBC People's War, Article ID. A2308105.
12. IWM Sound Archive 6901.
13. TNA ADM 199/786.
14. ibid.
15. TNA ADM 199/789.
16. TNA ADM 199/786.
17. ibid.
18. Alec Brew, *The Turret Fighters, Defiant and Roc* (Crowood Press, Marlborough, 2002), p.63.
19. Quoted on the 264squadron.co.uk website.
20. Quoted in Wilson, pp.50-1.
21. BBC People's War, Article ID A2349768.
22. TNA WO 106/1607.
23. http://www.bbc.co.uk/archive/dunkirk/14312.shtml
24. This unlikely tale is drawn from David Knowles, p.71.
25. Norman Wickman, 'A Royal Engineer at Dunkirk Tells His Story', *Warfare History Network*, September 2, 2016.
26. Smith, pp.10-11.
27. TNA ADM 199/786.
28. TNA ADM 199/786.
29. W.J.R. Gardner, p.45.
30. Quoted in Hammerton, p.636
31. BBC People's War, Article ID: A2270422.
32. TNA WO 361/19.
33. ibid.
34. Though written in 1940 whilst the officer was in hospital in Leeds, it was published in The West Australian on 16 June 1945.
35. BBC People's War, Article ID: A2306891.
36. Wake-Walker's report in ADM 199/792.

37. TNA ADM 199/786.
38. Churchill, Vol. II, p.94.

Chapter 7: Operation *Dynamo*: Day 5, Thursday 30 May

1. Gardner, p.46.
2. TNA ADM 199/789.
3. TNA ADM 199/792.
4. ibid.
5. Gardner, p.57.
6. TNA ADM 199/788A.
7. Russel Plummer, *Paddle Steamers at War 1939-1945* (GMS Enterprises, Peterborough, 1995), p.44.
8. M. Mace, They Also Served: *The Story of Sussex Lifeboats at War 1939-1945*, (Historic Military Press, Storrington, 2001), pp.7-8.
9. *Daily Mirror*, 20 June 1940.
10. Quoted in Jackson, p.117.
11. Quoted in Patrick Wilson, pp.148-9.
12. IWM, Catalogue no. 18204.
13. Tennant gives his name as Maud, TNA ADM 199/789.
14. Quoted in Sean Longdon, *Dunkirk, The Men They Left Behind* (Constable, London, 2008), pp.50-1.
15. Wilf Saunders, *Dunkirk Diary of a Young Soldier* (Brewin Books, Studley, 2010), p.78.
16. TNA WO 197/119.
17. TNA ADM 199/786.
18. Sebag-Montefiore, p.415.
19. Grehan & Mace, p.87.
20. ibid, pp.130-1.
21. Quoted in Norman Franks, *Air Battle Dunkirk, 26 May – 3 June 1940* (Grub Street, London, 2000), p.96.
22. Ellis, p.235.
23. Yesterday's Witness, One Man's Dunkirk, BBC Archive.
24. It has not been possible to validate the story of Berkshire Lass, which has an apocryphal feel to it. However, it is told by two men who were there, Lieutenant Colonel Ewan Butler and Major J. Selby Bradford, in *Keep the Memory Green, The First of Many, France 1939-40* (Hutchinson, London, nd.), pp.141-7.
25. Richardson's report was appended to Tennant's report in TNA ADM 199/789.
26. Captain Maund's report in Admiralty Records III, reproduced in W.J.R. Gardner, pp.63-4.

27. Ellis, p.232.
28. http://dkepaves.free.fr/download/bourrasque.pdf
29. TNA WO 197/119.
30. TNA ADM 344/83.
31. TNA ADM 199/786.
32. The D.G. cable on a (steel or iron) ship is its degaussing cable, i.e. when an electric current is passed through this DG cable the ship's magnetic signature is eliminated for several months. The ship will need to be 'wiped' (using the fixed DG cable) from time to time to maintain a very low magnetic signature and so be invulnerable to magnetic mines.
33. Danchev and Todman, p.72.
34. Bryant, Arthur, *Turn of the Tide*, (Doubleday, London, 1957), p.154.
35. TNA ADM
36. C. Vince, *Storm on the Waters: The Story of the Life-Boat Service in the War of 1939-1945* (Hodder & Stoughton, London 1946), p.29.
37. Quoted, unsourced, in Wilson, pp.102-3.
38. ibid, pp.104-5.
39. Ellis, p.226.
40. BBC People's War, Article ID: A2281312.
41. Ellis, p.230.

Chapter 8: Operation *Dynamo*: Day 6, Friday 31 May

1. Hammerton, pp.643-4.
2. Ellis, p.227.
3. Grehan & Mace, p.133.
4. Quoted in Jackson, p.137.
5. Lord, pp.198-9.
6. ibid, p.199.
7. TNA ADM 199/789.
8. 166 rescued by the corvette Widgeon, fifty by the trawler Wolves, twenty-one by the trawler Stella Dorado and fifteen by the Polish destroyer Blyskawica.
9. TNA ADM 199/788A.
10. Bob Tough, *One of the Many* IWM Document no.3797.
11. http://www.scoutsrecords.org.
12. The James Christmas Portfolio, IWM Document no.15674.
13. ADM 199/788A.
14. TNA ADM
15. Quoted in Sebag-Montefiore, pp.412-3.
16. TNA ADM 234/360.

17. Hammerton, p.644.
18. IWM Document no. 17393.
19. John Osborne, *Dunkirk – first-hand account of one of the small boats*, BBC WW2 People's War. Article ID: A2657270.
20. TNA WO 197/119.
21. TNA ADM 234/360.
22. TNA ADM
23. Dildy, p.69.
24. TNA ADM
25. Quoted in Alexander McKee, *Strike from the Sky the Story of the Battle of Britain* (Souvenir Press, London, 1960), p.27.
26. Alan C. Deere, *Nine Lives* (Crécy, Manchester, 2009), p.69.
27. Quoted, unsourced, in John Masefield, *The Nine Days Wonder: The Operation Dynamo* (William Heinemann, London, 1941), p.51.
28. TNA ADM 199/788A.
29. Hammerton, pp.645-6.
30. From thamestugs.co.uk, Dunkirk Logs.
31. Dildy, p.86.
32. IWM Sound Archive, Catalogue number 9341.
33. Lord, p.192.
34. BBC People's War, Article ID: A7445432.
35. TNA ADM 199/789.
36. Information from John Dell's website *Skuas Over Dunkirk*.
37. ibid.
38. TNA ADM 234/360.
39. TNA ADM 234/360.
40. Quoted, unsourced, in Masefield, pp,31-2.
41. TNA WO 106/1607.
42. TNA WO 167/350.
43. IWM Sound Archive, Catalogue no. 12305.
44. TNA ADM 199/787.
45. TNA ADM 199/799.
46. *Evening Express*, 1 June 1940.

Chapter 9: Operation *Dynamo*: Day 7, Saturday 1 June

1. ADM 199/787.
2. *New York Herald Tribune*, European Edition, June 1, 1940.
3. IWM Catalogue no.16722.
4. TNA ADM 199/786.
5. Quoted in Knowles, pp.171-2.

6. TNA ADM 199/786.
7. IWM Sound Archive Catalogue no. 9768.
8. IWM Document no.10167, Samuel Palmer, *M.V. Naiad Errant at Dunkirk 1940*, pp.2-3.
9. TNA ADM 199/788A.
10. TNA ADM 199/792.
11. Spears, p.323.
12. TNA ADM 199/792.
13. IWM, Catalogue no. 22385.
14. TNA ADM 234/360.
15. BBC People's War, Article ID: A2269424.
16. TNA ADM 199/792.
17. Robert Jackson, *Churchill's Moat: The Channel War 1939-1945* (Airlife, Shrewsbury, 1995, p.34).
18. www.hmshood.com
19. TNA ADM 199/786.
20. TNA ADM 199/786.
21. TNA ADM 199/792
22. T. J. Spiers, *Shot Down Over Dunkirk*, BBC People's War, Article ID:A2764235.
23. Quoted from an undated account written by Potter and held in the Andy Saunders' Collection.
24. This was the B-class destroyer's third run from Dunkirk. The previous day she had carried out two trips to embark troops, taking 338 troops on the first run and 357 on the second.
25. TNA ADM 197/119.
26. Lionel Tucker, *Memories of The Maid of Orleans*, BBC WW2 People's War, Article ID: A8408630.
27. Stewart, p.112.
28. TNA ADM 199/792.
29. See, Martin Mace, *The Dunkirk Evacuation in 100 Objects, The Story Behind Operation Dynamo in 1940*, to be published by Pen & Sword of Barnsley in 2017.
30. IWM Sound Archives, Catalogue no.19770.
31. Supplement to *The London Gazette*, 26 July 1940.
32. *British Medical Journal*, Vol.300, May 1990, quoted in Murland, p.216.
33. ibid, p.218.
34. Blaxland, pp.339-40.
35. Lord, p.234.
36. Quoted in Hammerton, p.631.
37. TNA ADM 197/119.

Chapter 10: Operation *Dynamo*: Day 8, Sunday 2 June

1. TNA ADM 199/789.
2. *London Calling: The 'Curlew' at Dunkirk* http://www.bbc.co.uk/archive/dunkirk/14416.shtml?page=txt
3. Quoted in Robert Jackson, p.171.
4. IWM Document no.23360.
5. TNA ADM 199/788A.
6. Quoted in Knowles, pp.186-7.
7. Christian Brann, *The Little Ships of Dunkirk* (Collectors Books, Kemble, 1989), p.94.
8. M. Henniker, *An Image of War* (Leo Cooper, London, 1987), p.59.
9. TNA ADM 199/786.
10. Derek Wood & Derek Dempster, *The Narrow Margin, The Battle of Britain and the Rise of Air Power 1930-1945* (Pen & Sword, Barnsley,2010), p.101.
11. Quoted in Norman Franks, p.145.
12. Quoted in Dunkirk Revisited, p.164.
13. Humphreys, 'Hawkinge' in Winston G. Ramsey (ed.) *The Battle of Britain, Then and Now* (After the Battle, Old Harlow,1982), p.105.
14. TNA ADM 199/788A.
15. Grehan & Mace, p.143.
16. Taken from Foremost 87's log, reproduced at http://thamestugs.co.uk.
17. TNA ADM 199/786.
18. Spears, p.295.
19. TNA WO 106/1607.
20. ADM 234/360.
21. TNA ADM 199/792.
22. John Masefield, *The Nine Days Wonder; The Operation Dynamo* (Heinemann, London, 1941), pp.45-6; Gardiner, p.110.
23. TNA ADM 199/787.
24. TNA ADM 199/787.
25. TNA ADM 199/787.
26. Divine, p.208.
27. 'Dunkirk – a Personal Perspective', BBC broadcast on 29 May 1950.
28. 'I helped keep Dunkirk rescue ship afloat', *Bath Chronicle*, 26 May 2010.
29. Quoted in Knowles, pp.193-4.
30. This is the wording of Tennant's signal as recorded in the Admiralty's Battle Summary No.41, in TNA ADM 234/360. However, Dildy, p.80 writes that this has been reworded for posterity, the original signal reading being 'Operation complete. Returning to Dover.'

Chapter 11: Operation *Dynamo*: Day 9, Monday 3 June

1. TNA ADM 199/787.
2. TNA ADM 234/360.
3. TNA ADM 234/360
4. TNA ADM 234/360
5. TNA ADM 234/360.
6. TNA ADM 199/789.
7. BBC Peoples War, W.E. Birtles, *Dunkirk Aged 17*, Article ID: A3475352.
8. TNA ADM 199/787.
9. ADM 199/788A.
10. W.J.R. Gardner, p.119
11. There was no HMS *Walrus* in Royal Navy service in 1940 and he must have misheard *Locust*.
12. TNA ADM 334/83.
13. TNA ADM 199/786.
14. *Gloucestershire Echo*, Tuesday, 4 June 1940.
15. *North Devon Journal*, 20 June, 1940.
16. Devine, pp.219-20.
17. Ellis, pp.245-6.
18. TNA ADM 199/786.
19. Max Arthur, *Forgotten Voices of the Second World War* (Edbury Press, London, 2004), p.69).

Chapter 12: The Dunkirk Spirit

1. Churchill, HC Deb 04 June 1940 vol. 361 cc787-98.
2. Julian Thompson, *Retreat to Victory* (Sidgwick & Jackson, London, 2008), pp.295-6.
3. Sir John Hammerton, *The War Illustrated*, Volume Two (Amalgamated Press, London, nd), p.626.
4. *Western Mail*, Wednesday, 4 June 1940.
5. John Masefield, *The Twenty-Five Days, The Flanders Campaign and the Rescue of the BEF from Dunkirk 10 May – 3 June 1940* (Pen & Sword, Barnsley, 2004), p.162.
6. Quoted in Max Arthur, pp.58-9.
7. *Nottingham Evening Post*, Thursday 27 June, 1940.
8. ADM 199/788A.
9. Thompson, p.296
10. Sinclair McKay, *Dunkirk, From Disaster to Deliverance, Testimonies of the Last Survivors* (Aurum Press, London, 2014), xv.
11. *Western Gazette*, Friday 21 June.

12. Longdon, p.11.
13. It has only been exceeded once since then in the debacle of Singapore in the winter of 1941/42.
14. BBC People's War, 'DWBD's War', Article ID: A6329216,
15. BBC People's War, 'Stretcher-bearers' by Hugh White, Article ID: A8992146.
16. BBC People's War, Henry Powell, Article ID: A2663660.
17. Ponting, p.91.
18. IWM Sound Archive, Catalogue no. 10478.
19. IWM Sound Archive, Catalogue no. 6825.
20. Spears, p.295.
21. Ironside, p,355.
22. C. King, *With Malice Towards None – A War Diary* (Sidgwick and Jackson, London, 1970), p.85.
23. Ponting, p.92.
24. BBC People's War, Article ID: A6667563.
25. Dr Alan Brown, *The Other Side of Dunkirk*, Youtube documentary.
26. Richard Collier, *1941 Armageddon* (Hamish Hamilton, London,1981), p.22.
27. This is one of the main themes in Clive Pontin's wonderful revisionist study *1940: Myth and Reality* (Ivan R. Dee, Chicago, 1991).
28. Warren F. Kimball, *Churchill and Roosevelt, The Complete Correspondence* (Princeton University Press, 1984), Vol. I, pp.65-6.
29. *Evening Telegraph and Post*, 5 June 1940.
30. Ponting, p.212.
31. Lynn Picknett, Clive Prince and Stephen Prior, *Friendly Fire, the Secret War Between the Allies* (Mainstream Publishing, London, 2005), p.201.
32. Theodore A. Wilson, 'The United States: Leviathan' in David Reynolds, *Warren F. Kimball and A.O. Chubarian Allies at War: The Soviet, American and British Experience, 1935-1945* (Macmillan, Basingstoke, 1994), p.214.
33. Addison and Crang, pp.71-9.
34. Quoted in Franks, pp.136-7.
35. Gardiner, p. xiii.
36. Hugh Dundas, *Flying Start: A Fighter Pilot's War Years* (St Martin's Press, London 1990), p.26.
37. Vigors, p.156.
38. Quoted in Franks, p.156.
39. Dundas, pp.25-6.
40. TNA ADM 199/789.
41. Hammerton, p.631.
42. Addison and Crang, p.75
43. Wallace, p.125.

Appendix I

1. Adapted from Lord Gort's Second Despatch on Operations, 25 July 1940.

Appendix II

1. Adapted from Lord Gort's Second Despatch on Operations, 25 July 1940.

Appendix III

1. Adapted from L. F. Ellis, *The War in France and Flanders 1939–1940* (HSMO, London, 1954), pp.372–3.

Appendix IV

1. Details from Ellis, p.327.

Appendix V

1. Details from Ramsay's despatch of 18 June 1940.

Appendix VII

1. Taken from IWM Document no. 3797.

Appendix III

1. Taken from IWM Document no. 3797.

Sources And Bibliography

Imperial War Museum

Buchanan, Lieutenant Commander A.G, Private Papers, Document no. Webb, Captain Lemon, Document no.17393.
Christmas, J.H., *The James Christmas Portfolio*, Document no.15674.
Samuel Palmer, Samuel, *M.V. Naiad Errant at Dunkirk 1940*, Document no.10167.
Tough, Bob, Collection of documents all relating to Tough Bros. a ship building company during the Second World War, Document no.3797.
Watson, Lieutenant Colonel J.S, Private Papers, Document no.16543.
Webb, Captain Lemon, Document no.17393.

IWM Sound Archive

Allen, Stanley Victor, Catalogue no. 6825.
Burton, Victor, Catalogue no. 18204.
Codd, Francis George, Catalogue no. 9341.
Curry, Frank, Catalogue no.19770.
Deere, Alan, Catalogue no. 10478.
Eldred, Ernest, Catalogue no. 6901.
Fahey, Brian Michael, Catalogue no. 10433.
Heron, Reginald, Catalogue no. 22385.
Joscelyne , William Joscelyne, Catalogue no. 9768
King, Thomas Philip Edward, Catalogue no.6973.
Ledger, George, Catalogue no. 16722.
McWilliam, W.L., Catalogue no. 12305.
Priest, Stanley William, Catalogue no.10695.

The National Archives, Kew

ADM 199/786, Operation 'Dynamo': evacuation of troops from Dunkirk, Vol.1.
ADM 199/787, Operation 'Dynamo': evacuation of troops from Dunkirk, Vol.2.
ADM 199/788, Operation 'Dynamo': evacuation of troops from Dunkirk, Vol.3.
ADM 199/789, Operation 'Dynamo': evacuation of troops from Dunkirk, Vol.4.
ADM 199/792, Operation 'Dynamo': evacuation of troops from Dunkirk

ADM 234/360, Battle Summary No.41, Evacuation from Dunkirk (operation DYNAMO) 26 May - 4 June 1940.
ADM 358/110, Lieutenant Commander R. G. K. Knowling, RN: lost overboard; HMS *Vimy*; 28 May 1940.
CAB 106/243, Headquarters, British Expeditionary Force, 1940: retreat to Dunkirk.
WO 106/ 350, British Expeditionary Force, France: War Diaries, 3rd Brigade.
WO 106/1607, Channel ports; defence of Dunkirk.
WO 197/134, Account of the evacuation from France and the quartering of the B.E.F. after Dunkirk May - June 1940.
WO 197/119, Evacuation of B.E.F: reports by Commander Dunkirk area and other Officers.
WO 361/19, Evacuation of Dunkirk: losses on SS Crested Eagle, 29-30 May 1940.

Other Unpublished Documents

Smith, Lieutenant Colonel David, *Retreat to Dunkirk* (unpublished memoir, HMP collection).
The Shropshire Regimental Museum, Account by Captain Jones, 1st Battalion King's Shropshire Light Infantry.

Published Sources

Addison, Paul, and Crang, Jeremy A., *Listening to Britain, Home Intelligence Reports on Britain's Finest Hour – May to September 1940* (Bodley Head, London, 2010).
Armengaud, J., *Le Drame de Dunkerque* (Plon, Paris, 1948).
Bartlett, Basil, *My First War: An Army Officer's Journal for May 1940 Through Belgium to Dunkirk* (Chatto and Windus, 1941).
Blaxland, Gregory, *Destination Dunkirk, The Story of Gort's Army* (William Kimber, London, 1973).
Brann, Christian, *The Little Ships of Dunkirk* (Collectors Books, Kemble, 1989).
Brew, Alex, *The Turret Fighters, Defiant and Roc* (Crowood Press, Marlborough, 2002).
Bryant, Arthur, *Turn of the Tide* ((Doubleday, London, 1957).
Butler, Ewan, and Selby Bradford, J., *Keep the Memory Green, The First of Many, France 1939-40* (Hutchinson, London, nd.).
Churchill, Winston S., *The Second World War*, Vol. II, *Their Finest Hour* (Cassell, London, 1949).
Collier, Richard, *1941 Armageddon* (Hamish Hamilton, London,1981.
Cooksey, John, *Boulogne 20 Guards Brigade's Fighting Defence – May 1940* (Pen & Sword Books, Barnsley 2002).
Cunliffe, Marcus, *History of the Royal Warwickshire Regiment, 1919-1955* (William Clowes and Sons, London,1956).
Danchev, A., and Todman, D., *War Diaries 1939-1940, Field Marshal Lord Alanbrooke* (Phoenix Press, London, 2002).

Deere, Alan C., *Nine Lives* (Crécy, Manchester, 2009).

Deighton, Len, *Blitzkrieg, From the Rise of Hitler to the Fall of Dunkirk* (Jonathon Cape, London, 1979).

Dildy, Douglas C., *Dunkirk 1940, Operation Dynamo* (Osprey, Oxford, 2010).

Divine, David, *The Nine Days of Dunkirk*, (Ballantine Books, New York, 1959).

Dobson, Alan P., *US Wartime Aid to Britain 1940-1946* (Groom Helm, Beckenham, 1986).

Dundas, Hugh, *Flying Start: A Fighter Pilot's War Years* (St Martin's Press, London 1990).

Ellis, L.F., *The War in France and Flanders, 1939-1940* (HMSO, London, 1953).

Franks, Norman, *Air Battle Dunkirk, 26 May – 3 June 1940* (Grub Street, London, 2000).

Gardner, Charles, *A.A.S.F.* (Hutchinson, London, 1940).

Gardner, W. J. R., *The Evacuation from Dunkirk, 'Operation Dynamo 26 May-4June 1940* (Frank Cass, London, 2000).

Grehan, J., & Mace, M., *The BEF in France, 1939-1940, Manning the Front Through to the Dunkirk Evacuation* (Pen & Sword, Barnsley, 2014).

Gunbuster, *Return via Dunkirk* (Hodder & Stoughton, London, 1940).

Hammerton, Sir John, *The War Illustrated, Volume Two* (Amalgamated Press, London, nd).

Harman, Nicholas, *Dunkirk, The Necessary Myth* (Hodder and Stoughton, Sevenoaks, 1980).

Hart, Basil Liddell, *History of the Second World War* (Putmam, New York, 1970).

Hay, Ian, *The Battle of Flanders 1940*, (HMSO, London, 1941).

Henniker, M., *An Image of War* (Leo Cooper, London, 1987).

Holmes, Richard, *War Walks 2, From the Battle of Hastings to the Blitz* (BBC Books, London, 1997).

Humphreys, Roy S., *Hellfire Corner - Reminiscences of Wartime in South East England* (Sutton, Stroud, 1994).

Jackson, Robert, *Dunkirk: The British Evacuation, 1940* (Cassel, London, 2002).

Jackson, Robert, *Churchill's Moat: The Channel War 1939-1945* (Airlife, Shrewsbury, 1995).

Kaufmann, E., & H.W., *Fortress France: The Maginot Line and the French Defences in World War II* (Connecticut, 2005).

Kimball, Warren F., *Churchill and Roosevelt, The Complete Correspondence* (Princeton University Press, 1984).

Kimball, Warren F. and A.O. Chubarian, A.O., *Allies at War: The Soviet, American and British Experience, 1935-1945* (Macmillan, Basingstoke, 1994).

King, C., *With Malice Towards None – A War Diary* (Sidgwick and Jackson, London, 1970).

Knowles, David J., *Escape from Catastrophe, 1940 Dunkirk* (self-published, Rochester, 2000).

Levine, Joshua, *Forgotten Voices of Dunkirk* (Edbury Press, 2010).

Longdon, Sean, *Dunkirk, The Men They Left Behind* (Constable, London, 2008).

Lord, Walter, *The Miracle of Dunkirk* (Allen Lane, London, 1982).

Mace, Martin, M. Mace, *They Also Served: The Story of Sussex Lifeboats at War 1939-1945*, (Historic Military Press, Storrington, 2001).

Mace, Martin, *The Royal Navy at Dunkirk: Commanding Officers' Accounts of British Warships in Action During Operation Dynamo* (Frontline, Barnsley, 2017).

Mace, Martin, *The Dunkirk Evacuation in 100 Objects, The Story Behind Operation Dynamo in 1940* (Pen & Sword, Barnsley, 2017).

Macleod, R., and Dennis Kelly (eds.), *The Ironside Diaries, 1937-1940* (Constable, London, 1962),

McKay, Sinclair, *Dunkirk, From Disaster to Deliverance – Testimonies of the Last Survivors* (Aunum Press, London, 2014).

McKee, Alexander, *Strike from the Sky the Story of the Battle of Britain* (Souvenir Press, London, 1960).

Masefield, John, *The Nine Days Wonder: The Operation Dynamo* (William Heinemann, London, 1941).

Murland, Jerry, *Retreat and Rearguard – Dunkirk 1940: The Evacuation of the BEF to the Channel Ports* (Pen & Sword, Barnsley, 2016).

Picknett, Lynn, Prince, Clive, and Prior, Stephen, *Friendly Fire, the Secret War Between the Allies* (Mainstream Publishing, London, 2005).

Plummer, Reussel, *Paddle Steamers at War 1939-1945* (GMS Enterprises, Peterborough, 1995).

Ponting, Clive, *1940: Myth and Reality* (Elephant, Chicago, 1993).

Prichard, S., *Life in the Welsh Guards 1936-46* (privately published, Wales, March 2007).

Ramsey, Winston G. (ed.), *The Battle of Britain, Then and Now* (After the Battle, Old Harlow,1982).

Rhodes, Anthony, *Sword of Bone, The Phoney War and Dunkirk 1940* (Severn House, London, 1975).

Rossiter, Mike, *I Fought at Dunkirk, Seven Veterans Remember the German Invasion of France* (Bantam Press, London, 2012).

Rowe, Vivian, *The Great Wall of France: The Triumph of the Maginot Line* (Putnam, London, 1959).

Saunders, Wilf, *Dunkirk Diary of a Young Soldier* (Brewin Books, Studley, 2010).

Sebag-Montefiore, Hugh, *Dunkirk, Fight to the Last Man* (Penguin, London, 2007).

Spears, Edward, *Assignment to Catastrophe* (Reprint Society, London, 1956).

Stewart, Geoffrey, *Dunkirk and the Fall of France* (Pen & Sword, Barnsley, 2008).

Thompson, Julian, *Retreat to Victory* (Sidgwick & Jackson, London, 2008).

Vigors, Tom, *Life's too Short to Cry: The Compelling Memoir of a Battle of Britain Ace* (Grub Street, London, 2006).

Vince, C., *Storm on the Waters: The Story of the Life-Boat Service in the War of 1939-1945* (Hodder & Stoughton, London 1946).

Wallace, Graham, *RAF Biggin Hill* ((Pace Reprographics, Denham,1975).

Wilson, Patrick, *Dunkirk, From Despair to Deliverance* (Pen & Sword, Barnsley, 1999).

Wood, Derek & Dempster, Derek, *The Narrow Margin, The Battle of Britain and the Rise of Air Power 1930-1945* (Pen & Sword, Barnsley, 2010).

Magazines & Newspapers

Britain at War Magazine
British Medical Journal
Daily Mail
Daily Mirror
Evening Express
Evening Telegraph and Post
Gloucestershire Echo
Liverpool Daily Post
New York Herald Tribune
Nottingham Evening Post
North Devon Journal
The Second World War Illustrated
The West Australian
Western Gazette
Western Mail

Internet sites/sources

bbc.co.uk/archive/dunkirk
BBC History Archive, 'Voices of Dunkirk'.
BBC People's War:
Ainsworth, Barry, Article ID: A6667563.
Birtles, W.E., *Dunkirk Aged 17*, Article ID: A3475352.
Bloom, Bob, Article ID: A2270422.
Bradley, James, Article ID: A2269424.
'DWBD's War', Article ID: A6329216.
Heath, Albert George, Article ID: A2306891.
Hogg, George, Article ID: A2528138
Lindsay, I.G.N., Article ID: A2308105.
Mewis, Stanley, Article ID: A4612484.
Morgan, Hector, Article ID: A2281312.
Munn, Harry, Article ID A2349768.
Nickholds, Benjamin, Article ID: A3542339
Osborne, John, *Dunkirk – first-hand account of one of the small boats*, Article ID: A2657270.
Perrin, Tom, Article ID: A2298495.
Brown, Dr Alan, *The Other Side of Dunkirk*, Youtube documentary

Potter, Ken, Article ID: A7445432.

Powell, Henry, ID: A2663660.

Spiers, T.J., *Shot Down Over Dunkirk*, Article ID: A2764235.

Lionel Tucker, Lionel, *Memories of The Maid of Orleans*, Article ID: A8408630.

Wampach, C. R., Article ID: A2663660.

White, Hugh, 'Stretcher-bearers', Article ID: A8992146.

www.*dunkirk-revisited*.co.uk.

Forces War Records Blog.

www.hmshood.com.

Medway Queen website: www.medwayqueen.co.uk.

Queen Alexandra's Royal Army Nursing Corps website, www.qaranc.co.uk.

Rickard, Dr John, *Operation Dynamo, the evacuation from Dunkirk, 27 May-4 June 1940*, http://www.historyofwar.org/articles/operation_dynamo.html.

http://dkepaves.free.fr/download/bourrasque.pdf.

http://www.scoutsrecords.org.

thamestugs.co.uk, Dunkirk Logs.

264squadron.co.uk.

Index

Index Of Persons

324   Dunkirk: Nine Days That Saved An Army

INDEX OF BRITISH MILITARY UNITS

INDEX OF ROYAL AIR FORCE SQUADRONS